This book represents the result of recent historical research by German and American scholars on German influences on education in the United States during the nineteenth century. The authors deal with all aspects of education, from kindergarten through primary and secondary education to universities. In analyzing German educational influences on the United States, the essays are concerned with reports of American visitors to Germany, as well as with accounts and activities of German educators in the United States. The book shows that in the context of an immigrant culture, the question of influence needs to be considered in an interdisciplinary setting. At the same time, the account recognizes that both Germany and the United States were mutually affected by the development and progress of their relevant educational theories and practices.

PUBLICATIONS OF THE GERMAN HISTORICAL INSTITUTE,
WASHINGTON, D.C.

Edited by Hartmut Lehmann
with the assistance of Kenneth F. Ledford

German Influences on Education
in the United States to 1917

The German Historical Institute is a center for advanced study and research whose purpose is to provide a permanent basis for scholarly cooperation between historians from the Federal Republic of Germany and the United States. The Institute conducts, promotes, and supports research into both American and German political, social, economic, and cultural history, into transatlantic migration, especially in the nineteenth and twentieth centuries, and into the history of international relations, with special emphasis on the roles played by the United States and Germany.

German Influences
on Education
in the United States to 1917

Edited by

HENRY GEITZ
Max Kade Institute for German-American Studies,
University of Wisconsin

JÜRGEN HEIDEKING
University of Cologne

JURGEN HERBST
University of Wisconsin

GERMAN HISTORICAL INSTITUTE
Washington, D.C.
and

 **CAMBRIDGE**
UNIVERSITY PRESS

CAMBRIDGE UNIVERSITY PRESS
Cambridge, New York, Melbourne, Madrid, Cape Town, Singapore, São Paulo

Cambridge University Press
The Edinburgh Building, Cambridge CB2 2RU, UK

Published in the United States of America by Cambridge University Press, New York

www.cambridge.org
Information on this title: www.cambridge.org/9780521470834

First published 1995
This digitally printed first paperback version 2006

A catalogue record for this publication is available from the British Library

Library of Congress Cataloguing in Publication data
German influences on education in the United States to 1917 / [edited
by] Henry Geitz, Jürgen Heideking, Jurgen Herbst.
p. cm. – (Publications of the German Historical Institute)
Includes bibliographical references and index.
ISBN 0–521–47083–8 (hardback)
1. Education – United States – German influences.   2. German
Americans – Education – History.   I. Geitz, Henry.   II. Heideking,
Jürgen, 1947– .   III. Herbst, Jurgen.   IV. Series.
LA216.G47   1995
370'.973 – dc20   94–17599
                                                                        CIP

ISBN-13 978-0-521-47083-4 hardback
ISBN-10 0-521-47083-8 hardback

ISBN-13 978-0-521-02624-6 paperback
ISBN-10 0-521-02624-5 paperback

Contents

v

Contributors

James C. Albisetti is Professor of History at the University of Kentucky.

Ann Taylor Allen is Professor of History at the University of Louisville.

Thomas N. Bonner is Professor of History at Wayne State University.

Ward W. Briggs is Professor of Foreign Languages at the University of South Carolina.

Henry Geitz is Director of the Max Kade Institute for German-American Studies in Madison, Wisconsin.

Bettina Goldberg is a Research Fellow at the John F. Kennedy Institute for North American Studies at the Free University of Berlin.

Karl-Heinz Günther is a member of the Akademie der Pädagogischen Wissenschaften in Berlin.

Jürgen Heideking is Professor of History at the University of Cologne.

Jurgen Herbst is Professor of the History of Education at the University of Wisconsin.

Juliane Jacobi is Professor of Education at the University of Bielefeld.

Konrad H. Jarausch is Lurcy Professor of History at the University of North Carolina.

Karl-Ernst Jeismann is at the Institut für Didaktik der Geschichte at the Westfälische Wilhelms University in Münster.

Sally Gregory Kohlstedt is Professor of the History of Science at the University of Minnesota.

Derek S. Linton is Associate Professor of History at Hobart and William Smith Colleges.

Jörg Nagler is Director of the John F. Kennedy House in Kiel.

Kathryn M. Olesko is Associate Professor of History at Georgetown University.

Gary K. Pranger is Professor of History at Oral Roberts University.

Anthony Gregg Roeber is Associate Professor of History at the University of Illinois at Chicago.

Gregory P. Wegner is Assistant Professor of History at the University of Wisconsin-LaCrosse.

Introduction

JURGEN HERBST

No one should expect the proceedings of a conference to bring together a complete survey and analysis of its announced subject. The often accidental and in some respects arbitrary conference arrangements of time and place, as well as the prior commitments of potential contributors, make such expectations illusory at the outset. Nonetheless, with much good will and persistent effort, it is possible to assemble a company of scholars – some seasoned and accomplished representatives of their fields, others at the early stages of their careers eager to bring their work to our attention – who will succeed in introducing us to recent scholarship on the announced subject. While not necessarily representative, such an effort can be sufficiently wide-ranging in its topics and varied in its approaches to permit a reasonably comprehensive and exemplary presentation.

The conference on German influences on American education was convened jointly by the German Historical Institute in Washington, D.C., the Max Kade Institute for German-American Studies in Madison, Wisconsin, and the School of Education of the University of Wisconsin – Madison. The sponsors and the editors of this volume hope that they have been successful in bringing together a group of essays that provide an overview of recent scholarship and permit us to arrive at insights and conclusions that deserve more extended discussion. The volume will have served its purpose if it stimulates and advances future work on intercultural influences in education.

As the essays amply demonstrate, a definition of the word "influence" is not without its perils. Does it refer to the mere appearance or presence of an actor or agency in an environment different from that of its origin? Does that presence have to remain visible for a particular length of time before we acknowledge it as such? And, most important, how effective does such a presence have to be or become in order to be recognized as influence? To what degree will the agent have to change its new environment, and

1

over how long a time will that effectiveness have to continue? And does influence always imply a positive action on the part of the imported actor, or may it be detected by the passive adaptation of the previously existing environment to the new presence in its midst?

Readers of this volume will discover that the editors did not demand of their contributors adherence to any one particular definition. Their expectations were that scholars, having detected the presence of German contributions to American educational institutions and practices, would inquire just what these contributions have been and what difference they made when they were added to or integrated into the American educational experience. Our authors were encouraged to arrive at their own conclusions in evaluating the significance of these items or episodes of cultural transfer from one society to another.

Why, it may be asked, did this conference concern itself with influences on American education? The current revival of historical studies in education is the major reason for this choice. Throughout the last three decades, the history of education has undergone a renaissance that has placed it at the center of some of the most active scholarship in social and intellectual history. As particularly the late Lawrence Cremin has shown so magnificently in his massive three-volume opus on *American Education,* the history of education is no longer restricted to the history of the school.[1] On both sides of the Atlantic, educational historians have come to claim large areas as legitimate targets of exploration. They have investigated childhood and adolescence, family and gender, science and popular entertainment, and their studies have enriched the existing historical literature. The essays in this volume reflect these developments, as did the conference itself.

Readers of this volume should also keep in mind that the conference organizers decided on the history of education as the principal field of scholarship and that they chose educational influences as their central theme. Thus they will not be surprised that the history of ethnicity, language use, and immigration does not receive major attention in this volume. But this is not to say that these topics are absent altogether. Some of the essays add significantly to our understanding of the German element in American culture and society. Jacobi's "Schoolmarm, *Volkserzieher, Kantor,* and *Schulschwester,*" for example, speaks directly to some of the questions recently raised in ethnicization history and, in that context, analyzes the different roles played by education in Protestant and Catholic midwestern immigrant

1. See my review essay of Cremin's work in *The American Scholar* (Winter 1991), 128–40.

communities.[2] The contributions by Roeber and Goldberg in the section on "German Schools in America" address topics familiar to students of immigration history and can also be read as case studies in the history of bilingualism.[3]

Most of the other essays, however, and particularly those in Parts One and Four, do not fall in the areas usually covered by the history of immigration or ethnicity. The contributions to Part One concern themselves with visitors traveling in both directions, and those in Part Four deal with higher education and the academic disciplines of theology, the classics, history, and medicine. Although school teachers and educational observers in general may be said to belong to the spheres of both popular and refined culture, the representatives of scholarship deal with matters of concern chiefly to the nation's cultural elite. Like visiting teachers and observers, they are usually temporary visitors in each other's country rather than immigrants.

Part of the special interest in the German influence on American education is that it moved on two levels: within and as part of the broad stream of popular immigration and on the more rarified plateau of higher education and elite culture. This, Kathleen Conzen pointed out in a comment on an earlier draft of this introduction, could not be said of French influences on American education. They were restricted primarily to elite culture. French immigrants contributed little to the history of American public schooling. German immigrants, however, did so in many ways, as secular supporters of public schooling or as adherents to confessional education. In addition, in the area of higher education, German immigrants and visitors were joined by American-born intellectuals who contributed their share in bringing German influence to bear on American culture. By the end of the nineteenth century, this twofold nature of German-American cultural relationships had created conditions out of which developed mutual exchanges and stimulation that continue to this day.

In this volume, we first turn to what German or American visitors had to say about the schools in each other's country.[4] This literature, well known

---

2. See the contributions by Kathleen Conzen, Mack Walker, and Jörg Nagler in *Making Their Own America: Assimilation Theory and the German Peasant Pioneer,* German Historical Institute, Washington DC, Annual Lecture Series, No. 3 (Providence, R.I.: Berg Publishers, 1990).
3. See Steven L. Schlossman, "Is There an American Tradition of Bilingual Education? German in the Public Elementary Schools, 1840–1919," *American Journal of Education* (February 1983), 139–86.
4. For an example concerning teacher education, see "The Atlantic Community of Whigs" in my *And Sadly Teach* (Madison: University of Wisconsin Press, 1989), 32–56.

to comparative educationists, joins the observational acumen of experienced educators with information on the host country's schools, thus bridging, as it were, the worlds of elite and popular culture. In the first essay, Jeismann evaluates the well-known and often discussed reports of Alexander Dallas Bache, Henry Barnard, and Horace Mann from a German point of view, asking what may be learned from them about the history of German education that has not usually been noted in the German historical literature on the subject.[5] Günther finds the significance of the exodus of German liberal educators in the wake of the unsuccessful 1848 revolutions to have been less in their effect on education in the United States than in the reports about democratic practices they sent back to Germany. Günther doubts that American schools were much influenced by German immigrants. He suggests that we take a closer look at the impact of the emigrants' reports on colleagues they left behind. Turning his attention to the closing decades of the century, Wegner tells us that admiration for and eagerness to learn from German models remained a powerful motive. He also notes a growing ambivalence of the American reporters toward the assumption that such intercultural learning could remain a one-way street. Eagerness to learn from Germany, he suggests, was restrained by caution. Linton's contribution, finally, moves us into the prewar years of the twentieth century, when the American interest in vocational education led to the adoption of the German system of continuation schools. Linton tells us how the Munich superintendent Georg Kerschensteiner succeeded, directly and indirectly, in providing a model for American vocational education, despite the many differences between the social and industrial structures of the two countries.

Whether the reporters discussed were Americans, as in Jeismann's, Wegner's, and Linton's essays, or Germans, as in Günther's, they intended their reports as ammunition in their efforts to reform the schools in their respective home countries. Thus Jeismann states that the first and direct result of Mann's reports in Massachusetts was to involve him in his quarrel with the Boston schoolmasters, and Günther finds that his protagonists aided the cause of liberal reform in Prussia. The passage of time did not alter this approach. Near the end of the century, Parsons and Prince, as Wegner relates, were sent by their respective state authorities in New York and Massachusetts to investigate German educational innovations for their possible introduction at home. Linton's essay on Kerschensteiner makes clear

---

5. For earlier discussions of these reports, see Edgar W. Knight, ed., *Reports on European Education by John Griscom, Victor Cousin, Calvin E. Stowe* (New York: McGraw-Hill, 1930), and Robert Ulich, *A Sequence of Educational Influences* (Cambridge, Mass.: Harvard University Press, 1935).

that the Munich model of industrial education was used to unify contending parties in the American debate over vocational education.

This is, I suppose, what one should expect. Our reporters were not intent on evaluating impartially the advantages and liabilities of what they observed. They did not hesitate to express disapproval as well as admiration, and they made few attempts to analyze and weigh the reasons for their reactions. They were men of practice, little inclined to contemplation and philosophical reflection. School organization and classroom management were their concerns. Thus, in their investigations, they tended to see what they were looking for and to ignore what did not fit into their preconceptions. Jeismann relates a good example of this when he tells us of Bache's approval of curricular differentiation in the German *Bürgerschulen* and of his criticism of the Humboldtian Latin-based general education offered in the same schools.

Reform of American schools was their primary concern. The fact that they thought reform was possible by selective adoption and adaptation of foreign models and practices reveals their assumption of what Jeismann calls the "relative autonomy" of an educational system. The reporters believed that an exemplary progressive educational system could exist within a politically backward society. How else could they have reconciled in their minds the existence of an educational system they admired within a political order they rejected? How else could they have conceived its transferability from one society to another?

Viewing themselves as champions of reform and having become advocates of a cause that borrowed heavily from a foreign example, they tended, despite their disapproval of aspects of the foreign system, to ignore or never perceive that the Prussian system itself was far from united in support of the reforms the observers had come to endorse. Thus Jeismann points out that the observers appeared to be oblivious to the conservative–liberal struggle in Prussia and failed to note or to report the poverty of German teachers and their desperate struggle to free themselves from clerical oversight. I am not sure whether that obliviousness to German shortcomings entitles them to be cited, as Jeismann does, for their "unbiased judgment" in their advocacy of Prussian examples for American reforms. Selective adaptation does not necessarily imply objectivity.

We get very much the same picture, but with the two sides reversed, when we read what Günther has to tell us of German teachers and travelers in the United States after the failed revolution of 1848. The German visitors, being liberals for the most part and committed to their ideals, wrote glowingly of the American schools as possible examples for German liberals. But whether their picture of American schools corresponded to reality, and whether the liberals can be accepted as representatives of German influences on the American school system, are quite different questions not addressed in Günther's essay.

The German teachers described by Günther by and large neither intended nor saw much reason to reform American schools. They frequently were aghast at what they considered American pedagogical backwardness, but they ascribed that situation to the relatively undeveloped state of the country. Rather than seeking to introduce improvements, they turned toward their fellow countrymen and taught in German schools. Being liberals, they fully endorsed such American practices as the separation of state and church, the emphasis in the public schools on knowledge rather than faith, coeducation, and the granting of equal rights to all children. Those like Diesterweg who visited for brief periods only wrote glowing reports on the achievements of schools in a republican society and described them as examples to be imitated back home in Germany. In this case, too, the reformers' concerns outshone any attempt at impartial reporting.

The essays by Wegner and Linton present much the same picture of Americans, seeking now to come to grips with the impact of industrialization, looking to Germany for suggestions on how the public schools might cope. Wegner's protagonists, not unlike Bache before them, look for curricula and schools that offer manual and industrial training in the elementary schools and vocational education in continuation schools. Their reports, published in the early 1890s, would eventually be vindicated in the Smith–Hughes Act on vocational education of 1917. As Linton then points out, by that time the influence of the Munich Superintendent Kerschensteiner's system of industrial continuation schools had served to join and harmonize conflicting interests of American educators, industrialists, and representatives of the labor movement. In this case, as Linton puts it, the German model became an institution of choice in the United States.

The question, then, of whether institutions and practices are transferable from one society to another admits of no unqualified answer. We have to remember that institutions do not transfer themselves. The key to the answer lies in the intentions and needs of those who propagate the transfer. Their needs and intentions shape the transferred and transformed institutions. Involved in every case has been a process of selection and adaptation.

The essays in Part Two focus on the person and role of the teacher involved in the transatlantic educational relationships. Jacobi's and Allen's essays both document, in different ways, the cultural tensions produced by the German tradition of teaching as a male profession and the American tendency to prefer women as teachers in schools for the young. Jacobi describes the German traditions of school teaching as an occupation for males when she writes of the German teachers of the 1848 generation. They were, by and large, liberals and freethinkers and belonged to the same circles reported on by Günther in his essay. Although they believed in bilingual education and the preservation of their native culture and language, they were at the same time intent on educating their students to become free American citizens. Eventually, these men, much like many of their English-speaking colleagues in the public schools, left their classrooms for administrative offices or positions in business. Their counterparts in parochial schooling were the Lutheran *Kantoren,* who arrived in larger numbers a decade later. They sought to join a parochial and academic education, training teachers and pastors for the Lutheran churches.

The women teachers described by Jacobi also fall into two groups, secular and religious. When young German immigrant women decided to teach, they seem to have joined their English-speaking sisters and gone to work in the public schools. Jacobi speaks of them as "Americanized." It is not very clear whether they were not readily hired in the German immigrant schools, or whether they preferred the public schools for reasons of their own. It is, however, the members of Catholic religious orders – Franciscans, Dominicans, and Sisters of Notre Dame – who could be considered professional teachers, making teacher training their main business, and establishing themselves as professionals working outside the traditional family setting. Their expulsion from Prussia in the 1870s established them as an important influence on women's education in the United States. Here again, we know little of what they accomplished and to what extent their teaching constituted a German influence on American education.

The issue of German education having a significant and positive influence on women's education in the United States is far more easily detectable in the case of the kindergarten and its champions. Allen focuses her essay on the Americanization of the kindergarten on the women teachers involved in this process, a process that was most significantly characterized by an ongoing dialogue between the two cultures. American women teachers were less drawn to the kindergarten as another classroom or playroom in which to teach and more attracted by the opportunities it offered to capitalize on their intellectual potential. Whether William Torrey Harris saw and advocated the kindergarten in the spirit of Hegelianism as a means of synthesizing American individualism and German social responsibility, or whether G. Stanley Hall used it as a forum in which to introduce science and child study, women teachers blended in their own professional advancement in science, social work, feminism, pacifism, and women's suffrage. As Allen points out, American women were eminently successful in making an impact on teaching and social work, thereby establishing the kindergarten as an accepted institution in American society. That happened at a time when, in Germany, the male-dominated professions held the kindergarten to be suspect and officially shunned. It also became quite apparent that by the turn of the century few new ideas concerning the kindergarten continued to come from Germany, and one-way German influences gave way to a transatlantic discourse.

Kohlstedt's essay on the natural history museums and Olesko's essay on the physics teachers highlight the subtle dialectic between German and American conceptions of science teaching. Throughout the nineteenth century, Americans took German museums and their educational practices as their examples. By the end of the century, it appeared that American educational museum exhibits had begun to overtake their German models. Similarly, the education of physics teachers for American secondary schools had by 1900 reached a level of complexity in a German-American dialogue that, not unlike the one between the devotees of the kindergarten, replaced earlier influences that had moved from Germany to the United States.

As Olesko makes clear, throughout most of the nineteenth century, German teacher training in physics had focused on disciplinary instruction and precision measurements. In the United States, the emphasis on precision was valued less for the training it provided in exact research techniques than for the ethics of work and efficiency that it was expected to convey. When toward the end of the century the improvements in instrumentation made such measurements routine and mechanical, American teacher training began to emphasize hypotheses, observations, experiment, induction, and efficient production as objectives of physics instruction. The German model, on the other hand, continued to involve to a far larger extent mathematical and deductive approaches. This shift from precision measurement to inductive procedures in high school teaching went hand in hand with high school teachers taking a dominant role in curricular decisions and limiting the influence of the universities over the school curriculum. To the extent that university influence has been associated with the German approach, by 1910 it remained in the United States only symbolically – like the Cheshire cat's smile, writes Olesko.

For the most direct impact of German culture on education in America, we have to look at the schools opened by German immigrants in the United States. It is in them and in the churches with which they were often, but not necessarily, associated that German culture and the German language initially gained their most tenacious hold. Bilingualism and bicultural education found a home in the German-American schools of Philadelphia, Cleveland, Cincinnati, Milwaukee, St. Louis, Indianapolis, Louisville, and Baltimore. Roeber and Goldberg introduce us to the issues raised by these schools in their essays on German religious and educational efforts during the eighteenth and nineteenth centuries.

In Part Three, Roeber describes how, in Philadelphia, Christian Helmuth (1745–1825) had fought to preserve his German Lutheran heritage in school and church. As pastor of St. Michael's and Zion, the largest German-speaking congregation of its time in North America, he organized a parish school, a Latin academy, and the von Mosheim Society for German adult literary education. In 1812 he published the *Evangelisches Magazin* to urge all German settlers, regardless of confession, to teach the German language to their children. Alas, by the mid-1920s, his efforts had come to naught.

Roeber's account shows us that it is difficult to disentangle and ascribe degrees of responsibility to the various factors contributing to Helmuth's failure. At heart, surely, Helmuth failed because he clung to the past and refused to adapt to the changing conditions of life in Pennsylvania. He closed his mind to the rationalist strains of thought of the Enlightenment. His dogmatic adherence to Pietist Lutheran theology and church practice ill disposed him to seek conversations and cooperation with fellow German Reformed and Lutheran groups, let alone with English-speaking Methodists and Baptists. His singleminded concern for the transmission of the German language and his firm conviction of the superiority of private over public schooling prevented him from working with German- as well as English-speaking countrymen who sought to promote public education. Last, but not least, his political views made him appear as a last-ditch defender of the old Federalism in a state with growing Republican sympathies.

Pennsylvania, the asylum of Europe's poor, served as an early stage for the development of ethnic and religious pluralism in America. Although German settlements and congregations could be found almost anywhere in the state, the political leadership, whether Quaker, Anglican, Deist, or Republican, was firmly in the hands of English-speaking people, whose language and culture became and remained dominant. Helmuth, as spokesman for a traditional German Lutheranism harking back to the Pietists of Halle, lost touch with the majority of Pennsylvanians. His case shows that, as the eighteenth century drew to its close, traditional ethnic-confessional ways could neither serve as ultimate authority for human relations in a multicultural society nor preserve and transmit a specific confessional and linguistic heritage to even its own members.

Goldberg's essay on Milwaukee shows us a quite different story. Though the founders of the German-English Academy, established in 1851, were strong believers in secular public education, they nonetheless created a private school because they were repelled by the strong Protestant influence over Milwaukee's public schools. The German-English Academy was to be bilingual, and its operation was to serve as a model for the city's public schools. Six similar schools were subsequently founded, until by the 1870s their number began to dwindle when Milwaukee's public schools introduced German instruction into their curriculum. By the beginning of the twentieth century, the demand for bilingual instruction waned, the German-English Academy was transformed into a university preparatory school, and by the late 1920s it ceased to offer German in the elementary grades.

In Milwaukee's German-English Academy, we observe the appearance of a bilingual private school spurred by the desire of German immigrants to offer alternatives to the existing low-quality parochial or public schools. Quite obviously, these German immigrants were dissatisfied with the state of American schooling, whether parochial or public. But they also were concerned about the preservation of German language and culture. Their intent and hope was to use their bilingual schools to offer their children the best of two worlds: an introduction to the English-language world of business of their neighbors, and a grounding in their own cultural and linguistic heritage. Milwaukee's German-American pedagogues were also intensely concerned with promoting knowledge and spreading information about the best available knowledge on education. They introduced a school museum and a kindergarten, and in 1878 sponsored the National German-American Teachers' Seminary. Their success spurred the opening of bilingual public schools, whose graduates appear to have furnished a disproportionally large number of high school students.

Although World War I brought the official termination of German instruction in the public schools of Milwaukee, neither the war nor its accompanying anti-German hysteria was responsible for the decline of the bilingual schools. Attitudes of the German-American population in the city had begun to change earlier. Although many German-American educators had seen in the teaching of the German language a means of preserving ethnic awareness and identity, it had become obvious that that aim had not been uppermost in the minds of most German-American parents and educators. Rather, parents were content with a minimal exposure to the German language, and Anglo-Americans valued German instruction for their own children as part of a college-preparatory instruction in a foreign language.

Goldberg reports that in Milwaukee the demand for German-language instruction had not come from below, but had been a concern of both German- and Anglo-American educators and school politicians. The chief aim, she tells us, had been to further the cause of Americanization by using the German language for that purpose. These educators were far more interested in preparing both German and American children for their life in the United States than in preserving German ethnic identity. By 1885 even the German-English Academy had given up a strictly bilingual curriculum, and English had received preferential treatment. Milwaukee's German-American citizens, concludes Goldberg, "were well aware that a thorough knowledge of the English rather than the German language was a necessary prerequisite for economic and social mobility in the new world." Assimilation of the immigrants had played its part, and the heyday of German-American bilingual schooling was past.

If we are to draw a common lesson from the six essays dealing with aspects of university-level education, it is that what we have referred to commonly as the German influence on American higher education may be more adequately characterized as an accommodation of American institutions and practices to German stimuli and innovations. There can be little doubt that in the half-century following the American Civil War, Americans began to look to Germany for suggestions and inspiration in coping with the mounting problems of a mushrooming industrial civilization. Not only were Americans eager to bring home specialized knowledge and expertise from abroad and to learn how to produce that knowledge by and for themselves, but they were also determined to find their own ways of putting that knowledge to use on this side of the Atlantic. As university scholars, they faced the first two tasks in their academic work. As citizens and professionals, they coped with the challenge of applying academic knowledge to tasks outside the universities. In either area they soon learned that successful accommodation required compromise and adjustment, and that as early needs stimulated willingness, even eagerness, to embrace and endorse the German imports, the very satisfaction of these needs, as well as the particular conditions of their appearance, significantly reduced their relevance. There emerges, then, a story of a rise and decline, which focuses on the production and transmission of knowledge.

By concentrating so closely on the production and transmission of knowledge, these essays give us aspects of what might be termed the "sociology of a guild." We are dealing exclusively with scholars engaged in or related to university study at various levels of proficiency. As Jarausch and Albisetti make quite clear, in their essays in Part Four, the majority of even the students who went to Germany, whether male or female, subsequently embarked on academic careers. The impulse of professionalism and the pursuit of an academic career characterize the individuals analyzed in these studies. The tensions that become obvious concern the relationship between the academics' professed ideal of the supposedly disinterested search for knowledge and their quite interested engagement in religious, political, or pecuniary aims. Pranger's essay clearly shows Schaff's involvement in ecclesiastical affairs – so different from Helmuth's in its search for adaptation of and adjustment to American circumstances. Nagler demonstrates von Holst's desire to apply historical knowledge to contemporary politics, and Bonner points to the clinicians' desire for outside income. These conflicting currents are neither German nor American; rather, they appear here as attributes of the emerging climate of professionalism on both sides of the Atlantic ocean.

One theme that emerges clearly from the essays dealing with the early years of the period under review is the power of the spirit of *Wissenschaft,* which inspired and moved the academics, both German and American. We find it in Philip Schaff (1819–93), who among Protestant theologians ranks to this day among the foremost representatives of nineteenth-century German historical scholarship. As Perry Miller put it: Through Schaff "the riches of German Protestant theology . . . flowed to the New World."[6] But it is caught best, I think, in the quotation Briggs gives us of what Basil Gildersleese wrote of his teacher Friedrich Ritschl: "One by one books, like men, drop into the night, and shade is lost in shadow. What is not lost, what lives forever, is the spirit of love to learning and love to the learner, which, once kindled, passes from teacher to learner, onward to the end of time." That spirit was real. We encounter it over and over in letters and memoirs. Jarausch testifies to it when he tells us that the most popular fields of the American students at Göttingen were mathematics, chemistry, history, and the classics – all fields of the philosophical faculty, among whom inquiry for its own sake ranked as the highest aim. He underscores it when he tells us that the American students at Göttingen cherished most the

---

6. See Perry Miller, "Editor's Introduction" to Philip Schaff, *America: A Sketch of Its Political, Social, and Religious Character* (Cambridge, Mass.: Harvard University Press, 1961), xi.

research seminar and the German notion of academic freedom as the students' freedom of choice.

Pranger's essay on Schaff also illuminates the particular suitability of German historical scholarship and mediating theology to the American environment. In Schaff's case, his easy adoption of the English language – married to an American wife, he spoke English in his home and advocated the use of English as the language of his church – and his advocacy of theological ecumenicism led him to avoid the rigidities that had earlier marked Helmuth's career. He quickly learned that a society and nation that rejected the confines of an established, state-supervised church made novel demands on those committed to the education of children and the training of future ministers. As the fountain of religious education for laypersons and ministers, theology had to accommodate inherited church doctrine and practice to the multifarious impressions that arose and incursions that took place from the presence of competing faiths and secular creeds. If flexibility, open-mindedness, willingness to compromise, and the desire to realize an ecumenical vision were the prime characteristics whose absence had stymied Helmuth's endeavors and whose presence fueled Schaff's success, then they were embodied in what has long been recognized as one of the key components of nineteenth-century German scholarship in the social and humanistic sciences: the historical approach.

Helmuth's failure and Schaff's success, I suggest, derive from their respective attitudes toward history. For Helmuth, an affirmation of history meant a defense of traditional dogma, language, and ways of worship. For Schaff, it embraced a recognition of history as development, in which the past was prologue to the present and the future developed out of new combinations of elements of the past and present. Whether, in Schaff's case, we attribute this understanding of history primarily to the writings of Hegel or the lectures of his teacher Neander matters little. The main lesson he received and made his own was that historical scholarship alone could do justice to both the tradition he had inherited and the significance of the events that marked his life in the new world he had entered.

The attitude of academics on both sides of the Atlantic toward the admission of women students to universities deserves special mention. Albisetti tells us that of the first twenty women graduating from American dental schools, twelve had come from Germany and returned to that country after graduation. Conversely, American women began to attend German and Austrian universities as early as the 1870s. As Jarausch shows for Göttingen, American women preceded their German sisters long before the latter were allowed to matriculate after the turn of the century. Apparently it was the threat of female competition for professional positions that persuaded academics on both sides of the Atlantic to bar formal admission to graduate degree programs for women of their own country.[7] Foreign women students apparently presented no such threat, and informal admission as auditors and even formal admission to degree programs were open to them relatively early. Reporting on American women students in Germany, Albisetti emphasizes that many of those few who made it across the ocean to attend the Victoria Lyceum in Berlin, to study medicine in Zürich and Vienna, or to enroll as auditors in the philosophical faculties of some German universities, on their return home entered teaching careers. Severe as the obstacles were for women students in both Germany and the United States, those pioneer students who succeeded in attending German institutions before 1900 cherished their German education as their most treasured possession.

As was the case in public education, the appeal of German *Wissenschaft* began to wane before the outbreak of World War I. Jarausch suggests that if we assume that the chief function of the German influence on American higher education had been to stimulate and encourage native American initiatives, then it was natural that with the growth of American graduate and professional schools the German presence would recede. That development is illustrated in the contrasting accounts given by Briggs on Gildersleeve and Nagler on von Holst. Gildersleeve, whose teaching career extended from 1856 to 1915, is presented as the model scholar who, through his superb command of German research methods, had become immensely productive in his research, in training his graduate students, and in his professional activities. At the same time, Briggs portrays him as impressively humane in his literary sensitivity, his admiration for Goethe, and his openess to English scholarly traditions. The combination of "the noble humanity of his style" and "the humbling regality of his learning" made him "the most important and influential classicist" in his lifetime and even today, sixty-five years after his death.

Von Holst, who took over the post of department chair and professor of history at the University of Chicago in 1892 and returned to Germany in 1899, belongs to a different generation. Born ten years later than Gildersleeve, he took over his teaching position when the Germanic influence on American academia was about to pass its high water mark. It was already too late for von Holst to play a pioneering role. The United States, writes Nagler, had already entered "a transitional period in which American uni-

---

7. Clara Zetkin made this point at the Vth Congress of the Communist International in 1924.

versities 'liberated' themselves from the European, especially German, academic predominance." Nagler argues that, except for the introduction of German methods in the training of American historians, the relationship between the two countries in the field of historical scholarship had become reciprocal and divergent. An emergent American university came to endorse values different from those taught in Germany. At the University of Chicago, Chancellor Harper stressed service and the needs of students, rather than, as von Holst did, faculty scholarship and academic freedom for professors. In historical scholarship in particular, German notions of *Rechtsstaat,* a national system of higher education, and the traditional hold of *Ideengeschichte* sounded "Germanic" and outmoded to many American historians.

Bonner's essay on clinical medicine may be read as a variant on the same theme of divergent and increasingly reciprocal relationships between German and American academic practice. By the late 1920s, Abraham Flexner's purist stand on the exclusively academic orientation of the clinical professor of medicine was effectively opposed by American clinicians, who were loath to give up their sources of outside income. Flexner's campaign was prompted by his admiration for the great scientific expertise of German clinical professors, yet he was effectively opposed by Americans, who pointed out to him that even the German clinicians were permitted an income from sources outside their professorial university duties. Thus, in different ways, all of our authors agree that what has been called the "German hegemony" in American higher education had come to an end, although there is disagreement about just when the waning of the German influence began.

At the outset I expressed my hope that this volume might stimulate and advance future work on intercultural influences in education. By stressing intercultural influences, I meant to highlight the relationships between and among cultures, relationships that involve mutual exchange, adaptations, adoptions, and assimilation, rather than unidirectional importations. I believe the essays in this volume bear out this contention. The influence of German ideas, institutions, and practices on American education affected American developments. At the same time, the American environment altered in many ways the thinking and behavior of those who had brought these German imports to the American shores. This was true for returning Americans as much as for German immigrants. Moreover, as Günther makes clear, the American experience of German visitors followed those who returned or transmitted itself through letters and newspaper stories back to their native country and influenced developments there.

One of the themes appearing repeatedly in these essays is the power of the Americanization process, which worked through and favored English-language public schools. The desire of families to prepare their children for business and life in an English-speaking society defeated attempts like Helmuth's to perpetuate German private schools. As developments in Milwaukee demonstrate, it also doomed efforts to preserve German-English schools, whether private or public.

By contrast, the work of Philip Schaff testifies to the far greater effectiveness of the strategy of assimilation and adaptation – at its best when seeking to fuse congenial elements in the traditions of the various immigrant groups. Assimilation and Americanization also meant that the German contributions to American education eventually lost their distinctiveness. Allen's essay on the kindergarten, Kohlstedt's on the natural history museums, and Olesko's on the physics teacher represent the fullest discussion of this fusion as the result of an ongoing dialogue between representatives of both cultures. In the case of the kindergarten, the German–American juxtaposition was accompanied by an equally apparent male–female contrast, and the ultimate outcome was another example of American developments having outpaced those in Germany.

The essays on the German immigrant teachers in America underscore once more how fragmentary our information is on this subject. It seems clear that those teachers, whether male or female, who taught in public schools chose assimilation and adaptation to English schooling as preferable for their students, although they opted, as long as possible, for the continuation of a bilingual German-American curriculum. Teachers, male or female, in the private, parochial schools, whether Lutheran or Catholic, appear on the whole to have held out far longer for the preservation of the German language.

Our contributors also warn us not to read the reports of American visitors to Germany or of German visitors to the United States solely as disinterested, complete, and accurate accounts of educational systems. Practicing educators themselves, most of the reporters arrived for and with a purpose that was shaped by the battles they fought at home and that was inspired by wished-for solutions. As Jeismann shows, this could benefit their hosts when the visitors pointed to aspects of educational practice that, by their daily familiarity, had escaped the natives' notice. More usually, as Günther, Wegner, and Linton describe, the reporting was selective to fit the exigencies of the situation at home.

The theme of accommodation and assimilation appears most starkly in the essays on higher education. The transmission of knowledge and the conventions of scholarship lie at the heart of modern higher education. Given the fame of the modern university tradition inaugurated at the century's outset in Berlin, it is only natural that the theme of German influence rings most loudly in this area. For our contributors, it begins with Philip Schaff and ends with the clinical professors of medicine discussed by Bonner. It is also quite revealing that the theme vanishes from the foreground and lingers – again, like Olesko's Cheshire cat's smile – behind the now ubiquitous façade of academic professionalism, an "ism" that is neither German nor American but, so to speak, purely and universally academic.

Perhaps this observation permits me to conclude that, whether we speak of German influences on America or mutual accommodations between two cultures, in their most intense way they took place in the academic area. As we glance back into history, we find that the most significant interaction between Germany and the United States occurred in education, science, and scholarship.

PART ONE

*Americans and Germans Look at Each
Other's Schools*

1

American Observations Concerning the Prussian Educational System in the Nineteenth Century

KARL-ERNST JEISMANN

All other reforms seek to abolish specific ills; education ministers to universal improvement. Horace Mann, "Reply to the Remarks of Thirty-One Boston Schoolmasters" (Boston, 1844), 3.

"Modernization" is a dominant perspective from which research in educational history in recent decades has examined the development of the educational system since the eighteenth century. The crucial question is whether and to what extent expanding school education contributed to the transition from the old estate society to modern civil society, to advanced industrialization, and to further participatory or even democratic structures. Following Talcott Parsons's definition of the three great revolutions that made the modern world – the industrial, the democratic, and the educational – and whose differential timing also influenced the differentiation of modern nations, one sees that in Germany, in contrast to other Western European states, the educational revolution preceded the industrial and political.[1]

This reversal of phases of modernization can be inferred from the different purposes and directions of the visitors who traveled abroad to study the newest developments. They hurried to Paris for the political revolution at the end of the eighteenth century, and they flocked to England in the first decades of the nineteenth century in order to learn the new technology and economy and to adopt it in their own countries. The same interest drew travelers to those places where modern educational institutions caused a stir. Their favorite destination in the 1830s was Germany and, above all, Prussia. In that respect, their journeys to Germany placed them among the other observers of advanced technologies and forms of organization of political,

---

1. Talcott Parsons, *Das System moderner Gesellschaften*, German ed. (Munich, 1972). Concerning educational revolution, see 120ff.

21

material, or intellectual culture. Despite the specific problems that the observation, criticism, or even adaptation of the new developments in the three sectors show, the international transfer of experience was not only a vehicle of progress but also evidence of the particular manner in which different nations behaved during the push for modernization.

In German historiography, the reports of the visitors from neighboring countries are well known, especially the famous report of Victor Cousin, written some years after his three-month tour through Germany in 1831. Dutchmen and Danes, but also Englishmen (Matthew Arnold being the most famous), followed in his tracks in the nineteenth century.[2] These journeys can be seen as a continuation of the pedagogical travels of the late eighteenth century, when individuals interested in enlightenment, education, and improvement of the human race went to observe those institutions and headmasters whom they viewed as models of pedagogical reforms. With regard to both time and matter, the famous travels to Pestalozzi in Ifferten mark the exact turning point that distinguishes the earlier and more personal travels of the eighteenth century, directed toward particular model schools, from the travels of the nineteenth century. The former still show a touch of the wish to hit upon curiosities; the latter were, above all, political expeditions with a public purpose. The interest no longer focused merely upon the improvement of education but upon the meaning of a general public education for state and society. The educators of the eighteenth century, one of them said, sought to solve the problem of how to ennoble the individual and also to make him a more useful and thereby a happier being in the existing social system.

In the nineteenth century, the double purpose of education became nationalized and politicized. How could a nation become better and at the same time more efficient by means of public school instruction? This was the question of the first half of the nineteenth century. Toward the end of the century, the national education system came to be considered a factor of national competition to increase economic and military efficiency. When William Torey Harris wanted to send a delegation of American educators to the World Exhibition in Paris in July 1889, he justified his application

---

2. Victor Cousin, *Bericht des Herrn Cousin . . . über den Zustand des öffentlichen Unterrichts in einigen Ländern Deutschlands, und besonders in Preussen,* trans. by J. C. Krüger (Altona, 1832, 1833, 1837). It was translated into English one year after its publication. Philipp Wilhelm van Heusde, ed., *Briefe über die Natur und den Zweck des höheren Unterrichts* (Heidelberg and Leipzig, 1830); E. F. Ingerslev, *Bemerkungen über den Zustand der gelehrten Schulen in Deutschland und Frankreich nach Beobachtungen auf einer pädagogischen Reise* (Berlin, 1841); Matthew Arnold, *Schools and Universities on the Continent* (London, 1868; newly edited by R. H. Super, Ann Arbor, Mich., 1964).

with the hint that it might be useful to observe the intimate connection of industry and education. For this purpose, he maintained that the German model should be paramount, because Germany since Frederick the Great had begun systematically to promote school institutions as an investment in the efficiency of the state. W. T. Harris drew a lesson: Nations that compete against each other and that do not endeavor to adopt new inventions or to educate their people soon fall behind.[3] The era of the so-called new imperialism had begun, and schools became instruments in the military and industrial competition of nations. In the competition over the purposes of public education, utility won out over improvement. Education no longer was an end in itself, as it still had been at the beginning of the nineteenth century, but a means.

I will not, however, follow this track, which can be read both from the reports of foreign visitors and from the domestic programs. I shall restrict myself to the early decades of the nineteenth century, which were from the pedagogical point of view still preindustrial and preimperialist, and during which the modern state educational system developed in Germany. Foreign travelers observed the European educational system as engaged educators, who tried to improve their own systems by their experiences. This intention must be taken into account when one examines the reports as a source for the observed circumstances, but it does not spoil the source. Quite the contrary: One may suspect that foreign eyes saw what escaped observations from inside – and those foreign eyes were sharp.

The following remarks are based on the reports of three Americans who traveled through several countries before the revolution of 1848 with the explicit purpose of inspecting educational systems. From 1836 to 1838, Alexander Dallas Bache visited Europe. He reported his observations of England, Scotland, Holland, the German states, and particularly of Prussia, France, and Switzerland, to the trustees of the Girard College for Orphans, on whose behalf he had undertaken his journey.[4] A year earlier, Henry Barnard had traveled to Europe. He first published his observations in 1851[5] but weaved into them publications and reports on the development of the educational system that had been published since 1848, as well as obser-

3. See Karl A. Schleunes, *Schooling and Society. The Politics of Education in Prussia and Bavaria 1750–1900* (Oxford, New York, and Munich, 1989), 236.
4. Alexander Dallas Bache, *Report on Education in Europe to the Trustees of the Girard College for Orphans* (Philadelphia, 1839). Hereafter cited as "Bache."
5. Henry Barnard, *National Education in Europe. Being an Account of the Organization, Administration, Institution and Statistics of Public Schools of Different Grades in the Principal States*, 2nd ed. (Hartford, Conn., 1854). The first edition of 1851 was not available. Hereafter cited as "Barnard."

vations on other travelers, such as Bache, Calvin E. Stowe from Ohio, and Joseph Kay, an English scholar and Traveling Bachelor at Cambridge.[6] The third report became much more widely known beyond the United States than the other two because of its author and because of the two controversial discussions that it set off. It was written by Horace Mann, who summed up his observations of a six-month journey in 1843.[7]

The three American travelers had a common motive for their observations, namely, to gain experience abroad that could be useful for the improvement of the educational system in their home country. They were above all interested in public education systems, which in the United States were still in their initial stage.[8] That explains why they, especially Horace Mann, paid special attention to the elementary school. Beyond that, their focus of interest lay in orphanages and in schools for the less well-to-do population. Alexander Bache traveled through Europe with a concrete mission from his board of trustees. The orphanage in Philadelphia was to be established as an educational institute comprising all grades from elementary school to college. The well-equipped orphanage had to reorganize its entire educational system, in both the lower and higher grades; the trustees therefore hoped for concrete, practical ideas from Bache's observations. Bache's report on his two-year journey is an intensive description of personal ex-

---

6. Calvin Ellis Stowe, married to the author of *Uncle Tom's Cabin*, wrote his "Report on Elementary Instruction in Europe" after he had traveled to Europe in 1836. In his report, he urged the authorities in Ohio to establish a public educational system after the Prussian model. His report was not available to me.

   Joseph Kay, Traveling Bachelor at Cambridge University, wrote *The Education of the Poor in England and Europe* (London, 1846) and *The Social Condition and Education of the People in England and Europe*, 2 vols. (London, 1850).

7. Horace Mann, *Seventh Annual Report of the Secretary of the Board of Education* (Boston, 1844). Hereafter cited as "Mann."

8. All three authors hold eminent places in American educational history. Bache, a great-grandson of Benjamin Franklin and a scientist at the University of Pennsylvania, was the first president of the famous Girard Foundation, an orphanage, since 1836 and organizer of the public educational system in Philadelphia; after 1853 he left the pedagogical field and dedicated himself both to his technical and scientific interests as head of the Coast Guard and to his tasks as first president of the National Academy of Sciences and the Smithsonian Institution. The *Encyclopedical Handbook of Education* of 1903 counts Henry Barnard and Horace Mann among the three major American educational reformers, the third being E. A. Sheldon, who was half a century younger than the two others. Barnard was the first Permanent Under-Secretary for Education in Connecticut. Later, in Rhode Island, he was president of several educational institutes and universities and, in 1867, first Commissioner for Education of the United States. In this office, which had no administrative authority, Barnard established historical educational science. He also endeavored to investigate and describe the development of school education in the most important European states from its beginning and to document this development in source compilations. Horace Mann, the most well known of these three educational reformers, was the most politically active. Through his work as a lawyer, he had already become president of the senate in Boston and, as secretary of the board of education, dedicated himself for more than a decade to the improvement of the public educational system of Massachusetts.

perience and shows distinctly what also characterized the other reports: that the visitors were less interested in philosophical-pedagogical conceptions than in practical ways of organizing school supervision, finance, class division, curricula, means and methods of teaching, school regulations and discipline, medical welfare, and maintenance. Bache's instructions indicated that his report should distinguish clearly "what is really useful from what is merely plausible in theory."[9] Thus all reports were characterized by their decidedly pragmatic approach.

Notwithstanding the common motives, the reports differed immensely in perspective and in tone. Though Horace Mann saw and reported less than Alexander Bache, because he was abroad for only six months, his report, which treated the experience of former travelers in a much more vivacious and engaged way than all the others, related his observations to the educational system in Massachusetts and scrutinized most carefully the relationship between educational system and the general political constitution in any given place. His report most clearly applied the "Tacitus" effect: He held up a mirror to the educational system in Massachusetts and, above all, to its teachers, and the image was not very favorable. The consequence was an extended and vehement quarrel between thirty-one Bostonian schoolmen and Horace Mann.[10] This quarrel was, if I am right, the first and most direct influence that the reports of American travelers exerted on the American educational system.

Henry Barnard's report, though it also served the concrete purpose of improving the educational system in Connecticut, because of its later publication and because of its reference to a number of other sources and reports, has a more detached and scientific character than the other two reports. Like all of his historical-educational writings, this report was written with a long-term, more general, and more indirect effect on the United States in mind. It therefore also contained historical surveys and perspectives.

The character of these reports, based as they were partly on each other or on other reports, does not make it seem advisable to analyze each one individually. I therefore confine myself to their remarks on the German

---

9. Bache, VI.
10. See *Remarks of the Association of Boston Masters upon his Seventh Annual Report* (Boston, 1844). Also see Horace Mann, *Reply to the "Remarks of Thirty-one Boston schoolmasters"* (Boston, 1840) and *Rejoinder to the "Reply" of the Hon. Horace Mann to the "Remarks" of the Association of Boston Masters* (Boston, 1845), as well as other material concerning the quarrel in the reprint of Mann's twelve most famous Annual Reports, edited by the Horace Mann League (Boston, 1949).

    Massachusetts opened its first teachers' seminary in 1839. In the following fifty years, almost 200 public and private teachers' seminaries were founded – a development that can be compared to the development of the Prussian teachers' training in the first half of the century.

educational system, although it would certainly be fascinating to follow the comparative reflections of the observers on the educational system of different European countries. I can only sum up briefly the extremely detailed reports. I divide this systematic approach into several topics that stand out clearly in the reports: organization of the public educational system; school forms; lessons; teacher training; and relation between the constitution and the educational system.

When the American observers used the term "national education," it did not have the same overtones or the complicated history of meaning that the term *Nationalerziehung* had in Europe, and especially in Germany, as early as the beginning of the nineteenth century. National education simply meant public education, in contrast to private education – a school system open to all and accountable to political authorities in the community and government. This term has a good reputation in a period in which the insight spread in the United States that education must be a general public affair. Against this background, it becomes understandable that the American travelers were above all interested in an already established education system. In this respect, they viewed Prussia as exemplary.[11]

Bache described carefully the structure of the Prussian school organization. The following elements seemed characteristic to him: general compulsory instruction or compulsory school attendance; establishment of elementary schools throughout the country; and a sufficiently broad availability of secondary school education. Although the Prussian system permitted private schools to exist, public financing of education made them unnecessary. To this system also belonged nationally regulated, systematic teacher training and a national supervisory school authority. Above all, the fact that the Prussian educational minister ranked equally with the minister of the interior or the minister of war impressed Bache. He described minutely the structure of the school administration and concluded that "there

---

11. "Arrange the most highly civilized and conspicuous nations of Europe in their due order of precedence, as it regards the education of their people, and the kingdoms of Prussia and Saxony, together with several of the western and south-western states of the Germanic confederation would undoubtedly stand preeminent, both in regard to the quantity and the quality of instruction. After this should come Holland and Scotland." Ireland, France, and Belgium followed at quite a distance but were on the same path. "England is the only one among the nations of Europe . . . which has not, and never has had, any system for the education of its people. Ant it is the country where . . . the greatest and most appalling social contrast exists – where, in comparison with the intelligence, wealth and refinement of what are called the higher classes, there is the most ignorance, poverty and crime among the lower."
So the Americans were not impressed by the polemics of the 1840s in connection with the discussion of the Factory Bill in England and directed against the Prussian educational system. These polemics appeared to them, with good reasons, to be political and rhetorical arguments in protection against demands to found a public educational system in England. See Mann, 21ff.

is a regular series of authorities from the master of the school up to the minister . . . and every part . . . takes its direction according to the will of the highest authorities. With such a system, under a despotic government, it is obvious that the provisions of any law may be successfully enforced."[12] Bache repeatedly expressed surprise that, in contrast to France, school regulations, especially the curricula, did not exist merely on paper but were put into practice. Also, within the school the system, of central authority ruled: "[T]he system of organization of the School resembles that of the government."[13]

All observers noted with surprise that these schools, governed by law and administration, "are not reduced to uniformity . . . the spirit of system not being allowed to check the growth of what is good." Though there was a tendency toward assimilation, as Bache stated in view of the general curricula for secondary schools of 1837, the respective interests of the population in the various regions were guaranteed by the fact that the regulations of the ministers were usually quite general and were only later specified in detail by the provincial authorities and local conditions. But above all, the teachers were free in their choice of methods. There was no prescribed opinion on pedagogical or methodological questions. Despite the standardizing effect that was spread by training and by the prevailing pedagogical views of the headmasters, there existed "some diversity of opinion and action. When we speak, then, of uniformity in the Prussian schools, it must be understood with great limitations, or we give a theoretical view of what might be, instead of a practical one of what is."[14]

How the structure of this educational system came to be was only of marginal interest. There are some references to early reforms in the eighteenth century, but for the American observers the real reform began with the foundation of the Ministry of Spiritual, Educational, and Medical Affairs in 1817. This shortened view may be the reason why conceptual but very real tensions and differences, already articulated in the concurrent German domestic discussion about governmental control of the educational system, were not perceived by the visitors. It is even more interesting to see that in this view, the tensions between the progressive tendencies of the reforms and the reactionary interventions of the restoration in the educational system did not appear at all. Diesterweg and Beckedorff pulled together for

---

12. Repeatedly they expressed surprise that such a general law did not exist at all; Bache cleared up the error of Victor Cousin, who had believed that the Süvern educational bill of 1819 had come into effect. See 220.

13. Ibid., 463.

14. Ibid., 231.

the improvement of the educational system as a public affair. Recent research has pointed repeatedly to the fact that during the Vormärz, improvement of the elementary schools in particular represented pedagogical
progress, regardless of whether it resulted from a liberal or a conservative
attitude. This view finds support in the reports. Generally speaking, and
from a far distance, opposites united in a common enterprise: "Prussia
seems, for a series of years, to have possessed patriotic and enlightened
citizens who devoted themselves to the cause of public instruction and
monarchs who have duly estimated and encouraged their exertions in this
cause."[15]

The definition of certain school forms and the discovery of their connections with each other was one of the most difficult problems of both
educational theory and practical organization that a national educational
system suitable for all adolescents faced. In the German states, this question
had been disputed since the eighteenth century and had been answered
controversially again and again. Today it is still a point of controversy. It
also remained controversial how to describe accurately the developing system of the school forms. Therefore, it is interesting to see how Americans
described this system.

Alexander Bache based his observations on the description of a fundamental choice in educational theory. One possibility is to have all pupils
pass through the same course, imparting to all an education identical in
principle, whether complete or at least partial, depending upon the time of
the pupils' leaving school. Alternatively, additional educational grades are
established beyond a common elementary form, gradually differing more
and more and in which the pupils can take their place, depending upon
their inclination and planned careers. Bache believed a segmented system
of education beyond elementary school to be both more reasonable and
more practical. Thus he implicitly and perhaps unknowingly sided against
the concept of the general education of humankind proposed by the neo-
humanists. This perspective led him to favor strongly a development that
pushed the establishment of specific professions in different forms of
schools.[16]

He regarded as first-rate the simple elementary schools, which he observed above all and which were generally schools for poor people, though
he did not think they were as outstanding as the Dutch ones. The better-
equipped *Volksschulen,* or burgher schools in town, lumped together under

15. Ibid., 221.
16. Ibid., 156.

the term "middle schools," he described as being excellent and first-rate. "The lower burgher schools . . . afford an elevated standard of true primary instruction and Prussia has special reason to be proud of the whole class."[17] He did not criticize the fact that these schools did not represent a higher grade of the general elementary school and that they were attended neither by the children in the country nor by the great number of children belonging to the poorer classes in the big cities because this division was in accordance with the pupils' future professional activity.

Concerning secondary education, the American visitors were interested above all in the higher burgher schools, or middle schools. For Bache, they were also exemplary for the organization of the educational system of the Girard foundation. He carefully described particular models: the Dorotheen school in Berlin and the even better-equipped higher burgher school in Potsdam. Today one could call the latter a real comprehensive school, where boys and girls were prepared for different professions in a general way and where, depending upon their interests and their choice of course, they would proceed to commercial or vocational school or even to secondary school. The variety of subjects and grades and the scope of choice impressed the observers, and the schools seemed to be excellent because they accommodated the different needs of the pupils. As with the middle schools, however, Bache was troubled by the Latin courses. The fact that these schools, corresponding to the conception of Humboldt and Süvern, prepared pupils at the same time for secondary school, seemed to him inappropriate and contrary to the system.[18]

Horace Mann was less interested in secondary schools, but Bache and, later, Barnard understood the secondary school as a pure learned institution that prepared pupils for the university. They approved of a clear distinction between university and secondary school, especially the provision for two years in the "prima" class, which actually belonged to the phase of "superior instruction."[19] The Americans did not remark upon the multifunctionality of Prussian secondary schools in their lower and middle grades. The problem for them was less whether and how the complete secondary class imparted a general higher education and much more how the secondary school, preparing students for the university, distributed the humanistic and modern subjects. Here Bache favored the Prussian utraquistic system and defended it against the attacks of the pure humanists and the resolute realists. He thought that the Prussian curricula of 1837 were well suited to prepare

17. Ibid., 231.
18. Ibid., 254 f.
19. Ibid., 362.

for studies at the university: "While the Germans have lost nothing in general literary culture by this system, they have gained much in other departments of knowledge."[20] He particularly approved of the fact that despite all governmental regulations, the state avoided uniformity and allowed a wide scope of tolerance. Bache presented three types of schools as examples of the breadth of variation: the Schulpforta, above all oriented to classical studies; the Cologne Realgymnasium, with its priority on modern subjects; and the Friedrich Wilhelm-Gymnasium in Berlin, in its endeavor to achieve "due equilibrium." "The spirit of toleration . . . constitutes a peculiar part of the excellence of the Prussian gymnasia, and is one source of the superior mental training which they afford."[21]

Bache was more interested in the middle schools than in the secondary schools. Although these schools were not permitted to have final exams until 1832, and although there were only twenty-nine of them in 1837, a little less than a quarter of the number of secondary schools, Bache's report presents them as a similarly important and legitimate part of the higher educational system. He considered the fact that they were clearly separated from the secondary schools to be an essential advantage. In the same way that the utraquistic curricula had elevated the secondary schools far above the English grammar schools, the acquired status of the middle schools had led them to the top of the other higher European schools.[22]

Thus the structure of school forms in Prussia already seemed to be a system that, in making distinctions between the main professional branches, had adjusted its basic outlines to modern working conditions. Residual incomplete segmentation, such as offering subjects in preparation for secondary schools, seemed a historically caused disorder that had to be overcome. Knowledge gathered primarily at schools in bigger cities or at model institutions such as the seminar schools in Weissenfels or Berlin undoubtedly did not give an exact picture of the school forms and their development in Prussia; with the strong emphasis on the higher municipal middle school system, however, the observer nevertheless had caught the dynamic of fu-

20. Ibid., 455.
21. Bache, who was in Prussia during the Lorinser quarrel, did not consider plausible the view that these schools, with their wide range of subjects, might overtax the pupils and affect their health. In England and the United States, more weekly hours of mental work would be demanded, and the lessons would be less lively and stimulating than those in the Prussian secondary schools. Bache also regarded the system of yearly promotion and six months' reports to be useful. He generally considered the exams at the higher German schools, which he himself had attended and not only read about in the exams regulations, to be much more appropriate than the French exams, which consisted of mere repetitionary knowledge (see 509). In the two essential issues on the secondary school during the Vormärz, the American visitors sided with the school administration rather than with its critics inside and outside school.
22. Bache, 503ff.

ture development and had foreseen what later asserted itself distinctly: the progressive differentiation of the system.[23]

The American visitors attended various forms of school, above all very large and very good schools. If one has some experience in dealing with foreign and expert visitors of schools, one is likely to develop a healthy skepticism about what one is shown. The American visitors already supposed that they had been shown lessons only from the very positive side and, being competent schoolmen, they took precautions.[24] The fact, however, that they reported unanimously, and with obvious surprise, only successful lessons could not have been based on pretense. They were interested in German teaching methods, just as Germans who visited English industry showed interest in new production processes.

I cannot describe here the minute attention with which the visitors took down questions and answers during many lessons, with the obvious intent of presenting the lessons for adoption in American schools. They were, above all, impressed by how much faster reading and writing abilities were developed than at home. They were especially surprised at the teachers' factual and methodological sovereignty, which allowed them to act in a flexible way, depending upon the circumstances and upon the pupils' reactions, and to adjust themselves to each pupil during the lessons. Freedom in choosing the method and control of various methods appeared to the observers to be the essential secrets of success in lessons. The fact that teachers, speaking offhand, built up their lessons systematically, in question-and-answer form, without limiting themselves to merely reading from a book, and that they organized and varied the single stages, depending upon the pupils' cognitive progress, must have been a new experience for the observers. They were impressed by the principle, dating back to Pestalozzi's conception, that pupils should understand what they learned in the lesson, and that they themselves should come up with solutions or ideas. The teacher should, above all, listen and understand how to challenge the pupils' ability to think independently, or even to challenge their contradictions with a little help at the right time.

The American observers admired the fact that German schools taught independence rather than mere knowledge. Horace Mann, otherwise very critical, reported that Dr. Vogel (a civil servant at the supervisory school

---

23. I will cut short the analysis of this aspect; one could continue the analysis with respect to vocational schools or to the carefully examined schools for the disabled or for socially menaced children such as the *Rauhes Haus;* one would also have to mention the criticism of the lack of any public and governmentally sponsored higher education for girls.
24. See the passage in Horace Mann in which he describes his procedure; Mann, 134.

authority) told him that failure to train pupils to do their own thinking was no mere fault or shortcoming, but rather a sin. "Alas! thought I, what explanation will be sufficient for many of us who have had charge of the young!"[25] Again and again, the observers emphasized German teachers' factual and methodological abilities, either in drawing complicated shapes or in presenting complex contexts. Even in more difficult parts of the lesson, the teacher would move freely in front of the class. He would not read from a book or let it be repeated but would teach entirely without a book in his hand: "[T]he Prussian teacher has no book. He needs none. He teaches from a full mind. . . . He observes what proficiency the child had made, and then adapts his instructions . . . to the necessity of the case. He answers all questions. He solves all doubts. It is one of his objects . . . so to present ideas, that they shall start doubts and provoke questions. He connects the subject of each lesson with all kindred and collateral ones."[26]

The consequence was obviously lively participation by the children and excellent discipline, which was unanimously praised as the consequence of the teachers' factual and methodological authority and "of familiar conversations between teachers and pupils."[27] Such a teacher prepared his lessons the way a lawyer or preacher prepares his arguments or sermons. The praise was directed toward elementary school teachers as much as toward learned schoolmen. It was said that a Prussian philologist would be considered as a professor at any American college or university. Prussian teachers felt obliged to work hard not only because they wanted to remain scientifically up-to-date but also because they strove to advance scientific research. This was a tendency that, as they observed rightly and not without skepticism, characterized the pure specialist teachers at secondary schools.[28]

Not only factual knowledge but, above all, methodological ability and the teachers' zeal called forth the visitors' admiration; in addition, they commented favorably upon the friendly and patient devotion to the pupils (something that they very much missed with Scottish teachers, who were similarly diligent).[29] They praised the teachers' pedagogical commitment and the fact that the teachers took the children seriously. Corporal punishment, thought not forbidden, was quite unusual: "Though I saw hundreds of schools and thousands – I think I may say . . . tens of thousands of pupils

---

25. Ibid., 119.
26. Ibid., 123.
27. Ibid., 117.
28. Bache, 456, 461.
29. Mann, 61ff.

– I never saw one child undergoing punishment. . . . I never saw one child in tears from having been punished, or from fear of being punished."[30]

The reports not only give such general descriptions, they also characterize the lessons, teaching aids, and methods used for each subject. I cannot reflect on them here but rather will proceed to the next issue, teacher training, with the question asked by Horace Mann: "Whence came this beneficent order of men scattered over the whole country, moulding the character of its people, and carrying them forward in a career of civilization more rapidly than any other people in the world are now advancing?"[31]

One could draw the indirect conclusion from the reports that in America the situation of teacher training was similar to that found in Germany until the last third of the eighteenth century. Teachers were young men "coming fresh from the plough, the workshop, of the anvil – or, what is no better, from Greek and Latin classics," without training for their profession.[32] Bache emphasized the examination rules for secondary school teachers in Germany, where there were special philological and pedagogical seminaries for the preparation of learned schoolmen and a compulsory examination for mastership, followed by more examinations in the course of their professional career.[33] The fact that even elementary and middle school teachers had to pass through a three-year training period, maintained during this time by large state scholarships and grants, impressed the American observers. Barnard (who quoted approvingly from the extensive reports by Joseph Kay), Bache, and especially Mann agreed in their admiration of the achievement of these teachers' seminaries. They attributed the progressiveness of the Prussian educational system to this kind of teacher training. They commented upon the careful selection of the successful applicants. The teaching profession, they noted, had such a high public reputation that no one who had failed in other activities would think of looking for a job as a teacher. "These considerations exclude at once all that inferior order of men, who, in some countries, constitute the main body of the teachers."[34] Common training and examination inspired a class consciousness. The secure social position, the regular (though not high) salary and pension, and the exemption from military service gave teachers social standing. Elementary teachers

---

30. Ibid., 133. Again and again, particular emphasis was placed upon the fact that discipline was excellent: "I never saw the discipline in better condition than in these schools." Bache, 463, 506 f. See also Barnard, 145.
31. Mann, 128.
32. Ibid., 124.
33. Bache, 478 f.
34. Mann, 129.

often came from families of farmers, "but in education and position they are gentlemen in every sense of that term, and acknowledged officers of the county governments."[35] Factual knowledge, methodological competence, and pedagogical ethos, as well as the feeling of dignity derived from their profession and social reputation, were the consequences of this professionalization of the teacher.[36]

Barnard's report remarks, not without an undertone of surprise, that as excellently qualified experts belonging to a respected profession, teachers were looked upon as persons able to represent the interests of the people. Barnard mentioned that teachers were delegates in the parliaments of German states and, after the revolution, also in the Prussian chamber of deputies.[37]

Despite all the praise of the state educational system and of the arrangement of the curricula, there were critical remarks. These criticisms concerned the absence of public secondary school for girls, the lack of physical exercise, the neglect of French, and the function of religious education in the public school system. But one will search in vain for critical remarks regarding the lessons or the training and social rank of teachers. All American reports underlined emphatically that here was an example that should be followed in many European countries and also in the United States. The observers did not even criticize the fact that there were hardly any female teachers and merely a beginning of private training for them.[38]

From the German perspective, these judgments were perceived with some surprise. To be sure, elementary school teachers enjoyed a rapidly advancing professionalization and a distinctly growing self-confidence, and they frequently maintained excellent factual and human connections with supervisory school authorities – as was reflected clearly in the domain of Natorp in the province of Westphalia. But as early as the 1830s, teachers in the opposition published protests against the conditions of their existence, their supervision by the parson, and their exclusion from the school com-

---

35. Barnard, 171.
36. What the church was for Europe in the Middle Ages – namely, the opening of the door to the talented of the lower classes to higher professions – the profession of elementary teacher was in Prussia in the nineteenth century. Quoting Kay, Barnard saw in this an overt political intention: "The German governments have been wiser . . . than our free countries. They have separated the fiery spirits from the easily excited masses, and converted them into earnest, active and indefatigable fosterers of the public morality, and into guardians of the common weal." Barnard, 178. Surprised and ashamed, Horace Mann noted the great number of pedagogical specialist periodicals in the German language: over thirty of them were published, whereas the indifference of the teachers and the absence of public interest in the United States permitted only two such periodicals to survive. Mann, 141.
37. Barnard, 169.
38. Mann, 140.

mittee. In the 1840s, Horace Mann could hardly have failed to notice some of the critical voices and publications, as well as the vehement calls for the promotion of the profession of elementary teachers and for the improvement of elementary school instruction, although he might not have noticed the more extreme critiques such as that of the Silesian elementary teacher Wander. Did the American visitors' wish to exert a stimulating effect in their homeland cause them to color their reports on the instruction and the teachers in Germany so positively, or did they consider the deficiencies marginal, in view of the gap that they noted between the methodological and didactic skills and the pedagogical virtues on the other side of the Atlantic?

The more the visitors from the United States emphasized the merits of the Prussian educational system, the more they had to ask themselves what they thought of the manifest contradiction that existed between Prussia's political and social constitution and its educational system. The sensitivity to the existence of such a connection was clearly developed, though they mentioned it only in passing. They all traveled with the conviction that they came from a free land with advanced political and social circumstances to an underdeveloped Europe that for centuries had gone astray under the sins of feudalism. Horace Mann underlined vigorously this advantage of the Americans, who had broken off from depraved Europe, which though blessed with many riches still was far from freedom and equality in living conditions, and where the masses lived in poverty while a small social stratum lived in abundance.[39]

In several respects, the observers had to explain how the educational system that they depicted could have been established under a despotic government and a feudal-aristocratic social system. The fact that the governmental organization and school authority worked and that the regula-

---

39. Horace Mann found amusing connections even between daily habits and the political system. During his stay at boarding schools and orphanages, he found a strange practice everywhere: The children slept between an underbed and a quilt, which obviously were both huge feather beds weighing ten to twenty pounds; the respective quilts of the teachers weighed up to forty pounds or more. I surmise that he experienced the same in the guest house where he stayed for the night. Wool blankets were given only at prisons; the denial of feather beds was considered one part of the punishment. "Every respectable man and child sleeps between two feather beds, summer and winter. The debilitating effect of such a practice both upon body and mind must be incalculable. If the leading members of the Holy Alliance wish to abase their subjects into voluntary submission to arbitrary power, – if they design so to enervate their spirits that they will never pant for the joys and the immunities of liberty . . . they can do no one thing more conducive to these ends, than to perpetuate this national custom of . . . sleeping between feather beds." On the whole, he found the want of hygiene, especially of good ventilation in the schoolrooms, deplorable: "Were one to attempt a philosophical explanation of that lethargy of character, that want of activity and enterprise, for which the Germans are so proverbial, I think he would fail of a just solution of the problem, if he left out of the account the errors of their physical training." Mann, 49.

tions were put into practice could still be reconciled with the efficiency of a disciplined administrative absolutism. However, the fact that, despite all fiscal economy, the state and its administration in the provinces and communities could spend such a great deal of money on the educational system, that it could finance a progressive system of teacher training, that the teacher candidates were modestly but safely provided for and respected, that the governmental supervisory school authorities promoted an instruction that would educate the people to independent thinking, that a high degree of liberality and eccentricity existed and was even encouraged throughout the system in general, and that teachers had great freedom in the use of their methods – all this was difficult to reconcile with the general conception of the political and social constitution and with the preconceptions that the reporters had about the German national character.

It has already been mentioned that the authors did not concern themselves with an explanation of this contradiction by means of historical analysis. Neither the long-term reform tendencies, which were controversial in themselves, nor the political opposition with which they had to contend came into their view. The rejection that resulted from the clash of reform and restoration went unnoted. That was why they perceived the contradiction as a clear and simple antagonism. For the Americans, two questions arose for the future. The first was directed to Prussia and Europe in general: What future development would result from that contradiction? The second question dealt with the chance of transferring the impulses of an excellent educational system in a despotic and feudal system to America.

Concerning the first question, Horace Mann presented a short formula: "The school is good, the world is bad."[40] With that, he touched on the big issue of the German educational policy discussion of the reform era: The "world" must be improved through the "intellect." The school therefore shapes society, and the reform of society must come from the school. But then Horace Mann described precisely why circumstances prevented the improvement of society through the school. First of all, at age fourteen, children left school far to early. Second, good books were lacking for young people, as was a network of good libraries in the otherwise excellent German literary culture. Journalism, operating under censorship, was poor and stimulated neither further education nor social activity. The most important reason for the inefficacy of good education in state and society was that what was learned at school could not be used in life. Neither the knowledge of the educated nor their good will and abilities found a field

40. Mann, 149.

of activity in the state or community. All was regulated by the authorities: laws, finance, war, and service. The subject could only pay and obey.[41]

To these concrete observations, Mann added a general remark that in his opinion applied not only to Prussia but to all European nations. The vices of the rulers and of the ruling classes, the depraved "cream" of society, which he considered feudal, had a perverting effect on the lower classes, who copied the vices of their superiors. Mann did not mention what these vices were; he took for granted the fact that they existed: "The power of the government presses upon the only partially-developed facilities of the youth, as with a mountain's weight."[42]

The picture that Horace Mann sketched of Europe in social, economic, moral, and political terms was somber; this was especially true for England, where in bigger cities children were born only "to be imprisoned, transported, or hung," and where not even an advanced education could be a counterweight, however weak, against the general grievances, as for example in the monarchical states.[43] Could these defects, having developed through centuries, be overcome through the influence of such an education? "It would be a revolution such as was never yet wrought in so short a period."[44] Horace Mann prognosticated: "No one who witnesses that quiet, noiseless development of mind which is now going forward in Prussia through the agency of its educational institutions can hesitate to predict that the time is not far distant when the people will assert their right to a participation in their own government."[45]

Other authors, such as Bache, Barnard, or Kay, the Briton upon whom Barnard relied for long quotations, who did not bring the contradiction between constitution and education into particular focus, nevertheless were of the same opinion and expected education to promote general progress in state and society. Barnard quoted approvingly Kay, who wrote against the generally accepted view in England that the Prussian teachers were merely instruments of the absolutist authority to educate the people to be passive subjects: "Many of the warmest friends of constitutional progress . . . have always been found among the teachers, and, it is a fact, . . . that liberal and constitutional ideas never made so rapid a progress in Prussia . . .

41. Ibid., 155ff.
42. Ibid., 159.
43. Ibid., 187. Mann noted only in Austria an even more negative system because of the connection of a despotic regime with the neglect of public education. See ibid., 144 f.
44. Ibid., 158.
45. He hoped that it was not true that King Friedrich Wilhelm IV "is adverse to that intellectual movement which is now so honorably distinguishing Prussia from most of the nations in Europe" and that the king "through a peaceful revolution by knowledge . . . can save a fiery revolution by blood."

as they have done since the establishment of the present system of education. I believe that the teachers and the schools of Prussia have been the means of awakening in that country that spirit of inquiry and that love of freedom which forced the government to grant a bona fide constitution to the country."[46]

If the answer to the first question was that public instruction in Germany was not an instrument of despotism but a means to its conquest, then the second question could also be answered positively. A bad political system did not discredit a good educational system but should incite politically more advanced nations "to a like care in their system of education."[47] Mann again argued more vehemently. If it were possible for an arbitrary government to use an excellent education for its own aims, how much better, then, could the Americans use such an educational system to support and develop their republican institutions? And in his enthusiasm for the improvement of the educational system, he even overcame for a short time his general condemnation of the despotic governments on the Continent. He refuted the argument that a public educational system with general compulsory school attendance could be introduced only in despotic systems by referring to those German states that had constitutions and broader franchises than some states of the United States. And in Silesia, the parliament had enacted a general school law in which the free representatives of a free people embodied general compulsory education. Referring to the Pilgrim fathers, Mann wrote that "we are not the descendants of an ignorant horde," and he appealed to his politically and socially well-advanced countrymen to remember their duty as "the depositaries of freedom and human hopes." If in a political system participation is possible and asked for, then "each child has the right to a public education."[48]

For Prussia it was true that "The world is bad, the school is good"; for the United States, the reverse applied: "The world is good, the school is bad." Prussia had well-educated men who were denied political and public activities; the United States had men who were poorly prepared for the tasks awaiting them. These observations ended with a glowing appeal to the moral message of America, demanding the promotion of education to first place on the political agenda. His countrymen should consider the huge possibilities of the American continent "not as tempters to ostentation and pride, but as means to be converted by the refining alchemy of education, into mental and spiritual treasures." They should not find satisfaction in the

46. Barnard, 184.
47. Bache, 230.
48. Mann, 193, 197.

expansion of their territory or their agricultural production "but in the expansion and perpetuation of the means of human happiness."[49]

I raise two concluding questions: First, is it possible to detect any effect that these reports had on the development of the educational system in the United States? I cannot answer this question myself but must pass it on to my American colleagues. I suppose that there are already studies on that issue in the United States that have not come to my knowledge.[50] Second, could the evaluation of these reports provide new insights into the historical research on education in Germany? I answer this question in the affirmative in two senses: Those reports can both supplement our factual knowledge and differentiate our judgments.

As far as I know, German research has not taken note of these reports as empirical evidence. Perhaps the reports are looked upon as unreliable sources because of their special perspective; perhaps they are denied authenticity because they base their description of facts on contemporary texts that are better and more extensively known to us. One should not, however, underestimate their informational value. The extraordinary precision of their observations of lessons makes them valuable complements to German pedagogical journals and to the reports that were usually drawn upon for the historical reconstruction of instruction in the nineteenth century. In that respect, they are original and broaden our knowledge, because they were written by experts with a different point of view and who at the same time included and compared experience from other European countries.

More important, however, is the evaluation pattern that underlies the reports. The criteria for judgment of the American observers, with their distinctly positive tenor, differ sharply from voices critical of the public educational system that had already been heard before the middle of the century, which escalated in the second half of the century into denunciations of "educational fraud." After the Second World War, this critique culminated in the reproach that the educational system had been politically functionalized to strengthen predemocratic political and social structures. The most resolute critics consider the history of the German educational system since the late eighteenth century to be an important factor in the

49. Ibid., 198; see the further remarks in Jonathan Messerli, *Horace Mann: A Biography* (New York, 1972), 404 f.
50. Messerli points to the pedagogic and administrative reforms coming into effect in consequence of the controversy started by Mann's report: "his ideas became institutionalized" – obviously not only to his satisfaction. See ibid., 422 ff. He does not refer to special literature.

German *Sonderweg,* which turned from the perpetuation of the aristocratic-absolutist state in a capitalist and finally imperialist and fascist direction. The extreme version of this theory understands the establishment of the public educational system as an experiment leading necessarily to a catastrophe. The formula of the "contradiction between education and domination government" (Heydorn) views the educational revolution in Germany as precisely *not* the important third link that Parsons envisioned between the two other revolutions – namely, the industrial and the democratic – but rather as a reactionary force leading to perversion in the hands of the government.[51] This crude interpretation is not representative but clearly shows a thought pattern that one also finds in more balanced judgments, and one that modern historical research on education shares with the social criticism of the nineteenth century, regardless of the specific current fashion: The world is bad. The school can be good only if it educates the pupil against his time so that he will some day bring forth a better one.[52]

The pragmatic opinions of the American observers run contrary to this dualistic-idealistic view of the relation between state and education. This contrary conclusion resulted from a more pragmatic relation to the Enlightenment that did not reduce it to dialectical oppositions. The American reports accepted the fact that a state, although politically backward, can establish sectors of partial progress. They did not reduce a "system" to one denominator but were led by their empirical observations to regard it as a polyfunctional political and social conglomerate. So they presumed, quite impartially, a relation between educational system and political structure that postulated a basic but not simultaneous parallelism of pedagogical and political progress. They saw that even where the educational system was established with a conservative intention as a strategy of "defensive modernization" (Wehler), it could serve the long-term encouragement of progressive forces. That allowed them an insight into the partial backwardness of free constitutional and social structures. This attitude also made it possible for them to consider the Prussian public education system as in many respects exemplary for the establishment of public education in the United

---

51. See, for example, Gerhardt Petrat, *Schulerziehung. Sozialgeschichte in Deutschland bis 1945* (Munich, 1987).

52. To word it classically with Schiller: "Eine wohltätige Gottheit reisse den Säugling beizeiten von seiner Mutter Brust, nähre ihn mit der Milch eines besseren Alters und lasse ihn unter fernem griechischen Himmel zur Mündigkeit reifen. Wenn er dann ein Mann geworden ist, so kehre er, eine fremde Gestalt, in sein Jahrhundert zurück, aber nicht, um es mit seiner Erscheinung zu erfreuen, sondern furchtbar wie Agamemnons Sohn, um es zu reinigen." Friedrich Schiller, *Über die ästhetische Erziehung des Menschen in einer Reihe von Briefen* (1794), ninth letter.

States – an unbiased judgment of which some English observers of that time were incapable.

Just as the emphasis on the positive side of the German and Prussian education system was a means to improve it, the liberal critique of the German educational system served as a means to improve the public educational system in America. Horace Mann expected such an inwardly directed critique to flow from his report and also a willingness to improve from his American teachers, and he was bitterly disappointed when they defended the old system.[53]

If for good reason we consider the American reports from a critical point of view, we must not misapprehend the German reports as direct reflections of reality. From the broadened perspective of international comparison, the criteria of judgment become detached from the suggestive polarization of fundamentally opposed constructions of ideas and become open again to the observation that the educational system is relatively autonomous and should be comprehended not only as a function of a political system but also as a factor for change of that system. This understanding, it is true, does not support the idea of a harmonious interlock of the three revolutions in the push toward modernization. The dislocating consequences of the Industrial Revolution and the quashing of the German political revolution through the conservative unification from above aggravated historical tensions and contradictions. A more intensive analysis of the American reports of the first half of the century could presage this outcome, and one can assume that reports from the second half of the century would show this still more clearly.

53. Mann, *Reply to the "Remarks,"* 4: "The spirit manifested in the greater part of the 'Remarks,' is not philosophic. . . . Education is treated not as an advancing, but as a perfected science; and the object of the 'Remarks' seems to be, to arrest and petrify it where it now is."

2

Interdependence between Democratic Pedagogy in Germany and the Development of Education in the United States in the Nineteenth Century

KARL-HEINZ GÜNTHER

Around the middle of the nineteenth century, democratic theories of pedagogy exercised a powerful influence in Germany. German liberal educators who were forced to emigrate to America after 1848 viewed the educational system that they encountered there through the prism of their democratic-liberal doctrines. Educational mediators such as Friedrich Adolph Wilhelm Diesterweg and Friedrich Fröbel drew from the experiences of German teachers in America to find confirmation of their theories and to continue their criticism of the Prussian-German educational system throughout the remainder of the century. Although the return impact of German democratic theories of pedagogy upon American schools reveals itself only in fragmentary form, it is nonetheless clear that since the mid-nineteenth century, these German theories and the course of the development of education in the United States have existed in a state of interdependence.

This interdependence proved to be possible because a tremendous number of Germans emigrated to the United States after the failed democratic revolution of 1848. Diesterweg himself had been a passionate supporter of that revolution. Although calculations differ, nearly 1 million people left Germany between 1849 and 1854, not only to escape the repression that followed the revolutionary events, but also to free themselves from the restrictive power structures of the reaction.[1] Among the emigrants were many who had been trained in Germany as teachers.

It is probably impossible to determine the exact number of teachers who emigrated to the United States after 1848; the literature often refers to "hundreds and hundreds" and points out the great importance of these emigrants for North American culture and education.[2] Karl Friedrich Wil-

---

1. See Karl Friedrich Wilhelm Wander, *Der Kampf um die Schule,* selected, introduced, and commented on by Gerd Hohendorf, 2 vols. (Berlin, 1979), 1:43.
2. See Karl-Heinz Günther, ed., *Geschichte der Erziehung* (Berlin, 1987), 291ff.

helm Wander, a coworker of Diesterweg, visited the United States in 1850 and 1851 and wrote from his own experience that "There was also a rather important number of teachers who went to the other side of the ocean and tried to found an existence in their professions."[3] In *Erinnerungen aus dem Leben eines Unbedeutenden,* Heinrich Börnstein wrote with regard to German immigrants after 1848:

> What a large number of *learned* people, talented disciples of science and art, experienced *instructors of young people* came to America in the period of a few years; what a mass of knowledge, scholarship, intelligence and skills were filled into the whole Union; the beneficial effect of this transfusion of fresh blood became evident after a short time, tremendous changes for the better emerged in the next ten years; in a surprisingly short time, huge changes in cultural and social fields took place not only in the lives of Germans but all North Americans. . . .[4] (italics in original)

Certainly such sources must be viewed with caution. Börnstein wrote as a German-American in 1880, when the wave of immigrants to the United States caused some people to fear a developing Germanization. Wander cautioned his readers against illusions about the New World and warned that hundreds of highly talented, scientifically or literarily educated men had been left alone in poverty and misery and had not survived the struggle for existence.[5] Wander urged teachers not to emigrate, saying that the teacher's job would not flourish in America because it was too new and the material ruled over the intellectual.[6]

As a rule, German teachers who emigrated spoke no English. Upon their arrival, therefore, they influenced mainly private German schools, some sponsored by associations. German schools developed into models that had local or regional influence. Good examples were Knapp's German-English Institute in Baltimore, founded in 1853; the German-American *Elementar- und Realschule* in Newark (1856); Beacon Street School in Newark (1858); and Hoboken Academy (1861). The first kindergarten in North America was founded in connection with the opening of German schools in 1856 (other sources say 1859) at German-English School 14 in Boston. Yet it remains doubtful that immigrant German teachers and German-American educational establishments were decisive in the foundation of kindergartens

---

3. Wander, *Kampf um die Schule,* 2:176.
4. Heinrich Börnstein, "Erinnerungen aus dem Leben eines Unbedeutenden," in *Der Westen* (Chicago) 40 (1888):1; quotation from Hermann Schuricht, *Geschichte der deutschen Schulbestrebungen in America* (Leipzig, 1884), 55.
5. See Karl Friedrich Wilhelm Wander, *Auswanderungskatechismus (Emigration Catechism) Ein Ratgeber für Auswanderer, besonders für diejenigen, welche nach Nordamerika auswandern wollen, in Bezug auf Kenntnis des Landes, Abreise, Überfahrt, Ankunft, Ansiedlung etc., und ein belehrendes Volksbuch für die Hinterbliebenen* (Glogau, 1852).
6. Wander, *Kampf um die Schule,* 2:178.

in the United States after 1850. The *United States Educational Report* first mentioned kindergartens in 1873: 42 kindergartens for more than 1,252 children. In 1881, the *Report* listed 272 kindergartens with more than 14,000 children educated by more than 600 kindergarten teachers.[7] These establishments were in such places as San Francisco, Wilmington, Belleville, Chicago, Indianapolis, St. Louis, Hoboken, Newark, and New York. Nonetheless, Germans clearly had special influence on the foundation of kindergartens in the United States, to which I shall return when discussing Adolph Douai.

To determine what pedagogical ideas and knowledge teachers brought into the German-American school system and hence into North America, we must ask why those teachers left Germany. The majority undoubtedly opposed Prussian-German educational policy, with its close connection between government school policy and the orthodox church. The teachers supported the separation of school and church, education that was not nonreligious but committed to the idea of religious tolerance. They objected to the manipulation of children in the interest of narrow feudalism but endorsed the inculcation of bourgeois freedom; they rejected forced manipulation and pursued a pedagogy that was to serve the free development of the personality. These theories were the reason that Diesterweg described the American school system several times in his *Rheinische Blätter.* His publication of these theories amounted to a retransfer of democratic educational ideas back to their place of origin, where they could not yet become effective.

The programmatic statements made by representatives of German-American schools reflected the democratic educational ideas held by immigrant pedagogues. The German school in Boston, for example, adopted a statement of purpose and covering by-laws that had been developed by Karl Heinzen, one of the most interesting personalities of the emigration.

Karl Heinzen was a radical democrat who was born in 1809 and emigrated to the United States in 1850. He edited the *Deutsche Schnellpost* in New York, which Karl Marx, with typical overstatement, called a *Saublatt* ("dirty rag") because of its anti-Communist stand.[8] Heinzen's *Deutsche Schnellpost* and the *Republik der Arbeiter,* edited by Wilhelm Weitling, were two of the German-language newspapers with which Wander became familiar and in which he followed efforts for social reform during his stay in the United States. Wander wrote, however, that "K. H. [Karl Heinzen] is

---

7. According to Schuricht, *Deutschen Schulbestrebungen,* 97.
8. Karl Marx and Frederick Engels, *Works,* vol. 27 (Berlin, 1962), 219.

called 'reactionary' in the Communist press because he fights against Communism most vehemently. He is one of the relatively small number of editors who work for the moral renaissance of the people by decisively improving the level of daily newspapers. The *Schnellpost* distinguishes itself by its noble attitude."[9]

Karl Heinzen also engaged in pedagogical work. He prepared the statutes of the *Boston deutsch-englischer Schulverein,* which, completely in the spirit of the democratic educational ideas of German pedagogues in 1848, stated that the task of the school was to disseminate knowledge, not belief. Proceeding from the principle of total religious tolerance, schools must not inquire about the religious creed of new pupils or imprint religion upon them. The serious task of the school is to develop in children a sense of the good, beautiful, noble, right, and true. Just as the Constitution of the United States dealt with religion, so too the school should proceed from the spirit of the Declaration of Independence with regard to the origin of its pupils. It was to be open to children of all nationalities. It should recognize the great principle of equal rights for all people, not only by its example and its teachings, but also by trying to become a guide for its pupils in their future lives. Boys and girls were to be taught together.[10] Freedom of worship in education, tolerance, the humanitarian aim of education aimed at the good, true, and beautiful, complete equal rights for all children in the schools, coeducation – these were principles of democratic German teachers in the Vormärz and in the revolution of 1848–9. Some of these principles can be found in identical wordings in the writings of Diesterweg.

These direct democratic German educational principles can be found in other governing documents of German-English schools and pedagogical associations that were founded by immigrant German teachers. For example, a German-American teachers' society was founded in Louisville, Kentucky, in 1870. It supported complete separation between school and church, rejecting any spiritual interference. It proclaimed that the educational task was "to develop free independent thinking and the receptiveness of the mind for all good and beautiful."[11] These words could have been formulated by Diesterweg, although there is no direct proof of his collaboration. The direct influence of democratic German pedagogy was even more evident in the Federal Constitution debated by the Second Teachers Congress of the German-American Teacher Association in Cincinnati,

9. Wander, *Kampf um die Schule,* 1:44.
10. Schuricht, *Deutschen Schulbestrebungen,* 57ff.
11. Ibid., 67.

Ohio, in 1871. Paragraph 2, for example, called for a naturelike (developing) teaching method, aimed for by German pedagogy, to be introduced into American schools.[12] Efforts aimed at establishing a symbiosis between democratic German educational ideas and the political conditions in the United States were shown in the expressed aim of educating truly free American citizens.[13]

In Germany itself, these ideas of democratic German pedagogy played a role only as alternatives to the Prussian-German training of children as subjects. These democratic ideas persisted for a long time, at least as long as democratic German teachers who had emigrated after 1848 maintained their influence on the German-American school system. The Eleventh Teachers Congress of the German-American Teacher Association met in Newark, New Jersey, in 1880 and adopted a constitution that expressed the relationship between specific American and traditional German democratic pedagogical traditions in a new way. Paragraph I gave priority of purpose for the Association to the task of educating free American citizens. The specific German democratic pedagogical tradition of making propaganda for naturelike (developing) education at home and at school was relegated to the role of a means to an end and subordinated to the main purpose: educating free American citizens.[14]

This shift in the function of German pedagogical traditions was understandable because, under the political conditions in the United States and the increasingly accepted ideas of equal rights and spiritual tolerance, it was no longer necessary to fight for educational policy principles that could not be fulfilled in the German states but had already become reality in the United States. Thus educational conditions in the United States could serve as examples for educational policy demands in Prussia-Germany; German pedagogical literature reflected this interdependence only to a small degree, especially because communication in the second half of the nineteenth century remained very difficult.

German influences were clear not only in pedagogical concepts but also in administration and organization. In this regard, the German-American Teacher Association and its Teacher Congresses were not particularly important. But they clearly followed the patterns of the German teacher movement in the middle of the nineteenth century. They were oriented to the works of the *Allgemeiner Deutscher Lehrerverein* – founded in Eisenach in 1848

12. Ibid., 71.
13. Ibid., 71.
14. Ibid., 67.

under the decisive influence of Wander – and the German *Lehrerver-sammlungen*.[15]

More detailed studies are still needed to recapture the story of teachers who had left Germany in the Vormärz and after the revolution of 1848 to begin a new life in America, some of whom later returned to Germany.[16] Doubtless the most influential, however, both in the United States and in other countries, was Adolf Douai.

Adolf Douai (born at Altenburg in Thuringia in 1819, died in New York in 1888) worked as a teacher at Altenburg. He was a left-wing republican and played a leading role in the democratic revolution in 1848–9. Active in the duchy of Saxony-Altenburg, he had to emigrate in 1852 because of his revolutionary activities. Like many other bourgeois democrats, he went to the United States and experienced a number of ups and downs in his life.[17] First, he lived in Texas, where he opened a school; then, with

---

15. See C. L. A. Pretzel, *Geschichte des deutschen Lehrervereins* (Leipzig, 1921).

16. A number of names are known, and they are mentioned in German-language literature. Many names of emigrated German teachers who were members of or affiliated with the German-American Teacher Association appear in Hermann Schuricht's *Geschichte der Deutschen Schulbestrebungen in America* (Leipzig, 1884). This book is rich in facts, but it is not without certain tendencies toward Germanomania. Disciples of Diesterweg and Fröbel, such as the outstanding democratic pedagogue Wander, left Germany, even if only for a short period, to work in the United States as teachers or journalists. Research on Diesterweg and Fröbel has also resulted in the discovery of others who emigrated to the United States, notably Karl Theodor Bayrhoffer (1812–88), professor of philosophy in Marburg since 1845, a German liberal who emigrated in 1853; Gustav Adolf Rösler (1818–55), teacher at a Gymnasium at Oels, member of the German National Assembly, imprisoned in 1849, who escaped and emigrated to the United States in 1850; Karl Schramm (1810–88), member of the *Burschenschaft* organization, imprisoned in 1833 as a "demagogue," sentenced to death for high treason, released in 1840, teacher at Langensalza, deputy of the Prussian National Assembly in 1848, who emigrated in 1852; Theodor Karl Gottlieb Hielscher (born in 1822), pupil of Diesterweg at the Berlin *Seminar für Stadtschulen* until 1847, imprisoned in 1851 because of democratic statements, who emigrated to the United States and became a teacher in Baltimore and San Antonio, Texas. Friedrich Adolph Wilhelm Diesterweg, *Sämtliche Werke*, ed. by Ruth Hohendorf, 9 vols. (Berlin, 1964–7).

     A number of supporters of Fröbel also emigrated to the United States after their kindergartens were closed by the Prussian government in 1851. Notable among these were the Swiss pedagogue Zeller, who had been a teacher at Fröbel's institution at Keilhau in Thuringia, and Fröbel's student Wilhelm Bähringer. Gustav Adolf Wislecanus (1803–75), a theologian and democratic supporter of the opposition, was imprisoned in Germany. He escaped to the United States and founded an educational establishment at Hoboken, New Jersey. Theodor Pösche was a representative of the *Freie religiöse Gemeinden* organization. He was a supporter of Fröbel and was sentenced to fourteen years of hard labor; in 1853 he emigrated to the United States. Minister Rudolph Dulon from Bremen was another leading member of the *Freie Gemeinden;* he also escaped to the United States, worked intensively on pedagogical problems there, and came back to Germany, where in 1866 he published his book *Aus Amerika über Schule, deutsche Schule, amerikanische Schule und deutschamerikanische Schule.* Helmut König, "Friedrich Fröbels Verbindungen zur kleinbürgerlichen Demokratie in der ersten Hälfte des 19. Jahrhunderts" (part 4), *Jahrbuch für Erziehungs- und Schulgeschichte* 27 (1987):96ff.

17. See *Beiträge zur Geschichte der Vorschulerziehung,* ed. by Edith Barow-Bernsdorff, Karl-Heinz Günther, et al., 7th edition (Berlin, 1986), 276ff; *Geschichte der Erziehung,* ibid., 370ff; Helmut

Karl Heinzen, he edited the *San Antonio Zeitung*. He energetically endorsed the abolition of slavery and initiated an antislavery assembly in San
Antonio in 1854. He was close to the ideas of Marx and Engels, although
he was never a Marxist in the dogmatic sense. Nevertheless, he was said to
be one of the pioneers of Marxism in the United States.[18] Because of his
fight against slavery, he had to leave the South; he went to Boston and became the headmaster of a German school. As a supporter of Fröbel's ideas,
he attached a Fröbel kindergarten to the school.[19] There is no doubt that
Douai contributed decisively in theory and practice to the dissemination of
the pedagogy of Fröbel in the United States and elsewhere. In 1871, his
book *The Kindergarten. A Manual for the Introduction of Fröbel's System of Primary Education* appeared. (It was later translated into Japanese, thus establishing an important basis for the dissemination of Fröbel's pedagogy in
Japan.)[20]

    When clergymen in Boston criticized Douai in 1860, he moved to New
York. There he worked until 1878 as a journalist and teacher. He wrote
first for the *New Yorker Demokrat* and became acquainted with U.S. representatives of the First International, especially Joseph Wedemeyer and
Adolph Sorge, who had close relations with Marx and Engels, and he conceived the idea (although he never carried it out) of translating the first
volume of Marx's *Capital*. Later he worked solely for the *New Yorker Volks-
zeitung*. As a pedagogue, he founded the well-known German-American
Hoboken Academy and headed it until 1868. His later creation of the Douai
Institute school in New York and his work at a school at Newark were not
as important. The German emigrant Rudolph Dulon wrote in 1866:

> Dr. Adolf Douai is a man of comprehensive general scientific education, of thor-
> ough philosophical and classical scholarship. We hold [that] he is one of the most

König, "Die Arbeiterbewegung und das progressive pädagogische Erbe Friedrich Fröbels," *Jahrbuch
für Erziehungs- und Schulgeschichte* 18 (1978):39; Ilse Schossig, "Zu den politischen, schulpolitischen
und pädagogischen Auffassungen des Mitglieds der I. Internationale Adolf Douai" (doctoral thesis,
Academy of Pedagogical Sciences of the GDR, Berlin, 1987). The following statements are based
on research work done by H. König and I. Schossig.

18. See W. Z. Foster, *Geschichte der kommunistischen Partei der Vereinigten Staaten* (Berlin, 1956), 26.
19. Dr. Douai's obituary in the New York newspaper *Der Sozialist* (1888) reported that "Douai had
    to leave the state of Texas in 1856. He went to Boston, founded a German-American school
    and the first kindergarten in America. This kindergarten still exists, and when its twenty-fifth
    anniversary was celebrated, Dr. Douai was named honorary member of the German-American
    Teacher Association owing to his merits of introducing the kindergarten and the educational
    system of Fröbel into America." *Der Sozialist* (1888), 1/28, No. 5, 1; quoted according to Schos-
    sig, "Adolf Douai," 81.
20. See Masako Shoju, "Die Fröbel Bewegung in Japan," *Jahrbuch für Erziehungs- und Schulgeschichte* 19
    (1979):284.

learned men whom Europe lost to America. He invested many years of pedagogical practice and working power in his directorate; there is an equally high degree of speed and staying power.[21]

All evidence indicates that Douai was one of the German democratic pedagogues who had a decisive influence on the educational system of the United States.

It is understandable that in Germany there was great interest in the work of democratically minded German teachers who had emigrated for political reasons and who defended the principles of the mid-nineteenth-century German teacher movement. This was reflected in articles in the *Rheinische Blätter*, edited by Diesterweg until his death in 1866. Although Diesterweg's articles about educational policy and pedagogical developments in the United States were not numerous, because the editor of *Rheinische Blätter* and *Jahrbuch für Lehrer und Schulfreunde* concentrated on providing German *Volksschule* teachers with direct, concrete support for their development,[22] the theoretical scope of the publications became larger and larger, and in the course of time Diesterweg found it necessary to report about pedagogical developments in other countries.

Diesterweg's publications made an essential contribution to the emergence of comparative foreign pedagogy. German teachers in the United States concentrated their effort on the implementation of those educational policy and pedagogical ideas for which they had been forced to leave their home country. Consequently, the activities of German teachers in the United States showed democratic pedagogues in Germany a positive and strengthening response, and they came to be seen as examples for Germany, although a cautious reserve against the unknown remained visible. Diesterweg expressed this belief as early as 1855, only a few years after many German pedagogues had emigrated to the United States because of political restrictions.

Diesterweg came to this conviction after reviewing Hermann Wimmer's *Die Kirche und Schule in Nordamerika* (Leipzig, 1853) in the *Rheinische Blätter*, writing that it brought North America closer, externally and internally: externally because of the speed with which steamships crossed the ocean and internally because of the "great number of German emigrants who raise

21. Rudolpf Dulon, *Aus Amerika über Schule, deutsche Schule, amerikanische Schule und deutsch-amerikanische Schule* (Leipzig and Heidelberg, 1866), 431.
22. See Blumenthal, "Amerikanische Schulnachrichten und Ansichten. Auszug aus dem siebenten Jahresbericht des Herrn Horace Mann," *Rheinische Blätter* 34 (1847):147ff; Wander, "Der deutsche Lehrerverein in Baltimore," *Rheinische Blätter* 47 (1852):251ff.; anon., "Aus einem Brief aus den Vereinigten Staaten Nordamerikas," *Rheinische Blätter* 8 (1859):85ff; Wander, "Wie es mir in den letzten zehn Jahren erging," *Rheinische Blätter* 13 (1864):99ff.

our interest."[23] There were also teachers among them; their number was increasing, and "most of them were driven out of their lovely home country against their will and wish."[24]

Therefore, the American church and school system would be of interest. In his review, Diesterweg proceeded from his own school policy and general policy goals, aimed at freedom of conscience and freedom of religion, as well as the strict separation between state and church. He concentrated upon the relationship between the ecclesiastical-religious spirit and freedom of religion and upon the question of whether freedom of religion would actually destroy religious conviction, as was said in Prussia. For him, the United States was the example that proved his view that religiosity would be promoted by freedom of religion and that forced religiosity (as it existed in his own country) would destroy it. He wrote that "in North America, there is freedom of religion in the most comprehensive sense. . . . In Germany there is no freedom of religion."[25]

American conditions justified the assumption that "the decline of religion was caused by the lack of freedom of religion in Europe, that the existence of freedom of religion in North America was the cause of lively religiosity and church life."[26] Based on this point of view, Diesterweg was especially interested in the lessons of the role of religion in the schools in the United States. He fully agreed with the fact that there were "very secular and lively activities" in those schools.[27] Generally, only one section from the Bible was read with the children; religiosity existed mainly in the families. Diesterweg wrote that it was necessary to learn from the Americans how to regain lost religiosity, and the way would be "unlimited religious freedom."[28] When considering Diesterweg's school policy struggles in the 1850s against the command of the orthodox church over the school, it is understandable that he placed great emphasis upon his conclusions from the American development, which he saw as a confirmation and consolidation of his own ideas. This also applies to other features of the American school system, because many varied developments may have contributed to the American mix, so that it would be impossible to reduce it to a common denominator. Diesterweg found the life-based and practice-based orientation of the educational program of American schools to be exemplary. He wrote:

23. Diesterweg, *Sämtliche Werke*, 12:39.
24. Ibid.
25. Ibid.
26. Ibid., 40.9.
27. Ibid., 41.
28. Ibid.

The practical American knows what the ability to read and write and other skills are good for. . . . The classroom is a working room at the same time. Children create everything the school needs in the school. . . . There they learn only what they practice in life. . . .[29]

American practice conformed to his education policy belief that all children should attend school. Schools were not schools only for the poor, and social differentiations did not seem to exist. There seemed to be an approximation of the democratic idea of general education for the people. For Diesterweg, the external conditions of American school life were also remarkable. For example, the high proportion of women teachers, completely unthinkable in Germany at that time, the size of the classes (no more than fifty or sixty children), new school buildings, and the fact that "our strict school discipline cannot be found in American schools" all met with his approval.[30]

Diesterweg wrote these views on the American church and school system in *Rheinische Blätter,* a practice-oriented paper for *Volksschule* teachers. Therefore, he felt committed to tell the German teacher whether it was right to go to America. He made no final judgment, because he knew very well that only political restrictions caused teachers to emigrate. However, if a teacher wanted to be successful in the United States, it would be necessary "to do away with all school rigidity, all the narrow European views, and to acquire a certain degree of entrepreneurial spirit, which is not in the Germans as everybody knows."[31]

A year later, in 1856, Diesterweg returned to this topic. His article "Amerikanische Stimmen über Schulangelegenheiten" contained the same political and school policy tendencies as the article written one year before.[32] Diesterweg used his analyses of German-speaking newspapers in the United States to elaborate three views; again, he referred to political and school policy conditions in the United States to support his own efforts.

Diesterweg first dealt with the political situation. He asked where "the sense of stay-at-home, brooding, philistinism . . . and evident political immaturity in Germany" had originated.[33] His answer was that Germans were not allowed to move freely in terms of policy, social affairs, and "as far as the foundation of associations is concerned."[34] American German newspapers, however, would be "fully democratic, republi-

29. Ibid., 42, 43, 44.
30. Ibid., 42ff., 43.
31. Ibid., 44.
32. Ibid., 25ff.
33. Ibid., 251.
34. Ibid.

can."[35] They are full of "hatred and abhorrence against monarchistic forms of government."[36] This was a very far-reaching formulation under prevailing Prussian-German conditions. He specifically pointed out the strict opposition of the German-American press to slavery in the southern states. He underlined the fact that democratically minded German emigrants vehemently opposed slavery.

Then Diesterweg again pointed out the idea and practice of freedom of conviction and freedom of religion; he referred to the large "variety of religious views and convictions and forms of the cult,"[37] whereas it was "one of the saddest signs of the time"[38] that it was still necessary to stand up for freedom of conviction and religion in Germany. Finally, Diesterweg dealt with the American school system in a more differentiated manner than he had the previous year. There were great differences in the school affairs of North America, supported by religious views in most cases. When church parties wanted to have strictly ecclesiastical confessional schools, they wanted "the community school of the Democrats or Republican,"[39] a "system of free schools without school pay, where children of rich and poor parents were sitting side by side."[40]

Diesterweg's most comprehensive utterance on this topic was called *Amerikanisches Schulwesen,* written in 1866, the year in which Diesterweg died, as a review of Rudolph Dulon's book on American schools.[41] Dulon had been attacked by his opponents in Germany as the "grand master of rationalism," had emigrated to the United States, and had founded a school in New York. When the venture failed, Dulon withdrew to the prairie and wrote his book in 1864–5. The book aroused Diesterweg's interest.

For the purpose of this essay, what Diesterweg said about Dulon's whole work, which dealt to a large extent with German pedagogical conditions, is not very interesting. Of interest are Diesterweg's views on those sections of the book devoted to the American school system and, in this context, what Diesterweg said about American school conditions. His reception was especially related to the democratic aspects of the American school system. He also expressed rather self-confident and nationalistic opinions about specific pedagogical problems, because Diesterweg, probably like German teachers in the United States, thought that there was a far higher level of

35. Ibid., 252.
36. Ibid.
37. Ibid.
38. Ibid.
39. Ibid., 253.
40. Ibid.
41. See Dulon, *Aus Amerika über Schule.*

professionalism, science, and thoroughness in the training of the German *Volksschule* teacher and in pedagogical and methodological work in Germany.[42] Repeating Dulon's words in some parts, Diesterweg pointed out several characteristics of the American school as especially remarkable.

First, he underscored the democratic character of the American school: "the aristocratic England," whose daughter the American school was, "had nothing that could be compared to the outstanding character of the state public school of the free people of America."[43] Diesterweg waxed enthusiastic about Dulon's remark that the American school was "free like sunlight."[44] And with a clearly critical reference to the German school, Diesterweg wrote that "there was no dignitary, no law-maker who could ever dare to make the place of national education a tool of stultification in the interest of the rulers. . . ."[45]

Second, in another indirect polemic against school conditions in Prussia, Diesterweg again pointed out the nonconfessional character, the "nonreligiosity" of the American school in the sense of the independence of confessions.[46] He wrote that "it [the American school] did not allow religion lessons that could crystallize to any church or sect; the American school did not suffer from priestly encroachment or interference by pious rulers."[47] On the contrary, by its nonreligiosity, it lit the "true religiosity in the hearts of the children."[48]

Third, Diesterweg dissociated himself from the *Volksschule* teacher training, because the view was widespread in the United States that those who had the knowledge would also have to be able to teach; this was a delusion similar to that in most German universities. He also dissociated himself from what he had heard about school methodologies at the American school. Working with a textbook based on questions and answers, the method of questioning would be a "method that had nothing to do with the teacher,"[49] and the method of "automatic training"[50] would dominate the lessons, because the general knowledge of the teachers was so bad that "they were not able to apply German school methods or even to understand

42. See Jurgen Herbst, *And Sadly Teach. Teacher Education and Professionalization in American Culture* (Madison, Wisc., 1989).
43. Diesterweg, *Sämtliche Werke*, 17:295.
44. Ibid.
45. Ibid.
46. Ibid.
47. Ibid.
48. Ibid.
49. Ibid., 293.
50. Ibid., 298.

them."[51] "Mechanical and automatic training at school"[52] would correspond to "rude, external discipline"[53] at the American school, which would be of a military character; it would be aimed at ambition stimulated by external things, such as wall posters displaying the best pupils and grades to the parents.

Certainly, these evaluations of the American school by Diesterweg can claim only limited value as truth; they were in fact based on extremely limited and one-sided information. This applies both to evaluations that criticized the Prussian-German school system by pointing out the democratic aspects of the American school and to those that express pedagogical superiority. Even at that time, schools in the vastness of America were so differentiated and varied that the study of a few writings could not have been enough to make competent evaluations. But this was surely not the reason Diesterweg dealt with this topic. He did so because of the school policy struggles in Prussia in his time; he wanted to know how his democratic ideas for school progress in Germany could be helped, supported, and confirmed by experience in other countries. Thus Diesterweg saw the American school through the spectacles of a German democrat who felt connected with German democratic teachers who had emigrated to the United States.

To sum up, we can say that the examples of Diesterweg and Fröbel show that the basic idea of democratic German pedagogy gained practical importance in the United States, especially in German-American schools. In a process of organic assimilation, this theory correlated with specific North American educational ideas based, above all, upon the Declaration of Independence and increasingly emerging from actual living conditions. It remains unclear whether and to what extent the ideas of German democratic pedagogy and school policy, as expressed in the Vormärz and the revolution of 1848 and in the works of Diesterweg and Fröbel, were introduced into North American pedagogical thinking through German-American schools and the German press in the United States. The answer can only be found by studying U.S. pedagogical literature. It is important to note that this was not a one-way development. German democratic pedagogical influence was very important for the educational system in the United States in the second half of the nineteenth century. However, as Diesterweg's examples proved,

---

51. Ibid.
52. Ibid., 299.
53. Ibid.

the emigration of German pedagogues to the United States initiated feed-back to Germany that decisively strengthened democratic educational thinking there. In this sense, one can say that an interdependence between democratic pedagogical views in Germany and in the United States existed after the middle of the nineteenth century.[54]

54. As far as the whole topic is concerned, see Friedrich Schneider, *Geltung und Einfluss der deutschen Pädagogik im Ausland* (Munich and Berlin, 1943), a book rich in material: "Franckes Missionsbe-wegung in den USA," 49; "Pestalozzi und USA," 90ff.; "Fröbels Kindergartenidee in den USA," 122ff.; "Herbert und die USA," 145.

3

Prussian Volksschulen *through American Eyes: Two Perspectives on Curriculum and Teaching from the 1890s*

GREGORY P. WEGNER

German knowledge of American schools remained very limited throughout most of the nineteenth century. The reverse was true for American scholars during this period, many of whom expressed growing interest in German education through their studies at Germany's renowned universities in Berlin, Jena, Heidelberg, and Göttingen.[1] Although the German university tradition still held the respect of many American educators crossing the Atlantic, an increasing number of American school people turned their attention to German methods of teaching, school structure, teacher education, and the curriculum in elementary and secondary schools.

German schools aroused the curiosity of American educators long before the unification of Germany in 1871. Horace Mann, an American champion of the common school, published in 1846 one of the first assessments of the Prussian school system to appear in the United States. His conclusions reflected the great American idealistic faith in the power of republican government to form free and democratic schools. Mann's faith in American education was strong enough for him to proclaim that Americans "do not desire to copy or study the systems of foreign nations, usually so different from our own; we hope rather that they will study and copy ours."[2]

There were those educators in a succeeding generation who would not share Mann's idealism concerning the ability of American schools to educate a democratic citizenry. Like Mann, these writers saw meaningful possibilities in studying the schools of Germany as a way of opening a new discussion on the reform of American education. However, by the 1890s, some fifty years after the appearance of Mann's *Report,* new and disturbing

---

1. Dietrich Goldschmidt, "Transatlantic Influences: History of Mutual Interactions between American and German Education," in *Between Elite and Mass Education: Education in the Federal Republic of Germany* (Albany, 1979,) 1–65.
2. Horace Mann, *Report of an Educational Tour in Germany, and Parts of Great Britain and Ireland* (London, 1846), 7–9, 70–1.

questions were being raised about the form and function of the American school curriculum. The arrival of millions of new immigrants to the shores of the United States, the breakneck pace of urbanization, and the dazzling array of technological changes wrought by such devices as the telephone, the railroad, and the printing of mass circulation newspapers toward the end of the nineteenth century resulted in a social transformation hitherto unwitnessed in American history. These profound changes in American life would ultimately influence the national dialogue on the role of schooling in American society in a world that was already decidedly different from that experienced by Horace Mann and the fledgling common school in an earlier age.[3]

The late nineteenth century witnessed another set of changes on the international scene that, combined with a sense of instability about developments in the United States, urged educators to emulate certain aspects of German schools. The years following the political unification of Germany in 1871 and the establishment of the Second Reich affirmed Germany's growing economic prowess in international markets. Germany's success in world trade drew the attention of American educational reformers, some of whom saw in the German tradition of technical schools and the finely tuned apprenticeship system the foundation for German economic achievement and an attractive model for the besieged American school system.

The National Association of Manufacturers, founded in 1896, established a Standing Committee on Education that worked on a long-term public relations campaign to persuade American educators to emphasize German-inspired technical training. The committee feared that America might fail in its competition with Germany over world markets. Its president, Theodore Search, announced that a newly formed school curriculum was needed to give us "skilled hands and trained minds for the conduct of our industries and our commerce."[4]

That American schools were simply out of touch with the new world of international economic competition and vocationalism was an assumption that motivated the publication of two relatively obscure studies of German schools by Americans during the 1890s. Their perceptions of curriculum and teaching in German public schools were part of an unending debate

---

3. For an examination of the underlying philosophical conflicts relating to the formation of the American school curriculum since the 1890s, see Herbert Kliebard, *The Struggle for the American Curriculum, 1893–1958* (London, 1987), 1–29.
4. "Resolutions Regarding Technical Education," *Proceedings Regarding the Second Annual Convention of the National Association of Manufacturers*, 92–3; Theodore Search, [President's Annual Report]. *Proceedings of the Third Annual Convention of the National Association of Manufacturers*, 3–32.

concerning the propriety of transferring school practices from one culture to another.[5]

Andrew Draper, Superintendent of Public Instruction for the State of New York, instructed James Russell Parsons, formerly the school commissioner for Rensselaer County in New York from 1885 to 1888, to examine Prussian elementary schools to "enable us to see more clearly the strong points and discern the weak points of our own [school] system."[6] The assignment appeared daunting to Parsons since he was appointed at the same time to Aachen as United States consul and, moreover, arrived without any prior direct experience with Prussian schools.[7] The findings from Parsons's report, *Prussian Schools through American Eyes,* were eventually transmitted to the New York State legislature on January 6, 1891, and by Draper's direction were to "reach all interested in the educational progress of the State."[8]

The second study, appearing in 1892, was commissioned by the Massachusetts board of education, the body formerly headed by Horace Mann. John Tilden Prince (1844–1916), the director of the study, brought to the position a publishing background with Ginn and Company in American curriculum and teaching methods. In the years following his survey on methods of instruction in Prussian schools in 1892, Prince's writings on education addressed a broad range of topics including school administration, reformatory schools for delinquents, and industrial training.[9]

5. The failure of American educators to transfer essential elements of the social studies curriculum from the United States to Germany after the fall of the Third Reich, ostensibly to facilitate the democratization of postwar German schools, is examined in Gregory Wegner, "The Power of Tradition in Education: The Formation of the History Curriculum in the *Gymnasium* of Berlin (U.S. Sector), 1945–1955" (Ph.D. diss., University of Wisconsin–Madison, 1988).

6. James Parsons, *Prussian Schools Through American Eyes* (Syracuse, 1891), iii.

7. Prussia, in the usage of Parsons's study, will refer to the unified nation of Germany, established as the Second Reich in 1871 and divided into fourteen provinces, including East Prussia and West Prussia. The terms "Germany" and "Prussia" will be used interchangeably in this essay unless they refer to the separate province of Prussia before the unification of 1871.

8. The apparent optimism that accompanied Draper's initiation of *Prussian Schools Through American Eyes* under Parsons's hand was evident in the following introduction:
To make them of the greatest value to us, foreign school system must be seen through American eyes, and must be described by an intelligent friend of our school system, who is so anxious for its improvement that he is willing to seize upon anything which will improve it, no matter where he may find it, and yet who has the power of discriminating sufficiently to enable him to see not only what is good; but to determine what is practicable and advisable in this country. (See Parsons, *Prussian Schools,* iii.)

9. John Prince, *Course and Methods: A Handbook for Teachers of Primary, Grammar and Ungraded Schools* (Boston, 1886). The book also appeared in four subsequent editions in 1888, 1892, 1895, and 1896. Among his other works completed after the publication of *Methods of Instruction of the Schools of Germany for the Use of American Teachers and Normal Schools* (Boston, 1892) was *Arithmetic by Grades for Inductive Teaching* (Boston, 1893–4), which was eventually expanded into a five-volume series.

The writings of Parsons and Prince, like those of their predecessor, Horace Mann, looked across the Atlantic to assess what German school traditions might enhance American education. The two men, writing during a period of increasing concern about the purposes of schooling in the republic, reflected enthusiastic support for the German school model. Those searching for a penetrating critique of the *Volksschule* would do well to look elsewhere.[10] As the two studies soon reveal, the search for what was admirable in German schools meant that the school traditions and practices of the young American democracy would come under the severest scrutiny.

The strongest similarities between the writings of Parsons and Prince concerned German educational policies they felt to be most appropriate for adoption by American elementary schools. Among the issues the two authors examined were compulsory school attendance, teacher education, centralized school administration, a nationalized curriculum, and manual training. It is the purpose of this essay to examine how Parsons and Prince articulated these five German elementary school traditions for what they believed were necessary elements in a thorough reform of American primary schooling.[11]

THE STRENGTHS OF GERMAN SCHOOLS: A CASE FOR POSSIBLE CROSS-CULTURAL TRANSFER OF SCHOOL PRACTICES

Parsons and Prince strongly supported the German compulsory school attendance laws for children aged six through fourteen but differed on the means of administering such laws. Unlike Parsons, Prince seriously ques-

---

He also published *A Practical English Grammar for Upper Grades* (Boston, 1910); *School Administration Including the Organization and Supervision of Schools* (Syracuse, New York, 1906); *Report upon Schools for the Deaf and Blind, Reformatory School for Boys and Girls: School for the Feeble-Minded and County Truant Schools* (Boston, 1906); and *Report on Educational Conditions, School Incentives, Time Limits and School Sessions, Industrial Training, Special Classes for Delinquents and Defectives* (Boston, 1907).

10. Douglas Skopp, "The Elementary School Teachers in Revolt: Reform Proposals for Germany's *Volksschulen* in 1848 and 1849," *History of Education Quarterly* 22 (Fall 1982): 341–1.

11. Similar to the Massachusetts report published by John Prince, James Parsons's work, *Prussian Schools Through American Eyes*, relied upon a small collection of official school sources for statistical information and other factual data on school structure, curriculum, teaching, and a variety of other German school traditions. Parsons drew heavily from Giebe's *Verordnungen betreffend das gesammte Volksschulwesen in Preussen* (1882, 1884, and 1887 editions) and *Preussische Statistik 101*. Prince also relied on these two sources but also used Kockle's *Lehrplan fuer die einfachen Volksschulen des Koenigreiches Sachsen, Dresden* (1890); A. Richter, *Paedagogischer Jahresbericht* (1899); and R. Goetz, *Gesetz ueber die Gymnasium, Realschulen und Seminare* (Leipzig, 1877). Abridged versions of the concluding chapter from Prince's study can be found in *Atlantic Monthly* 66 (September 1890): 413–19 and *Educational Review* 2 (October 1891): 231–7.

tioned whether America could "adopt the same rigorous policy of coercion which Germany enforces with her strong military spirit and her complete state police system." The New Englander stood behind compulsory attendance laws primarily because they safeguarded the republic against "the dangers of an ignorant citizenship" and "the evils of illiteracy."[12] The call for uniformity in school attendance laws and the forty-week school year based on the Prussian model were at the heart of Parsons's reform plan for American schools. Without this change in elementary education, Parsons insisted, American pupils "could not compete with the children of the average school district in Prussia."[13]

The prospects for reforming American education appeared even bleaker when Parsons and Prince addressed the daunting challenge of reforming teacher education. On this issue, above all others, the two men expressed the strongest agreement. Using figures gathered from the U.S. Commissioner of Education from 1886 to 1887, Prince estimated that as many as three-fourths of all teachers in America entered their work "without the slightest theoretical knowledge of the science or art of teaching." Since only about 25 percent of teaching candidates completed normal school studies, Prince castigated the American public for its toleration of widespread mediocrity among an "army of novices." This regrettable group, he wrote, caused an enormous waste of money and brought irreparable injury to children through their "experiments and mistakes" in the classroom.[14]

These two reformers left no doubt in the minds of their readers which Western nation provided the best model for the professionalization of American teachers. Parsons and Prince dutifully recorded the rigorous German tradition of the three-year normal school for prospective elementary teachers. Once having passed the first teacher examination, the candidate practiced as an assistant teacher for at least two years under the direction

12. Parsons, *Prussian Schools*, 2–4; Prince, *Methods of Instruction*, 226.
13. Parsons, *Prussian Schools*, 3–4.
14. Prince, *Methods of Instruction*, 219–20. Note also that at about this time, Joseph Mayer Rice, a former medical doctor, became one of the first persons to enter the arena of educational reform through investigative journalism. After studying pedagogy in German universities in 1888, Rice returned to the United States, where he eventually visited schools in over thirty American cities. What he witnessed in these extensive classroom observations led to a scathing attack on the American school system in a series of articles published in *The Forum* (1892–3). Rice directed his strongest condemnations against the inadequate state of teachers preparation, the unqualified people sitting on school boards, and school superintendents who were out of touch with the realities of school life – some of the same themes sounded by Parsons and Prince. His writings drew enraged reactions from school administrators and teachers. See Joseph Rice, "The Public School Systems of Chicago and St. Paul," *The Forum* 15 (1893): 200–15; Rice, *The Public School System of the United States* (New York, 1893), 12–58.

Table 1. *Course of study for the German normal school*

| | Years | | |
Classes	One	Two	Three
Pedagogics	2	2	3
Religion	4	4	2
Language	5	5	2
History	2	2	2
Arithmetic	3	3	1
Geometry	2	2	1
Natural history	4	4	2
Geography	2	2	1
Drawing	2	2	1
Writing	2	1	0
Gymnastics	2	2	2
Music	5	5	3
Foreign languages	3	3	2
	38	37	22

Source: James Parsons, *Prussian Schools Through American Eyes* (Boston, 1891), 56.

of a master teacher.[15] Only then did the candidate take his second and final examination.

The teacher education curriculum for the German normal school included a broad array of courses (see Table 1). Parsons reprinted the official syllabi for all normal school courses, which showed that, in contrast to their American counterparts, the German candidates competing for teaching positions in the *Volksschule* took more courses and spent more time in the normal school. American teachers in rural areas often prepared for their careers without normal school training, and those few who had such training usually attended for a year at most.[16] Inspired by German educational tradition, Parsons and Prince called for higher admissions standards for candidates entering the American normal school, and for a three-year program and graduation for all elementary teachers.[17]

15. Parsons, *Prussian Schools*, 5, 55–63; Prince, *Methods of Instruction*, 35–43.
16. Andrew Gulliford, *Country School Legacy* (Washington, D.C., 1982), 92–106.
17. Parsons, *Prussian Schools*, 52–6; Prince, *Methods of Instruction*, 220–1. Some of Prince's assumptions about the relative independence of the German school teacher were not wholly accurate. In an especially idealistic portrait of the Prussian school master meant to highlight the weaknesses of the American teaching profession, Prince praised the pedagogues of the Second Reich for their ability to virtually shape public opinion on matters of educational policy through the press and their political influence with the government. The German teacher, he said, "does not take his cue from anybody," especially "fledgling members of school boards," in the initiation of school reform (229). Prince failed to recognize that it was the *Gymnasium* teacher, not the *Volksschullehrer*, who even

Just how far American educators should go in imitating the curriculum of the German normal school was an entirely different and exceedingly complicated matter left unaddressed by Parsons and Prince.[18] Moreover, Prince took the position that public school teaching in America could not be called a profession in its present state unless standards were raised to the level of the German model. Again, neither Prince nor Parsons commented on the cultural transformations necessary in American society to realize these changes. Unlike Parsons, Prince even advocated the use of state force if there was an unwillingness in America to reach teaching standards as high as those in Germany.[19]

As before, the representative of the Massachusetts board of education was much more adamant than Parsons in his insistence that Germany alone provided the best model for the reform of American school administration and teaching. The criticism and direction of teaching methods, he wrote, must follow the German tradition of professionalism under a set of uniform standards administered under the auspices of the state. In remaining consistent with his earlier approaches, Prince declined to specify in detail what these standards should be other than abolishing the popular election of school superintendents.[20]

The push for centralization extended to the formation of the elementary school curriculum. After denouncing the power and independence of America's local school boards to determine textbook selection and the direction for courses of study, Parsons and Prince countered with a Prussian-style bureaucratic model designed to secure a nationalized curriculum.[21] The course of study defined for the *Volksschule* provided that desired conformity (see Table 2).

The two Americans praised the German curriculum in manual training for the middle and advanced classes and the continuation schools in voca-

---

came close to approximating this idealization. The German elementary school teacher did not enjoy the relatively high status given the teachers of the elite *Gymansia,* who exercised much of their influence through their professional associations. See Konrad Jarausch, "The Crisis of German Professions, 1918–1933," *Journal of Contemporary History* 20 (1985): 379–8.

18. One readily notes, for example, the important place of religious instruction in the first and second years of study, with the weekly number of course hours (four) exceeded only by those devoted to natural history, music, and language. The church–state relationship reflected in the German historical tradition of schooling and public finance was of an entirely different nature in the United States, where strict separation of church and state remained a centerpiece of American constitutional tradition. Religion as a school subject for future pedagogues was therefore alien territory for the American educational establishment.

19. Prince, *Methods of Instruction,* 220–1.

20. Prince, *Methods of Instruction,* 226–7.

21. Part of John Prince's critique of American schools has a contemporary ring. The local school board, wrote Prince, "is made up of men who can, it may be, run a farm or factory, but who have no special fitness to direct teachers in respect to subjects of study." See *Methods of Instruction,* 223.

Table 2. *Course of study for the Volkschule*

Course	Lowest class	Middle class	Advanced class
Religion	4	5	5
Language	11	10	8
Arithmetic	4	4	4
Geometry	0	0	1
Drawing	0	1	2
Realien			
(geography, history, natural science)	0	6	6
Music	1	2	2
Gymnastics			
(manual training)	0	2	2
	20	30	30

Note: The lowest class included the first two years, the middle class the following three, and the highest class the remaining years. Children first entering school had to receive six months of practice in reading and writing the German script. See source note, 32.

Source: James Parsons, *Prussian Schools Through American Eyes* (Syracuse, 1891), 32.

tional education. Prince was particularly taken with the manual training traditions established in Leipzig and Berlin. Parsons extended his purview to include industrial training courses for girls. He noted that the courses were practical, thorough, and inexpensive. The young charges learned "only plain household work" fitting them for domestic life. Parsons recommended that a similar course be introduced in New York elementary schools.[22]

Other age-old German curricular traditions caught the attention of the observers. One of these concerned the practice of promoting love of the fatherland through music, geography, history, and language. Prince remained cautious on this issue, fearing that the traditional Prussian cultural relationships between the individual, the state, and the military would be disastrous if transferred to the fledgling American democracy. This, however, contradicted his earlier advocacy of force in raising the standards of teacher education.[23] Instead, Prince asked for exemplary teaching methods in the teaching of arithmetic and geography. He admired the German emphasis on the use of illustrative lessons and mental arithmetic in teaching primary mathematics. He was even more enthusiastic about the pedagogical features of geography instruction, even though he admitted that geography, like history, too often centered on things German, to the exclusion of a

22. Prince, *Methods of Instruction*, 59–67; Parsons, *Prussian Schools*, 18, 36.
23. Prince, *Methods of Instruction*, 221.

world view.[24] Nonetheless, Prince insisted that American geography instructors apply some of the eternal principles of good teaching:

1. The teacher had a definite plan and followed it.
2. There was a constant association of ideas.
3. Pupils made inferences from known causes.
4. The teacher relied on constant repetition in classroom lessons.
5. Pupils expressed themselves fully and accurately.
6. The teacher exhibited great patience with pupils.[25]

Most of these teaching methods were part of the teaching tradition established in the Herbartian schools, which Prince also observed. Just how much of the Herbartian curricular philosophy could be successfully integrated into American schools was an issue on which Prince remained silent. The vast majority of German and American elementary schools in the 1890s still used the dominant method of recitation, a method that neither Prince nor Parsons openly criticized.[26]

Parsons, in sharp contrast to Prince, assigned a vigorous role to patriotism in breathing new life into the school curriculum. He cited the long German school tradition of teaching patriotic songs to "awaken love toward the Fatherland" in music classes, geography, and history. The latter two subjects were apparently devoid of meaning in the minds of many American pupils, and there was no subject in our public schools "so imperfectly taught," Parsons insisted, as U.S. history. By contrast, he continued:

In Prussian schools the utmost pains are taken to foster the spirit of patriotism. The law requires that a likeness of the Emperor be placed in each school-room. Courses of study improve every opportunity to call attention to the importance of cultivating a national spirit. From the cradle, the Prussian child learns the national songs.[27]

CONCLUSION

The reports of John Prince and James Parsons represent a curious legacy. The powerful and growing economic influence of Germany during the late nineteenth century provided the pretext and justification for Massachusetts and New York to commission the ambitious projects studying Prussian elementary teachers and their curriculum.

24. Prince, *Methods of Instruction*, 132–8.
25. Prince, *Methods of Instruction*, 139.
26. Prince, *Methods of Instruction*, 183–204.
27. Parsons, *Prussian Schools*, 19.

Collectively, the reports had just as much to say about what was wrong with American schools as what was right and admirable about Prussian schools. On the equally important problem of the weaknesses of German elementary schools, Parsons and Prince were much less concerned. Beyond castigating Prussian school authorities for requiring pupils to study the written and printed characters of the German script and for dark and over-crowded classrooms, Parsons said little else about the potential drawbacks of the German elementary school.[28] For Prince, a serious philosophical problem rooted in German culture remained unresolved. He concluded that Prussian schoolmasters imposed exceedingly harsh discipline through the severest means. In reforming this excess, he suggested that German educators could learn wisdom from American pedagogy, although he did not mention what educational thinkers could be tapped for this purpose. This could only happen, Prince added, when conditions no longer compelled Germans to train their children for war. The Massachusetts native, one will recall, was also the person who advocated the stern use of state force if American teacher education institutions refused to adopt standards at least as high as those in Prussia. Given his uncompromising aspiration, he was to be bitterly disappointed.[29]

On one level, a derivative of the German school legacy was to find fulfillment. Support for the German model of industrial education and vocational instruction would grow among circles of American educators and businesspeople, leading to the passage of the landmark Smith–Hughes Act in 1917. Several subsequent American studies of Prussian schools affirmed the serious consideration given by Americans to the German model of industrial education and apprenticeship programs.[30] The Smith–Hughes Act, which legitimized vocational education in American public schools with federal funds, drew from the spirit of Prussian traditions in industrial training so highly praised by John Prince and James Parsons. By the time the sociologists Robert and Helen Lynd completed their notable study on schooling in *Middletown* in 1929, vocational education had become a central part of the American school curriculum.[31]

By its very nature, the cultural rootedness of schooling calls into question

28. Parsons, *Prussian Schools*, 13–15, 26–7.
29. Prince, *Methods of Instruction*, 236–7.
30. T. W. Gosling, "Annual Report for 1915–1916 of the Superintendent of Schools of Cincinnati," 248–9; U.S. Bureau of Education, "Industrial Schools in Germany," *The Pedagogical Seminary* 19 (1912): 112–15; L. R. Klemm, *Public Education in Germany and in the United States* (Boston, 1911), 106–9;
31. Robert Lynd and Helen Lynd, *Middletown: A Study in Contemporary American Culture* (New York, 1929), 46–58.

the advisability of transferring elements from one nation to another. During the years leading up to World War I, John Dewey sounded a note of caution among his contemporaries concerning the German model of vocational education. He insisted that German education be viewed within its unique historical context. Education in Germany became closely associated with the ideal of the national state, a relationship addressed generations before through the philosophies of Kant, Hegel, and Fichte. Subsequently, the social aim of education for "human welfare and progress," central to Dewey's ideal in school and society, was never realized in Germany because of the political subordination of the individual to the state and a heightened nationalism.[32]

The dilemma of emulating school traditions from abroad for the purposes of national advancement was not unique to the generation of Parsons and Prince. In a subsequent period of history, the German–American interaction over school reform resurfaced in an order reversed from the focus of studies completed by the two writers. Events following the fall of the Third Reich in 1945 revealed that Dewey's apprehension over the transference of school practices from one nation to another still remained unheeded when American educators came to Germany with ideas on reforming German schools with a democratic idealism once inspired by Horace Mann.

32. John Dewey, "A Policy of Industrial Education," *New Republic* 1 (1916): 11–12.

4

American Responses to German Continuation Schools during the Progressive Era

DEREK S. LINTON

The development of vocational education was long treated as the neglected stepchild of American educational history. In recent decades, however, historians have reaffirmed the conclusion already reached in 1921 by Paul Douglas, professor of labor relations at the University of Chicago, that the campaign for vocational education was probably the most important educational movement in the United States during the first two decades of this century.[1] At its height, between publication of the Douglas Commission Report in Massachusetts in 1906 and enactment of the federal Smith–Hughes Act of 1917, this often controversial campaign was conducted by such powerful interest groups as the National Association of Manufacturers (NAM), the American Federation of Labor (AFL), the National Educational Association (NEA), and the National Society for the Promotion of Industrial Education (NSPIE). Leading educators including John Dewey, George Herbert Mead, and Charles Eliot formulated positions on industrial education.

Recent historiography has evaluated this campaign from several ideological perspectives. Whereas some historians have viewed the campaign as a positive attempt to adapt education to the increasingly industrial and technological society emerging in the United States at the turn of the century, others have argued that vocationalism meant an accommodation by the schools to the labor force needs of nascent corporate capitalism and entailed the abandonment of equal educational opportunity.[2] Recently, educational

1. Paul H. Douglas, *American Apprenticeship and Industrial Education* (New York, 1921), 11. The best general introduction to this movement, its ideas, and its controversies is still probably Arthur G. Wirth, *Education in the Technological Society* (Scranton, Pa., 1972). A representative sample of key documents from the movement is contained in Marvin Lazerson and W. Norton Grubb, *American Education and Vocationalism* (New York, 1974).
2. Wirth, *Education,* and Lawrence A. Cremin, *The Transformation of the School* (New York, 1964), 34–57, represent this former school, although they expressed some misgivings about the outcomes of the movement, as did the more critical piece by Sal Cohen, "The Industrial Education Movement, 1906–17," *American Quarterly*, Vol. 20 (1968), 95–110. The revisionists of the 1970s are best rep-

historians have begun to research the campaign at the state and local levels. In light of their work, industrial education programs appear much more as vector sums of clashes between business and labor in shifting alliances with educators and professionals, rather than merely as the result of functional congruence with changing labor demand.[3] But placing the campaign in local contexts, while offering more subtle explanations of the introduction of vocational education, has tended to push the international dimensions of the campaign into the background.

Few practical results have followed from Lawrence Cremin's observation that "the very concept of an American education became problematical in a metropolitan era as the extension of ideas and institutions across boundaries accelerated."[4] Certainly, educational historians have noted in passing the fascination with German vocational education within the campaign, but the German challenge and the U.S. response have not been explored thematically or systematically.[5] Here this omission will be made good, in part by treating four problems concerning the reception of German vocational education during the Progressive era.

First, how was the growing industrial might of Germany used to justify the U.S. vocational education movement? Second, what descriptions of German vocational schools were available, and how were they deployed in American debates over vocational education? Third, what did the various contenders in the campaign conceive to be the limits to the transferability of the German industrial education model and why? Finally, what was the significance of the admiration for Georg Kerschensteiner, the Munich school superintendent, and the Munich model, the most celebrated and imitated German vocational education system within the U.S. movement?

From the very beginning of the movement for vocational education, government officals and businessmen considered the challenge of German industrial competition one of the most compelling reasons to establish a comprehensive system of secondary vocational education in the United States. Indeed, the notion that Germany's system of vocational and technical

resented by Samuel Bowles and Herbert Gintis, *Schooling in Capitalist America* (New York, 1977), 191–200, and Paul Violas, *The Training of the Urban Working Class* (Chicago, 1978), 127–93.

3. An earlier work along these lines was Marvin Lazerson, *The Origin of the Urban School* (Cambridge, Mass., 1971), 142–201. More recent examples include Julia Wrigley, *Class Politics and the Public Schools* (New Brunswick, N.J., 1982), 48–90, and Ira Katznelson and Margaret Weir, *Schooling for All* (New York, 1985), 86–120.

4. Lawrence A. Cremin, *American Education: The Metropolitan Experience 1876–1980* (New York, 1988), 12.

5. Raymond E. Callahan, *Education and the Cult of Efficiency* (Chicago, 1962), 11–14; Cremin, *Transformation*, 52–3; Wirth, *Education*, 25, 35, 41.

education had contributed substantially to the empire's rapid rise to industrial eminence became one of the uncontested commonplaces of the campaign.[6] Thus, at the Tenth Annual Convention of the NAM in 1905, a section of the newly formed Committee on Industrial Education's report was entitled "Why Germany's Competition Is to Be Feared." According to this document:

> The German technical and trade schools are at once the fear and admiration of all countries. In the world's race for commercial supremacy we must copy and improve upon the German method of education. . . .Trade education has made Germany an all-round competitor with all of the world; she is the only nation we have to be afraid of.[7]

Such mixed expressions of admiration and apprehension soon became joined with the argument that as cheap resources dwindled and conservation became essential, the United States would have to funnel more resources into investment in human capital. German trade and technical education served as a successful synthetic substitute for absent natural resources. This position was expounded at the first conference of the NSPIE in 1906 by Frank Vanderlip, Vice President of the National City Bank of New York, who, after remarking on Germany's barrenness of soil, its lack of mineral wealth, its high agrarian tariffs, the commercial antagonism of its neighbors, and its laborers' supposed lack of native ingenuity, nonetheless asserted that Germany was the one great competitor of the United States:

> On what does Germany rest her ability thus to compete with us even in the face of the prodigal aid which nature has given us and withheld with such niggardly hand from the great nation over the sea?. . . .You know as does every manufacturer know, that Germany's superiority in international commerce rests almost wholly on Germany's superior school system. . . . It has put Germany, in spite of her natural disadvantages, in the forefront of commercial nations.[8]

Literally dozens of such statements could be culled from the convention proceedings of the NAM, NEA, and NSPIE between 1905 and 1915.[9] Justification of industrial education in terms of improving competitiveness

---

6. The common assumption of this close relation between Germany's technical education and economic growth was already noted in the *Seventeenth Annual Report of the Commissioner of Labor 1902: Trade and Technical Education* (Washington, D.C., 1902), 871.

7. *Proceedings of the Tenth Annual Convention of the National Association of Manufacturers of North America held at Atlanta, Ga. May 16, 17 and 18, 1905* (New York, 1905), 145–6.

8. National Society for the Promotion of Industrial Education, *Bulletin No. 1*, 21–2. Jane Addams, however, cautioned against adopting Germany's technical education while ignoring Germany's welfare system and rich cultural life, 39.

9. See, for example, National Education Association, *Journal of the Proceedings and Addresses of the Forty-Eighth Annual Meeting Held at Boston, Massachusetts, July 2–8, 1910* (Winona, Minn., 1910), 605

vis-à-vis Germany, however, seems to have resonated most strongly in business audiences. State and local reports were more likely to cite the role of industrial education in decreasing dropout rates, confronting problems of dead-end youth jobs, or combating delinquency.[10] But the pervasive rhetoric of national efficiency within the campaign would be incomprehensible without recognizing the widespread diffusion of the belief that Germany had become a major industrial rival largely because of the superiority of its technical and vocational training.

Of course, simply pointing to the importance of vocational schools in stimulating German industry did not resolve the problem of what sort of educational response was desirable in the United States. Many of the early calls for a system of vocational education were vague, as were ideas about the German system the United States was supposed to emulate. To remedy this deficiency, however, government officials and educators began to produce extensive reports on German vocational schools. Initially, such reports aimed only at demonstrating the comprehensiveness and efficacy of the German system and showing that it offered concrete models for the United States.

The first official document to discuss German industrial continuation schools (*gewerbliche Fortbildungsschulen*) was the 1902 report of the U.S. Commissioner of Labor on trade and technical education in the United States and Europe. This report devoted six pages to surveying German industrial continuation schools, which were characterized as the "keystone to the whole scheme of industrial education as offered to the laboring classes."[11] In industrial centers, these part-time evening or Sunday schools for young workers between the ages of fourteen and eighteen had been transformed "first from schools of ordinary instruction to those for general technical or industrial education and then to trade schools" with courses designed to "apply specifically to the prevailing trades of the locality in which it was situated." According to the report, because these schools supplemented shop floor instruction and concentrated on theoretical issues or such skills as drawing and bookkeeping, they enjoyed the advantage of being inexpensive since they required no workshops. Although recognizing the importance of mandatory industrial continuation schools within the German system of vocational education, both this report and the special consular report of 1905, *Industrial Education and Industrial Conditions in Ger-*

---

10. The Douglas Commission of Massachusett's *Report of the Commission on Industrial and Technical Education* (Boston, 1906), 18–21, and Susan Kingsbury's appended report on school dropouts became the prototype, although most at least mentioned German vocational schools.
11. *Seventeenth Annual Report of the Commissioner of Labor 1902,* 890–1.

many, depicted these schools in very broad terms and supplied far more detailed accounts of the organization and curricula of more specialized trade schools (*Fachschulen*).[12] Presumably the reason for this weighting was that during the early phase of the U.S. campaign for vocational education, businessmen, to whom the Commerce Department and consuls catered, were committed to building a system of trade schools that corresponded to lower-level German *Fachschulen.*

The focus of interest would soon change, however, from the *Fachschulen* to the industrial continuation schools, especially those developed by Georg Kerschensteiner in Munich. In large part, this shift was effected by the tireless propagandistic efforts of such American educators as Paul Hanus, founder of Harvard's education department, and Edwin Cooley, former superintendent of Chicago's schools. This new interest was then solidified by Dr. Kerschensteiner's speaking tour of the United States in 1910 under the auspices of the NSPIE.

It was Hanus who, after a sabbatical spent in Munich in 1904–5, first brought the city's experiment in industrial education and the work of Dr. Kerschensteiner to the attention of American vocationalists. His article, "The Industrial Continuation Schools of Munich," was widely circulated, appearing in the *Boston Transcript,* in the University of Chicago's *School Review,* and as an appendix to the 1907 report of the Massachusetts Commission on Industrial Education, which Hanus chaired. In this article Hanus avowed:

[I]n spite of the absence of great industries and great business enterprise, it [Munich] nonetheless maintains a unique and wholly admirable system of technical continuation schools, whereby those who leave school at about thirteen or fourteen years of age are well trained for the several callings on which they enter, . . . due partly to the general principle recognized in Germany, that efficiency in any calling . . . requires special training. . . ; but chiefly to the energetic and farsighted superintendent of schools, George Kerschensteiner, who saw that the ordinary continuation school failed to supply a much needed technical training for beginners in the trades and in business.

Hanus also recognized the enormous importance of keeping young people between the ages of fourteen and seventeen under systematic educational influence for their moral and social welfare. He saw that by combining good general education, good technical education, and good education in the rights and duties of citizenship, he might expect to exert on them a permanent influence for good – moral, intellectual and techni-

---

12. Department of Commerce and Labor, Bureau of Statistics, *Industrial Education and Industrial Conditions in Germany* (Washington, D.C., 1905), 37–43.

cal.[13] With their fusion of general and technical education and their practical orientation, Hanus claimed, the Munich continuation schools "solve the problem of how to keep under appropriate educational influence during the period of adolescence that great body of youth who are obliged to leave school when only thirteen or fourteen years old."[14]

The second major American educator to propagate the Munich model was Edwin Cooley, who after serving as superintendent of Chicago's schools from 1900 to 1909 became the educational adviser to the Commercial Club of Chicago, a prestigious association of Chicago's leading businessmen.[15] It was in this latter capacity that Cooley spent 1910 in Europe observing vocational training programs.

The end product of this investigative trip was his influential book *Vocational Education in Europe*. The chapter on continuation schools, by far the longest, examined the Munich schools. Not only did Cooley approve of Munich's school workshops, but he also made it clear that for Kerschensteiner, vocational education was conceived to further moral and social ends. Kerschensteiner

connected the work in drawing, in mathematics, in civics – in fact all of the work – with this shop practice. He believed that only in this way can apprentices become interested in the various subjects taught in the schools – only in this way can a genuine joy in the work of the school and shop be produced. He believed that dexterity must be based on insight; and if the boy is to become an efficient workman, he must comprehend his work in all its relations to science, to art and to society in general. Efficiency in work will lead to joy in work and joy in work will lead to good citizenship. The young workman who understands his trade in its scientific relations, its historical, economic and social bearings . . . will take a higher view of his trade, of his powers and duties as citizen and member of society.[16]

In his conclusion, Cooley touted part-time day continuation schools based on the Munich example as the model for industrial education in the United States.[17]

In addition to explaining Kerschensteiner's positions through his own writings, Cooley persuaded the Commercial Club to commission a trans-

13. "The Industrial Continuation Schools of Munich" in Paul H. Hanus, *Beginnings in Industrial Education and Other Educational Discussions* (Boston, 1908), 90–2. The German-born Hanus, like Kerschensteiner, was an ex-mathematics teacher who had turned to educational theory and administration.
14. Ibid., 97–8.
15. For Cooley, see Wrigley, *Class Politics*, 62–90. Because Cooley was Kerschensteiner's foremost promoter in America, Wrigley tends to collapse all tensions between their positions, tensions Dewey certainly perceived. She also overlooks the fact that the Munich schools were largely designed for craft apprentices not factory laborers.
16. Edwin G. Cooley, *Vocational Education in Europe* (Chicago, 1912), 99–100.
17. Ibid., 333.

lation of Kerschensteiner's *Staatsbürgerliche Erziehung* (*Civic Education*), in which the Munich superintendent first elaborated on the social and industrial role of continuation schools, and to publish his *Three Lectures on Vocational Training* delivered in the United States during the fall of 1910.

In the course of his U.S. tour, Kerschensteiner lectured in most major cities of the Northeast and Midwest, including New York, Boston, Cincinnati, and Chicago.[18] Apart from presenting an insider's perspective on the organization and curriculum of the Munich schools, Kerschensteiner took great pains to allay any misconceptions that the continuation schools were pure trade schools and to underline the communitarian nature of his project. Education for community service and citizenship were just as important as imparting trade skills. Such education was all the more necessary to offset the one-sided training afforded by modern industry, with its minute division of labor. Moreover, since most employers regarded their young laborers as cheap hands, joy in work had to be cultivated outside the workshop.[19] Despite his discussion of modern industry and the division of labor, however, Kerschensteiner's prototype of the young worker was the craft apprentice, and his notion of joy in work depended on the artisan's commitment to his trade. As Kerschensteiner acknowledged, given the differences in apprenticeship between Germany and the United States, there was at least some question about the direct transferability of the Munich model.[20]

Clearly, by 1910, the Munich continuation schools and the work of Dr. Kerschensteiner were widely known and admired in the United States. In 1912 George Herbert Mead chaired a committee of the City Club of Chicago, a major society of Progressive professionals, that urged the city to establish day continuation schools in commercial and industrial subjects in which the work should be "of the same general character as that of the continuation schools in Munich."[21] The same year, Frank Leavitt, professor of industrial education at the University of Chicago, in his book *Examples of Industrial Education,* attributed the success of the Munich schools to the strong and optimistic personality of Kerschensteiner.[22] A picture of Dr.

18. For Kerschensteiner's U.S. tour, see Emil Otto Toews, *The Life and Professional Work of Georg Michael Kerschensteiner 1854–1932* (unpub. diss., UCLA, 1955), 154–62.
19. "The Fundamental Principles of Continuation Schools" in George Kerschensteiner, *Three Lectures on Vocational Training* (Chicago, 1911), 6–7.
20. Ibid., 15–16.
21. *A Report on Vocational Training in Chicago and Other Cities* (Chicago, 1912), 24. Kerschensteiner's *Three Lectures* was cited several times in the report, 20–1, and the entire plans of the Munich continuation school for young building trades workers and unskilled laborers were incorporated in the report, 119–27, 204–7.
22. Frank Mitchell Leavitt, *Examples of Industrial Education* (Boston, 1912), 223.

Kerschensteiner graced the cover of the journal *Vocational Education* in 1913, and the accompanying editorial lauded him as the man "who has done more than any other perhaps, to focus popular attention on the problems of industrial education."[23]

After 1910, literature produced by the U.S. government also reflected this new interest in the Munich schools, as well as the more sharply focused debates on the nature of industrial education within the U.S. movement. Representative in this respect was *German Industrial Education and Its Lessons for the United States,* issued by the Bureau of Education in 1913. Its author, Holmes Beckwith, had spent the summer of 1911 investigating German vocational schools in Berlin, Hamburg, and Munich. He was especially interested in "industrial education for the masses, for rank and file workers," an area in which Germany excelled and had the most to teach the United States.[24] In treating the Munich schools, which he considered the most vital experiment in industrial education in Germany, Beckwith, with his single-minded dedication to the cult of efficiency, fretted that Kerschensteiner's civic and ethical approach might pose the danger that "as in our manual-training movement, the industrial results may become but slight."[25] He also repeated criticisms of the Munich experiment vented by many master artisans: that instruction sometimes undermined shop floor training, that it was overly theoretical, and that Kerschensteiner ultimately aspired to usurp the role of the master artisan and teach the whole trade. Nonetheless, Beckwith cautioned against prematurely dismissing the Munich model since "the trade improvement schools of Munich must be looked upon as an experiment not long enough established to have final judgment passed upon them. Their future development and results on industry will be of the greatest interest to those desirous of promoting industrial education and efficiency the world over."[26]

Moreover, what seemed disadvantageous about the workshop system in Munich, with its long history of craft apprenticeship, might be particularly applicable in the United States, where the apprenticeship system was disappearing and specialized labor was more prevalent. Beckwith avowed that the United States not only needed a system of mandatory part-time continuation schools, but that because of specialization within American industry, workshops that could promote flexibility by introducing young

23. *Vocational Education,* Vol. III, no. 3 (January 1913), 176, 237–40.
24. Holmes Beckwith, *German Industrial Education and Its Lessons for the United States,* U.S. Bureau of Education, Bulletin 1913, No. 19 (Washington, D.C., 1913), 7.
25. Ibid., 120–1.
26. Ibid., 119–21. The quote appears on 121.

workers to a wider variety of operations and procedures were all the more necessary, despite the higher cost of shop-based instruction.[27]

Beckwith also used the German example as a springboard to intervene in the sharp debate over control of vocational education that arrayed the NAM and other business groups against the AFL. The former favored separate vocational education boards with heavy business representation (dual control), whereas the latter wanted to place vocational education under the supervision of the democratically elected boards of education (unit control). Beckwith espoused a hybrid position, supporting separate boards of vocational education but arguing that although "employers should be represented on school boards as in Germany, but as is seldom done there, workers should also be allowed a place. The industrial schools should keep in closest touch with each of these classes. Only by such close touch with, and real control by, the two classes most directly affected can our industrial education be both efficient and truly democratic."[28]

By contrast, in his pamphlet *Problems of Vocational Education in Germany*, published by the Commissioner of the Bureau of Education in 1915, George E. Myers, a leader of the movement for vocational guidance in the United States, supported unit control. Myers affirmed that the dual control system as it existed in Prussia, where continuation schools were supervised by the Ministry of Commerce and Industry rather than the Educational Ministry, had some clear advantages. He agreed with most Prussian educators that the Commerce Ministry was more attuned to the needs of industry. But he did not regard the dual system as indispensable for the success of these schools and in fact discerned a number of drawbacks. As a result of the administrative separation of the continuation schools, industrial education had little influence in the primary schools, where manual training and guidance counseling were shortchanged. Thus the system of dual control led to "widening the gap between elementary education and industrial life – the gap which industrial education seeks to bridge." Moreover, "the one city in Europe which has done significant work in putting real life into the elementary schools is Munich, the largest city where unit control is in effect."[29]

As such interest and the paeans cited earlier testify, after 1910 Kerschen-

27. Ibid., 143.
28. Ibid., 143.
29. George E. Myers, *Problems of Vocational Education in Germany with Special Application to Conditions in the United States,* U.S. Bureau of Education, Bulletin, 1915, No. 33 (Washington, D.C., 1915), 35–42. The quotes appear on pp. 42 and 40, respectively. A similar position had already been put forward in E. George Payne's "How Industrial Education Is Controlled in Germany," *The Survey* Vol. 30, no. (21 June 1913), 405.

steiner and the Munich industrial schools achieved an enviable reputation among American vocationalists. But this acclamation gives rise to several questions. First, did it have any practical consequences? Second, what were the limits of transferability of the Munich model? Finally, what was the significance of the Kerschensteiner phenomenon for the U.S. industrial education movement?

In response to the first question, suffice it to say that such "Kerschensteinerians" as Hanus and Cooley played pivotal roles in the institutionalization of vocational education in the United States and that the Munich model was imitated in the Northeast and Midwest. Thus, as a direct result of Hanus's tenure as chair of the Massachusetts Commission on Industrial Education, a number of cities launched evening or day continuation schools.[30] With its Commercial Club imprimatur, Cooley's *Vocational Education in Europe* was apparently instrumental in convincing the NAM to abandon trade schools and endorse continuation schools in 1912.[31] The congressional report of the Commission on National Aid to Vocational Education in 1914, which laid the foundation for the Smith–Hughes Act, also used his book to assess German vocational education.[32] Even before passage of the Smith–Hughes Act in 1917, seven states had adopted legislation empowering local boards of education to require continuation schools for employed youths between the ages of fourteen and sixteen. Major industrial cities in Ohio and Wisconsin created extensive systems of continuation schools for young workers and apprentices, although the heyday of such schools would follow passage of the Smith–Hughes Act.[33] In 1921 Paul Douglas reflected:

The real movement for the establishment of part-time continuation schools began in 1910 when Ohio passed the first law definitely referring to continuation schools. More important still was the tour of the country the same year by Dr. Kirschen-

---

30. Although not without opposition from unions over training skilled workers, from municipalities over finance, and from educators over control. See Lazerson, *Origins,* 158–71, and Paul H. Hanus, *Adventuring in Education* (Cambridge, Mass., 1937), 166–74.
31. *Proceedings of the Seventeenth Annual Convention of the National Association of Manufacturers of the United States of America held at New York, N.Y., May 20, 21 and 22, 1912* (New York, 1912), 150, 158–60. The NAM was already moving in this direction the previous year, when the Committee on Industrial Education praised the Munich continuation schools and cited Kerschensteiner on trade and civic education. *Proceedings of the Sixteenth Annual Convention* (New York, 1911), 189–93.
32. U.S. House of Representatives, *Vocational Education: Report of the Commission on National Aid to Vocational Education* (Washington, D.C., 1914), 17, 88–91.
33. Leavitt, *Examples,* 223–34; Douglas, *American Apprenticeship,* 253–62; Warren Dunham Foster, "Wisconsin Plans for the Extension of Industrial and Agricultural Education," *The Survey,* Vol. 26 (20 May 1911), 303–5. For the 1920s, see Charles A. Prosser and Charles R. Allen, *Vocational Education in a Democracy* (New York, 1925), 318–19.

steiner [sic], the celebrated founder of the Munich system of continuation schools. Dr. Kirschensteiner's influence was increased by the prestige then popularly attached to German "efficiency" methods. Dr. Kirschensteiner very much emphasized the fact that the German system of industrial education was not based on the all-day trade school, as people had assumed, but instead upon the part-time continuation school. Drawing upon his own experience, Dr. Kirschensteiner pled for the adoption of the system in the United States. As a result of Dr. Kirschensteiner's visit, the leaders of the movement for industrial education in this country came to understand the real nature of continuation school and many of them became enthusiastic advocates of it. From this time on, the continuation school gained ground with every year.[34]

The victory march of the German-style continuation school, however, was never quite as untroubled as Douglas's account implies. American educators regularly voiced some reservations about the importation of these schools without modifications. Their reservations were grounded in perceptions of significant differences between Germany and the United States, several of which stood out in bold relief.[35]

First, the institution of apprenticeship in the United States differed markedly from its German counterpart. American industry was more highly specialized, and the division of labor was more highly refined than in Germany. In the United States the artisanal sector was negligible. Apprenticeship, although not moribund, had been declining for decades since most employers found the system unprofitable.[36] Apprentices constituted approximately 1 percent of the U.S. labor force. Moreover, those firms that did offer apprenticeships only accepted youths sixteen years of age or older, in contrast to the standard fourteen in Germany. Several different conclusions could be drawn from this institutional distinction. As previously mentioned, Holmes Beckwith claimed that workshop training in continuation schools was more needed in the United States than in Germany. Kerschensteiner proposed that the school-leaving age should be raised to sixteen or that U.S. employers should be induced to take younger apprentices.[37] Other educators concluded that U.S. continuation schools would have to provide prevocational education that concentrated on machinery and industrial safety. But whatever the concrete recommendations, all agreed that differences between apprenticeship in the United States and Germany necessi-

---

34. Douglas, *American Apprenticeship*, 252.
35. See, for example, the warnings against crude imitation of German trade schools by the president of the University of South Dakota before the Congressional Commission on National Aid to Vocational Education. U.S. House of Representatives, *Report of the Commission on National Aid to Vocational Education: Vol. II Hearings* (Washington, D.C., 1914), 165.
36. Douglas, *American Apprenticeship*, 74–80; Beckwith, *German Industrial Education*, 133–6.
37. Kerschensteiner, *Three Lectures*, 15.

tated a different approach. Apart from exceptional cases, continuation schools could not be strictly a supplement to apprentice training.

Second, American educators and labor leaders feared that industrial education along German lines might impede social mobility and make the United States a more rigid and hierarchical society. No matter how enthusiastic they were about the German vocational education system, American observers uniformly deplored its inability to foster the advancement of diligent young workers. They decried the absence of German Horatio Algers and indeed sometimes regarded the German emphasis on industrial education as a residue of the commitment to immobile estates (*Stände*).[38] George E. Myers thought it unfortunate that "so many bright capable boys who might render valuable service to society in skilled industrial, commercial or even professional pursuits are bound to lives of unskilled labor simply because their parents are poor."[39] Although remarking that this happened to some degree everywhere, "it is to be regretted . . . that the German scheme of industrial education, which is so comprehensive in character and has so many admirable features, should not only fail to provide a remedy. . . , but should actually close the door of opportunity on these boys." American proponents of vocational education such as Paul Douglas were not entirely certain about how to make continuation schools pathways for mobility, but they were convinced that opportunities had to be available for further education that could enhance prospects of moving up the career ladder.

Third, such concerns about hardening class lines were sometimes coupled with a critique of the goals for which industrial education had been developed in Germany, namely, nationalism and the interests of manufacturers. This critique was stated most vigorously by John Dewey, who accepted continuation schools as a stopgap measure to aid youths compelled to quit school at age fourteen but who generally suspected that pro-Germanism within the vocational education movement barely concealed admiration for Germany's hierarchical social system and undemocratic polity.[40] The interests of the state and industrial competitiveness, not the well-being of the laborer, motivated industrial education in Germany. German policies were irrelevant in the United States, with its different history and conditions. "There is a grave danger that holding up as a model the educational methods

38. Earl Dean Howard, *The Cause and Extent of the Recent Industrial Progress of Germany* (Boston, 1907), 95–6; Hanus, *Adventuring*, 167.
39. Myers, *Problems*, 16.
40. "Should Michigan Have Vocational Education under 'Unit' or 'Dual' Control?"; "A Policy of Industrial Education" in John Dewey, *The Middle Works, 1899–1924: vol. 7, 1912–14* (Carbondale, Ill., 1979), 90–7.

by which Germany has made its policy effective will serve as a cloak, conscious or unconscious, for measures calculated to serve the interests of the employing class."[41]

In keeping with his distaste for dualism, Dewey also denounced dual control of vocational schools, since this would separate trade from cultural education, sharpen class lines, and benefit only employers. On such grounds, in 1914 Dewey sharply attacked the Illinois vocational education bill, written by Edwin Cooley, that would have set up a system of vocational schools segregated from the regular public schools, a system to be governed, moreover, by a state board of vocational education with heavy employer representation. In assailing the Cooley bill, however, instead of completely rejecting the German model, Dewey invoked the educational philosophy of Kerschensteiner that Cooley had done so much to popularize.

The segregation will work disastrously for the true interests of the pupils who attend so-called vocational schools. Ex-superintendent Cooley of Chicago, who is understood to be responsible for the proposed bill in its present form, has written a valuable report on "Vocational Education in Europe." He quite rightly holds in high esteem the work and opinions of Superintendent Kerschensteiner of Munich. It is noteworthy that this leading European authority insists upon all technical and trade work being taught in its general scientific and social bearings. Although working in a country definitely based on class distinctions (and where naturally the schools are based on class lines), the one thing Superintendent Kerschensteiner has stood for has been that industrial training shall be primarily not for the sake of industry, but for the sake of citizenship, and that it be conducted therefore on a purely educational basis and not on behalf of interested manufactures.[42]

Dewey's rhetorical invocation of Kerschensteiner, which both established a common reference point with Cooley and simultaneously clarified Dewey's differences with him over the Illinois bill, raises the final point about the function of Georg Kerschensteiner and the Munich schools within the American industrial education movement. Although by 1910 there was a broad consensus on the need for some sort of vocational education, the nature and goals of this education were controversial and unfocused. The NAM desired trade schools that could turn out specialized skilled craftsmen, whereas the AFL endorsed general industrial education. Some educators wanted purely practical instruction; others held that young workers required further cultural and civic education. Such divisions threatened to condemn the movement to quarrelsome impotence.

---

41. Ibid., 945.
42. "Some Dangers in the Present Movement for Industrial Education," in Dewey, *The Middle Works: Vol. 7*, 101.

The Munich system provided a common model around which American vocationalists could define, shape, and concretize their programs. In part, Kerschensteiner played the role of the esteemed outsider, who could mediate among divergent positions. It was notably the NSPIE, which was trying to forge a compromise between business and organized labor, that sponsored Kerschensteiner's U.S. tour. The Munich schools seemed to show that some of the dichotomies that split the U.S. movement could be dialectically transcended, that industrial education could be trade related without training surplus skilled laborers, as the unions feared. Rather than counterposing vocational and cultural education, Kerschensteiner asserted that vocational instruction could be directly related to civic and cultural themes. Kerschensteiner could partially overcome the division between the NAM and the AFL, the former proponents of national efficiency and the latter who believed that industrial education should improve the laborer's life chances and prospects for civic participation. Even in the most bitter debate, over unit versus dual control, an examination of the German schools provided the distance that enabled vocationalists to hammer out a compromise, largely along the lines recommended by Beckwith, with separate vocational boards but with joint labor and business representation.

Obviously, there were many reasons why part-time continuation schools became the vocational institutions of choice in the United States: relative cheapness, the increasing recognition by industrialists that they needed flexible workers rather than specialized craftsmen, and the AFL's endorsement of general industrial education. But American vocationalists could crystallize their positions around the image of the Munich schools. Certainly this image was projected on a quite different industrial, social, and political screen than in Germany. Despite accommodation to specific American conditions, much of Kerschensteiner's message and the Munich model seem to have survived transatlantic transmission.

Acknowledgment

I would like to thank Professor Robert Huff of the Hobart and William Smith History Department for his comments on an earlier version of this essay.

PART TWO

*Varieties of Teachers and
Styles of Teaching*

5

American and German Women in the Kindergarten Movement, 1850–1914

ANN TAYLOR ALLEN

Boston reformer Elizabeth Peabody, though duly respectful of the awesome intellectual and bureaucratic authority wielded by St. Louis School Superintendent William Torrey Harris, had no hesitation in arguing with him. In 1877, Harris wrote that the Froebel kindergarten, which he had introduced into the St. Louis school system in 1873, would have to be "Americanized" in order to meet the needs of American children. Peabody responded indignantly, "I hope . . . that you will distinctly say that by Americanizing it you do not mean departing from Froebel's principle. . . .Froebel in his lifetime specially recognized the fact that the spirit of society in America was more coincident with his system than that of his Fatherland. He thought of emigrating to establish it here." Historians of American early childhood education such as Michael Steven Shapiro often picture the Americanization of the kindergarten chiefly as a movement away from its German counterpart in response to uniquely American conditions. However, this process did *not* show American rejection of foreign influences, but rather the continuing relationship of German and American cultures. Although the American kindergarten developed differently from its German counterpart, German influences were important at each stage in its development from 1856 to 1914. German and American kindergarten activists stayed in contact, visited each other, and often used the differences in their situations and ideas as a basis for cross-cultural dialogue.[1]

The popularity of the kindergarten cause among educated, middle-class American women in the period from 1870 to 1914 suggests the complex

---

1. Peabody to Harris, January 19, 1877. Harris Papers, Missouri Historical Society. For historical views of the divergence of the American kindergarten movement from its German models, see Michael Steven Shapiro, *Child's Gardens: The Kindergarten from Froebel to Dewey* (University Park, Pa., 1983), 29–45; and Agnes Snyder, *Dauntless Women in Childhood Education* (Association for Childhood Education International, Washington, D.C., 1972), 173–81; Snyder describes the development of the American movement as "Changing Directions through an Indigenous Philosophy" (173) and "Changing Directions through an Indigenous Psychology" (178).

and shifting meanings of the concept of "Germany" in American intellectual life. The fact that Froebel accorded high honor to motherhood and recommended the involvement of professionally trained women in education does not in itself explain his appeal to American women. In the later decades of the nineteenth century this idea was much more influential in America than in Germany, and many American writers, among them Catharine Beecher, had expressed it in considerably less abstruse and more readable form. A more important reason for the appeal of kindergarten pedagogy to some women, however, was the prestige accorded in America during this period to German philosophical and scientific learning. Many of the female kindergarten founders, German and American, were drawn much more to intellectual speculation than to the practical work of early childhood education. "For though I am a woman and thus terribly driven by practical work," wrote Peabody to Harris, "yet I find my heaven in speculative philosophy."

But women's opportunities for intellectual self-expression were very limited; childrearing was one of the few subjects on which they could speak with authority. Kindergarten theory gave them an impressive philosophical and scientific vocabulary with which to comment not only on childrearing, but on a host of related issues. Their use of this vocabulary enabled women kindergarten activists to enter the major intellectual and political discourses of their era; to legitimate their own intellectual, professional, and political agendas; and to gain a hearing from their male contemporaries. They used kindergarten theory as male intellectuals used other kinds of German learning – to argue for the integration of American individualism with alternative ethical values, supported by German ideas, stressing social responsibility and community spirit. The impact of German ideas was important to three major stages through which the American kindergarten movement passed during this period – the establishment of the first public school kindergartens and kindergarten training programs in the 1870s, the development of new methods based on the scientific field of child study in the 1880s and 1890s, and the incorporation of the kindergarten into social reform movements in the period from 1890 to 1914.[2]

The coming of the kindergarten to America, as ritualistically recounted in kindergarten literature, became a legend of the thwarted potential of the Old World and its realization in the New. Friedrich Froebel, founder of

---

2. Peabody to Harris, April 25, 1871; on the various stages of the kindergarten movement, see, among many other sources, Shapiro, *Child's Gardens;* and Ann Taylor Allen, "Let Us Live with Our Children: Kindergarten Movements in Germany and the United States," *History of Education Quarterly* 28 (Spring 1988): 24–48.

the kindergarten, envisaged his new institution as an alternative to traditional authoritarian forms of education and as a seedbed (or garden) of a new generation of citizens. Three aspects of Froebel's theory were particularly important to his American disciples. Drawing on post-Kantian philosophy, his pedagogical approach stressed the relationship of the part to the whole, of the individual to the group, and of freedom to responsibility. He regarded the mother–child relationship, in which self and other were perfectly merged, as the natural basis for these social virtues. Even more important was his assertion that children's development followed certain scientific laws that must be studied and used in education. Child nurture, he asserted, did not rest merely on instinct or emotion, but was a science that must be learned through an extensive program of education and training. And he insisted that early childhood education must be based on play, directed but not controlled by the maternal discipline of the teacher, rather than book learning.

Kindergarten method, originally designed for the use of mothers in the home, was adapted to an institutional setting in 1840, when Froebel founded the first kindergarten in the small Thuringian town of Blankenburg. Though this educational experiment attracted little attention at first, the kindergarten movement became a major form of social activism among liberal German women in 1848. It acquired the taint of radicalism and godlessness largely through its central place in the curriculum of the Hamburg Academy for Women, a daring educational experiment in which both Friedrich Froebel and his nephew, Carl, were involved. The Academy, based on ideas derived from dissenting religious sects and from utopian socialist theory, was open for only two years, from 1850 to 1852, when it closed in response to the reactionary political atmosphere created by the suppression of the 1848 revolutions. In 1851, largely because of its association with religious and political movements now defined as subversive, the Froebel kindergarten was banned in Prussia and in some other German states. The Prussian ban was not lifted until 1860.[3]

Though Froebel himself, who died in 1851, never realized his dream of emigrating to America, many of his followers joined the flow of liberal exiles to the New World. The first kindergarten in the United States was founded by Margarethe Schurz, wife of the eminent politician Carl Schurz,

---

3. On the history of the German kindergarten, see, among many other sources, Günter Erning, Karl Neumann, and Jürgen Reyer, eds., *Geschichte des Kindergartens*, 2 vols. (Freiburg, 1987), 1: 29–46; Ann Taylor Allen, "Spiritual Motherhood: German Feminists and the Kindergarten Movement," *History of Education Quarterly* 22 (Fall 1982): 319–40; and Catherine N. Prelinger, *Charity, Challenge and Change: Religious Dimensions of the Mid-Nineteenth-Century Women's Movement* (Westport, Conn., 1987), 94–100.

in Watertown, Wisconsin, in 1855. Other emigrants from Germany or the German-speaking world, such as the Swiss William Hailmann and the German socialist Adolf Douai, also founded kindergartens that at first served to preserve German traditions and German language among the children of emigrants. Emigrants who were not political exiles sometimes returned to Germany for training. Caroline Louisa Frankenberg of Eddigehausen (near Göttingen), for example, founded a school (not a kindergarten) in Columbus, Ohio, in 1836. In about 1840, discouraged at the failure of her efforts, she returned to Germany, lived at Froebel's institute at Keilhau for six years, and then taught in Germany until 1858, when she returned to Columbus and set up a kindergarten. She recalled that curious neighbors peered through the windows of the kindergarten, astonished that children could learn without books. In 1862 Louise Pollock (originally Plessner), a German emigrant from East Prussia who had settled in Boston with her American husband and had received kindergarten literature from her family in Germany, opened what she claimed was the first "pure" kindergarten in America under the auspices of Nathaniel Allen, principal of a school in West Newton. In 1870 she sent her daughter Susan to study kindergarten methods in Berlin, where she herself also studied briefly in 1874.[4]

The spread of the kindergarten to the broader English-speaking constituency was largely the work of Elizabeth Peabody, a Boston intellectual and educator, whose interest in German ideas had already been awakened by the transcendentalist movement. Peabody learned about kindergarten methods from Margarethe Schurz. In 1860 she set up her own kindergarten in Boston, using chiefly English kindergarten guidebooks. In 1867 she traveled to Germany to study with the then most prominent female kindergarten founder in Germany, the Baroness von Marenholtz-Bülow. Marenholtz, who had worked with Froebel, believed that the new institution must create social peace by teaching the virtues of citizenship and social responsibility, especially to working-class children. Peabody, now persuaded that all existing American kindergartens were useless because they did not conform to the German model, persuaded some German kindergartens, including Maria Boelte (whom she met in England) and Emma Marwedel, to come to America. In 1868, Matilda Kriege, a student of Marenholtz-Bülow, set up a "German kindergarten," later expanded into a training school, in Boston. In 1873, Maria Boelte (later Kraus-Boelte)

4. Elizabeth Jenkins, "Froebel's Disciples in America," *German-American Review* 3 (1936–7): 15–17; Shapiro, *Child's Gardens*, 29–45; "Louise Pollock," in Frances E. Willard and Mary A. Livermore, eds., *A Woman of the Century* (Buffalo, N.Y., 1893), 578–9; *Letter and Data relating to the Early History of the Kindergarten in America*, (Washington, D.C., n.d.), 1–3.

established a two-year training program in New York. Marwedel emigrated first to Washington, D.C., in about 1870 and set up a kindergarten with Susan Pollock, the daughter of Louise Pollock. Kriege, Marwedel, and Boelte trained most of the best-known members of the first generation of American kindergartners.[5]

In 1873 William Torrey Harris, superintendent of schools in St. Louis, set up the first public school kindergarten system there. Harris was persuaded both by the German-American Teachers Association and by Elizabeth Peabody, who started an extensive correspondence with him in 1870. Harris was at first reluctant, objecting that the climate of St. Louis was less suitable to the kindergarten than that of Germany. "If St. Louis is not too hot for children to be born there," replied Peabody, "it cannot be too hot for the mind as well as body to grow on nature's plan of development, which is just Froebel's kindergarten plan."[6]

Harris was a Germanophile and amateur philosopher who, along with some German immigrants, had founded a society called the St. Louis Hegelians in 1858. His argument for public school kindergartens was based on a conception of the dialectical relationship of German and American cultures that proved influential in the American kindergarten movement, of which he was a prestigious advocate. Many German emigrants of 1848 had taken a negative view of the oppressive regime that had suppressed the kindergarten. Peabody, who identified herself strongly with these German exiles, did not admire German culture, and compared its "uninventive" and "bookish" spirit unfavorably with Yankee independence and ingenuity. But Harris reached the opposite judgment on the relative merits of practical and "bookish" learning. In a speech to the German-American Teachers Association, he declared in 1872 that the Anglo-Saxon tradition, dominant in America thus far, had emphasized practicality at the expense of intellectual depth. "Born as I was, among the rugged hills of Connecticut, I can still remember the immense astonishment I felt when I first came to learn of the province and scope of German thought. . . .To comprehend – *Begreifen* – is a German achievement and he who would attain that highest gift of man must aid himself with the works of German genius."

For Harris as for many postbellum reformers, a major consequence of the Anglo-Saxon tradition of individual freedom was disorder and disunity: "doubt and denial . . . skepticism, vice and corruption." He identified the

---

5. On the coming of the kindergarten to America, see Jenkins, "Froebel's Disciples in America"; and Shapiro, *Child's Garden*.
6. Peabody to Harris, May 18, 1870, and August 25, 1870; W. T. Harris, "German Reform in American Education," *The Western: A Review of Education, Science, Literature and Art* (September 1872): 327.

German philosophical tradition that defined freedom within, rather than apart from, the social organism as the essential corrective to this malaise. The kindergarten was a practical application of German philosophical theory to pedagogy. Using the dialectical method, Harris explained that the kindergarten would reconcile the freedom permitted by the family with the order demanded by the school. The initiation of the kindergarten in St. Louis served a practical purpose as well; Harris had observed that most working-class children left school at the age of ten; thus the inclusion of younger age groups in the public school system was the best means of increasing its effectiveness.[7]

The meaning of the kindergarten, and of the German culture that it represented, to some American-born women in the 1870s and 1880s may be illustrated by the career and ideas of Susan Elizabeth Blow, to whom Harris assigned the leadership of the St. Louis public school kindergartens in 1873. Blow was born in 1843 into the family of a wealthy businessman who later became a politician and diplomat. According to a friend of the family, philosopher Denton Snider, Blow's early education, supervised by a German tutor, reflected the high prestige accorded German culture in St. Louis in the 1850s and 1860s. But, though exposed to German learning, she was not encouraged to pursue it; her teacher regarded her passion for philosophy as unfeminine. She herself was dissatisfied with her education, which was completed at a New York boarding school, and supplemented it with a personal program of reading that included much German philosophy and literature.[8]

Temperamentally unsuited to the ornamental role of young lady, Blow longed for a vocation, but was prevented from taking up a profession both by a lack of training and by the opposition of her conservative father. Blow's only experience of meaningful work had been in childrearing, for she had helped to raise her numerous brothers and sisters. In the American culture

7. Peabody to Harris, October, 1878 (no day); Harris, "German Reform in American Education," 327; *Twenty-Fourth Annual Report of the Board of Directors of the St. Louis Public Schools, for the year ending August 1, 1873*, 18–19. On St. Louis Hegelians, see Denys P. Leighten, "William Torrey Harris, the St. Louis Hegelians, and the Meaning of the Civil War," *Gateway Heritage: Quarterly Magazine of the Missouri Historical Society* 10 (Fall 1989): 32–45. On the more general discourse on American individualism and its problems, see William Leach, *True Love and Perfect Union: The Feminist Reform of Sex and Society* (New York, 1980), passim; and Jurgen Herbst, *The German Historical School in American Scholarship: A Study in the Transfer of Culture* (Ithaca, N.Y., 1965), 66–71, 130–59.

8. Denton J. Snider, *The St. Louis Movement in Philosophy, Literature, Education, Psychology* (St. Louis, 1929), 296; Blow to Harris, July 9, 1892, Harris Papers, Missouri Historical Society. On Blow's early life, see also Margaret Hilliker, "Life and Work of Susan Blow," typescript, 1953, Missouri Historical Society, 1–26; Snyder, *Dauntless Women in Childhood Education*, 59–63; Committee of Nineteen, *Pioneers of the Kindergarten in America* (New York, 1924), 185–7; and Shapiro, *Child's Garden*, 45–65.

of the 1850s and 1860s, however, mere practical experience with children was increasingly devalued by experts, who called for more scientific approaches and defined childrearing as a social, rather than simply an individual and familial, responsibility. Thus, in order to speak and act with authority, women such as Blow needed academic credentials and a public or social field of activity. Froebelian pedagogy, which emphasized both the intellectual prestige and the public importance of child nurture, provided both. In 1876 Blow, who had already visited Germany with her family, once again traveled there to study with Marenholtz-Bülow, whose training course in Dresden was then widely regarded as the most faithful to Froebelian tradition. Because Froebel had defined kindergarten work as a highly altruistic calling – in Peabody's words, "a vocation from on high" – it could be done as a volunteer activity, without the stigma of paid work. Blow functioned as a volunteer worker, and so, at the beginning, did many of her assistants. By 1880, there were fifty-eight public school kindergartens in the St. Louis system.[9]

Blow, who was not a gifted teacher of small children, became famous chiefly as an author and a teacher of teachers. In 1888, she left St. Louis and embarked on a career as a lecturer and teacher that culminated in an appointment to Teachers' College, which she held from 1896 to 1906. The many works published during this period used concepts derived from German philosophy and pedagogy to create a theory of child development that emphasized the central role of woman as private and public nurturer. Blow had become a convert to German idealism chiefly because its concept of an orderly universe that could be understood by human reason provided an attractive alternative to the grim Calvinist religion in which she had been raised. She regarded Froebelian pedagogy as "a marvellous application of those verities to the interpretation of childhood."

Her methods were designed to initiate the child into the order of the universe through symbols conveyed by stories and games. Along with Froebel, she believed that this process was based on the mother–child bond, as experienced from the first days of life. Much of Blow's later career was devoted to a series of commentaries on Froebel's *Mother and Nursery Songs,* a book of songs and games for mothers and infants. Blow explained the deep ethical and philosophical truths conveyed by the "Falling Game," in

---

9. On Blow's decision to adopt kindergarten teaching as a profession, see Blow to Harris, July 9, 1892; on her visit to Marenholtz-Bülow, see Blow to Harris, Dec. 3, 1876; on changes in idea of childrearing, see Mary P. Ryan, *The Empire of the Mother: American Writing about Domesticity* (New York, 1985), 97–114; on Peabody's idea of the kindergarten profession, see Barbara Beatty, "A Vocation from on High: Kindergartening as an Occupation for American Women," in Joyce Antler and Sari Biklen, eds., *Change in Education: Women as Radicals and Conservatives* (Albany, N.Y., 1990), 38–9.

which the mother lets the baby fall for a few seconds and then catches it. According to Blow, the game taught trust, which began with the mother and was then extended to other human beings and ultimately to God. Blow used maternal love as a metaphor for an idea of social order based on responsibility, cohesion, and community. This idea was derived originally from Pestalozzi, but Blow applied it specifically to the American scene: "Children must trust parents . . . we must all trust the tradesmen with whom we deal . . . the economic system upon which depends the fair participation of each man in the labor of all men, the government which orders and protects other institutions. . . . Faith is the beating heart of the body corporate."[10]

Blow's influential works proposed a vital role for women, not just in education but in the tempering of American individualism through new forms of social order. The order of the kindergarten classroom, anticipating the order of adult society, was achieved not through coercion, but through a freely accepted responsibility conveyed through the maternal pedagogy of the teacher. Kindergarten theorists and teachers during the period from 1870 to 1914 often used the kindergarten classroom as a metaphor for their ideal of community. "Froebel provides exercises in the Kindergarten for private duty and public," wrote Frances Lord of Boston in 1889. "Take the simplest circle game; it illustrates the whole duty of a good citizen in a republic. Anybody can spoil it, yet no one can play it alone."[11]

In the 1880s, as Jurgen Herbst has noted, philosophy gave way to science as the most influential field of German learning in the United States. The new scientific interpretations of child development, or "child study," that eventually displaced Froebelianism as the basis of kindergarten theory were originally based on German research. American psychologist G. Stanley Hall, usually identified as the first to apply these theories to kindergarten method, had studied with Wilhelm Wundt in Leipzig and was deeply influenced by German child psychologist Wilhelm Preyer. He used a German project, carried out by a group of Berlin teachers, as a model for his article "The Content of Children's Minds," which is often identified with the beginning of the child study movement in America.

But the new psychological and physiological ideas had another important early adherent in the United States. Emma Marwedel, who was born in

---

10. Susan E. Blow, *Letters to a Mother on the Philosophy of Froebel* (New York, 1899), 11–12; on Blow's conception of German idealism and its significance, see Blow, "The Service of Dr. Harris to the Kindergarten," *Kindergarten Review* 20 (June 1910): 592–3.
11. Frances Lord, "The Kindergarten as a School of Public Spirit," *Kindergarten Magazine* 2 (1889–90): 1. For more on the pedagogy of the kindergarten, see Allen, "Let Us Live with Our Children."

Minden in 1828, had been head of a girl's industrial school in Hamburg, to which a kindergarten training program was attached, and was also active on the leading committee of the German Women's Association, the first German feminist organization, which she joined in 1865. Marwedel, who (as we have seen) emigrated to America in about 1870, moved from Washington, D.C., to California, where with the help of wealthy philanthropists she established the state's first free kindergarten, open without cost to poor children, in Oakland. After 1879 she moved again, to San Francisco, where she became director of another such institution, Silver St. Kindergarten. This kindergarten was sponsored by a fellow German emigrant, Felix Adler, who had founded an organization, the Ethical Culture Society, that promoted secular ethical training through educational institutions. The head teacher at Silver Street was Marwedel's student, Kate Douglas Wiggin. Marwedel, who like Blow was a self-educated intellectual, had apparently known Preyer in Germany, and by 1880, even before the publication of Hall's article, was already interested in incorporating scientific ideas into kindergarten training. In 1881 (thus before the publication of Preyer's major work, *The Mind of the Child*) the curriculum for her training school included books by Marenholtz and Froebel, but also by Huxley and Spencer. Her book, *Conscious Motherhood,* published in 1887, was promoted by Elizabeth Peabody and became a well-known kindergarten text.[12]

Marwedel's scientific approach to childhood was very different from that of Susan Blow. Blow, who remained a philosophical idealist and orthodox Froebelian, was deeply troubled by scientific theories that seemed to emphasize the child's animal rather than spiritual nature. But both women looked to Germany as a source of intellectual inspiration. Marwedel characterized Preyer's book, *The Mind of the Child,* as "a remarkable book – the first of its kind in range and profundity," that answered "every query . . . which mothers and other educators should ask concerning the earliest physical, mental and emotional needs of the child." Both Blow and Marwedel used ideas derived from Germany to legitimate the claims of women to education, professional activity, and social influence. Women, claimed Marwedel, must be educated to "conscious motherhood," now based on scientific knowledge. "The characteristic of the nineteenth century," she

12. Herbst, *The German Historical School,* 67–71; the only biography of Marwedel is Fletcher Harper Swift, *Emma Jacobina Christiana Marwedel, Pioneer of the Kindergarten in California* (Berkeley, Calif., 1932); on her German background, see 149–54; on her career, see 154–80; on the curriculum of her training school see 173–4. Another discussion of Marwedel's career is Snyder, *Dauntless Women,* 97–101. On child study and its effect on kindergarten pedagogy, see (among many other sources), Shapiro, *Child's Garden,* 107–30; on Hall's own debt to Preyer, see G. Stanley Hall, *Life and Confessions of a Psychologist* (New York, 1924), 378–9.

wrote, "is its craving for truth. . . . .Man not only puts the almost invisible parasite and worm under the microscope, but he subjects himself to the same investigation. . . .Is woman's moral and physical relation to her child not to be adjusted by the same laws which control the universe, from the star to the atom?"[13]

Marwedel also shared with Blow, Harris, and other kindergarten advocates a view of the kindergarten as a microcosm of a new form of social order. Like her contemporaries, she feared that the American spirit of liberty could turn to license if not tempered by a new spirit of responsibility, of which women as "conscious mothers" must be the proponents. America, she wrote, had the divinely appointed mission to solve "on free soil . . . the problem of social equality and not to turn her great future into a most fearful chaos of human passions and destructive forces." Against the specter of anarchy, Marwedel invoked the efficacy of private and public motherhood in the struggle for "moral reform" and against "the causes and effects of crime, idiocy, insanity, poverty and suicide." Because the new science showed that most characteristics were hereditary, the science of childhood included that of eugenics, which upheld the right of the child to be "well born." But hereditarian theories of personality development did not make the mother's role irrelevant. On the contrary, Marwedel believed, they underscored the need for scientific knowledge as a basis for guidance and education, for "the right unfolding of its higher inborn faculties into a good and happy being." Though Marwedel, who died in 1893, did not herself participate in the major revision of kindergarten pedagogy during the period 1890–1914 under the influence of Anna Bryan, Patty Smith Hill, Hall, and John Dewey, her students, especially Kate Douglas Wiggin and her sister Nora Archibald Smith, played influential roles in that movement.[14]

Marwedel's free kindergartens were among the first examples of a new and wide-ranging application of kindergarten theory and practice in the urban environment. The idea of the urban free kindergarten (or *Volkskindergarten*), which originated with Marenholtz in the 1860s, was developed in the 1870s and 1880s in America, where many groups, including male and female reformers, set up kindergartens providing care and education for the children of the urban poor. The first free kindergarten had been

13. Emma Marwedel, *Conscious Motherhood, or the Earliest Unfolding of the Child in the Cradle, Nursery and Kindergarten* (Chicago, 1887), 15, 19. On the role of scientific knowledge in the feminist arguments of this period, see Leach, *True Love and Perfect Union,* 64–99.
14. Marwedel, *Conscious Motherhood,* 73, 79, 137. For another view of Marwedel's work, see Barbara Beatty, "From Conscious Motherhood to Children's Rights: The American Kindergarten Movement and Child-Rearing in the Early Progressive Era," paper delivered at the convention of the History of Education Society, Oct. 29, 1989.

founded by the New York Ethical Culture Society in 1878; by 1890, there were 115 free kindergarten societies, maintaining 223 schools, in American cities. Kindergarten practice, which emphasized the teacher's involvement with the personal as well as the intellectual development of her pupils, provided an influential model for the developing field of social work. Many settlement houses, including Chicago's Hull House, included kindergartens; some of the settlements, such as Neighborhood House in Louisville and Elizabeth Peabody House in Boston, grew out of urban kindergartens. The kindergarten idea – order, cooperation, and community, mediated through a regime of maternal love – acquired a new significance in cities where an influx of immigrants had aroused the fear of social unrest and of the erosion of American culture through foreign influences. The evolution of kindergarten theory in the period 1880–1914 was shaped by the gender, class, and ethnic consciousness of the first generation of American kindergartens, almost all of whom were white, Protestant, middle-class, and native born. These women won acceptance for the kindergarten from many school boards, philanthropic organizations, and local government by emphasizing the importance of exposing foreign-born children to American culture, and poor children to middle-class values at the earliest possible age.[15]

American kindergartens, though adapting their methods to uniquely American conditions, nonetheless maintained contact with their German colleagues and learned from German examples. Until 1890, the most influential German kindergarten theorist in America had been Bertha von Marenholtz-Bülow, an orthodox Froebelian. After 1890, the interest of American kindergartners shifted to another German kindergarten founder, Henriette Schrader-Breymann, a great-niece of Friedrich Froebel. In 1873, Schrader-Breymann had founded a kindergarten training institution, the Pestalozzi-Froebel House, in Berlin. The school at first included an urban kindergarten serving the children of the poor as well as a training program; in the 1880s it developed many other services, including a day nursery, a school lunch program, and a school of domestic arts. From the beginning of her career, Schrader-Breymann had criticized Froebel's methods and had developed her own approach to early childhood education, which included practical activities such as housework, handicrafts, and gardening, nature study, and field trips. These methods reflected both a Pestalozzian belief in

---

15. On free kindergartens, see Shapiro, *Child's Garden*, 85–106; Barbara Beatty, "Child Gardening: The Teaching of Young Children in American Schools," in Donald Warren, ed., *American Teachers: History of a Profession at Work* (New York, 1989), 76–81; on kindergartens in settlement houses, see Allen F. Davis, *Spearheads for Reform: The Social Settlements and the Progressive Movement, 1890–1914* (New York, 1977), 44–7.

"learning by doing" and a conviction, also shared by Americans such as G. Stanley Hall, that exposure to nature was a vital part of the education of the urban child.[16] The transition from Froebelian routines to activities based on practical activities and nature study was the most important, and most bitterly disputed, change in American kindergarten practice in the 1890s. Opponents of these changes cited the authority of Marenholtz-Bülow; proponents looked to Schrader-Breymann. The Pestalozzi-Froebel House became known to American kindergartners at least by 1880, when a visitor to Berlin published a very favorable report in Henry Barnard's *American Journal of Education*. Doubtless, the transition away from Froebelianism in America, as in Germany, was chiefly a pragmatic response to the practical demands of urban kindergarten teaching. In 1883, Wiggin wrote to Peabody that an article on teaching methods by Schrader-Breymann's coworker, Mary Lyschinska, had so closely resembled one that she had just written that she feared the suspicion of plagiarism. Anna Bryan, sometimes identified as the first to use the new methods, acknowledged no German influence on her experimental kindergarten in Louisville in 1887.

But the Pestalozzi-Froebel House was an important source of ideas to some American kindergartners, for kindergarten training in the 1880s and 1890s, still dominated by Blow, Kraus-Boelte, and their students, remained traditional. For example, Elizabeth Harrison, the head of the Chicago Kindergarten Training School, was surprised in 1889 by the pedagogical methods used by a German student who had previously studied at the Berlin institution and decided to travel to Germany in order to learn more about these methods. Cordially received by Schrader-Breymann, Harrison was at first shocked at her German colleague's abandonment of Froebelian orthodoxy. But she soon realized that training in practical activities was an effective means of achieving the goal that she and other American kindergartners had developed: the teaching of orderly and cooperative behavior. The Schraders, she wrote, were "striving as best they could to educate the inhabitants of this district into better ideas of cleanliness and economy." After her return to the United States, Harrison put some of these methods into practice in her training school, renamed the Chicago Kindergarten Training College, which became a center of kindergarten training. She also applied her ideas about the reformative potential of such methods in her

16. On the Pestalozzi-Froebel House, see Mary Lyschinska and Henriette Schrader-Breymann: *Ihr Leben aus Briefen und Tagebüchern zusammengestellt und erlätert*, 2 vols. (Berlin and Leipzig, 1922), 2: 1–50, and Henriette Schrader-Breymann, *Der Volkskindergarten im Pestalozzi-Froebel Hause* (Berlin, 1890).

work at Hull House, which was founded by Jane Addams and her colleagues in the same year, 1889.[17]

The visibility and prestige of the Pestalozzi-Froebel House were increased by the exhibit that it sponsored at the Chicago World's Fair of 1893. The editor of *Kindergarten Magazine,* the central organ of the American movement, was Amalie Hofer, a German immigrant who often visited Germany and publicized German developments. An editorial in this magazine asserted that a thorough study of the exhibit was "of vital import to the revival of natural methods" in the United States. Other Americans also pictured the Pestalozzi-Froebel House as an example of both the scientific expertise and the devotion to communal welfare that they considered characteristic of Germany. Hall, who visited the school shortly after the opening of its new buildings in 1898, characterized it as "the finest kindergarten installation in the world today." He praised the institution's emphasis on practical activities, nature study, and physical health and hygiene, contrasting its spirit of scientific rationality to the outmoded methods of his conservative rival and adversary, Susan Blow.[18]

Another example of the influence of the Pestalozzi-Froebel House was the creation of a student residence hall, known as the House of Gertrude, at Chicago Kindergarten College. Annette Hamminck-Schepel, a former student of Schrader-Breymann, who supervised the exhibit at the World's Fair, encouraged her Chicago colleagues to provide its trainees with a residence closely modeled on the Pestalozzi-Froebel House. Like their counterparts in Berlin, the Chicago trainees lived in an all-female residential community, sharing domestic, professional, and social activities. The purpose of the Chicago residence, named after Pestalozzi's heroine, was to train "young women in homemaking ideals, believing this to be the true foundation for their professional training." The building, located in a poor neighborhood, contained dormitory rooms, a dining hall, and a kindergarten. The residents, who combined practice teaching with domestic work,

---

17. A. Aldrich, "Mrs. Schrader's Kindergarten in Berlin," *Barnard's American Journal of Education* 30 (1880): 880–8; Kate Douglas Wiggin to Elizabeth Peabody, February 9, 1883, Elizabeth Peabody Papers, Massachusetts Historical Society; Elizabeth Harrison, *Sketches Along Life's Road* (Boston, 1930), 116–21; quotation, 121; on Bryan and the development of the American kindergarten, see Snyder, *Dauntless Women,* 239–50, and Shapiro, *Child's Garden,* 115–22.
18. "The Exhibit of the Pestalozzi-Froebel Haus of Berlin," *Kindergarten Magazine* 7 (1894–5): 10. Examples of other American responses to the Pestalozzi-Froebel House: "The Kindergarten Department Meeting at Denver," *Kindergarten Magazine* 8 (1895–6): 4; Laura Trefft, "The Transition and Elementary Classes at the Pestalozzi-Froebel House," *Kindergarten Magazine* 2 (1889–90): 414; "Pestalozzi-Froebel House: Twenty-Fifth Anniversary; Dedication of New Buildings," *Kindergarten Magazine* 11 (1898–9): 168–9; Amalie Hofer, "Death of Frau Henriette Schrader," *Kindergarten Magazine* 12 (1899–1900), 107; G. Stanley Hall, "The Pedagogy of the Kindergarten," in *Educational Problems,* 2 vols. (New York, 1911), 1: 16–17.

developed a sense of community through meetings, discussions, and rec-
reational activities. Thus forms of female communal life that were practiced
in many other kindergarten training schools, as well as in social settlement
houses and women's colleges, were also encouraged by the example of the
Pestalozzi-Froebel House. These substitute families provided young women
professionals with emotional support and space for personal development.[19]

By the 1890s, both the American and the German kindergarten movements were well on their way to modifying or rejecting both Froebel's
theories of child development and many of his methods. It is therefore all
the more interesting that Froebel himself lost none of his stature as a symbolic figure. Froebel, a man who respected women, loved children, and
honored motherhood, represented an appealing ideal of male behavior to
women who aspired to tame the male-dominated world through the power
of female influence. The effects of the feminization of childrearing and
teaching in the latter half of the nineteenth century were apparent in portrayals of Froebel, who in his own lifetime had played the highly male-
identified roles of soldier, patriot, philosopher, and teacher, as an
androgynous and saintly figure resembling this period's image of Christ.
"Let them [the kindergarten children] feel that the dear, good Froebel looks
down with gratitude and happiness on the children's love and joy," wrote
Wiggin on the occasion of the founder's birthday in 1895. The religious
overtones of the movement were also apparent in the custom of the "Froebel pilgrimage" – a tour of Froebel's homeland of Thuringia, including the
important sites of the early kindergarten movement. In 1899, German kindergartner Eleonore Heerwart, then president of the International Kindergarten Union, took advantage of this tourist traffic by appealing for
American financial support for the creation of a Froebel museum, a library,
and a home for retired kindergarten teachers in Blankenburg, where the
first kindergarten had been founded. Lucy Wheelock, head of a Boston
kindergarten training program and a national leader of the American kindergarten movement, cooperated with Heerwart to plan a Froebel pilgrimage for American kindergartners. By appealing to her American colleagues
to rescue a project that had apparently found little support in Germany,
Heerwart implicitly acknowledged America as the international center of
the kindergarten movement.[20]

19. Ruth Grey, "The Keilhau of America," *Kindergarten Magazine* 10 (1897–8): 619–29; on Schepel's
    visit to America, see Jenkins, "Froebel's Disciples," 18 and Annette Hamminck-Schepel, "Mittei-
    lungen aus Chicago an Frau Henriette Schrader," *Vereins-Zeitung des Pestalozzi-Froebel Hauses* (Oc-
    tober 1896), 1–2.
20. As an example of a Christ-like image of Froebel, see the bas-relief sculpture over the entrance of
    Wheelock College, Boston; Kate Douglas Wiggin, "On Froebel's Birthday," *Kindergarten Magazine*

The responses of Wheelock and her seventy colleagues who participated in the 1911 Froebel pilgrimage to Germany suggest a change in the American kindergarten movement's perception of Germany. To Harris, who admired Germany from afar, and to Hall, who often traveled there, Germany was the land of scientific and social progress. Wheelock also knew, visited, and admired, impressive institutions such as the Pestalozzi-Froebel House. But in her account of her travels, she emphasized chiefly the backwardness of Thuringia, which she sometimes described as sinister rather than picturesque. In 1903, her tour of Froebel's birthplace, Oberweissbach, included "the dark closet in which Froebel's stepmother used to shut him up for punishment," and she commented on the town's poverty and lack of modern conveniences. "It is the most primitive place that I have seen."

The Froebel pilgrims of 1911 learned from their German colleagues that the kindergarten cause had received far less official and popular support in Germany than in America. By 1900, many major American school systems supported kindergarten classes, and kindergarten teaching had been recognized as a department of the major teachers' organization, the National Education Association, since 1884. By contrast, in Germany, the majority of public school teachers still firmly resisted the idea of incorporating the kindergarten, or indeed any form of education for children under six, into public school systems. A major reason for this difference was the differing status of women in the two nations; the professions of teaching and social work, which in America were dominated by women, in Germany remained dominated by men. "The development of kindergarten remained outside the German school system," lamented one speaker in her welcoming address to the Americans. "Our German government, our German school officials, all those who had power and influence in educational matters, have not shown the slightest interest in the matter in the fifty years that followed Froebel's death." American visitors to Germany also noted that most male educators there, including those in university departments of education, had little knowledge of Froebel or of the kindergarten. By contrast, kindergarten teaching had been incorporated into the curricula of the University of Chicago and of Teachers' College by 1900.[21]

8 (1895–6): 549; an account of one Froebel pilgrimage is in Helen K. Mills, "A Froebel Birthday Celebration," *Kindergarten Magazine* 8 (1895–6): 733; on the Froebel Museum project see "An International Froebel Memorial," *Kindergarten Magazine* 12 (1899–1900): 106–7; and "Regarding the Future Froebel-Haus," *Kindergarten Magazine* 16 (1903–4): 315. On American support for this project, see Barbara Beatty, "Lucy Wheelock's Education and Vocation," in *Wheelock College: 100 Years* (Boston, 1988), 7–8.

21. Lucy Wheelock, "My Life Story," typescript, Lucy Wheelock Collection, Archives, Wheelock College, 66; Lucy Wheelock, *Letters from Europe* (Boston, n.d.), 16; "The Froebel Pilgrimage," *Kindergarten Review* 21 (1911): 488; other materials on the Froebel pilgrimage are held in the Lucy

A similar view of Germany as backward rather than advanced was expressed by John Dewey. Dewey, who acknowledged Froebel as an important influence on his own educational approach, nonetheless argued that the kindergarten had been deformed by its authoritarian German environment. Froebel, Dewey asserted, based his games on abstruse symbolism because he "could not regard the occupations of the schoolroom as literal reproductions of the ethical principles involved in community life – the latter were often too repressive and authoritarian to serve as worthy models." Only under the more "progressive" conditions of American life could Froebel's central ideal of education for citizenship be realized. Thus, after the turn of the century, many American educators echoed the sentiment of American kindergartner Alice Fitts, who while standing at Froebel's grave felt that "he was not dead, but living in America." The anti-German sentiment aroused by the First World War only intensified this change in kindergartners' image of Germany, which they now regarded as the home of tyrannical "Prussianism" rather than as the land of learning, order, and progress.[22]

The relationship of the American to the German kindergarten movement suggests that, in this as in other cases, international contacts served less as sources of absolutely new ideas than as sources of cross-cultural dialogue, leading to a deeper insight into the participants' own cultures and their position within them. Most of the ideas introduced by the kindergarten movement to America were not absolutely new. The forms of female professionalism and social activism that it encouraged were already developing in America by the 1870s, when the kindergarten movement became popular among educated, middle-class American women. After a short initial period of dependence on German models, American kindergarten activists found innovative and inventive applications for kindergarten theory. For most of this period, German culture, as experienced through contacts with German colleagues, served the Americans less as a model to be imitated than as a symbolic "other" against which to assess the strengths and weaknesses of American culture.

By encouraging some women to acquire and use the prestigious vocabulary of German philosophy and science, the kindergarten movement enabled them to discover their intellectual potential, to overcome some

Wheelock Collection; see also Beatty, "Lucy Wheelock's Education and Vocation," 7–8; and Allen, "Let Us Live with Our Children."

22. John Dewey, "Froebel's Educational Principles," in *The School and Society* (New York, 1899; rpt. New York, 1967), 131; the quotation from Fitts is in Mills, "A Froebel Birthday Celebration," 734; Shapiro, *Child's Garden*, 184–5. On the incorporation of the kindergarten into the public schools in Germany and the United States, see Allen, "Let Us Live with Our Children."

cultural barriers to women's public self-expression and activity, and to gain a hearing from their male contemporaries. German and American women, moreover, did not worshipfully accept the wisdom of male pedagogues; they revised and transformed these ideas, often in ways that would have shocked their original proponents. By the 1890s, female kindergarten activists had incorporated kindergarten theory into arguments for many feminist causes, including educational and social reform, pacifism, and women's suffrage. Pestalozzi and Froebel, declared kindergarten teacher Eudora Hailmann (the American wife of German immigrant Wilhelm Hailmann), had recognized women as "the most important agency in the evolution of mankind. From the cradle to the grave it is woman who inspires, sustains, restrains, urges and guides." Their creative use of these ideas suggests that, for many of these women, the study of the child had provided the basis for a new understanding and affirmation of the self. "The child, any child I had almost said," wrote Kate Douglas Wiggin, "is the Columbus of the undiscovered world within you, in your heart, that goes without saying, but in your mind as well."[23]

23. "Kindergarten Department Meeting at Denver," *Kindergarten Magazine* 8 (1895–6): 4; Kate Douglas Wiggin, "The Training of Children," in *The Woman's Book* (New York, 1894), 319.

6

German Ideas and Practice in American Natural History Museums

SALLY GREGORY KOHLSTEDT

In the nineteenth century, sometimes dubbed the "century of science," formal learned institutions in Europe and throughout its imperial systems consolidated activity in the natural sciences. Research previously done by individuals and through informal correspondence now became concentrated in major urban museums administered by voluntary societies and state governments. Although museums were by no means new – the Greek muses resided in such facilities – they took on distinctive and expanded dimensions in the period of exploration and colonial expansion. Natural history museums became the principal agencies for research in the natural sciences. Created to serve primarily local and national constituencies, these major museums were nonetheless deeply engaged in international communication and exchange. Their collective agenda in the nineteenth century was to catalog all specimens in the natural world, and increasingly, their intention was to find the historical and dynamic (environmental or ecological) relationship among them.

During the "golden age" of museum building in the nineteenth century, these facilities were viewed in a number of ways – as temples to science, facilities for preservation and research, cultural centers demonstrating urbane sophistication, and, increasingly over the century, as instruments for education. The definitions of museum education were provided in general and often rhetorical terms, following a presumption that visitors were responsible for their own learning. Early in the nineteenth century, museum proprietors claimed only that their displays could stimulate "rational amusement." Exhibits of abnormal specimens or shelves arrayed with minerals, stuffed birds, pinned insects, and shells, institutions at midcentury paid relatively less attention to broad public needs than to preservation and publication. Their evident complacency, however, was challenged by school administrators, especially those who had been trained in normal schools and who advocated the need for a graded and comprehensive "system" in education and were attracted to "object teaching."[1] In many cases, museum activities experimented with innovative ideas and, indeed, with the kinds of pedagogic practices advocated by contemporary educational reformers. By the end of the century, the education techniques in museums were much more didactic, with descriptive labels and posters, printed handbooks, and volunteer guides to translate what visitors saw. Although the incentives that pushed museums into educational programs were multiple and complex, German scientific visitors and émigrés who carried with them German educational philosophies, with their emphasis on nature and object study, influenced the museum movement in specific and significant ways.

Some barriers to German influence were presented by the tendency of citizens in the early republic to look to England and France for models. In the 1810s, the astronomer Nathaniel Bowditch lamented in the *North American Review* that the inability of Americans (and the British) to speak or read German meant that important work on German science was not readily accessible.[2] Jurgen Herbst has argued, with regard to historical studies in the nineteenth century, that there was never a wholesale transfer of that German science (or scholarship) to America.[3] Museum proprietors and curators of the early republic most often referred to English, and sometimes to French, public and private collections when promoting their institutions. Yet evidence exists to demonstrate that German examples were important, particularly in the promotion of museum holdings for educational purposes, but also with regard to the building and display of collections. George Brown Goode, for example, a dedicated Anglophile and principal museum theorist at the end of the nineteenth century, downplayed the importance of the German influence. At the same time, his arrangement of the anthropological collections at the Smithsonian Institution was significantly influenced by what he saw in Berlin and elsewhere in continental museums.[4]

The mechanisms for both the interchange of ideas and the transfer of scientific material among museums came in a number of ways. This essay examines several examples of these mechanisms in order, first, to explore the particular connections that existed between Germans and North Americans and then to highlight the sometimes explicit and sometimes subtle

1. Frank Forest Bunker, "Rise of the Graded School" in *Reorganization of the Public School System*, U.S. Bureau of Education, Bulletin No. 8 (1916), pp. 20–9.
2. John Greene, *American Science in the Age of Jefferson* (Ames: Iowa State University Press, 1984), p. 2.
3. Jurgen Herbst, *The German Historical School and American Scholarship* (Ithaca, N.Y.: Cornell University Press, 1965), p. 128.
4. Sally Gregory Kohlstedt, ed., *The Origins of Natural Science in America: The Essays of George Brown Goode* (Washington, D.C.: Smithsonian Institution Press, 1991).

ways in which elements of German museum practice were incorporated here.

Like other Europeans, Germans came to the new nation to visit and study the natural and social landscape of a wilderness society. Americans, in turn, went abroad to study the formal institutions in which such information was analyzed. Foreign travel in both directions across the Atlantic involved the consequent transfer of scientific information. Museums coordinated the exchange of publications and thus reinforced the global connections of the largest natural history museums. Natural scientists who participated in personal or institutionally sponsored exploration and who attended international conventions returned with a determination to expand and improve facilities at home in order to make them comparable to those they visited abroad. Museum curators, of necessity, worked collaboratively, but they were also highly self-conscious and competitive.

The steady in-migration of German scientists and educators, a traffic that ebbed and flowed, encouraged émigré commitment to familiar and effective programs that could sustain their intellectual and social life. The influence of such migrants can be found in the Academy of Natural Sciences in Philadelphia during the early national period. Later it spread to the frontier cities in the Ohio river valley that had a substantial German population, such as Cincinnati and St. Louis. Perhaps the most notable example was in Milwaukee, where German educators created a significant and unusual base for a public museum.

Ethnic sensibility and local pride, however, were counterbalanced by the recognition that natural history research was developing as an international enterprise. At the outset, the Europeans and English were best equipped for the comprehensive collecting and taxonomic analysis that led to theory, whereas colonial naturalists were encouraged to provide the raw data, especially unidentified or controversial species in the Americas, Southeast Asia, and other parts of the world. Some elements of these imperial connections have recently been described in Susan Sheets-Pyenson's *Cathedrals of Science,* which documents the difficult and often heroic efforts of museum managers in the colonial outposts of Australia, South America, and Canada.[5]

Essentially no attention has been paid, however, to the ways in which German ideas and practices were adopted and adapted in the young United

---

5. Susan Sheets-Pyenson, *The Cathedrals of Science: The Development of Colonial Natural History Museums during the Late Nineteenth Century* (Montreal: McGill-Queen's Press, 1988).

States. Although English and French connections and institutions were important, it may well have been the Germanic strand of influence that really shaped educational activities and outcomes.

INTERMITTENT CONTACTS AND IMPORTED INFLUENCE

Significant numbers of German travelers came to the young American republic, apparently inspired as much by German romanticism regarding Native Americans and the still untamed Western wilderness as by the political experiment that so intrigued the French observer Alexis de Tocqueville. As William H. Goetzmann has pointed out in his studies of western exploration, these independent travelers of the 1820s and 1830s were often inspired by the work of Alexander von Humboldt. Frederick Paul Wilhelm, Duke of Württemberg, a student of George Cuvier and Humboldt, made four such trips, the first in 1822. His account of his initial journey and his scientific observations were published when he returned to Stuttgart. More well remembered was the trip of Duke Paul's friend Prince Maximilian of Weid-Neuwied, whose published field notes, books, and especially superb illustrations done by Karl Bodmer provided an unprecedented record of the American West. Prince Maximilian visited the utopian socialist community of New Harmony, Indiana, as well. The site had earlier been settled by a community headed by George Rapp, a Lutheran sectarian and avocational naturalist. When his followers regrouped in Economy, Pennsylvania, they again established a special building for their collections of plants, minerals, birds, and Indian artifacts.[6] The prince was impressed by the educational experiment conducted there under the financial sponsorship of William Maclure and the philosophical leadership of Madame Fretegot, a former student of Pestalozzi.[7]

Quite a number of German and other European scientists participated in the federal exploring expeditions that surveyed the American West. One of the most notable was Henrik Baldwin Mollhausen, who joined the Whipple transcontinental railroad survey and, in an already well-established tradition, returned to Germany to publish a two-volume account of his

---

6. Karl J. R. Arndt, *George Rapp's Harmony Society, 1785–1847* (Philadelphia: University of Pennsylvania Press, 1965).

7. Goetzmann, *Exploration and Empire: The Explorer and the Scientist in the Winning of the American West* (New York: Vintage Books, 1972 [1966]). Duke Paul of Wurtemberg's account, "First Journey to North American in the Years 1822 to 1824," trans. William Bek, is in *South Dakota Historical Collections, XIX* (1938), pp. 7–474; Prince Maximilian of Wied-Neuwied, *Travels in the Interior of North America in the Years 1832 to 1834* (London: Ackerman and Co., 1843), is also reprinted in Reuben Thwaites, *Early Western Travels*, 32 vols. (Cleveland, A. H. Clark, 1904–7), vols. XXII–XXV.

western adventures.[8] These and less prominent naturalists and collectors visited natural history museums, deliberately sought out naturalists here, and continued correspondence and exchanges after their return.

Traffic went in the opposite direction as well. Americans journeyed to Europe on their postgraduation tours, often in order to study with prominent scientists like Justus Liebig. On their return, they communicated not only specific scientific knowledge but also impressions about institutional developments abroad. Museums and laboratories figured prominently in the discussion of facilities that could advance science and, not incidentally, education, particularly higher education. By the 1840s, natural history collections were becoming a fundamental part of the cultural landscape and a presumed necessity on college campuses.[9] Then, in 1846, Louis Agassiz came to the United States, bringing with him a vision of museum building that seemed irresistible, as well as experience in European museums that made his ideas credible. The Swiss-born zoologist and geologist had studied in Lausanne, Zurich, and Heidelberg before taking a Ph.D. at the University of Erlangen and an M.D. at the University of Munich.[10] The *Wunderkind* came to the United States in 1846 and quickly became a leader of the scientific establishment, in part because he was such a charismatic public advocate for science. Everywhere he went on lecture tours, he stated his conviction that "great scientific institutions are essential to the very existence and maintenance of an advanced civilization."[11] Often he spoke about the ways in which local collections, common on the European continent, proved an inspiration to children, citing his own experience as a reference point. At the Museum of Comparative Zoology, which he founded at Harvard, he concentrated his efforts on postgraduate students, but he also spoke of the educational importance of his collections to the girls in his wife's small school, to Horace Mann's teachers' institutes, and to teachers in training at the Framingham Normal School just outside Boston.

In important ways, Agassiz dissociated himself from his European past and committed himself to establishing resources in this country for the study and dissemination of scientific knowledge. Apparently as a result, very few of his postgraduate students went abroad for extended study and Ph.D.s.

8. William H. Goetzmann, *Army Exploration in the American West, 1803–1863* (Lincoln: University of Nebraska Press, 1979 [1959]), pp. 309–11. He was also known as the German Fenimore Cooper because of his novels.

9. Sally Gregory Kohlstedt, "Collections and Cabinets: Natural History Museums on Campus, to 1860," *Isis*, 79 (Fall 1988): 405–26.

10. Perhaps it should be noted that the King of Prussia controlled the area of Canton Fribourg, where Agassiz's father was a pastor.

11. Quoted in Edward Lurie, *Louis Agassiz: A Life in Science* (Chicago: University of Chicago Press, 1960), pp. 55–7.

The cadre educated at Harvard in the 1850s and 1860s instead caught and extended his vision of a public museum. Their stated goals were to forge institutions comparable and perhaps even superior to those abroad; and, using the rhetoric of democracy, they explained that the collections were invaluable for public instruction. In the last third of the century, Agassiz's graduates built or became prominent curators at nearly every major public museum in the United States, and all carried with them a commitment to scientific education at some level.

Those building natural history museums were eager to study systematically the methods and content of museums abroad. So, although few took degrees abroad, many naturalists took transatlantic trips in the 1870s and 1880s to investigate the techniques for preservation, storage, and display in what were thought to be preeminent institutions. Alpheus Hyatt at the Boston Natural History Museum, Albert Bickmore at the American Museum of Natural History in New York, and George Brown Goode at the Smithsonian Institution in Washington, D.C. – all former students of Agassiz – went on tours that extended for weeks and sometimes months. London's British Museum (Natural History), being built on the new site in South Kensington, was certainly a standard destination. Even more widely discussed, however, in the journals and notes of these travelers were the natural history and ethnological museums in Paris, Hamburg, Munich, Berlin, Vienna, and Copenhagen.[12] The traveling administrators emphasized such practical matters as acquisition record keeping, display techniques, and various technical concerns such as lighting and ventilation; but considerable attention was also paid to the ways in which ethnology and anthropology were presented in the context of natural history. Should specimens be arranged to show relationships of similar objects across cultures or, alternatively, to demonstrate multiple features of a single cultural group? The problems were complex and not easily resolved, but curators returned to the United States aware that the presentation of objects in their museums did in fact represent scientific theory.

RE-CREATING NATURAL SCIENCE EDUCATION

If international visits were useful, and if certain immigrant "stars" like Agassiz played some role in shaping museum developments, those self-

---

12. Sally Gregory Kohlstedt, "International Exchange and National Style: A View of Natural History Museums in the United States, 1850–1900," in Nathan Reingold and Marc Rothenberg, eds., *Scientific Colonialism: A Cross-Cultural Comparison* (Washington, D.C.: Smithsonian Institution Press, 1987), pp. 167–89.

conscious migrants who joined German-speaking communities had a particularly direct and fundamental influence on programs. Philadelphia, the cultural capital of the early republic, by the early nineteenth century had attracted a sizable German population. The Philadelphia Academy of Natural Sciences, founded in 1812, reflected Pennsylvania's diversity from the outset. The study of natural history had important bases in Charles Willson Peale's proprietary museum and in the well-established American Philosophical Society, but the founders of the Academy needed to collaborate in order to build a library and study collection in mineralogy, zoology, botany, and chemistry. Philadelphia merchants and physicians joined with a number of European émigrés to write a constitution and to build a resident and corresponding membership. Prominent among them was Gerard Troost, a Dutch immigrant who had brought with him an impressive collection of mineralogy acquired during his study with crystallographer Abbe Hauy in Paris, with Abraham Gottlob Werner at Frieberg, and on tours in Germany and Switzerland. He was readily elected the first president.[13] Troost was a museum advocate and urged his colleagues to put their efforts into building and maintaining a collection that would make it possible for the Academy to engage in exchange with similarly specialized societies elsewhere. The goal was to have organized and accessible collections.

Naturalists in New York, Boston, and Charleston created similar societies in the 1810s, but none was as initially successful and well grounded as the Academy of Natural Sciences in Philadelphia. It concentrated its efforts on mutual improvement and education among the local membership, but it also opened its facilities to the public and sponsored evening lectures with a liberality that was distinctive among its peer societies.[14] When, however, William Maclure, a Scottish émigré, took his "boat load of knowledge" to the socialist experiment in New Harmony, Troost went along in order to extend his research and to teach in the experimental school. His subsequent career (after disharmony in New Harmony) took him farther into the frontier regions of Tennessee, along with his minerals, fossils, shells, Indian artifacts, birds, and fishes. There his new neighbors regarded him as an eccentric virtuoso who amused colleagues and students by carrying tamed snakes casually on his shoulders and collecting whatever curiosities came his way. Troost's decision not to return to Philadelphia is somewhat puzzling

13. Records of the Academy are available on microfilm and summarized in the guide *Minutes and Correspondence of the Academy of Natural Sciences of Philadelphia, 1812–1924* (Philadelphia: Academy of Natural Sciences, 1967).
14. Minute books record these activities, and a circular for 1829 indicates that by that date the collections numbered 3000 minerals, 3500 petrification and geological specimens, 1200 specimens, 300 shell specimens, 120 crustaceous animals, 500 plants, and some reptiles.

and hints at the kind of ambiguity surrounding "foreign-speaking" (i.e., those who spoke with an accent) immigrants. German philosophy may have been more easily integrated than German immigrants.

In Tennessee, Troost became the state geologist and taught at the state university; his research showed his lack of regular scientific contacts, and he relied on fresh field recruits from the local area as assistants. Moreover, his contribution has been obscured. Just before his death, he sent to the Smithsonian Institution a monograph with illustrations on the crinoids of Tennessee. Reviewer Louis Agassiz kept the manuscript for five years, and James Hall of the New York State survey never returned it; in subsequent years and after Troost's death, most of the species were described by Hall under his own name. Back in Philadelphia, the legacy of international correspondence and exchange to which Troost contributed sustained the Academy in the face of numerous financial challenges.[15] However, the Academy lost for a time during the 1830s and 1840s its goal of being educational, and took on a character of introverted self-study activities that more closely paralleled societies in New York and Boston, which in turn took their lead from the Linnaean Society of London.

Where Germans congregated in considerable numbers, they also brought with them a commitment to establish institutions comparable to those they left behind – leading some immigration historians to suggest that where homogeneity and reconstituted lifestyles existed, the proper term should be simply "migration" rather than "immigration." Outposts along the inland waterways, especially the Ohio River and the Erie Canal, drew new immigrants and their institutional traditions. Social and cultural associations based on models from Europe, sometimes translated by experiences in the eastern United States, appeared quickly along the western frontier from Texas to Wisconsin.[16]

In St. Louis, for example, German children constituted nearly half of the school-age population at midcentury, and the German language was so prevalent that the bulk of the scientific correspondence seems to have been with colleagues in Germany. As in Philadelphia and other Eastern cities, the earliest natural history displays were by entrepreneurs. Albert Koch

15. See Henry Grady Rooker, "A Sketch of the Life and Work of Dr. Gerard Troost," *Tennessee Historical Magazine*, Series 2, vol. 3 (1932): 3–19. Some contemporaries believed that Louis Agassiz appropriated work by Troost on freshwater crinoids after his death. See, for example, J. G. Anthony to A. A. Gould, 12 May 1857, Gould MSS, Houghton Library, Harvard. Also see James X. Corgan, "Early American Geological Surveys and Gerard's Troost's Field Assistants, 1831–1836," in James X. Corgan, ed., *The Geological Sciences in the Antebellum South* (University, Ala.: University of Alabama Press, 1982), 39–72.
16. Gilbert Giddings Benjamin, *The Germans in Texas: A Study in Immigration* (Philadelphia: reprinted from *German American Annals*, VII, 1909), pp. 112–19.

created his St. Louis Museum on the model of that by Charles Willson Peale and sought an audience of children and adults. The museum had a bit of everything: Wax figures, cosmographic views of battles, and exhibitions of the infernal regions were combined with "the whole illustration of natural history, consisting of beasts, birds, and creeping things."[17] His presentations verged on the bizarre. A visitor reported that one of the mounted alligators was made to "look more poetical . . . [with] a stuffed Negro in his mouth." Koch himself, however, was interested in paleontology. He searched the Middle West for fossil remains and, after recovering a massive skeleton from Benton County, Missouri, on tour in 1840, he sold it in London, where the British Museum's curator, Richard Owen, gave it the name *Mastodon americanus*. National and ethnic connections were important but not inevitably overriding.

The intellectual and organizational leader of those who clustered in the St. Louis Academy of Science (established in 1856) was George Engelmann. Born in Frankfurt am Main, he emigrated in 1832 and eventually settled and established a medical practice in St. Louis. An active botanist, he became a "botanical gatekeeper" for those collecting specimens for herbaria from the American West. He gathered reference materials that laid the foundation for the Missouri Botanical Garden and conducted an extensive correspondence on botanical matters with naturalists around the world. He collaborated as well with German scholars like Frederick Wislizenus, who had fled Frankfurt and set up a medical practice in Illinois, not far from St. Louis.[18] (It is worthy of note that although there is extensive correspondence of Engelmann in the Botanical Garden as well as at the Brooklyn Botanical Garden, the fact that a considerable portion of it is in German script has deterred anyone from producing a full biography of this central figure in nineteenth-century American science.) Not exclusively wed to things German, he nonetheless valued the German connections and self-consciously sought to establish a scientific center that would benefit the local community and its education, as well as the international scientific community. The Academy foundered and never built the institutional base that Englemann envisioned. The German educational incentives, however, were evident when his friend, William Torry Harris, became superintendent of schools in the city and made natural science a key component of

17. See Frederick Marryat, *A Diary of America with Remarks on Its Institutions, 1837–1838* (New York: Knopf, 1962 [1838]), p. 218; John Francis McDermott's "Forward" to Dr. Albert Koch, *Journey Through a Part of the United States of North America in the Years 1844–1846* (Carbondale: Southern Illinois University Press, 1972), pp. xi–xxxv.

18. Biographical information is in F. A. Wislizenus, *A Journey to the Rocky Mountains in the Year 1839*, trans. Frederick A. Wislizenus (St. Louis: Missouri Historical Society, 1912), pp. 5–13.

the curriculum.[19] During the latter part of the nineteenth century, educational activity in St. Louis attracted national attention and led to Harris's appointment as the U.S. Commissioner of Education.

Milwaukee provides a second, particularly interesting case to examine. In the 1850s there were two distinctive natural history societies in Milwaukee, both with the ambitious title "Natural History Society of Wisconsin." One was associated with Increase A. Lapham, physician and leading naturalist, who later headed the Wisconsin state geological survey.[20] Its members were drawn primarily from the English-speaking merchant and professional classes. The other society was organized by Peter Engelmann (no known relation to George Engelmann), who was principal of the German-English Academy. A "48er" who had a degree from Berlin and had taught at the Gymnasium, Engelmann was outspoken in his enthusiasm for Friedrich Froebel's educational theories. He sponsored a natural history society in order to develop and sustain an object collection at the Academy. That society flourished, rooted in a well-established school and with interested and literate adult participants. Within a decade, it had attracted over 500 members and raised $800 to pay for maintenance. The parallel society, by contrast, foundered. In the late 1860s, Lapham put his personal collection on the market. The successful bid of the German-English Academy added specimens to their collection, which reached a total of 23,000 objects by 1877. The Milwaukee Public High School's principal during that period, George W. Peckham, also established an assembly room for the study of natural history – an activity not typical of public high schools elsewhere in the country and probably a modest imitation of that at the German-English Academy.[21]

One of Engelmann's students, Carl Doerflinger, had fought in the Civil War, lost a leg in the Battle at Chancellorsville, and returned to Milwaukee. Although born in Baden and German-speaking, Doerflinger, more like second-generation immigrants, was eager to make the German-English Academy's museum – by this time the largest in the city – available to the

19. Selwyn K. Troen, *The Public and the Schools: Shaping the St. Louis System, 1838–1920* (Columbia: University of Missouri Press, 1975); and David Detjen, *The Germans in Missouri, 1900–1918: Prohibition, Neutrality, and Assimilation* (Columbia; University of Missouri Press, 1985).
20. The papers of what became the Milwaukee Public Museum are in the Milwaukee Public Library, including the incoming correspondence of the director. See also Walter B. Hendrickson, "The Forerunners of the Milwaukee Public Museum," in *Lore* (Milwaukee Public Museum), 22 (Summer 1979): 99–103; and Nancy Lurie, *A Special Style: The Milwaukee Public Museum, 1882–1982* (Milwaukee: Milwaukee Public Museum, 1983); also see the small pamphlet by C. H. Doerflinger, *The Genesis and Early History of the Wisconsin Natural History Society at Milwaukee* (n.p., [1907]); Kathleen Neils Conzen, *Immigrant Milwaukee, 1836–1860: Accommodation and Community in a Frontier City* (Cambridge, Mass.: Harvard University Press, 1976), p. 190.
21. Dr. R. M. Strong, "In Retrospect" (copy in Milwaukee Public Library Archives).

English-speaking public. In 1879 the Society received a state charter. By 1882 its members launched a campaign to make the museum a publicly supported facility.[22] Not coincidentally, a major exposition that same year brought the merchant naturalist Henry A. Ward to town. His display of plaster casts of famous fossils (most from European museums) and his well-mounted skins and skeletons led to a campaign to purchase the entire display. This material, together with the holdings of the Natural History Society of Wisconsin, were housed in the Exposition Building after 1884, when the exhibition closed.

What is particularly significant in the history of museums in this country is that the City Council accepted the Natural History Society's donation of its collection and promised funds sufficient to open the new Milwaukee Public Museum to the public free of charge. No other major museum in the country was open so freely or enjoyed the guarantee of funding as that in Milwaukee. In 1889 the Council, in another virtually unprecedented move, established a tax levy of 1/50 mil for each dollar of assessed property evaluation to go to the museum and public library. Museum attendance that year reached a new high of 83,000. Doerflinger was director from 1883 to 1887, and devoted much of his time to providing programs for teachers and materials for the schools of Milwaukee. He also went on a tour of museums in the eastern United States (and later Europe), where he met museum directors like Spencer F. Baird of the Smithsonian Institution. He created a network somewhat distinct from that of most English-linked institutions.[23] Files of the Milwaukee Public Museum indicate considerable correspondence with German suppliers like bookseller William J. Gerhard of Philadelphia, as well as curators in Germany and even in colonial settings, like Adolph Hemple in São Paulo, Brazil.

Urban-based museums were particularly visible, but there were also numerous college museums built and furnished in the United States after 1840, collections that expanded on older cabinets of curiosities and the specialized collections of individual faculty members. This activity has been largely overlooked because historians of higher education have tended to concentrate primarily on graduate study and on the development of the laboratory in new or transformed universities at the end of the century. Before and

22. See Laws of Wisconsin Concerning the Public Museum (330A), approved March 31, 1882. The City of Milwaukee accepted the Natural History Society's collection to be "kept, supported, and maintained by said city as a free museum" (p. 23). The paper by Bettina Goldberg in this volume emphasizes that by the 1880s the Academy was also facing somewhat harder financial times.
23. He went east in March and April 1883; see letters to Spencer F. Baird in RU 189, Smithsonian Institution Archives. Henry Nehrling, director in the 1890s, also began his administration with a tour of museums in 1892; see Milwaukee Public Museum, *Annual Report, 1892–1893*.

beneath that movement for graduate education, however, was a changing bachelor's degree; in fact, it was the availability of science education in four-year college programs that made postgraduate education here and abroad possible. Numerous college catalogs mention the existence of natural history collections along with the library facilities as a basic facility, and by 1873 there were at least seventy scientific schools in the country. In many of the state universities from South Carolina to California, and at some private schools as well, the collections were based on the results of state surveys whose specimens were permanently deposited. These college facilities have yet to be studied in detail, but the fact that many of the faculty were being educated abroad, often taking advanced degrees at German and Swiss universities, suggests an element of importation as well as local incentives.

The examples in this essay point to a pattern of involvement by Germans in American museums in the nineteenth century that emphasized, among other things, the educational potential of museum materials. Historians of education have indicated that science in public as well as private schools derived more from German than English philosophy and practice in the nineteenth century. There was an evident parallel in museums, which pulled and in some cases were pushed by local school officials and teachers to provide resources and special instruction. The German influence, however, was inevitably complex, and the outcomes were unpredictable.

In 1900, A. B. Meyer, director of the Royal Zoological, Anthropological, and Ethnological Museum in Dresden, toured American museums. His 300-page published report concluded that "museum affairs in general are on a higher plane [in North America] than in Europe."[24] What particularly impressed him was an emphasis on instruction nearly everywhere, from displays and handbooks within museums to outreach programs involving school teachers and children. Thus, ironically perhaps, the ideology and practices that American museum leaders had earlier imported from the Continent, especially Germany, had by the end of the century, in one expert opinion at least, now surpassed those of the originators.

24. A. B. Meyer, "Studies of the Museums and Kindred Institutions of New York City, Albany, Buffalo, and Chicago, with Notes on Some European Institutions," *Report of the National Museum . . . for 1903* (Washington, D.C.,: Government Printing Officer, 1904), Appendix 2, p. 323.

7

Schoolmarm, Volkserzieher, Kantor, and Shulschwester: German Teachers among Immigrants during the Second Half of the Nineteenth Century

JULIANE JACOBI

German-speaking immigrants formed the largest group of non-English-speaking immigrants to the United States during the second half of the nineteenth century. They set up a distinctive German-American cultural environment in various parts of the United States. Among the most prominent German-American areas was the Midwest, and the 1900 census revealed that about one-third of the population of Wisconsin was of "German stock." Schools shaped that ethnic culture, and teachers who immigrated from Germany, as well as teachers who were daughters and sons of German immigrant families, contributed to the newly established American school systems, both public and private parochial. Studying the contribution of these school teachers to the cultural assimilation of immigrant children offers further insight into the relationship between the German cultural background of the immigrants and the various ways in which immigrants encountered and coped with new educational challenges.[1]

This essay deals with four different groups of teachers among German immigrants that I came across while investigating elementary schools for German immigrants in Wisconsin. Two variables, gender and religious affiliation, divided teachers into four different categories: (1) the female public elementary school teacher, ridiculed as "schoolmarm"; (2) the German-American non-church-affiliated teacher, that is, the *Volkserzieher;* (3) the Lutheran parochial school teacher, that is, the *Kantor;* and (4) the Catholic school sister. Separate teacher training institutions were established for the last three of these groups. Thus the easiest way to examine the four groups

---

1. This article is based mostly on material from a larger investigation into elementary schools that served German immigrants in Wisconsin: Juliane Jacobi-Dittrich, *"Deutsche Schulen" in den Vereinigten Staaten von Amerika. Historisch-vergleichende Studie zum Unterrichtswesen im Mittleren Westen (Wisconsin 1840–1900),* Marburger Beiträge zur vergleichenden Erziehungswissenschaft und Bildungsforschung, vol. 20 (Munich, 1980).

is according to what their training schools claimed their graduates should become. Besides this inquiry, this essay traces ideas of the hiring communities about what their teacher should be like. Finally, this essay asks: How did these ideas connect to German teachers' images during the nineteenth-century emigration (1840–80)?

The essay deals with the different groups according to their degree of modernization. It starts out with the most advanced type, the wage-earning woman, followed by the German-American teacher who considered himself modern. Most historians of education consider the church-affiliated Lutheran male teacher and the Catholic school sister as the least modern types of school teacher. What did this mean in the most democratic modernized society of the era?

The most Americanized type of schoolteacher was the young female elementary teacher who came from an immigrant family and taught school for a couple of years. How did it come about that women taught school, an event still quite unusual in German *Volksschulen?*[2] Settlements by Germans who had no strong church affiliations – in the Midwest, these settlers usually came from higher social ranks in Germany and owned larger farms – usually started a public school soon after settling. School was taught for seven to nine months during the year. During the first years, school was taught by both male and female teachers, and the large bulk of biographical material on German immigrants in the State Historical Society of Wisconsin indicates that there were various types of immigrant school teachers unconnected to the political upheavals of the 1840s. Protestant or Catholic, they were just looking for a better standard of living. As other studies of the American public school system have shown, the employment policies of local authorities shifted from male to female teachers during the century, and the same shift took place in German settlements in Wisconsin.[3]

After 1865, young women (ages sixteen to twenty) from the community taught school with no specific teacher training except perhaps some high school attendance. This type of school teacher, who taught school for a few years and then either got married or went on to gain further education, was strongly representative of Midwestern school teachers in rural areas.[4] The

---

2. Whereas in the United States the percentage of female teachers in public elementary schools reached 65 percent in 1890 in 1900, in the German state of Prussia it did not exceed 12 percent.
3. See Jacobi, *"Deutsche Schulen,"* 150–62.
4. See Jurgen Herbst, *And Sadly Teach: Teacher Education and Professionalization in American Culture* (Madison, Wisc., 1989), 109–39.

graduation lists of one Wisconsin normal school, founded in 1866 in an
area with strong German immigration, show that only a few German students attended during the first two decades of its existence. A later source
from Milwaukee shows that German-American students did attend Milwaukee Normal School, founded in 1882.[5] Female immigrants' participation in state teacher training is still fairly unexplored. Talking about these
young female public school teachers underlines the sharply contrasting ideas
about teaching that existed simultaneously among German immigrant
groups – ideas and ideologies connected to gender and ethnicity that were
explicitly German-American. The way these young women performed
their jobs was not exceptional in the American school system of the time.
At the same time, there were strong German voices that did not appreciate
the female teacher. Germans considered school teaching a rather serious
business:

For the same money that our school authorities now pay to an Anglo-American,
Irish, or French-Canadian schoolmarm, often of doubtful knowledge and other
merits, we can get a right good German-American [male] teacher with those abilities, and one need not even spell out how valuable exactly such energies would
be precisely in young aspiring communities, the care for the souls of whose individual members should never be neglected. There are enough male teachers who
willingly would come into our wilderness, and we and our children would be
better served with such male teachers than with female teachers who view their
call to teaching only as a guest appearance or as an opportunity to earn money a
few months in the year in a more or less comfortable way, money with which they
can spend their leisure time heaven knows where during the remainder of the year.
And the public schools ought not be a form of public support for the nieces or
female cousins of members of the school board. We Germans think of school as
something else, something better.[6]

The speaker spoke in the wake of the conflicts about the Benett Law,
an attempt to repress parochial private schools, as he sought to organize a
German *Schulverein*.[7] He expressed a view of school teaching that might
have been shared by the limited group of the German-Americans of Wisconsin. He clearly pointed out that the American type of female elementary
school teacher was by no means a desirable choice for a German-American
school board. What type of teacher was desirable to this group?

5. See Jacobi, "*Deutsche Schulen*," 186.
6. Address to the Pioneers of Chelsea and Greenwood Township of Taylor County for the purpose of
   organizing a German School Association, Germans in Wisconsin, State Historical Society of Wisconsin–Madison, Manuscript Collection.
7. On the Benett Law, see Thomas L. Hunt, "Catholic Educational Policy and the Decline of Protestant
   Influence in Wisconsin's Schools during the Late Nineteenth Century" (Ph.D. diss., University of
   Wisconsin, Madison, 1971).

The well-trained *Volkserzieher,* servant of the state and the people, was the idea of the teacher expressed by the *Deutsch-Amerikanische Lehrerseminar Volkserzieher.* Although recent research indicates that there were relatively few teachers among the refugees of 1848–9, and especially very few elementary school teachers, the *Deutsch-Amerikanische Lehrerverein* proclaimed a vision of school and teaching shaped by the idea of the so-called Forty-Eighters.[8] In the German-American community, the *Verein* organized the foundation of the German-American Teachers Seminary to spread bilingual instruction and freethinking education. Organized efforts to establish training facilities arose at a time when the State of Wisconsin and other midwestern states had just founded normal schools to train teachers to serve the country.[9] The *National Deutsch-Amerikanische Lehrerseminar* opened its first course in 1877 after ten years of organizing and fund-raising activities. The director of the newly founded seminary declared:

It is my firm conviction, by which I propose to proceed in the acceptance of candidates as well as in the placement of pupils, that the seminary will fulfill its task better, will serve its country more faithfully by the formation of one tactful, freethinking teacher, enthusiastic for his profession, than it could through the production of a great number of mass-produced teachers [*Dutzendware*].[10]

Without a doubt, *Dutzendware* refers to the state normal schools' graduates. Nine years later, the director of the school humbly resolved:

Despite the fact that more than 75 percent of the pupils at our public schools take part in German instruction there [i.e., Milwaukee], that did not at all mean that they entered the German-American seminary in order to prepare themselves for the teaching profession. In general they preferred to attend three years of high school first, and then one or two years at a public normal school. The recognition of this disparity would have to show us that we have had too little contact with the public school.[11]

8. On the social background of participants in the upheaval of 1848, see Franzjörg Baumgart, "Lehrer und Lehrervereine während der Revolution von 1848/49," *Mentalitäten und Lebensverhältnisse. Beispiele aus der Sozialgeschichte der Neuzeit. Rudolf Vierhaus zum 60. Geburtstag* (Göttingen, 1982), 173–88; Hans-Josef Rupieper, "Die Sozialstruktur der Trägerschichten der Revolution von 1848/49 am Beispiel Sachsen," in Hartmut Kaelble et al., eds., *Probleme der Modernisierung in Deutschland* (Opladen, 1978), 80–109; Hans-Jürgen Rupieper, "Die Polizei und die Fahndungen anlässlich der deutschen Revolution 1848/49," *Vierteljahrsschrift für Sozial- und Wirtschaftsgeschichte* 64 (1977):328–55.

9. In 1866 the first four state normal schools of Wisconsin were founded in Whitewater, Platteville, Oshkosh, and River Falls; in 1882 the Milwaukee Normal School was established.

10. Festausschuss der Engelmannschen Schule, ed., *Kurzgefasste Geschichte der Deutsch-Englischen Akademie des Nationalen Deutsch-Amerikanischen Lehrerseminars und des Turnlehrerseminars des Nordamerikanischen Turnerbundes* (Milwaukee, 1901), 45.

11. *Jahresbericht über das nationale deutsch-amerikanische Lehrerseminar und die mit demselben als Übungsschule verbundene deutsch-englische Akademie Milwaukee* (Milwaukee, 1886).

The founding regulations from 1871 claimed three educational essentials: bilingual instruction, introducing teaching in a natural way (*naturgemässe [entwickelnde] Lehrweise*), and education of free American citizens.[12] In this way, the seminar intended to take care of the spiritual and material interests of German teachers in America. During the following years, members submitted to the annual meeting of the *Verein* elaborate papers that claimed ethnic identity as opposed to *Engländertum* of the ruling American culture. The political ideas of this group of German-Americans reflected the national spirit of the decade after the *Reichsgründung*. Yet toward the turn of the century, the national voice became less explicit, and bilingual instruction as the right of German immigrant children remained the main issue of the *Verein*.

Strong claims do not necessarily correlate with strong influences, and we cam see that the influence of the German-American teacher who considered himself a *Volkserzieher* in the romantic and emphatic sense remained rather limited. The National German-American Teachers' Seminary trained a very limited number of teachers and shared the structural problems of institutions of higher learning in the United States at the time. Only a small part of the student body remained for the whole four-year course, and only half of them became teachers. Of eighty-one students who attended during the first ten years, only twenty-one graduated. Among those sixty-seven students who left the seminary before graduation, thirty-six went into teaching, thirteen of them women. The male students who went into teaching took administrative positions in schools in communities with a large German population in Texas and the Midwest. The majority of the male students who graduated went on to the university.[13] The college originally meant to train teachers turned into a school, giving German-Americans a chance to prepare for a professional or administrative career. In 1901, about fifteen years before it closed in the great doomsday of German-American culture, it advertised itself as "national, modern, liberal, and *wissenschaftlich!*"[14]

Unlike the National German-American Teacher Seminary, the Lutheran synods were regional, traditional, conservative, and Christian. The foun-

---

12. I am not dealing with the related history of educational thought in this essay, but I want to point out that the German words refer to the work of Friedrich Fröbel, the outstanding romantic pedagogue.

13. *Jahresbericht über das nationale deutsch-amerikanische Lehrerseminar und die mit demselben verbundene deutsch-englische Akademie Milwaukee* (Milwaukee, 1886), 15–16. For a similar pattern, see Herbst, *And Sadly Teach*, 135, on Wisconsin's normal schools.

14. *Kurzgefasste Geschichte*, 42.

dation of the Wisconsin Synod and the Missouri Synod, associations of German Lutheran parishes with centers in the Midwest, dated back to the 1840s. The spiritual origin of their leading clergy was the evangelical confessionalism of the 1830s and 1840s, partly influenced by the aftermath of the church conflict over the Prussian Union. In the twentieth century the two synods, with the Missouri Synod in the lead, developed a large school system with schools on every level. In the beginning, spiritual and personal ties to Germany were still strong. This essay does not attempt to give a complete picture of how and why this school system took shape. Both the German Lutheran and the Catholic school systems came to flourish only around the turn of the twentieth century, but the roots of this boom stretch back to the 1860s and 1870s. Ethnic origin, religious affiliation of non-Anglo-American immigrants, and Anglo-American school policies during those decades of intense immigration were major reasons for the boom in various parochial school systems.[15]

Both synods founded teacher training facilities. The Missouri Synod established its first school in 1854 in Milwaukee and soon transferred it to Addison, Illinois. The Wisconsin Synod's Northwestern University (now called Northwestern College, Watertown, Wisconsin) served as a general institution of higher learning, both for pastor and for teaching training. A close look at its early history shows the vagueness of ideas about higher education, as well as the process by which a successful institution finally took shape.

Originally founded in the 1860s to provide pastors to the synod's parishes – after a series of more or less unsuccessful attempts in the evangelical milieu of Germany – Northwestern University was given up by its founders within the first five years. They became victims of the synod's turn from a moderate evangelical confessionalism to a rigid Lutheranism that went hand in hand with a self-concept of being German-American, in contrast to Anglo-American Protestantism. In 1870, a new attempt was made under the leadership of two learned teachers, Notz and Ernst, graduates of Tübingen and Göttingen, who taught at a Lutheran college in Pennsylvania before they came to the Midwest. Although the initial founders had not decided whether Northwestern would serve Watertown's immigrant community as a high school as well as a community college or train young men from a larger area for the pastorate, Professor Ernst, as principal, was determined

15. On religious schools in the United States, see James C. Carper and Thomas C. Hunt, eds., *Religious Schooling in America. Historical Insights and Contemporary Concern* (Birmingham, Ala., 1984). On Lutheran schools, see John Diefenthaler, "Lutheran Schools in American," in ibid., and Stephen A. Schmidt, *Powerless Pedagogues* (River Forest, Ill., 1972).

to make the school an institution of higher learning modeled after the German *Gymnasium*. The university's second yearbook declared:

The term "education" is frequently understood as a sum of information and skills that fits one for higher business and social life and from which everything must be appropriated that would be of use in entering and conducting one's self in that life. Whoever has this information and skill is considered an "educated man," and the transmission of these skills is viewed as the proper task of higher schools. Such schools – and this is far and away the opinion held by most in our country – do not transcend the role of mere training institutions, which differentiate themselves from trade schools only in that they lack the strictly unitary tendency of trade schools, and that they therefore are in the greatest danger, even in the transmission of information, of losing themselves in the most vapid superficiality and delivering far less satisfactory results.[16]

"*Erziehender Unterricht*" – educating instruction – the Herbartian idea and Christian higher education, were the two ingredients of Northwestern's concept of higher education. Whether the genealogy of Saxon *Landesschulen, Frankesche Stiftungen,* and Thomas Arnold's Rugby meant anything more than rhetoric seems doubtful. But the "classical department," as well as the "academy or normal school," translated by its teachers as *Gymnasium* and *Realzweig* or normal school *Zweig,* were considered to be Christian institutions with a German idea of *Bildung*. The normal school *Zweig* complemented the academy by *Erziehungslehre, Katechetik, Musik-, Klavier- und Orgelspiel*. Thus teacher training intended to educate teachers according to the German model of the Christian school teacher serving his church. Yet in the context of a college-type educational system, enabling graduates to continue professional training after graduation, the seminary served a larger range of purposes than the German *Seminar* training organized in the aftermath of 1848, with its exclusive aim of training teachers.[17] In 1893 the Normal School Department was dismissed, and Dr. Martin Luther College at New Ulm, Minnesota, now became the teachers' training college for the newly found Lutheran Synod of Wisconsin and other states. Northwestern remained a preparatory college for pastors of the Wisconsin Synod.

School attendance data are fragmentary. The academy always had higher enrollment than the classical department, and until 1880 it had a preparatory

---

16. *Zweiter Jahresbericht der Northwestern University zu Watertown, Wisconsin, für das Schuljahr 1872* (Watertown, Wisc., 1873), "Über die Erziehung unserer Anstalt und die wünschenswerte Förderung derselben durch die Eltern und Zöglinge," 5.

17. For the problem of *Berechtigungen zum Hochschulstudium* connected with teacher training in German states, see Michael Sauer, *Volksschullehrerbildung in Preussen. Die Seminare und Präparandenanstalten vom 18. Jahrhundert bis zur Weimarer Republik* (Cologne, 1987), 42, 43, 134. Except for Saxony, there was no regulation that awarded credit for university entrance on the basis of the state's teaching certificate.

department that served Watertown's young as a high school. The average
yearly attendance in the academy during these years was between 50 and
111 students. The ratio of graduates from the Normal School was rather
low: in 1894, the last group to graduate had seven members, among them
two women, out of roughly twenty-five students.

The question of coeducation was never definitively settled. In its early
days, a large group of girls attended the academy (1870: twenty). From
1882 to 1888 no girls were admitted, but when enrollment sagged, girls
were again accepted. In 1880, the synod thought about establishing a Female Seminary. Thirteen girls enrolled in 1881, but the experiment was
dropped. From other data on the school's development, we can see that
the more the Wisconsin Synod became a conservative and distinctly orthodox Lutheran Church, the more higher education became exclusively male.
The idea of the parochial school teacher as a servant to his church did not
permit women to attain the same status. Until 1980, both churches, in
Missouri and Wisconsin, discriminated between the male teacher, who was
"called" by the church, and the female teacher, who was only "hired."
Only in the 1930s did both churches start to hire a considerable number of
female teachers.

Both institutions of higher learning – the National German-American
Teachers' Seminary and Northwestern University – aimed at educating
teachers. Their promotional literature addressed only male applicants. Both
had in mind bilingual instruction. The foundation of these institutions coincided with the general attempt to establish state-run teachers' training
facilities in the United States. Neither school expanded during the first
decades of its existence. The Lutheran churches gained much vigor through
the conflicts about public and private religious schooling during these years,
eventually established a self-sufficient, autonomous teacher training system,
and by the 1880s they definitely did not want to hire teachers from Germany.[18] The National German-American Teachers' Seminary became a
multifunctional college-type institution of German-American background.
Among German immigrants there was only one group that established female teachers training facilities: the Catholic orders.

Among those groups who established teacher education for young women
from German immigrant families in the Midwest, three Catholic orders
dominated parochial schools in parishes with a German population.[19] All

---

18. On recruiting teachers from Germany, see Diefenthaler, "Lutheran Schools."
19. All of these communities were orders of lower commitment in their vows; thus, they should
    properly be called congregations.

orders established mother houses in the new country. Milwaukee had always been a center of German immigrant Catholicism, especially reinforced after German-speaking Swiss Bishop Henny took office in 1844 and supported the establishment of an ethnically oriented parochial school system. At first sight, one would expect that self-concept, community, expectations, and motivation for the work among women who joined teaching orders would differ widely from those of the three other types. Since amazingly little attention has been paid to teaching orders in the history of education in the nineteenth century, this essay focuses on their origins, their activities, and their self-concept, as interpreted within the broader framework of women and religion as well as women and work.[20] As an unknown nineteenth-century Catholic author stated:

> The history of the individual houses and their sisters is hard to write because the sources are only rarely available to us; their chroniclers are only the angels who inscribe all noble actions in the hidden book of the living, while the remembrance of the sisters, like a Herculean manuscript, immediately humbly decays after it is copied.[21]

In Catholic areas of Germany, exclusively female teaching orders shaped nineteenth-century girls' education, both elementary and secondary. The Catholic church's own history speaks of an *Ordensfrühling* that took place between the 1830s and the 1860s. A closer look reveals that this blossoming involved mainly women's orders, which dedicated their activities to social and educational "caring" work outside of the cloister. There were comparatively few male foundations at the time.

The Franciscans and Dominicans of the third order and new foundations of various groups of "sisters" who lived according to *Augustinger Chorfrauen* rules were the most flourishing of the new congregations.[22] Between 1830 and 1870, the Franciscans founded twenty-six mother houses in the German states (not including Austria), and eleven of them sent sisters to the United States during the second half of the century. From scattered numbers provided by Heimbucher, I would estimate that at the turn of the century in the United States, there were 3,000 or 4,000 Franciscan sisters among those from orders of German origin. Six of eleven orders considered teaching their major task. In two mother houses among those eleven, teacher training

20. The recent dissertation by Wolfgang Schaffer, *Schulorden im Rheinland. Ein Beitrag zur Geschichte religiöser Genossenschaften im Erzbistum Köln zwischen 1815 und 1875,* Kölner Schriften zur Geschichte und Kultur (Cologne, 1988), sheds new light on this aspect of the history of education.

21. Max Brandt, *Die katholische Wohltätigkeits-Anstalten und-Vereine sowie das katholisch-soziale Vereinswesen insbesondere in der Erzdiozöse Köln* (Cologne, 1895), 64

22. Max Heimbucher, *Die Orden und Kongregationen der Katholischen Kirche,* 2 vols. (Paderborn, 1934).

is well documented, though there may have been more facilities. In the Upper Midwest, the Franciscans from Ehrlenbach, who left the state of Baden because of the *Kulturkampf*, founded the largest house, which became *Generalmutterhaus* of the order. In the 1880s, partial remigration took place to the state of Baden, where the order actively engaged in teaching and caring for female university students.

The Dominicans of the third order had taught school since the Middle Ages. During the 1850s and 1860s, a large number of new foundations could be counted in Germany. In 1853, the Regensburg congregation sent sisters to the United States, where within a few years they established five mother houses. The inhabitants dedicated their lives to teaching and teacher training on various levels – elementary, secondary, and vocational.

The third group working among German immigrants, the School Sisters of Notre Dame, a German Bavarian foundation from the 1830s, founded their first American mother house in 1849 in Milwaukee under the leadership of their head, Theresa Maria Gerhardinger. They became the largest teaching order of German origin in the twentieth century, with four mother houses in 1930 and 5,014 teaching sisters. The American *Generaloberinnen* were of German origin until 1917.

The thriving, religiously motivated teaching among immigrants gained further support after Adalbert Falck's decree was issued in Prussia in 1872. The decree excluded all members of Catholic orders from teaching in Prussian schools. About 1,000 school sisters were expelled. Furthermore, the Law of 1874 suspended all Catholic orders in Prussia except those engaged in nursing. It caused sisters to immigrate at a high rate. The presence of large numbers of nuns who were trained in mother houses founded by German sisters correlates with the fact that between 1880 and 1900, members of German origin formed their largest group among non-English-speaking American Catholics. The female teaching orders ran the parochial school system of the Catholic church in the big cities of the Northeast and Midwest and in the rural areas of the Midwest and West. The German contribution to its establishment was significant. Its founders were competent and determined organizers. As an example, I quote from a letter that Mother Theresa Gerhardinger sent to her confessor in 1849, shortly after she arrived in the New World:

In our earlier letters we asked our order for three or four house sisters. Now that we have been in Baltimore for three months, we know that in this case, things have developed entirely differently from what we originally planned. In case not everyone comes, send us only teachers. I would like to remind you that these should be healthy, strong, robust and courageous, each must be capable of filling the post of superior, and must be a competent teacher in the elementary school and the Industrial Arts department. The requirements for German are not as rigid here as in Munich. Great prudence is needed to manage the children and their parents successfully and only a keen insight and strong will can meet and conquer the various difficulties that arise in the school room and outside it. Neither are mannish, rough sisters acceptable. They would be a torment to themselves, to the children, to their parents and the priests, and they could accomplish nothing, bringing shame and disgrace upon the order.

We cannot use sisters and young ladies who desire only to live a quiet, retired conventual life, those who cannot be employed in school; unless they bring with them considerable funds which bear a yearly interest of at least 200 dollars. . . .[23]

The letters of Theresa Gerhardinger cover funding problems, personnel management, and school policies concerning the English–German problem. Besides, Mother Theresa also gave careful consideration to the different way in which American children were socialized and why teaching them was so different from teaching Bavarian children. The writer was not only a powerful organizer but also a competent educator.

Mother houses that sent their members to teaching had teacher training facilities, and the newly founded orders recruited their new members from among trained teachers.[24] The history of education usually looks at female teachers in the elementary school system in Germany at the time as a *quantité négligeable*. In Catholic areas of Germany, large numbers of sisters were engaged only in girls' schools at various levels of rural and urban elementary schools systems (i.e., Aachen, Augsburg), In the big cities of the United States, they also taught only girls. The shift to coeducation occurred only recently. In rural areas, the parochial schools that I have investigated always instructed both girls and boys, and thus differed from elementary schools in Catholic areas in Germany, but efforts were made to segregate the sexes. This seems especially remarkable since both American and German Catholic journals of the time claimed that Catholic schools were pedagogically superior *because* they were noncoeducational.[25]

The successful efforts to provide work outside the family for young women suggest that the role of these orders as contributors to the establishment of the nineteenth-century school system should be reconsidered.

23. Quoted from Mary Ewens, O.P., "The Leadership of Nuns in Immigrant Catholicism," in Rosemary Radford Ruether and Rosemary Skinner Keller, eds., *Women and Religion in America*, 3 vols., vol. 1, *The Nineteenth Century* (San Francisco, 1981), 124.
24. For information on recruiting practices and training opportunities among these congregations in Germany, I benefited from Relinde Meiwes, "Katholische Frauenorder und- Kongregationen in Preussen, 1803–1875" (unpublished master's thesis, University of Bielefeld).
25. See, e.g., "Die Vereinigten Staaten von heute," *Historisch-politische Blätter für das katholische Deutschland* 36 (1876):501–17.

Because male teachers by far outnumbered female teachers in Germany in
the nineteenth century, we tend to neglect the contribution of the Catholic
female teacher who belonged to an order. Her work may offer a key to a
further explanation of the different pace of the feminization of this profession in different countries that goes beyond labor market or ideological
arguments. The former are usually applied to the United States, where
scarcity of labor was prevalent throughout the century; the latter are more
often developed in the case of Germany, where the state-oriented, patri-
archal society offered limited opportunities to women in the public school
system during the nineteenth century.

From scattered data on the fathers' social status of the founders of the
tätige Kongregationen in Germany, we know that they came mostly from
middle-class families. We also know that the orders intentionally recruited
from middle-class families – those of professionals, affluent craftsmen, and
rich merchants. Young Catholic women who joined an order apparently
found a way of living outside their families. In Germany this took place at
a time when living as an independent working woman was virtually impossible. The story of these Catholic nuns who dedicated their lives to
teaching can be seen as a chapter in the century-long story of women's
work outside the family. A comparison of the two religious groups of
women who were prevalent in nineteenth-century Germany, the deaconesses and the sisters of the "working orders," supports the British historian
Susan O'Brian's view that the experience of religious women was ahead of
the general development of professional life for women.[26] Franz Schnabel's
judgment on the formative aspects of religious forces in nineteenth-century
German history should be reconsidered for a general view of the development of teacher training and the formative forces of the profession.[27] For
the purpose of this essay, it would explain in a broader framework why
Catholic sisters were so successful in teaching among German immigrants,
while at the same time the progressive National German-American Teachers' Association vanished fairly quickly during the first decades of immigration. A comparison between the work of the Catholic sisters, both in
Germany and in the United States, the schoolmarm, the *Kantor,* and the
modern *Volkserzieher* casts new light on the American the German development of the teaching profession.

An explicitly German background can be found for three of the four groups
discussed in this essay. The Lutheran teacher considered himself the *Kantor*

26. Susan O'Brian, "Terra incognita, the Nun in Nineteenth-Century England," *Past and Present* 121
    (1988):115.
27. Franz Schnabel, *Deutsche Geschichte im 19. Jahrhundert,* vol. 4, "Die religiösen Kräfte," 2nd ed.
    (Freiburg, 1951), 4.

of his church, providing a Christian denominational education, being bilingual, and thus contrasting with the American environment. The German-Americans who claimed ethnic autonomy without religious support and the Catholic sisters who considered education of the Catholic German immigrants' children to be their field of work both intended to pursue bilingual education. During the first years of their existence, all three groups struggled in a foreign environment that was often hostile toward them. A similar bewilderment about the children of German immigrants and the difficulties of teaching them can be found among all three groups. They clung to traditional views of the educational relationship and to the idea of superiority to the American school. Only the young women teaching public school in nondenominational communities merged with the American public school teachers without any overt tension.

The two religiously affiliated groups survived the turn of the century. Though being German became less important than being identified with non-Anglo-American religion, they taught in an important sector of the American school system. The Lutheran teacher was more regionally confined than his Catholic colleague. Both shaped American education in its private sector. For both groups, there are still many unanswered questions, and church history has not answered them. We know little about their social background and even less about their occupational patterns, especially among the Lutheran teachers. Although the feminization of the occupation took place in the Lutheran schools, it has never been investigated thoroughly. The Catholic female orders of the United States are considered to be the most modernized of the Roman Catholic church in the twentieth century. Was the teaching success of the large parochial school system one reason for the outspoken claim for equal rights in the church? The most striking result of my investigation is the highlighting of the importance of religion in a field that certainly was a creation of modern secular forces: the educational system established in both Germany and in the United States during the nineteenth century. That "behind the thoroughly secular leading and formative forces of the age, a completely different nineteenth century still lived," as Schnabel states, is not too surprising and finds support for the German case in Nipperdey's famous essay on "*Volksschule und Revolution im Vormärz.*"[28] Recent research on schools of immigrant churches in the United States suggests a similar interpretation.[29] Further research in

---

28. Thomas Nipperdey, "Volksschule und Revolution im Vormärz," in *Politische Ideologien und nationalstaatliche Ordnung. Festschrift für Theodor Schieder* (Munich, 1968), 117–42.
29. Reinhardt Dörries, *Iren und Deutsch in der Neuen Welt: Akkulturationsprozesse in der amerikanischen Gesellschaft im späten 19. Jahrhundert* (Wiesbaden, 1986); Harro W. van Grummelen, *Telling the Next Generation: Educational Development in North American Calvinist Christian Schools* (Lapham, 1986).

the field of teacher training in both countries should investigate the impact of this argument systematically.

The history of women in education points out that the traditional bounds, which Schnabel claims to have been saved only for a certain time through "*Romantik und Restauration,*" were highly supportive of the efforts of women to enter the teaching profession and thus gain access to an influential field in modern society. This access meant hard work under hostile conditions, poorly compensated, and taken for granted by the male church hierarchy and the parish members. Looking on immigrant sisters, the story of women entering the teaching profession was sharply double-edged: Teaching meant unpaid female work, as well as "a widening sphere" both occupationally and geographically.

8

German Models, American Ways: The "New Movement" among American Physics Teachers, 1905–1909

KATHRYN M. OLESKO

The "new movement" among American physics teachers, which began at a midwestern regional science teachers' meeting in 1905 and ended with a national symposium in early 1909, marked a major turning point in American high school physics education. Before the new movement, American physics teachers had adopted a style of physics instruction that had its origins in the university community. They remained, however, poorly trained in the discipline that they taught. Moreover, they had not yet taken the direction and content of the high school physics curriculum into their own hands, and they had no national organization in which their interests could be represented. After the new movement, physics teachers had not only seized curricular control over school physics, but had also forced a reconsideration of teacher training and founded two fledgling national organizations.

German models of school physics instruction and teacher training played crucial roles in the new movement. American high school physics teachers, under the guiding hand of university physicists, had adopted by the late 1880s a physics curriculum based on laboratory exercises, especially precision measurement, that had proven so successful in Germany and that had its origins in the system of German science seminars, the institutional predecessors of the large-scale German science laboratories of the late nineteenth century. But lacking the training and especially the exposure to research of their German counterparts, American teachers soon found such practical exercises sterile. In the late nineteenth century, the introduction of exact experimentation into the classroom was sustained only by ideologically interpreting measurement in ways different than had been done in Germany. But as a result of the new movement, and of the criticisms of measurement and quantification in physics instruction that had led up to it, not only did the ideology justifying physics instruction change, but so did American views of the content and significance of the German model of school physics instruction.

I

Together with the redefinition of the role of the philosophical faculty as a place both for learning *Wissenschaft* and for training secondary school teachers at the beginning of the nineteenth century and the inauguration of state teaching examinations in 1810, science seminars were one of the three means by which science teaching became professionalized in Germany. Between 1825 and 1888, fifteen science seminars were founded within the boundaries of what eventually became the German Empire; graduates of these seminars were responsible for the enhancement of science instruction, especially *Prima* and *Secunda* physics classes, during the years when German science attained hegemony in the Western world. Although these seminars varied in the quality of the instruction they offered, collectively they came to represent the unity of teacher training and disciplinary instruction to which several educational institutions of industrializing nations aspired.

Four of these seminars, among the earliest, were for the collective natural sciences. These proved to be either overambitious ministerial expressions of outdated philosophies linking all sciences into a single whole (as they were at Bonn, Königsberg, and Freiburg) or ill-formed amalgamations of faculty demands for the educational priorities of their own subjects (as was Halle's seminar for the natural sciences and mathematics).[1] All four natural science seminars experienced operational problems almost from the start; they were the first seminars to disband. Nine others (at Königsberg, Göttingen, Munich, Giessen, Breslau, Heidelberg, Tübingen, Erlangen, and Rostock) were more successful, having been narrowly conceived primarily as seminars for physics alone or for mathematics and physics combined.[2] Physics instruction in these seminars benefited from the prominent role of mathematics in the neohumanist *Gymnasium* curriculum and from the growing importance, especially to the state, of precision measurement in economic administration and planning. In addition, two pedagogical sem-

1. On the natural sciences seminars, see Gert Schubring, "The Rise and Decline of the Bonn Natural Sciences Seminar," *Osiris* 5 (1989): 57–93; Hans-Jürgen Apel, "Gymnasiallehrerbildung zwischen Wissenschaft und fachdidaktischer Orientierung: Konzeption und Praxis der Lehrerbildung am Seminar für die gesamten Naturwissenschaften der Universität Bonn zwischen 1825 und 1848," *Vierteljahrschrift für wissenschaftliche Pädagogik* 62 (1986): 289–319; Kathryn M. Olesko, *Physics as a Calling: Discipline and Practice in the Königsberg Seminar for Physics* (Ithaca, N.Y., 1991), esp. chaps. 1 and 2.
2. On the mathematico-physical and physical seminars, see Olesko, *Physics as a Calling*, esp. chaps. 3–8, 10; Christa Jungnickel and Russell McCormmach, *Intellectual Mastery of Nature: Theoretical Physics from Ohm to Einstein*, 2 vols. (Chicago, 1986), 1:78–107, 2:121–5.

inars in physics were established relatively late, which incorporated well-established patterns of teacher training and accentuated the professional function and didactic usefulness of teaching and learning precision measurement: one for teachers of mathematics and physics in Berlin (directed by the pedagogue and ministerial advisor Karl Schellbach) and one for physics teachers at Giessen University (directed by the physicist Karl Noack). The usefulness of all fifteen seminars was short-lived. Almost all disappeared by the first decades of the twentieth century, their functions having been passed on to the more amply endowed science institutes and laboratories beginning in the 1870s.

Although, like other university-based seminars, German science seminars were identified with the institutionalization of the "research ethos," their actual accomplishments were much more modest but nonetheless significant. Especially where physics was concerned, German science seminars were responsible for the consolidation of pedagogical changes in the sciences. These began in the late eighteenth century, when review sessions first appeared as supplements to lecture courses, and then revolutionized the nature of science instruction in the nineteenth century, when those exercises metamorphosed into practical laboratory exercises in the rudiments of scientific investigation. As had occurred in other disciplines, education in the sciences was enhanced considerably by reading clubs, exercise sessions, and student societies that appeared especially in the early decades of the nineteenth century, often as private gatherings at the institutional fringes of the universities and intended especially as aids for the training of secondary school teachers. Although the neohumanist and Humboldtian reforms have traditionally been identified as responsible for German instructional innovations, especially for the introduction of the research ethic into university teaching, those reforms were the culmination rather than the origination of these pedagogical changes, especially in the sciences. Rhetorical appeals, on the part of prospective seminar directors, to neohumanist educational ideologies for the purpose of enhancing and even changing science instruction were merely convenient ploys designed to draw attention to, and hopefully achieve institutional parity for, the natural sciences.[3]

Contemporary observers praised science seminars for their provision of practical exercises under "the guiding hand and intelligence of a master,"[4]

3. See, e.g., Karl Ernst von Baer et al. to Kultusministerium, 15 September 1828, Zentrales Staatsarchiv Merseburg [hereafter ZStA-M], Acta betr. eines Seminars für die naturwissenschaftlichen Studien auf der Universität zu Königsberg, Rep. 76Va, Sekt. 11, Tit. X, Abt. X, Nr. 21, [1827–76], fol. 7.
4. C. F. Lentz, "An- und Aussichten die Mathematik und Physik an den Gymnasium betreffend," *Programm*, Friedrichs Collegium zu Königsberg, 1836–7, pp. 4–5.

but historians since then have concluded that most science seminars suffered, to various degrees, from tensions generated by the incompatibility of teacher training and disciplinary instruction. In the mathematico-physical seminars of Erlangen, Heidelberg, and Munich, and in the Königsberg and Bonn natural sciences seminars, didactic exercises designed to improve teaching skills existed side by side with more scientific ones. Elsewhere – most notably in the mathematico-physical seminars at Königsberg and Göttingen – didactic objectives were either nonexistent or implicit in the more discipline-oriented training that dominated their operation. Even in Prussia, the state purportedly most interested in furthering *Wissenschaft,* the educational ministry occasionally looked askance on sophisticated seminar exercises that appeared ill-suited for training teachers. August Leopold Crelle, Berlin mathematician and esteemed advisor to the *Kultusministerium* in the mid-1840s, criticized the exercises of the Königsberg mathematico-physical seminar because, in his view, their emphasis on the written solution to scientific and mathematical problems failed to elicit what was important in teaching: "Future teachers," he admonished, "instruct not by writing but by speaking." It was through oral presentations that students proved "that they possess the gift and the ability to communicate their views to those who do not know them, as is found in the vocation of teachers."[5] Also in Prussia, the two early seminars founded with explicit intentions to train secondary school teachers, the natural science seminars at Bonn and at Königsberg, had curricula that were comprehensive but that failed to help students fulfill the requirements of the state's teaching examination, especially in mathematics. The Bonn seminar directors reported that one prospective teacher bluntly told them that attending a seminar that did not include mathematical instruction was nothing short of a "hardship."[6]

Not even the Prussian state teaching examination of 1866 was an unequivocal expression of disciplinary over didactic ends in teacher training. To be sure, the examination enhanced the scholarly attributes of teachers through several means. It added a written requirement that was for all practical purposes equivalent to a doctoral dissertation. It required an intensification of specialized study, including study in physics, where a candidate had to have "knowledge of the theories of mathematical physics and its methods, along with a precise understanding of physical instruments and

5. A. L. Crelle to Kultusministerium, 20 August 1845, ZStA-M, Math.-phys. Seminar Königsberg, fols. 126–30; on fol. 129.
6. Directors of the Bonn Natural Sciences Seminar to Kultusministerium, 10 January 1831, ZStA-M, Acta betr. die Einrichtung eines Seminars für die naturwissenschaftlichen Studien auf der Universität zu Bonn, Rep. 76Va, Sekt. 3, Tit. X, Nr. 4, Bd. I: 1823–31, fols. 197–8; on fol. 198.

exercises in their use." And it increased the importance attached to seminar attendance, which had to be listed on a candidate's curriculum vitae.[7] But when Friedrich Julius Richelot, the mathematician who had been instrumental in shaping these changes, pressed for even greater specialization on the examination, the educational ministry reminded him that evidence of a candidate's possession of "practical teaching skills" was in the state's best interest.[8]

The state's admonitions aside, science seminars trained teachers principally through the mastery of disciplinary knowledge, and the seminars excelled in their task. What made science seminars so influential in shaping instruction — especially in physics, the science best represented in them — was their commitment to obligatory practical exercises in precision measurement as supplements to lecture courses *before* teaching laboratories were commonplace. That those exercises were chosen from among a larger field of pedagogical possibilities requires explanation beyond pointing out that throughout the German states in the first half of the nineteenth century the dominant approach to physics was experimental. The introduction of French mathematical physics into German universities in the 1830s and 1840s was one factor contributing to the choice, for French theories lacked adequate empirical confirmation, yet made what to German thinkers were outrageous claims to certainty and truth. A second factor was more contextual and concerned especially the Prussian state's interest in measurements useful to it. Between the 1830s and the 1850s, Prussia commissioned more precise measurements of its standard of length, its land, and the heating power of fuels — all matters of pressing economic concern.[9]

Seminar exercises in precision measurement were not examples of the original research believed accomplished in German institutes, nor were they necessarily always intended to cultivate the pursuit of *Wissenschaft* for its own sake. More often, they were designed to aid the understanding of introductory material, and in this they helped to achieve the pedagogical consolidation of disciplinary knowledge by which a larger number of stu-

7. "Reglement für die Prüfung der Candidaten des höheren Schulamts, 12. Dezember 1866," *Centralblatt für die gesammte Unterrichtsverwaltung in Preussen* 8 (1867): 13–35; "Ausführung des neuen Reglements für die Prüfung der Candidaten des höheren Schulamts," ibid., 209.
8. Kultusministerium to the Director of the Wissenschaftliche Prüfungskommission in Königsberg, 31 July 1869, rpt. in Gert Schubring, *Die Entstehung des Mathematiklehrerberufs im 19. Jahrhundert* (Weinheim/Basel, 1983), 289.
9. The principal results of those investigations were: F. W. Bessel, *Darstellungen der Untersuchungen und Maassregeln, welche, in den Jahren 1835 bis 1838, durch die Einheit des preussischen Längenmaasses veranlasst worden sind* (Berlin, 1839); idem and J. J. Baeyer, *Gradmessung in Ostpreussen und ihre Verbindung mit preussischen und russischen Dreiecksketten* (Berlin, 1838); Phillip Wilhelm Brix, *Untersuchungen über die Heizkraft der wichtigeren Brennstoffe des preussischen Staates* (Berlin, 1853), 6.

dents could be educated in the sciences. They incorporated training in research methodologies and skills only insofar as they became more complicated and rigorous in advanced courses. The amalgamation of functions in science seminars where learning physics was combined with teacher training resulted in a mixed form of instruction having explicit disciplinary elements and implicit didactic ones. The case of the Göttingen mathematico-physical seminar, founded in 1850, is instructive in this regard. When Friedrich Kohlrausch took over the seminar's practical exercises in 1866, he codified them, adjusted several for beginning students, and identified as one of the four functions served by these exercises (which were still overwhelmingly disciplinary, not didactic) "training teaching candidates in how to use instructional apparatus."[10]

The professionalization of the German *Physiklehrer* was certainly aided by instruments of certification, such as the state teaching examination; by organs of publication, such as *Grunert's Archiv für Mathematik und Physik* and, later in the century, pedagogical journals; by professional organizations; and by special summer schools in physics. But it was these practical exercises that contributed most to the training of physics teachers. Not all future physics teachers took a doctoral degree, so these exercises determined the nature and extent to which they were exposed to research methodologies and the depth of their learning in physics. Former seminar students adapted these exercises to school instruction and made them standard rather than occasional features of physics courses; used them to shape their workaday world, especially in building up physical cabinets; and found in them a common bond with introductory physics instruction at the university. The professional identity of the *Physiklehrer* as a carrier of specialized knowledge rested not on a knowledge of how a child learned science or of how to teach it, but on a knowledge of the intricate and delicate investigative practices in physics.

But not all physics teachers found their professional image harmonious or satisfying. At times constrained by institutional conditions and unable to offer or execute these exercises, physics teachers felt the disparity between what their training had made them and what their daily professional lives required. One former seminar student faulted the system that equated esoteric learning with teacher training: "the instruction which a natural sciences teacher receives in a seminar," Emil Schinz wrote in

10. Friedrich Kohlrausch, *Leitfaden der praktischen Physik,* 4th ed. (Leipzig, 1880), pp. iii–iv [foreword to 2nd ed., 1872].

1849, "is too general, too high, and penetrates too little into life."[11] Near the end of the century, when the training of science teachers began to incorporate considerations of science pedagogy in addition to scientific practice, physics teachers even questioned the pedagogical usefulness of precision measurement, which had "meaning . . . for the physicist who later has a well equipped laboratory at his disposal" but was "of little significance for the prospective school man."[12] Yet even in spite of such criticism, the training of science teachers in nineteenth-century Germany remained oriented to the acquisition of knowledge and investigative skills rather than to child psychology or other pedagogical and didactic concerns. Hence, although in 1901 Thomas Mann attributed to Dr. Marotzke, the chemistry teacher in *Buddenbrooks,* "the reputation of being an original thinker," when relating Marotzke's teaching style he resorted to the military metaphors so pervasive in descriptions of nineteenth-century German scientific practice.[13]

II

The expansion of laboratory practica in physics in the last third of the century, both in Germany and in America, signified the full acceptance of the educational ideology of the seminar, which maintained that lecture courses were incomplete without exercises that applied what had been learned. Although practical exercises in physics had begun to appear in American secondary schools in the 1870s,[14] it was not until 1887, when the Harvard physicist Edwin H. Hall published the first nationwide announcement of laboratory exercises for high school physics courses, that such exercises began to become commonplace. Hall and his followers considered such exercises emancipatory, freeing both the high school teacher and the student from a "blind and helpless dependence upon textbooks" and providing them with the means for a type of training that was "partly of the

11. Emil Schinz, "Vorträge über den naturwissenschaftlichen Unterricht in Volkschulen," *Verhandlungen der Schweizerischen Naturforschenden Gesellschaft* (1849): 50–8; on 52.
12. "Das physikalische Studium auf der Universität (Von einem praktischen Schulmann H. G. M.)," *Zeitschrift für mathematischen und naturwissenschaftlichen Unterricht* 15 (1884): 638–45; on 643.
13. "He was, besides all this, a reserve officer, and very enthusiastic over the service. . . .He set more store by discipline than any of the masters: he would review the ranks of sturdy youngsters with a professional eye, and he insisted on short, brisk answers to questions." Significantly, Mann went on to identify Hans Hermann Kilian as the "best in the class . . . because of his desire to become a military officer." Thomas Mann, *Buddenbrooks,* trans. H. T. Lowe-Porter (New York, 1961; orig. publ. 1901), 575.
14. Sidney Rosen, "A History of the Physics Laboratory in the American Public High School (to 1910)," *American Journal of Physics* 22 (1954): 194–204.

senses and partly mental."[15] Yet the rapid acceptance of these exercises threw into disarray older ways of teaching physics, resulting initially in a considerably more unmanageable situation, a free-for-all in which students, without supervision, were left to rediscover the laws of physics on their own. Far from being liberating, laboratory work, it was found, required its own variety of authoritative guidance in the form of craft supervision in order to be successful. Finding that a student had to have "a clearly defined idea of what he is doing" and "a good degree of skill in conducting an investigation," authors of some school physics textbooks of the 1890s initiated a rethinking of didactic practices "to render intelligible the chaotic work of the laboratory."[16] By the end of the decade, a harmonious integration of the textbook and the laboratory seemed to have been reached when the College Entrance Examination Board, established in 1899, made E. H. Hall's list of experiments mandatory for college-bound high school seniors.[17]

But in terms of what it meant to become and to be a physics teacher, these university-driven pedagogical changes were problematic. American physics teachers possessed neither the degree of professionalization nor the culture of science that had surrounded their counterparts in Germany. Professionalization of secondary school teaching, including specialized, discipline-specific training (especially in the sciences) was hardly apparent; teachers were trained at heterogeneous institutions that varied widely from region to region. The establishment of departments or chairs of education at major universities by the end of the century, sometimes cited by contemporary commentators and later historians as a step toward professionalization, merely served to underscore the intellectual foundation of school teaching in the subjects of pedagogy and psychology and to distance teaching even further from the kind of training secondary school teachers received in Germany.[18] The low caliber of school science teachers was not lost on E.H. Hall, who knew that "probably only a small portion of the teachers of physics in the preparatory schools have had such a training as would enable them to arrange and conduct the proposed course [or laboratory exercises] without considerable effort and some mistakes." Although Hall

15. E. H. Hall, "Experimental Physics for the Schools," *Science* 10 (1887): 129–30; on 129; see also Albert E. Moyer, "Edwin Hall and the Emergence of the Laboratory in Teaching Physics," *The Physics Teacher* 14 (1976): 96–103.

16. Henry S. Carhart and Horatio N. Chute, *The Elements of Physics* (Boston, 1892), iii, iv.

17. Moyer, "Edwin Hall," 101.

18. B. A. Hinsdale, *The Training of Teachers,* Monographs on Education in the United States, ed. N.M. Butler, no. 8 (New York, 1900), 33–47.

made a feeble attempt to instruct teachers on how to teach his exercises (his most substantial recommendation, however, was to remind them to "be in the laboratory whenever work [was] going on there"), for the most part he relied on on-the-job training, hoping that in two years' time, teachers would know what they were doing.[19] Between 1880 and 1900 several normal schools inaugurated laboratory courses intended to train teaching candidates the practical aspects of physics instruction;[20] but they were never enough to acclimatize teachers to pedagogical practices whose origins were found outside the school.

It was a distinctly American cult of science, rather than a scientific culture, that facilitated the assimilation of practical exercises in precision measurement into high school physics classes at a time when almost all American physics teachers lacked discipline-specific training. During the last two decades of the century, scientific thinking and techniques entered the innermost recesses of American culture: All that was known and observed – including the most banal activities of daily life – was submitted to objectification, quantification, and systematization. Education itself was objectified with the creation of formalized courses, textbooks, degrees, standardized examinations, and, of course, the objectification through psychology of that most confounding member of the human family, the child. For late-nineteenth-century Americans, according to Burton Bledstein, science "established a rational and orderly process of development beneath the fragmented experiences of American life."[21] It became the foundation of industrial efficiency, the source of professional authority, and the guarantor of moral certainty.[22]

Science also became a source of ethical values, for it forged links between a disciplined work ethic and the moral efficacy of labor in ways that, as David Hollinger has made clear, other professions such as law could not.[23] According to Thomas Chamberlin, geologist and president of the University of Michigan in 1888, "narrow and loose habits of thought, prejudiced attitudes towards evidence, bias from previous opinions and feelings, shallowness and superficiality in observation, and carelessness in reasoning are

19. Hall, "Experimental Physics for Schools," 130.
20. Rosen, "A History of the Physics Laboratory," 198.
21. Burton Bledstein, *The Culture of Professionalism: The Middle Class and the Development of Higher Education in America* (New York, 1976), 326.
22. Ibid., 89–90; Rosen, "A History of the Physics Laboratory," p. 196; G. Stanley Hall, "Research: The Vital Spirit of Teaching," *Forum* 17 (1894): 558–70, esp. 565 (division of labor, as exemplified in the *Physikalisch-Technische Reichsanstalt*) and 569 (military power and industrial growth).
23. David Hollinger, "Inquiry and Uplift: Late Nineteenth-Century American Academics and the Moral Efficacy of Scientific Practice," in *The Authority of Experts*, ed. Thomas L. Haskell (Bloomington, Ind., 1984), 142–56, esp. 143–4.

appropriate subjects of moral reproof" and could be modified by following
the scientific methods of "the *seminar,* the laboratory, and the field."[24] His
views were shared by other eminent educators, including those active in
the redesign of school physics instruction, such as the social scientist and
university president G. Stanley Hall who found in research methods "a high
and positive religious character."[25] For these educators, digressions from the
straight and narrow path of upright behavior could be corrected by following the methods of science. Here the model of research was distinctly
German but remolded to fit American conditions. German students studied
Wissenschaft and learned its methods so as to achieve *Bildung,* the cultivation
of personality and talents; American students, in contrast, could find in
research "the spirit of democracy" and "free and full individuation."[26]

Yet the methods of research were many. Which ones could best achieve
morally uplifting ends? Chamberlin's answer, written only a year after E.H.
Hall's practical exercises were introduced into American secondary schools,
revealed the high regard in which the exact sciences were held in certain
American circles. Chamberlin considered the methods par excellence to be
found in the elaborate practices of precision measurement, which quantified
both the observed and the actions of the observer:

The astronomers, geodesists and other precise observers have set us an example
worthy of imitation in all departments of thought. It is their practice to ascertain
by careful tests their habitual errors, and then to correct their results as conscien-
tiously for their own personal defects as for the systematic errors of their instruments. This application of the personal equation should be extended beyond the
field of observation and applied to all impressions, inferences, interpretations, in-
ductions and opinions. It is indeed less easy to determine the personal error in these
more recondite and complex processes of the mind, but the effect is none the less
wholesome, none the less important to trustworthy results.[27]

The personal equation, discovered by the astronomer Friedrich Wilhelm
Bessel in 1823, expressed in quantitative terms the disturbances contributed
by the observer in the act of measuring; adjusted for personal error, measurements were believed to approximate better their "true" value. Applied
to human thinking, the personal equation, Chamberlin suggested, could
help individuals rectify faulty mental processes.

Significantly, Chamberlin neglected to mention the most complex ana-

24. Thomas C. Chamberlin, *The Ethical Functions of Scientific Study,* An Address delivered at the Annual
    Commencement of the University of Michigan, June 28, 1888 (Ann Arbor, 1888), 3–4, 6 (emphasis
    in the original).
25. G. S. Hall, "Research: The Vital Spirit of Teaching," 558.
26. Ibid., 559.
27. Chamberlin, *Ethical Functions of Scientific Study,* 10.

lytic correction for experimental error: the computation of accidental errors by the method of least squares, which German astronomers, geodesists, and some physicists had infused with moral content by identifying it as the most reliable index of the trustworthiness and integrity of the observer.[28] Yet even in those corrections for errors that Chamberlin did mention – they were among the most complicated components of precision measurement – he found ethical benefits. Their potential to educate secondary school pupils morally, he urged, should not be overlooked:

> The school work may be only secondary or imitative research, but it may and should have in itself all essential qualities of original investigation. The minor problems, the tests and the determinations of the student in the laboratory, the field and the seminar may and should involve the same mental and moral characteristics as the more weighty work of the true discoverer. The scientific child in training should foreshadow the scientific man in creative work.[29]

The ease with which Chamberlin saw an ethics in the mental disciplining of scientific ways of thinking – methods that cultivated "a lofty moral courage systematically to discount one's own work for one's persistent errors"[30] – is indicative less of science's actual ability to inculcate disciplined behavior (for there were other kinds of activities, some of them socially undesirable, that also required disciplining) than of the unexamined cultural assumption, held by Chamberlin and others of his generation, that science in itself was good: in its results and in its intolerance of deceptive pride, faulty reasoning, and the moral weaknesses common in humankind.

Chamberlin's views encapsulated the ideology justifying the inclusion of precision measuring exercises in school physics at the end of the century. It was an ideology of discipline tied to a morally uplifting work ethic, not one of creativity and discovery tied to an intellectually stimulating research ethic, as it had been in Germany. As the well-known Ann Arbor, Michigan, physics teacher Horatio Chute wrote in 1894, "the educational value of practical physics does not lie in the so-called discovery of laws, nor in the experimental demonstration of principles," but in "the training it gives in attention to details, in the cultivation of accuracy in observing the smallest changes, in the formation of systematic methods of working, in developing the ability to reason to a general law from a particular set of observations, and in cultivating habits of precise expression of ideas and principles on the pages of the notebook."[31] Chute's physics guided students in the habits of

28. Olesko, *Physics as a Calling*, chap. 10.
29. Chamberlin, *Ethical Functions of Scientific Study*, 11 (emphasis in the original).
30. Ibid., 10.
31. Horatio N. Chute, *Physical Laboratory Manual for Use in Schools and Colleges* (Boston, 1894), iv.

disciplined behavior: to be "orderly and neat" in manipulation; to "economize time" by preparing beforehand and by combining tasks; to be exact and methodical.[32] Still, the scientific element was not completely expunged in such exercises; their goal remained "to secure the highest degree of accuracy," but only that which was "attainable with the quality of apparatus used and the amount of time that can be devoted to the problem."[33] The practical laboratory problem for students to work their way through was thus not that of achieving an ideal (truth through refined measurements), but of the efficient management of resources. Pity the poor unwitting student who could not "see accurately, manipulate carefully, and adjust with precision." Chute saw "nothing in store for him but failure," whereas the systematic, orderly, neat, exact, and careful student achieved a "consciousness of power" and a knowledge appropriate "to welfare, correct living, and to rational conduct."[34] The American cult of science thus created the ideological framework within which precision measuring exercises were legitimated as worthwhile assignments in physics classes.

By the first half-decade of the twentieth century, however, the combination of precision measuring exercises and an ideology of work, discipline, and ethical principles proved unsustainable. A major reason for this union's weakening had to do with the technical improvements in instrumentation made possible by America's growing industrial strength and overall economic wealth. Within a decade, this instructional improvement would prove to be the envy of German physicists. That Americans were able to purchase such equipment with the help of private funding prompted the Göttingen physicist Woldemar Voigt to conclude in 1912 that "many physical problems are to a certain extent monopolized in America" as a result.[35] The immediate effect of increased and improved instrumentation on American school physics, however, was subtler but nonetheless profound. The production of and introduction into the classroom of more elaborate instruments meant that students had to spend much less time, and deploy much less skill, in getting measurements whose accuracy easily exceeded that which was obtainable under more primitive conditions. This technological change weakened arguments that measuring exercises disciplined students in proper work habits; now the fear was that the student might

32. Ibid., xiv.
33. Chute, *Physical Laboratory Manual* (1903 ed.), 15.
34. H. N. Chute, "The Teaching of Physics," *School Science and Mathematics* [hereafter *SSM*], 6 (1906): 255–61, 360–6; on 257, 365.
35. Woldemar Voigt, *Physikalische Forschung und Lehre in Deutschland während der letzten hundert Jahre: Festrede im Name der Georg-Augusts-Universität zur Jahresfeier der Universität am 5. Juni 1912* (Göttingen, 1912), 16.

"degenerate into an 'organ-grinder' " because the corrections, judgments, and evaluations concerning accuracy formerly made by students were now incorporated directly into the instrumentation.[36]

Doubts also began to be expressed about the functional role of physics instruction in the life of the high school student. What could an exact experiment with precise measurements and intricate analyses of errors mean to a student who did not, in his daily experience, encounter phenomena on such a refined level? "It is stupid," John Woodhull of Columbia University Teachers College told physics teachers, to expect students to be interested in experiments such as "whether a rod of iron will expand by one twelve-millionth part of its length for one degree rise in temperature."[37] Mechanics, the subject long considered the most appropriate pedagogical introduction to physics, which almost 100 years earlier began to be utilized pedagogically for the mathematical analysis of exact experiment and precision measurement, came especially under fire for being too abstract and difficult for students to handle.[38] It was not objectification that a student needed to understand modern industrial and commercial life, American critics argued, but rather demystification, so as to comprehend "the cause of the many mysteries about him, and the secrets of machinery."[39] One detects beneath this rhetoric of criticism an attempt to use physics instruction to alter undesirable or immature attitudes toward technology. Physics instruction thus had to shed many of its layers of quantitative dressings to be practically meaningful to daily life, the cultivation of common sense, and even the maturation of a child's ability to reason.[40]

A far more pressing concern raised in the wake of the reaction to exact experimentation and measuring exercises, however, was the training and workaday practices of physics teachers. Decades earlier, they had participated little in a transformation that had been orchestrated largely by college and university physicists. Since then the Northwestern University physicist Henry Crew had noted that some school teachers had unwittingly pushed the student laboratory "too far"; the Chicago physicist Robert Millikan,

36. Henry Crew, "Recent Advances in the Teaching of Physics," *Science* 19 (1904): 481–8; on 483.
37. John F. Woodhull, "Modern Trends of Physics and Chemistry Teaching," *Educational Review* (1906): 236–47.
38. Ibid., pp. 235–7; R. A. Millikan, "Present Tendencies in the Teaching of Elementary Physics," *SSM* 6 (1906): 119–24, 187–93, on 122; W. B. Tower, "What Amount of Mechanics Is It Desirable to Introduce Into a First-Year Course in Physics, and in What Position Should It Come?" *The School Review* [hereafter *SR*] 13 (1905): 69–72.
39. C. H. Perrine, "To What Extent Is It Possible to Introduce Into the High-School Course in Physics a Study of the Practical Applications of Physics to Industry?" *SR* 13 (1905): 73–5, on 73; see also Millikan, "Present Tendencies," 124.
40. See also Woodhull, "Modern Trends," 237.

active in secondary school physics instruction similarly decried the "tyranny of the university over the high-school."[41] Justifiable as such criticisms of physics teaching might have been, it is noteworthy that even an observer as perceptive as Crew failed to appreciate the professional tensions that threatened physics teaching. During the crucial last decade of the nineteenth century, the training of physics teachers had not perceptibly changed, and yet they were called upon to direct the same classroom tasks that their German counterparts oversaw with the benefit of more substantial backgrounds in physics. On the one hand, Crew acknowledged that directing measuring exercises required a different kind of teacher training, especially "a more profound scholarship on the part of the instructor."[42] "The young teacher without special training," Crew warned, "navigates uneasily a stream beset with small craft hailing him for information about the trolley line, about the automatic telephone, about the transformer, about liquid air, about radium."[43] Yet, on the other hand, he viewed measuring exercises as a way of empowering students to become their own teachers, thus eliminating teachers from the instructional loop entirely and making any argument for their improved training superfluous.[44] At a time when it was becoming even more apparent that science was a worthy "handmaid, or better still, the adviser, of the state," Crew clung to the ideal that the best laboratory instructors aimed for their students "to acquire what is known in military circles as skill in scouting" and "to learn that accuracy of speech and thought which is at once the first step in morality and the best preparation for action."[45] As is suggested by the contradictions in Crew's thinking, American physics teachers were thus caught between a training ideal that, because it assumed advanced knowledge of physics, was institutionally unrealizable; and a professional ideology of discipline and work that defined their social role as the guardians of students' character and that imputed a moral significance to the precision measuring exercises they taught.

III

It was not until the Chicago physicist and pedagogue Charles R. Mann orchestrated what became known as the "new movement" among physics

---

41. Crew, "Recent Advances," 484; Millikan, "Present Tendencies," 121; see also Moyer, "Edwin Hall," 102–3.

42. Henry Crew, "What Can Be Done to Make the Study of Physics a Better 'Training for Power'?" *SR* 8 (1900): 520–7; on 525.

43. Crew, "Recent Advances," 486.

44. Crew, "What Can Be Done to Make Physics 'Training for Power'?" 526.

45. Crew, "Recent Advances," 486, 487, 488.

teachers that physics teachers were themselves drawn directly into the revision of their curriculum and considered, in more sustained ways than had
been possible in the past, the alignment between the content and ideology
of their teaching. The new movement began at the December 1905 meeting of the Central Association of Science and Mathematics Teachers, where,
in the Physics Section, a "committee of three" was appointed to survey
faculty at schools, normal schools, colleges, and universities on their pref-
erences for and pedagogical interpretation of experimental exercises in
physics.[46] Although never explicitly identified as such, the intent of the
survey was to challenge directly the curriculum that had been set up by
Edwin H. Hall almost two decades before, sanctioned by the College Board
at the end of the century, and overemphasized measurement as the essence
and goal of physics instruction.[47] As Mann put it: "we have fallen heir to a
set of arid, parched, and lifeless experiments."[48] The new movement initiated the strongest challenge yet to the German model of physics instruction that had been adapted to American conditions.

Between 1906 and 1908 the organizers of the new movement distributed
thousands of surveys; received hundreds of responses from high schools,
colleges, and normal schools nationwide; and published six circulars eliciting
information and reporting responses. Responses were never unanimous, nor
did they always indicate a plurality of opinion. Nevertheless, the new movement marked a watershed in the history of pre–World War I physics education because it mobilized physics teachers to think about a single issue,
laboratory exercises, in broad but discipline-specific professional terms: that
is, in terms of the reorganization and redefinition of the elementary physics
course. Pedagogical knowledge that had hitherto been a means to social
ends rather than an end in itself, and that had been largely controlled by
forces outside the high school, now became an object of intense concern
for the teachers themselves.

The committee of three – and, later, members of other science and mathematics teachers' associations affiliated with the new movement – compiled
responses into narrative paragraphs with qualifying clauses indicating dis-

---

46. The committee of three consisted of Mann and two high school teachers, C. H. Smith of the Hyde
Park High School in Chicago and C. F. Adams of the Detroit Central High School. C. R. Mann,
C. H. Smith, and C. F. Adams, "A New Move Among Physics Teachers," *SSM* 6 (1906): 198–
202.
47. Although not so expressed in the circulars of the new movement, Mann, in his own publications,
thus framed the factors motivating a reform in physics instruction. C. R. Mann, "The Aims and
Tendencies in Physics Teaching," *SSM* 6 (1906): 723–30, esp. 723. In Mann's view, by concentrating so much on the methods and apparatus of physics instruction, "the art of teaching boys and
girls" had been "entirely lost." Ibid., 724.
48. C. R. Mann, "On Science Teaching (V)," *SSM* 6 (1906): 194–7, on 197.

senting opinions. A majority of the initial questions concerned the types of experiment that should be offered; but the most interesting answers came in response to the few questions that sought teachers' opinions on the character and role of physics instruction. "Physics," the new movement's second circular reported, "should be closely co-ordinated with the daily life and experiences of the student." To accomplish that end, respondents thought, the "numerical relations between portions of phenomena" and "quantitative work in the laboratory" should be deemphasized in favor of "observation and the study of phenomena as such." As to the type of teacher training best suited to a reformed instruction, respondents were vague, emphasizing "good teaching" but having little idea as to how that could be achieved (respondents were divided between those who thought that personality made the best teacher, and those who thought that rigorous training in physics did). Mann and his committee interpreted the diversity of responses they received as an indication that "we teachers do not comprehend two things as clearly as we should; namely (1) we fail to understand the nature and needs of the adolescent mind; and (2) we comprehend even less the real nature of science and the real meaning of her services to civilization."[49] The organizers thus set the stage, in their second questionnaire, for focusing on style rather than content: on how and why physics should be learned rather than on what knowledge and skills should be incorporated into physics classes.

Hoping to focus respondents' answers, Mann took, in the third circular, what proved to be a decisive move, one that attempted to reintroduce a German model for physics instruction by playing proposed American reforms off against similar changes then taking place in Prussia, where it was recommended that physics instruction emphasize the observational ideal of the experimental natural sciences rather than the mathematical rigor of exact science, as the new movement's second circular had also advocated. The American commentator on German developments, J. W. A. Young, in fact viewed German developments in the same light as American ones: as aiming for "the better adaptation of the instruction to the needs and capacities of the pupil and to the spirit and requirement of our twentieth century civilization."[50] Mann not only considered German developments an inspiration

49. C. R. Mann et al., "A New Movement Among Physics Teachers: Circular II," *SR* 14 (1906): 429–37; on 432, 433, 435.
50. J. W. A. Young, "The Movement in Prussia for the Reorganization of the Instruction of Mathematics and the Natural Science in the Secondary Schools," *Science* 23 (1906): 773–8; on 778; see also H. E. Cobb, "Proposals for Reform of the Teaching of Mathematics and Science in the Nine-Class Higher Schools of Prussia," *SSM* 6 (1906): 708–10.

for what Americans might do, but also gleaned from French and especially German reform reports the "theses" that he believed had guided reform in those countries, translated and edited them for an American audience, and then asked for his readers' opinions on how they should be rewritten to fit the experiences of American physics classes. Three crucial theses concerned quantification and measurement: (1) the role of laboratory apparatus in furnishing "the means of determining quantitatively the relations summarized by law"; (2) the approximate nature of a scientific law, which measurements approach only by degrees, for the law is truly realizable only in an ideal case; and (3) the function of measurement as the "determination of efficiencies" rather than "the verification of laws."[51] These three represented to Mann a quintessentially German approach, one especially prominent in physics seminars, to measurement and scientific truth as represented in the mathematical expression of physical laws. Yet, although the first two clearly were characteristic of German science, the third was not. Through it Mann was trying, it seems, to introduce a physics more reflective of modern experiences, for the term "efficiency" was associated with work and energy and hence with machines and industry. Despite his earlier criticism of measuring exercises, Mann considered these theses fundamental precepts of modern science that he viewed as "Teutonic," for "the German not only acknowledges that laws are approximations, but he also is content to use these approximations until better ones are found. Herein lies the power of the Teutonic science: for unless we are willing to consider every scientific conclusion as an approximation, no growth in science is possible." So, in addition to relating science instruction to "a pressing necessity of social life," Mann believed students should be aware of "the method invented and developed by Teutonic men."[52]

Followers of the new movement, disagreeing with Mann's Teutonic views, went further in their revision of the old physics than Mann probably thought they would in distinguishing American and German views of science and science education. They struck from the first two theses every reference to quantification and reworded each thesis to express a relation not between measurement and experiment, but between hypothesis and experiment. So (1) "laboratory experiments furnish the means of converting hypotheses into laws"; (2) "every law is a tested hypothesis," but because of experimental errors "the law is always a statement of what we believe

---

51. [C. R. Mann], "A New Movement Among Physics Teachers: Circular III," *SSM* 6 (1906): 696–702; on 701 (theses 6, 7, and 8).
52. Mann, "The Aims and Tendencies in Physics Teaching," 728, 729.

true in an ideal case."[53] Essentially these physics teachers replaced the mechanical thinking associated with quantitative exercises in precision measurement with the more philosophical and abstract thinking associated with the hypothetico-deductive method. To underscore that point, an eleventh thesis was added to the ten originally circulated, this one addressing the need to keep clear in the student's mind the distinction between facts and speculation (or hypothesis).[54] As to the third "German" thesis, new movement physics teachers agreed with the idea that in "laboratory work it is often more profitable to place the emphasis on the determination of efficiency rather than on the verification of laws," but they wanted nonetheless to redefine the "value of quantitative knowledge" in physics pedagogy. Whereas earlier the quantitative techniques of exact experiment, including precision measurement, had instilled a disciplined work ethic and cultivated moral rectitude, now the "practical use of experiment," with its emphasis on efficiency, "prevents false notions of the mechanical advantage of machines" and "helps to make clear the importance of this concept in the world's work."[55] Thus school physics was recast ideologically in terms of the social needs of a more aggressive industrial economy where value and work were defined first in terms of the efficient mechanical production of material goods and second (if at all) in terms of the toil and discipline of human labor.

There is a remarkable quality to the new movement that went beyond its rhetorical success in redefining the purpose of experiment and quantification in school physics instruction, divorcing it from essentially German ways of teaching physics and of viewing scientific knowledge. The new movement acted as a centripetal force on the collectivity of physics teachers in the United States, bonding them to one another without alienating the university physicists against whose earlier conception of physics instruction they rebelled. In this the movement contributed to the professionalization of physics teachers by creating the conditions under which organizations, nationally based and dedicated to professional goals, could be established. The leadership of the new movement was shared by high school and university representatives, but the membership was overwhelmingly drawn from the former. From the committee of three spawned by the Physics Section of the Central Association of Science and Mathematics Teachers,

---

53. [C. R. Mann], "The New Movement Among Physics Teachers: Circular V," *SR* 15 (1907): 290–8; on 291.
54. Ibid., 292.
55. Ibid., 291.

the new movement quickly grew to embrace a dozen regional school science teaching associations and the American Physical Society, the professional organization of American physicists. With the movement's third circular in 1906, a National Commission on the Teaching of Elementary Physics was created, with Mann as its chairman. It was joined two years later by the formation of the American Federation of Teachers of the Mathematical and Natural Sciences, whose purpose was the betterment of the teaching of mathematics and the natural sciences; Mann was active here, too, serving as the federation's first secretary. Through its affiliation with the American Association for the Advancement of Science, the federation was able to integrate the pedagogical concerns of physics teachers further into the national context of professional science.[56]

But it was the national commission that was initially most effective in helping to bring physics instruction under the control of physics teachers themselves. In the new movement's fourth circular, the commission published part of its proposed new physics syllabus, which it offered as a "basis of discussion" in which everyone was supposed to "express his opinion freely." Consistent with the rhetoric of an industrial economy that had reframed the ideological orientation of physics courses in critical remarks preceding the new movement, the proposed syllabus made its focus and organizing principle "energy transformations and transferences," rather than measurement or the mechanical equations of motion, as courses and textbooks up to then had emphasized. Work and efficiency were thus central notions in this new syllabus, which tried to make physical principles concrete by relating them to the performance of machines. Devices that in German physics teaching had been interpreted either as illustrations of the principles of motion or measuring instruments, such as the pendulum, were presented in this new syllabus as examples of how "mechanical energy may be measured by work." Every attempt was made to introduce topics "from the general experiences of the student" so that the student could learn how to think inductively.[57] Especially this last pedagogical strategy recast physics as an observational science rather than a mathematical one wherein deduc-

---

56. C. R. Mann, "The American Federation of Teachers of the Mathematical and the Natural Sciences," *SSM* 8 (1908): 78, 335–7.
57. [C. R. Mann], "The New Movement Among Physics Teachers: Circular IV," *SSM* 6 (1906): 787–794; on 787, 791, 788. Remarkable is the fact that the rhetoric of industry, energy, efficiency, work, and machines that characterized the new movement predated the transition in American manufacturing to mass production (with its attendant labor problems), which began with the introduction of the assembly line at the Ford Motor Company in Detroit in 1913. David A. Hounshell, *From the American System to Mass Production: The Development of Manufacturing Technology in the United States* (Baltimore, 1984), 9–13, 217–62.

tive thinking was more common. This new American syllabus thus proved to be more like a well-known British one of a half-century earlier[58] and less like German ones, still organized around measurement and the mechanics of motion. Bringing teachers nationwide directly into a discussion of curricular matters, this new syllabus marked the first time physics teachers became involved on a widespread basis in curricular reform. Pedagogical knowledge came under their control.

Now centrally organized and offered the opportunity to voice their own opinions, regional science teaching associations were spurred to adopt their own resolutions on physics instruction, ensuring teachers of their freedom to construct courses without considering national recommendations. At its first two meetings, on November 30, 1906, and December 29, 1906, the commission took additional steps to transfer curricular control to physics teachers by addressing the construction of the new syllabus; by questioning the influence of examining boards on teaching physics; and by reaffirming the freedom of teachers to construct their own courses. Thus the new movement was successful in relocating curricular authority in physics, taking it from the hands of university physicists and the College Board, and giving it directly to those who grappled with the problems of teaching physics in their daily professional lives.[59]

Answering the national commission's circulars also gave physics teachers the opportunity to vent their frustrations over their professional obligations, identity, and status, and hence to express a professional self-consciousness that might not otherwise have been articulated and hence developed. Their wants were many: for a free period in their schedules for preparing laboratory work; for "rank and standing" for belonging to professional organizations "so that people would recognize that [they were] not mechanician[s], carpenter[s], janitor[s], and scrub-lad[ies] combined"; and for "ways of controlling entry into the profession, as is done in medicine, law, theology, etc." And, of course, they wanted the freedom, which they did achieve, to develop their own style of teaching, unencumbered by the College Board or other agencies.[60]

Ironically, however, the new movement's highly advertised symposium on the purpose of physics instruction in secondary schools, which was intended to climax the movement by refining the national commission's

58. William Thomson and Peter Guthrie Tait's *Treatise on Natural Philosophy* of 1867. Crosbie Smith and M. Norton Wise, *Energy and Empire: A Biographical Study of Lord Kelvin* (Cambridge: Cambridge University Press, 1989), 348–95.
59. Mann et al., "A New Movement Among Physics Teachers: Circular II," 429, 436–7; [Mann], "The New Movement Among Physics Teachers: Circular V," 297–8.
60. [Mann], "A New Movement Among Physics Teachers: Circular III," 698.

newly proposed syllabus, merely underscored the bankruptcy of the old, university-directed school physics pedagogy. The voices of the symposium were largely those of post–secondary school educators: of the ten participants, only three (the teachers and textbook authors G. R. Twiss and H.N. Chute and the Wisconsin school inspector H. L. Terry) were from the secondary school community. Not surprisingly, Twiss was the only participant to mention an issue concerning the status of teachers. Disgusted by the low wages science teachers received, he urged schools to pay "the market price for trained science teachers."[61] Among college and university professors, only Crew defended them, reminding his audience that "accuracy and order are the first steps toward morality" because laboratory work helped students respond "reasonably and ethically" and cultivate "a keen sense of responsibility."[62] Most other university physicists condemned precise measuring exercises, thereby acknowledging what secondary school teachers had long argued. The symposium did make one point especially clear: the German model, although not entirely abandoned, nonetheless became a caricature of what it had been. Notably, what Americans now considered important in German practices were those things that resonated with their newly developed ideology of industry, work, and energy. So G. Stanley Hall, who advocated more description and application in physics courses, believed that Americans had "much to learn from the Germans with their many colored wall maps for boys in the early teens illustrating the steam engine, the electric motor, the mechanism of wireless telegraphy, aërial navigation, etc." and that the toys that "abound in Germany" for introducing younger students to science might be used with profit in the United States.[63]

What began as a curricular reformation questioning essentially German ways of teaching physics thus ended up as an emergent stage in the professional self-definition and hence in the professional training that these American physics teachers never really had. The adaptation and then rejection of exact measuring exercises that had had their beginnings in German science seminars proved to be these teachers' "sentimental education" because, by exploiting the opportunity to examine and question their workaday world, they gained control over it. The reorganization and rethinking of the high school physics course became a way for physics teachers to set their own goals, which Mann believed all teachers had to have to do their jobs effec-

61. G. Stanley Hall et al., "Symposium on the Purpose and Organization of Physics Teaching in Secondary Schools," *SSM* 8 (1908): 717–28; 9 (1909): 1–7; on 7.
62. Ibid., 722, 723.
63. Ibid., 2, 3.

tively. Mann described this purpose as a "personal possession" that bore the stamp of the teacher's "individuality" to an extent greater than "the purposes that impel . . . other actions." For Mann it was both a "privilege" and a "duty" for teachers to form their "own purpose[s]" for themselves, even though "this finding of one's individual purpose may require considerable time, for it is impossible to reach the goal without much contemplation and careful thinking."[64] Physics teachers who participated in the new movement or who followed Mann's advice thus belatedly partook of the nineteenth-century American "culture of professionalism" described by Bledstein as embodying

a more radical idea of democracy than even the Jacksonian dared to dream. The culture of professionalism emancipated the active ego of a sovereign person as he performed organized activities within comprehensive spaces. The culture of professionalism incarnated the radical idea of the independent democrat, a liberated person seeking to free the power of nature within every worldly sphere, a self-governing individual exercising his trained judgment in an open society.[65]

IV

German physics teachers observed with interest the evolution of the new movement. Their queries cast the self-examination among American physics teachers in both new and old molds. They revealed an underlying factor the new movement scarcely mentioned – the declining enrollments in high school physics courses – but the kinds of questions they asked of enrollment data suggested that a simple decline in the number of students in physics courses was a grossly insufficient reason for taking drastic actions in recasting all of physics instruction. German observers considered other qualitative demographic factors to be far more important. They asked: How many "colored pupils" and girls were included in the counting? How many women instructors taught physics at boys' schools, girls' schools, or coeducational schools? That they even thought to pose such questions suggests that to them "perturbing" factors in the population base had to be eliminated before any serious assessment could begin.[66]

With Mann, German physics teachers recognized that fundamentally the problem in American physics instruction was a problem of teachers. They considered Mann's commentaries on a teacher's need for goals "valuable,"

---

64. C. R. Mann, "On Science Teaching: IV," *SSM* 6 (1906): 29–35; on 30, 31, 35.
65. Bledstein, *The Culture of Professionalism*, 87.
66. H. Hahn, "Die neue Bewegung unter den Physiklehrern in den Vereinigten Staaten," *Zeitschrift für den physikalischen und chemischen Unterricht* 20 (1907): 189–95, 259–63; on 189.

but they decried the tearing apart of the lists of experiments that had been
the mainstay of physics instruction until the new movement because it
implied an undesirable separation of classroom and laboratory work and the
loss of substance in the measuring exercises that did remain. Their remarks
show how powerfully the ideology of seminar instruction, with its rigorous
disciplinary learning and introduction to research methodologies, was still
a part of their own professional self-image, as well as of their conceptions
of teacher training and physics teaching. Changes in the American list, they
believed, "could easily lead to the result that in the practical exercises,
routine will suppress research methods. Without a doubt that would be a
step backward." But what troubled them most was what they believed the
national commission missed in its review of how the child learned. "The
commission also has not recognized," they continued, "that the pupil repeats in abbreviated form the struggle of humanity in order to fight out
internally a physical world view. Instead it one-sidedly emphasizes the practically important problem, neglecting the great problem of 'how, in pathbreaking human knowledge, factual thinking and ideas accommodate one
another.' "[67] To the German observer, Americans had eliminated the opportunity to cultivate the creative thinking associated with the research ethic
and the pursuit of *Wissenschaft.*

Engaged at the same time in a review of both the physics curriculum
and the training of physics teachers, German teachers also began to question thoroughly the pedagogical usefulness of precision measuring exercises.[68] But their efforts were directed not at changing their methods of
teacher training, but at substituting for one intellectual foundation of that
training another less tied to the teaching and execution of precision measurement. Teacher training, rigorous as ever, still followed the shape of disciplinary knowledge.[69] Hence in 1907 the American normal school teacher
E. A. Strong found it appropriate to invoke the emotionally laden industrial manufacturing term "Made in Germany" when he reported on how
physics teachers were trained there.[70] Matters remained quite different in
America. The new movement had coincided with a nationwide review of
the qualifications of secondary school teaching that emphasized the profes-

67. Ibid., 263.
68. "Das physikalische Studium auf der Universität," 643, 644, 645.
69. See, e.g., E. Grimsehl, "Ueber den Hochschulunterricht für künftige Lehrer der Physik," *Zeitschrift für den physikalischen und chemischen Unterricht* 20 (1907): 1–6; Karl T. Fischer, "Vorschläge zur Hochschulausbildung der Lehramtskandidaten für Physik," ibid., 65–78; K. Noack, "Die Vorbil-dung der Physiklehrer," ibid., 147–53.
70. E. A. Strong, "How Teachers of Physics are 'Made in Germany'," *SSM* 7 (1907): 57–9. I thank Margaret Rossiter for bringing this article to my attention.

sionalism achieved by individual choices and the study of psychology over the professionalism achieved by conformity to rigorous, detailed requirements and by advanced knowledge of subject matter, as had been the case in Germany.[71] Much as the German method of teacher training was still admired, and even cast as a model,[72] it was incompatible with fundamental American beliefs such as individualism, opportunity, and decentralization, and even with American's social system, more fluid that Germany's. American students of the German *Oberlehrer,* such as William S. Learned in 1914, may have argued that "the high and uniform degree of professional training" of the German secondary school teacher "furnishes an irresistible object-lesson," but the standardized examinations that he identified as the chief route to that professionalization were not possible in a federal system.[73]

Bledstein has written that in nineteenth-century America, the professional person came to represent someone who had "mastered an esoteric but useful body of systematic knowledge."[74] Commenting on the new movement in 1906, Edwin H. Hall attributed the "mature and weighty" opinions "concerning the proper range and the best method of physics teaching" expressed by physics teachers in the new movement to the cumulative "influence" of the Harvard list of experiments.[75] In this he was only partially right. Control over knowledge was important in the new movement, more so than were other aspects of professionalization, such as the establishment of national organizations. It was not, however, the Harvard system per se but rather the negative reactions to it that initiated the movement and created the occasion for school physics teachers to express several matters of pedagogical and professional concern.

The central importance of knowledge to this movement may be viewed in another way. The new movement was part of a larger political struggle to secure for physics the dominant position in the secondary school science curriculum, then overloaded with a plethora of sciences, many of which have since passed out of existence.[76] The curricular position for physics that

71. Reuben Post Halleck [chairman, Committee of Seventeen], "The Professional Preparation of High School Teachers," *SR* 15 (1907): 489–507; Frederick E. Bolton, "The Preparation of High-School Teachers: What They Do Secure and What They Should Secure," ibid., 97–121.
72. Bolton, "The Preparation of High-School Teachers," 113, 118–19, 120, 121; Halleck, "The Professional Preparation of High-School Teachers," 501.
73. William S. Learned, *The Oberlehrer: A Study of the Social and Professional Evolution of the German Schoolmaster* (Cambridge, Mass., 1914), 124–40; on 129, 124.
74. Bledstein, *The Culture of Professionalism,* 86–7.
75. Edwin H. Hall, "Discussion of the New Movement Among Physics Teachers," *SSM* 6 (1906): 628–31; on 628.
76. Expressions of the struggle may be found in, e.g., George H. Mead, "Science in the High-School," *SR* 14 (1906): 237–53, esp. 243, where Mead chooses sciences on the basis of their relevance to

American teachers struggled to attain had been the norm in Prussia for 100 years; in Bavaria, for 50. In the ideology of utility and social relevance, other sciences (e.g., physiography) seemed more suitable than physics in the American high school curriculum. But physics teachers did not want to leave the decision to chance, and their repeated appeal to German models (despite their denigration of measuring exercises) seems in this context to have been part of their ploy to ensure that chance alone would not rule. The triad of sciences – physics, chemistry, and biology – that dominate the secondary school curriculum today would both please and appear strange to physics teachers early in the century. What lies behind this larger struggle, especially the role of German models in it, deserves further study.

One lesson of the new movement is that there was no single or simple way in which the German model was used or viewed. In light of the multiple forms that the German model of school physics instruction took in the new movement, it seems woefully inadequate merely to say that it was molded to fit local conditions. Much more seems to have been at work, and at stake, in the interaction between two cultures of science. Americans admired and at times argued for the German model of training physics teachers, but what they understood by it amounted to an ideal abstraction that ignored the tensions that had grown within it. American physics teachers may have adapted the German model of school physics instruction, with its emphasis on precision measuring exercises, but not even the different ideological dressing that Americans gave them prevented the generation of dissonances and destabilizations that led to the new movement. The invocation of the German conception of scientific truth and the recommendation that German maps be used in American physics classes were attempts to retain a German connection in the new movement, but that connection seems to have functioned only symbolically, like the smile that remains after the Cheshire cat's body disappears. Ironically, after World War I, it was none of these German models, but rather the recognition of the importance of the tremendous advances in modern physics – in which the atom was speculated to be a source of energy – that led to the introduction, into high school physics and the training of physics teachers, of the intellectual values and the ideology associated with the German research ethic.[77]

daily life; and H. R. Linville, "The Relationship of the Sciences in the High School," *SSM* 8 (1908): 777–8.

77. Kathryn M. Olesko, "Secondary School Education in American Physics, 1870–1930," unpublished essay presented at the annual meeting of the History of Science Society, 30 December 1988, Cincinnati, Ohio.

PART THREE

German Schools in America

9

The von Mosheim Society and the Preservation of German Education and Culture in the New Republic, 1789–1813

ANTHONY GREGG ROEBER

Justus Heinrich Christian Helmuth arrived from Halle to assume pastoral responsibilities in Lancaster, Pennsylvania, in 1769. This representative of Halle pietism, who subsequently moved to Philadelphia in 1779, later succeeded Heinrich Melchior Mühlenberg as first pastor to the largest German-speaking Lutheran congregation in North America, the parish of St. Michael's and Zion. Before he arrived in America, Helmuth had already formed a commitment to education at the pietist center of Halle, where he had taken to heart the emphasis of the Franckes, father and son, for whom pedagogy lay at the heart of their pietist institution's commitment to both personal and social renewal. Between 1785 and 1818, Helmuth labored to erect a comprehensive system of German education ranging from parish elementary schooling to the von Mosheim Society, which he founded in 1789 as an adult literary society for the perpetuation of German language and culture.

Helmuth's adult educational effort, the von Mosheim Society, never extended far beyond Philadelphia, although corresponding members in New York and South Carolina did appear on the membership rolls. His plans to erect a *Gymnasium* in Philadelphia to prepare German youths for university training and for careers in the ministry and education also ended in frustration, despite temporary success with a truncated version of his plan from 1785 to 1815. Between 1811 and 1817 he founded and edited the *Evangeliches Magazin* for German speakers, regardless of denomination, urging them to educate their children in both German and English. Most of Helmuth's suggestions and efforts built upon earlier educational theories and practices imported from Halle or attempted in the charity school tradition of colonial Pennsylvania. Yet, even before his death in 1825, Helmuth and his vision of yoking classical and practical learning, pietist Lutheran doctrine, and the German language together had all been repudiated. When the city

157

of Philadelphia established its own secondary school system in 1818, it took no notice of Helmuth's plans.

Helmuth arrived in Pennsylvania, a colony with a long history of charity schools, when German-speaking Lutherans were involved in debating how best to develop a schooling program at the largest parish in North America. The successful founding of an academy at Germantown in 1761, only a few years before Helmuth's arrival, encouraged him to hope that a more elaborate system of education could be created in Philadelphia. Helmuth also took a keen interest in the work of his colleague, pastor Johann Friedrick Kunze, who was also from Halle and who successfully started a preparatory seminary in Philadelphia in 1773 that actually combined aspects of *Gymnasium* training with theological seminary work. After the Revolution, Kunze was appointed professor of classics at the new University of Pennsylvania. When Helmuth succeeded Kunze in this post, he had good reason to hope that his own plans for extending these educational efforts would reach fruition.[1]

The outbreak of the Revolution in 1776, however, interrupted both the initial efforts of Kunze and contact with Halle, where since 1763 Gotthilf August Francke had been skeptical in his response to news that an elaborate school plan was being debated in Philadelphia. To his senior missionary, Heinrich Melchior Mühlenberg, Francke wrote that if one could prepare young men in Philadelphia to become schoolmasters in the parish school, well and good. But in his opinion, plans for a more extensive system that envisioned preparation for the ministry and university training lay far in the future.

Francke's skepticism, which echoed similar negative judgments voiced by Reformed authorities against the German Reformed plans for Franklin College, did not discourage the German Lutherans of North America. Despite warnings from Halle about the need for elaborate financial support to sustain such ventures, Helmuth and his allies built upon Kunze's seminary of 1773 to expand the venture into an academy in Philadelphia that would use the parish school at St. Michael's and Zion and tie these efforts to the collegiate institution that would soon become known as the University of Pennsylvania. To elicit support for these plans, Helmuth began to write

1. See, in general, Lawrence A. Cremin, *American Education: The National Experience 1783–1876* (New York, 1980), 388–400; Samuel Edwin Weber, *The Charity School Movement in Colonial Pennsylvania* (New York, 1969, orig. pub. Philadelphia, 1905); J. P. Wickersham, *A History of Education in Pennsylvania* (New York, 1969, orig. pub. Lancaster, 1886), 143–7; Paul Monroe, *The Founding of the American Public School System: A History of Education in the United States*, 2 vols. (New York, 1940), I, 216–17, 296–303; for a full bibliography, see Jurgen Herbst, *The History of American Education* (Northbrook, Ill., 1973).

pamphlets that reveal his objectives and attitudes about creating such a system inspired by Halle's example and how he thought the public authorities of Pennsylvania should support such efforts. His initial *Gymnasium* opened in 1785, and one year later, as the legislature struggled to save the failing Dickinson College, Helmuth seized the opportunity to write a pamphlet on the wisdom of using public funds to sustain successful private educational systems such as the one he was developing at St. Michael's and Zion.[2]

Helmuth's aspirations reflected the underlying assumptions of Halle's pedagogical methods and institutions. He also built upon the Pennsylvania tradition of educating the indigent in private charity schools. Like Prussian reformers such as Wilhelm von Humboldt, he envisioned the proper kind of state supporting education but essentially allowing control of the schools to remain insulated from state interference.[3] But by the late 1780s, the general thrust of other Pennsylvanians' assumptions about education – Benjamin Rush's, for instance – lay more in the direction of Enlightenment emphases on "system," "harmony," and "mechanical" views of persons and education, all of which Helmuth sharply rejected. Deeply troubled by the French Revolution and the corrosive effects of the European Enlightenment upon the American republican experiment, Helmuth withdrew into a sectarian retreat at St. Michael's as the only hope for preserving both pietist doctrines and German-language culture. The connection to Halle, which helped to sustain financially some of Helmuth's enterprise, also alarmed him, as the effects of French rationalism became increasingly evident in this former bastion of Prussian pietism. To his dismay, indifference both to issues of doctrine and to German language and culture among his own coreligionists finally undercut his efforts decisively.

The pedagogical efforts of August Hermann Francke at Halle developed in the larger context of late-seventeenth-century educational reforms. The emphasis on practical experience and knowledge that underscored pedagogical treatises after 1648 help account for the reason why Francke's emphasis on interior experience summarized his larger preference for

---

2. For G. A. Francke's warning, see his letter to Mühlenberg, No. 291 18.02.1764, in Kurt Aland, ed., *Die Korrespondenz Heinrich Melchior Mühlenbergs: Aus der Anfangszeit des Deutschen Luthertums in Nordamerika,* vol. 3: 1763–72 (Berlin, 1991). I thank Professor Aland for providing me with the page proofs of this volume. Mühlenberg was heartened by George Whitefield's typically enthusiastic support for the educational plans, as he informed Halle on November 11, 1764 (Letter No. 355). On financial support for educational institutions from Halle's benefactors, see below.

3. See Wilhelm von Humboldt, *The Limits of State Action,* ed. with an introduction by J. W. Burrow (London, 1969); on Prussian educational practices and notions in general, see Anthony J. La Vopa, *Prussian Schoolmasters: A Profession and Office, 1763–1840* (Chapel Hill, N.C., 1980). Helmuth, although never explicitly noting the Prussian monarchy's support for Halle, which also had largely left the running of Francke's Institute autonomous, surely was aware of this relationship.

experiential knowledge. In various writings on education and the rearing of children, Francke discouraged recreation for its own sake as a waste of time and a potential occasion of sin.

Yet, despite the strict, regimented quality of training followed in Halle's *Pädagogium,* considerable time was devoted to model building, the collection of nature specimens, and discussion among the staff about how to move from more theoretical and abstract views of life to what experience could teach. The potential grimness of Francke's serious inclination may have been modified by the staff's willingness to awaken curiosity for learning in all areas of life with which students came into contact. By 1709, the theology students who worked in the *Stiftung* met regularly in the *Seminarium praeceptorum* to exchange ideas about teaching experiences. Not surprisingly, Francke reserved some of his most trenchant criticisms about society in the famous *Grosser Aufsatz* for the teaching profession.[4]

Helmuth revealed in his letters and in the diary that he assiduously kept from 1769 until the early years of the nineteenth century relatively little about his own study of pedagogy at Halle. He made it clear in his letters to Halle and in modest financial gifts he sent to his mother until her death in 1794 that he was devoted to his mother and credited her with both his religious conversion and his interest in the pastoral ministry and education. Helmuth also never forgot his older brother, who walked him partway to his departure for Halle, and the centrality of his family connections remained at the heart of his assumptions about the need for comprehensive education for all members of his parish. In one of the few letters in which he explicitly reflected upon his time at Halle, Helmuth suggested in 1800 that he attempted to perpetuate the "old Method" that previously had been common in all of Germany, namely, "to teach youth according to the simple Cathechism [*einfältige Catechismo*], and in this manner to bring them to the fear of God." The rise of the Enlightenment, in Helmuth's mind, was a "swindle" that had worked to the detriment of the common man, who had profited nothing from it and perhaps had even lost ground in both educational opportunity and social standing.[5]

4. For an overview, see Karl-Heinz Günter et al., eds., *Geschichte der Erziehung* (Berlin, 1987), 149–52; Francke's own collected ideas can be surveyed in *August Hermann Franckes Schriften über die Erziehung und Unterricht* (Berlin, 1871); Friedrich de Boor, "A. H. Franckes Hamburger Aufenthalt im Jahre 1688 als Beginn seiner Pädagogischen Wirksamkeit," and Franz Hofmann, "Zur Stellung des Pietismus in der Geschichte der pädagogischen Theorie," both in Rosemarie Ahrbeck and Burchard Thaler, eds., *August Hermann Francke 1663–1727* (Halle/Saale, 1977), 29–36, 75–85; Paulus Mensch, *Die Pädagogik A. H. Franckes* (Wuppertal, 1969).
5. Helmuth began a *Lebenslauf* in his diary for 1769; q.v. under PH 48 A 1767–69, Lutheran Theological Seminary Archives, Philadelphia. Helmuth's gifts in memory of his mother are detailed in a letter dated September 10, 1794, Archiv der Franckeschen Stiftungen, Universität Halle/Saale, 4 D3 Phi-

Helmuth's plans for schooling that built upon the parish school at St. Michael's and Zion in Philadelphia were put into effect almost as soon as he reached that city in 1779. As early as December 1781, he reported to Halle that "our schools, especially the German-Latin School blooms." For Helmuth, the decision of the new State of Pennsylvania to charter and incorporate the University of Pennsylvania upon the foundations of the old prerevolutiony college seemed to promise a connection between his parish-level work and an advantageous berth in the new state-supported institution. His vision of an elementary parish education followed by a *Gymnasium*-style classical academy that would prepare students to become pastors or teachers would then be topped by admission to the university, where his colleague Johann Kunze was named professor of a classics department to be taught in German.[6]

Helmuth was especially pleased to note that the German Society of Pennsylvania had voted, beginning in 1780, to provide scholarship funds for promising young men to pursue advanced study at the university, provided that they had the recommendation of pastors like Helmuth. Based upon these events, and noting that the interest in his schooling plans apparently enjoyed broad support in Philadelphia, Helmuth now proposed to enlist the new state's aid in a decisive manner to support already existing private education that had historically functioned primarily for poorer children.

In 1786, Helmuth wrote in detail about his vision of combining German methods of education with traditional Pennsylvania state support for charity schools whose purpose would be to provide education for poorer students. The reason for these essays can be found in the decision of the Pennsylvania Assembly in that year to attempt to realize the obligation set down in the Constitution of 1776 to provide for common schooling. The same notion, repeated in the Constitution of 1790, obligated the state to provide "for the establishment of schools throughout the state in such manner that the poor may be taught *gratis*."

After granting the charter to the University of Pennsylvania in 1779, however, the assembly's next action was to provide immediate relief for failing Dickinson College in 1786. In the relief statute, the state specified that 60,000 acres were to be set aside for endowing public schools in each county. Despite further recommendations six years later that a county-level

---

ladelphische Schriftwechsel, 1791–6; for his letter to Halle referred to earlier, see 4 D 5, Schriftwechsel, 1800–4, Helmuth to G. C. Knapp, July 28, 1800, 24–6.

6. AfSt 4 C 20, December 28, 1781, 11–13; on the vexed history of the new university and the impact upon the German speakers, see Edward Potts Cheyney, *History of the University of Pennsylvania, 1740–1940* (Philadelphia, 1940), 132–3, 145–83.

tax should also be imposed to support secondary schools, nothing was done. Helmuth had good reason to be optimistic, given Pennsylvania's attitude toward private charity schools, that his time had come. Kunze's seminary, begun in 1773, had closed with the Revolution and is not mentioned again after 1785 in the reports of the Pennsylvania Ministerium's deliberations. The field was open, therefore, in 1786 for Helmuth to build upon the primary education already available at St. Michael's and Zion, which also since 1780 had expanded into a German-Latin school that provided at least some elements of the *Gymnasium* emphasis upon classical learning. In this respect, Helmuth's plans closely resembled the colonial British pattern of English grammar schools; the Latin grammar schools for boys that emphasized Latin, Greek, history, and mathematics; and the academies that mixed some of both of the first two types but functioned sometimes as boarding schools as well.

Helmuth's essays built upon a memorandum he sent to Halle in October 1784. In his argument, he pointed out that a third of Pennsylvania's inhabitants were Germans, were equal members of society, and were entitled by their participation in the Revolution to education. Arguing for the continued privilege of sending his academy students to the university, he pointed out that schoolmasters and pastors could hardly be gotten from Germany "on Account of the great Alteration taking Place with respect to toleration in the Dominions of Several Roman Catholic Princes." The Germans in America ought "to receive their Instruction through the medium of their own Language, ell's [sic] they never can convey their Ideas to others in the Same in a clear manner, as another Language, which has been made use of by them in their Studies, wil allways be predominant and make them very poor in Expression and deficient in Pronunciation." Pointing out that six German boys "of a lively Genius" were being supported gratis at his academy, he noted that another six were soon to arrive. Surely, he argued, the Germans had made good use of the public funds already made available to them (£300) for educating German speakers at the university. Faced with a faltering economy, however, the state began to debate whether the funds should be redistributed among the English-speaking majority. Against this, Helmuth argued that German speakers made "destitute of any Instruction whatsoever will be very unusefull and troublesome Members of Society, yea easily turn Heathens or Indians, if not prevented one Way or another by Assisting them, in providing young Men in this Institution, that will be able to instruct them."[7]

Helmuth never abandoned this unsubtle threat of potential social disorder

7. AfSt 4 C 20, October 6, 1784.

among German speakers bereft of the civilizing effects of education. His own perceptions of the country folk in Lancaster, where he had served, had done nothing to encourage him in the belief that, left to their own devices, the common people of North America would improve their lot. Instead, he feared that the barbarization that always lurked just beyond the bounds of transplanted European institutional life would inevitably spill over into society at large. Delighted at the decision of the Assembly in 1786 to guarantee Germans continued participation in the University of Pennsylvania, Helmuth noted that society at large remained godless, because "the sorrowful war has let loose frightful disorders and made for breaches that can hardly be healed."[8]

In an undated pamphlet, the "Colloquium of two friends concerning the blessings of a good education," Helmuth again encouraged parents to send their children to school, warning that false economy and tight-fistedness would rob rural German speakers of any future. The rural son, Peter, sorrowfully reflects that he has no chance to go to Philadelphia, for he is poor and his father sees no profit in educating a son in such a fashion. The luckier and wealthier student convinces his father to convert the student's inheritance to tuition for his hapless friend. What, he asks rhetorically, will it help me to have many horses and cows if I remain as stupid as they are? Both set off for the school in Philadelphia, quoting the father's proverb, *"Wer etwas weiss, den hält man wehrt, des eigenständen Niemand begehrt."* Should anyone in city or country miss the point, Helmuth concluded that no better inheritance could be given children than providing them with an education.[9]

In this same year, Helmuth composed an essay that further revealed his long-range plans for combining the perpetuation of German language and culture with support for educating poorer Germans in Pennsylvania. Helmuth based his essay "Humble Suggestions of a Plan How Religious Schools Might Be Established" upon the experience of St. Michael and Zion parish, as well as upon his own conviction that Philadelphia was the only possible location for a systematic development of education modeled on German pietist conceptions.[10]

---

8. Ibid., Helmuth to Halle, January 24, 1786, No. 60, 251–2.
9. Lutheran Theological Seminary Archives, PH 48 Z 20. For the identical sentiment, see George Lochman's "Fragen eines Lehrers an seine Gemein-Glieder" (Lancaster, Pa., 1802): "Bekümmern wir uns aber wenig um ihre Erziehung, lassen wir sie in der Unwissenheit, in der Dummheit, in der Zügellosigkeit aufwachsen . . . Schicket eure Kinder fleissig in die Schule, damit sie in denen nöthigen Wissenschaften Unterricht bekommen. Gewis, liebe Eltern, wir können unsern Kindern kein besseres Vermögen geben, als eine gute Erziehung" (PL 82 H).
10. Lutheran Theological Seminary Archives X/16; both texts are handwritten and apparently were never published, but they may have circulated privately among Helmuth's acquaintances and allies in Philadelphia.

In the "Humble Suggestions," Helmuth advocated a general tax to be levied in favor of schools founded by any religious society or "any number of People that freely associate for this purpose," namely, to achieve the constitutionally mandated goal that "poor Children may be taught *gratis.*" Incorporated trustees, such as those enjoyed by St. Michael and Zion since 1762, should be chosen to select teachers, and superintendents chosen by the inhabitants of the county or township would give warrants to the trustees for their share of the tax monies in proportion to the number of students and the percentage of the bounty lands of the state that the locality was entitled to use. Funds collected were to be distributed in proportion to the numbers in each society, and the superintendents were to ensure that poor children were cared for and provided with skills in reading, writing, arithmatic, orthography, and religious principles. The yearly examination of the children by the superintendents completed Helmuth's view of the governance of such schools. Should surplus funds exist in a given society for a year, books were to be purchased or "Cloathing for the poor Children" to be distributed on examination day as a premium "for good behaviour and Diligence." Those societies not deserving of a dividend or not calling for it would see such funds given by the state "to the use of the poor in general." Alternatively, Helmuth thought that half of the bounty lands offered by the state could be used by schools already established in proportion to the number of poor children taught gratis, the other half to go toward erecting schools for the poor where there were none.

Apparently not content with the statutory provision setting aside 60,000 acres, Helmuth urged adding 40,000 more, then dividing the total by each religious society in proportion to the number of poor children already being educated free, with 50 acres for each child. Since the Lutherans already had such a system in operation in Philadelphia and elsewhere, he suggested using them as a test case. It was better, he concluded, to do this than to give land to various counties, since in the more remote places "this Land will lay dead and useless . . . for a long time."

In 1789, three years after these reflections were set down, Helmuth reported his enormous gratification that the Pennsylvania assembly had voted a grant in the amount of 5,000 acres to establish a free school for poor Lutheran boys in addition to a grant in 1787 that provided for a "German College and Charity School" to be open to both sexes and all denominations.[11]

---

11. *Statutes at Large of Pennsylvania, 1682–1809* (Harrisburg, Pa., 1898–1915), XIII, 182–4; the evolution of Franklin Academy into Franklin College corresponded to the closure of the German

Ironically, as Franklin College in Lancaster opened, Helmuth's difficulties in centering activities at Philadelphia deepened. He did not favor the dissipation of German-language efforts to the back country town in the midst of uninterested Palatines and Württem-bergers. He and his colleague, Schmidt, sent a letter to Halle on October 8, 1789, reporting that even German students "now have so much English pride, that none wishes to be a German preacher, and therefore the number of students has shrunk from 600 to 300, because they cannot learn in the German school what they need. They go to the English schools, forget their German, and become strangers to the church." The hopes that had been placed in the university were partly dashed by the constant infighting between the old trustees of the College of Philadelphia and the new university, which had favored the Germans with various privileges confirmed since 1785 by the assembly. But now, "we regard it as most necessary, if German Lutheranism in Pennsylvania, and especially in Philadelphia, is not to die out within a few years, that a German School Center be established in which young people receive the necessary instruction in order to be useful in the life of our church and schools." Only Philadelphia could support such an effort, Helmuth and Schmidt reported, despite the foundation of the college at Lancaster. It was not only the lack of children that would doom Lancaster, Helmuth thought, but "the attitude [*Gemüthart*] of country people, who give not the slightest thought to such affairs." The Halle fathers received similar gloomy messages from Heinrich Mühlenberg, who wrote to Sebastian Andreas Fabricius in December of the same year. His hopes for the Franklin College were high, but here, events were "as everywhere in America where the rich allow their children to become lawyers or doctors or something else, but not preachers . . . and the middling or poor send a promising youth here, but cannot bear the costs although the tuition in Lancaster is lower than anywhere else."[12]

In this context, one appreciates all the more the decision of Helmuth in 1789 to found the von Mosheim Society, the Philadelphia-centered adult literary society that was intended to be the capstone of his efforts to provide a systematic educational program from elementary school to adulthood in which German culture and language could be directed under the auspices of Halle-inspired Lutheran teachers and and pastors.

Helmuth's decision to found a society dedicated to the memory of Jo-

---

classical department at Penn, where Helmuth's hopes for funneling his students from the German Latin academy had not worked out.
12. AfSt 4 D 2, Helmuth and Schmidt to Halle, October 8, 1789, 77–83; Mühlenberg to Fabricius, December 14, 1789, 59–60.

hann Lorenz von Mosheim, the preeminent Protestant church historian of the eighteenth century, was based upon years of admiration for this man. Halle's missionaries had used various parts of von Mosheim's essays and his massive *Institutiones historiae ecclesiasticae* in their North American libraries, and Helmuth himself owned a copy of von Mosheim's treatise, ordered from Halle. As the first chancellor of the university at Göttingen, von Mosheim represented a more orthodox strain of Lutheran theology than that reputed to be taught at Halle. But the former professor from Helmstedt was nonetheless highly regarded by pietist missionaries, perhaps because of his historical perspective that traced the degeneration of the early apostolic church not only to Rome, but also to the further excesses of free church radicals and the Reformed tradition after the Reformation. As a preeminent educator and church historian, von Mosheim must have appealed to Helmuth as the exemplar of an orthodox but learned writer possessed of an elegant prose style in both German and Latin.[13] Yet in none of his letters to Halle did Helmuth discuss the founding of this society, and even in his diary entries, he only obliquely referred to the organization's founding in the fall of 1789. In the entry for August 28, 1789, Helmuth recorded his "Considerations for ensuring the maintenance of the German language in Philadelphia or Pennsylvania." The first and primary point was his concern that the future of the Lutheran faith depended upon the maintenance of German, lest the coming generation lose all contact with the religion of their fathers. Second, however, Helmuth noted that God had blessed the Germans richly over the past thirty to forty years, especially in Philadelphia's churches and schools. But in secular life as well (*im bürgerlichen Leben*), if one passed through the richest houses and most flourishing shops and businesses of Philadelphia and asked to whom they belonged, one would have to answer that, to an astonishing degree, they were in the hands of the formerly poor Germans who had arrived but a short time before. The answer to the riddle lay "in the German mode of living and mores" (*Lebensart und Sitte*). But what would become of this people in the future? Helmuth asked. The new generation, increasingly estranged from their language, style, and tradition of hard work, would raise their children "after the English fashion and in the English language." It was clear enough to Helmuth that Germans not only in Philadelphia but in Pennsylvania were better off remaining Germans and not trying to make themselves into poor copies of the English.[14]

---

13. For further details, see Roeber, "Citizens or Subjects? German-Lutherans and the Federal Constitution in Pennsylvania, 1789–1800," *Amerikastudien/American Studies* 34 (1989), 49–68.
14. Helmuth Diaries, Lutheran Theological Seminary Archives, K. 1.3, June–December 1789.

Yet, neither here nor elsewhere in his diaries did Helmuth discuss the von Mosheim Society at length. The surviving yearly orations held before the Society also betrayed little about the history of the group, although the rules make clear how Helmuth intended to prevent gradual anglicization from taking over this group, as he feared had already happened to the German Society of Pennsylvania, with which he increasingly now came into conflict, especially in the person of his own parishioner, Friedrich Augustus Mühlenberg.

The rules published for the von Mosheim Society in Germantown in 1791 stipulated that the members were obligated to bring every four weeks a written work in German, although exceptions were allowed for interested members without a sufficient foundation in the language. The society met weekly, with one-half of the membership constituting a quorum, and discussions were allowed only in German, although the president could also make exceptions to this rule. Discussions and disagreements that took place *within the society* were strictly forbidden to be revealed to outsiders, and two-thirds of the membership had to agree to expulsion for breaking these rules. Prospective members could only be suggested by the membership and voted into office by the membership, upon which three shillings and nine pence paid for initial membership, after which the "sixteenth part of a dollar" was to be paid monthly.[15]

The membership lists of the society seem not to have survived, although Wilhelm Händel in New York and Friedrich Schubert in Georgia were corresponding members in the first years of the society's existence. Certainly not only Helmuth, but also his promising student Christian Endress, who later delivered one of the yearly addresses, were members, as was the physician Benjamin Schultz, who delivered the annual address in 1795. Almost certainly, the core membership came from among Helmuth's friends and parishioners at St. Michael's and Zion. That Helmuth intended this society to take an active interest not only in adult debates but also in preparing appropriate literature for German-speaking children is obvious from surviving contextual evidence. And in this respect the society seems to have been in competition with the older German Society of Pennsylvania, of which Helmuth was also a member, though increasingly an unpopular one.

Within a short time of the von Mosheim Society's founding, Helmuth received a letter from a woman of his parish who complained that insufficient attention was being devoted to providing suitable literature for

---

15. *Regierungsverfassung der Mosheimischen Gesellschaft in Philadelphia* (Germantown, Pa., 1791); incomplete copy, Lutheran Theological Seminary Archives, Gettysburg, Pa.

German-speaking children, especially young women. English-speaking girls, "Maria" argued, enjoyed enormous advantages since, from their earliest childhood, books were provided them, whereas German girls languished. Could not the pastor provide something better than the common foolish tales circulating among the Germans in Pennsylvania? "What is planted in childhood, fool of nonsense or error is not easily rooted out later; such books that are about nothing other than the holy Genovea and Welusina and many others wholly unworthy of being committed to memory ought to be completely rooted out." This parishioner suggested that "innocent stories are no sin when they bring children to a correct understanding of religion and virtue." Surely, she hoped, the pastor would respond to her plea.[16]

The continued connection between the von Mosheim Society and exemplary literature for children (the *Erbauungsliteratur* dear to pietists) continued at least into the early nineteenth century.[17] In 1808, the society underwrote the costs of a book for children as an example for other interested people outside Philadelphia. The moral tales of children dutiful to parents and attentive in German-language church services, historical explanations of who Luther was, and an *"Amerikanisch Deutsches Lied"* were supplemented by woodcuts provided by English-language printers. Lacking historically accurate scenes, the printers bestowed empire-style clothing on Luther and his mother, and the holy Salomé emerged as a swooning, sorrowful Greek maiden seated under a bower-covered arch. The heavy-handed moralism of little Louise dying a holy death at age three illustrates the mixture of didacticism and sentimentality that were the hallmarks of the pietist movement, which now fit rather easily into the growing cult of sentimentality in early republican letters. The iconography of a ladder composed of baptism and the Lord's Supper and the rungs consisting of God's promises marked the unmistakably Lutheran character of the booklet.[18]

---

16. Lutheran Theological Seminary Archives, Helmuth Correspondence, PH 48 E 7, February 25, 1790. The letter is semianonymous, intentionally as the woman indicates, out of fear of offending Helmuth by the boldness of her suggestions from one of his former confirmands in the parish. On the tales of St. Genoveva, the most popular and widely distributed piece of literature among Pennsylvania Germans (and still in print today), see Roeber, " 'The Origin of Whatever is not English among Us': The Dutch-speaking and German-speaking peoples of Colonial British America," in Bernard Bailyn and Philip D. Morgan, eds., *Strangers Within the Realm: Cultural Margins of the First British Empire* (Chapel Hill, N.C., 1991), 220–83.

17. See Hartmuth Lehmann, *Pietismus und Weltordung in Württemberg* (Göttingen, 1969).

18. *Unterhaltungen für deutsche Kinder* (Philadelphia, 1808), Library Company of Philadelphia Am 1808 Unt [published by Conrad Zentler in Second Street, near the corner of Race]. For samples of the broader literature of the day, see Gordon S. Wood, ed., *The Rising Glory of America, 1760–1820* (Boston, 1974); Cathy N. Davidson, *Revolution and the Word: The Rise of the Novel in America* (New York, 1986), 125–40, 254–62.

Identical sentiments and didactic moralism shaped the 1805 poem composed for the society by an unknown author. In this heroic composition, reminiscences on youth and childhood open a praise of God's blessings, followed by the "Thoughts of the Mosheim Society concerning the Good Fortune of the Germans in America who yet understand German." The Germans in America stand in the train of Luther, Johannes Arndt, the pietist fathers Spener and Francke, and Mosheim, "himself a light unto the British" to be proud of, and yet a heavy responsibility for Germans never to betray. Only where "German blooms in church and school/ taste we the purest air" of free America. Arndt, Franke, Spener, and Paulus Gerhard, whose poetry graced the most favored hymns of German Lutherans in North America, are all remembered in heroic verse. Finally, however, this literary effort ends by shrinking from the day when such great figures will be silent and speak to younger generations no longer, or about the Savior. "No! the loss would be too great for us; we will learn German and German will preserve us a great people."[19]

Despite these auspicious offerings, Helmuth's plans for Philadelphia as the center for a comprehensive educational system were undercut by various events in the 1790s. Even as he constructed his comprehensive system, in 1792 a group of Philadelphians led by Albert Gallatin founded the Society for the Establishment of Sunday-schools, intended to provide both secular and religious training for poor boys who worked during the week. Although it was unsuccessful, in late 1794 a committee of the House of Representatives began work on how to establish free schools throughout the state through academies – precisely the plan Helmuth had pioneered at St. Michael's and Zion for years. Despite support, the bill died in committee in 1795, perhaps leading to Helmuth's decision to write his essay on the *Einrichtung der Schulen in der Deutschen Lutherischen Gemeine in und bey der Stadt Philadelphia.*[20]

The internal debates among German speakers about the wisdom of perpetuating the language now reached a new height. In 1793 Northern Lib-

---

19. *Aufmunterung zur gemeinschaftlichen Erbauung. Abgesungen für die Mosheimische Gesellschaft; Gedanken der Mosheimsichen Gesellschaft über das Glück der Deutschen in Amerika, welche noch Deutsch verstehen wollen;* both bound together and published (Philadelphia? 1805); State Library of Pennsylvania, Harrisburg. Helmuth had decided by 1806 to found his *Geistliches Magazin für unsre deutsche Kinder,* perhaps recognizing that the Von Mosheim Society's numbers and resources were too small to sustain the task of publishing for children. See his letters of July 31 and August 14, 1806, to pastor Jacob Goering of Yorktown, Lutheran Theological Seminary Archives, PH 48/D1.

20. Wickersham, *History of Education in Pennsylvania,* 255–63; Helmuth's essay is in the Lutheran Theological Seminary Archives, H 10 P5 M 6 1796.1. On Lutheran responses to the general trend toward religious education via the Sunday school, see R. H. Thurau, "A Study of the Lutheran Sunday School in America to 1865," Ph.D. diss., University of Pittsburgh, 1946.

erties Lutherans asked for a new school to serve their part of the city. Helmuth's diary entries and the vestry minutes reveal that he led an intense battle against the anglicizing forces marshaled behind Friedrich August Mühlenberg, who opposed extending schools whose major purpose was to preserve the German language. Barely able to contain his anger, Helmuth recorded in May 1793, after a heated exchange in the vestry, that Mühlenberg predicted that German must eventually vanish, to which the pastor retorted that "admittedly little by little it can be proposed that as one wishes to push along the idea that it ought to vanish," the language surely would.[21] Mühlenberg and his adherents, David Saeckel and other elders, became more deeply committed to the Democratic-Republican Club in Philadelphia and alienated from the staunch Federalism of Helmuth, Endress, and other von Mosheim members. Undoubtedly, as well, Helmuth's plans and hopes for his system were deeply disrupted by the outbreak of yellow fever in Philadelphia in 1793, in which the pastor's heroic reputation was secured both by his essay on the disease and by the public acclaim he won for ministering to its victims.[22]

By the time the epidemic passed and Helmuth turned to the issue of schooling again, the German Lutherans possessed three schoolhouses, one of which was a boys' school in Cherry Street, where the first class was taught the alphabet, something from the Catechism and Psalter, sayings, and the beginning of writing in German. The second class was divided into Old Testament and New Testament groups, and more elaborate Bible lessons and scholastic tasks were done in German, but with each class receiving English instruction every other week. A school for girls that may have sprung from Helmuth's receipt of the 1790 letter was established separately in the house on Fourth Street near Zion, where girls learned basic spelling, reading, arithmetic, the Catechism, and German and English writing lessons. This school too had an English class where reading, spelling, and knitting were taught in English. The Camptown school was just beginning as Helmuth wrote, and few details were provided about its functioning. For all schools, however, the same rule held: poor children unable to pay tuition

---

21. Helmuth Diary entry April 1793 (n.d.), K.1.19, Lutheran Theological Seminary Archives. For earlier conflicts in the German Society, see also December 15, 1790 (K.1.7); for confrontation in the vestry, see January 6, 1791 (K.1. 8).

22. Helmuth published his essay both in German and in English, and his colleague Schmidt reported to Halle its success; see Johann Friedrich Schmidt to Halle, September 3, 1793, on the outbreak of yellow fever and the death of his own wife, as well as on Helmuth's heroic labors, AFSt 4 D 3 No. 45, p. 45; Helmuth, *A Short Account of the Yellow Fever in Philadelphia for the Reflecting Christian* (Philadelphia, 1794); on the epidemic, see John Harvey Powell, *Bring Out Your Dead: The Great Plague of Yellow Fever in Philadelphia in 1793* (Philadelphia, 1949); for details on the political strife within the German-speaking community in Philadelphia, see Roeber, "Citizens or Subjects."

were to be instructed free, with parents and children reporting to the school committee to examine their financial affairs and provide the children with an admission slip as scholarship students, to be renewed each year.

In his "Reflections concerning the School Bill," written in response to the law debated in 1795–6, Helmuth managed to combine his own pietist convictions with some of the predispositions he must have known occupied the minds of more secular proponents of education like Benjamin Rush. Beginning with the opinion that "civil Government without Religion is like a Fabric without any foundation, and will soon vanish away," Helmuth opined that "The Religion of the Bible is doubtless the most rational of all other Religions that are know [sic] of." Arguing that since members of both houses of the Pennsylvania assembly were in some way connected to scriptural religion, the principles of religion that would promote "the true Happiness" of the republic ought to be encouraged in youth. Citing the "natural Connection between Religion and a School," Helmuth pointed to "The Germans in the old country and here, not only in the City but likewise in the country who unite both together and cannot do otherwise as long as they intend to see their future Generations prosper as religious Generations." If Pennsylvanians wanted an example, Helmuth pointed to New England, "the Eastern States," where the "happy Effects this sort of Education has had . . . is [sic] obvious to every thinking mind." Knowing, as he did, that Timothy Pickering of Luzerne County, the transplanted Massachusetts Federalist, had been the leading advocate of such schools, Helmuth seems to have reasoned that Pickering and his friends could carry the argument before the legislature seeking to carry out the provisions of the conservative constitution of 1790.

Pennsylvania's already flourishing religious schools, whether Quaker or German, Helmuth stated, ought to provide the legislature with the model needed. The provision under the First Amendment of the new national Constitution forbidding the state to "meddle itself with religion" could not possibly be construed by "any serious thinking person, that they only could mean, they would or could not meddle with opinions and principles of the different religious Denonimations to encourage the one more as the other much less could it ever have been expected that under such a Constitution a Bill should be framed by which an indirect Tax would be laid on religious Opinion." Firmly opposed to a general assessment, Helmuth insisted that schools should be supported as they had been in the past, each "look'd upon as a Congregational, religious property." The Pennsylvania legislature now had the chance, Helmuth wrote, "to wipe off that Imputation as if all free Republican Governments in our times by their Nature must pave the

Way to Irreligion and that therefore can be no permanency in them."
Rather, religion and a republican government could coexist exactly when
a government gave "full Scope to liberty of Opinion and religious principle." The worst development of all would be an interpretation of the legislature's actions as meaning that "Religion . . . [is] a thing that had nothing
to do with the Education of Youth; and this to appear at the height of
infidelity in our present times must necessarily darken the prospect with
regard to the happyness of future Generations in our western hemisphere."

Helmuth identified ignorance, not differences of opinion in religion, as
the enemy of the republic. If the legislators were to take a "bold, but manly
and Virtuous Step," they would become the "warm Patrons of Religion,"
making America a citadel against the "dark and destroying power of Infidelity – Hundreds of virtuous families would be induced on that account
to transmigrate to this blessed Spot of the Globe, where Religion free and
unfetter'd should sway its enlivening Scepter."[23]

Helmuth's dogged insistence on tying the future of the German language
firmly to his own religious convictions and Halle's traditions of education
doomed his impressive work. To be sure, he could report to Halle in 1797
that the schools were flourishing – 185 children in the Philadelphia and
Camptown schools. As late as 1810, the Episcopalians had established only
one free school for boys and another for girls; the Reformed congregation
and the Catholics two; and the Presbyterians one. The Lutherans ran six
schools in the city. But the tide was slowly turning to a broader, secularized,
and anglicized preference in education with which Helmuth could not
agree. In 1799 the Philadelphia Society for the Establishment and Support
of Charity Schools opened as a night school for poor children. Ironically,
they obtained $13,000 from the bequest of Helmuth's deceased parishioner,
Christopher Ludwig, the former baker for the revolutionary army. The
bequest establishing free education for poor children contained the fatal
proviso that this was to be provided without regard to nationality, race, or
religious persuasion, thus effectively preventing Helmuth from using the
bequest for his own schooling system.[24]

By the early nineteenth century, Halle also was in decline, finally closed
in the dissolution of the Holy Roman Empire in 1806. Halle's mission
account for the Pennsylvania mission field never recovered from the effects
of the Revolution, and for the years between the Revolution and 1806 it

23. Lutheran Theological Seminary Archives, X/16 (1796).
24. Helmuth to Halle, February 8, 1797, AFSt, 4D4, No. 71, 31; see also Wickersham, *History of
    Education in Pennsylvania,* 279–82.

actually ran at a deficit of 50 to 100 Reichstaler. Interest from two bequests, the Streit and the Solms-Rödelsheim legacies, also did not return the amount for schooling that was intended.[25] Support for Helmuth's system therefore had to come from within the German-speaking community of Pennsylvania, especially Philadelphia. By 1806, however, a group of younger German Lutherans led by former general Peter Mühlenberg, restive under their sixty-one-year-old pastor's insistence upon the use of German in worship and in the Pennsylvania Ministerium's business, organized Saint John's Church as an English-speaking Lutheran congregation.

Helmuth's predecessor as German professor at the University of Pennsylvania, Kunze, had perhaps divined earlier than his successor the doomed quality of the enterprise. In a depressed letter to his brother in Germany, and in a similar report to Halle from New York, Kunze favored turning their efforts toward Indian missions. But German, he concluded, could only die out. "There is not much fruit here from the preaching office, although a little. What hinders it is that the people here are completely English, the coming generation understand no German and no new Germans are arriving here." The founder of the 1773 seminary repeated even more bitterly in 1796 to his brother the fact that the preaching office was held in contempt in New York; the role of a learned German clergyman was impossible to fulfill in such surroundings.[26]

Perhaps Helmuth's dogged insistence upon Lutheran pietist doctrine and his determination to preserve German even as Pennsylvania and American society at large turned to ever more anglicized and dogmatically indifferent notions of civic religion explain adequately how completely his work has been forgotten. But perhaps, too, his methods of pedagogy suffered atrophy as the years went on. Reputedly a spellbinding preacher in both English and German, Helmuth also had enjoyed considerable success in his pastoral years in Lancaster and Philadelphia among younger people. As he grew older, however, there is some evidence that he fell back on a rote use of drilling students in the Catechism and in German even when it was obvious that they were not understanding the content of what he wished them to

25. The financial arrangements are exceedingly complex and too involved to follow here. I trace some of these developments in *Palatines, Liberty, and Property* (Baltimore, 1993); ironically, because of the closure of Halle in 1806, the Solms-Rödelsheim legacy continued to accrue interest, and between 1818 and 1825 was used by the Philadelphia congregation, contributing yearly about $270 for St. Michael's and Zion on an invested capital that in 1825 was still worth $22,133.45. See AFSf 4F3, Correspondenz zweischen dem Herrn Dr. Helmuth . . . das Solms Roedelsheimschen Legats betreffend.

26. AFSt. 4 D 2, Johann Christoph Kunze to Halle, October 27, 1789, 71–6; and 4D3 No. 11, July 18, 1796, to Johann Carl Kunze in Langenwezendorf near Nürnberg.

learn. Despite similarities between Halle's own methods and the Lancastrian schooling that had become the rage in North America by the 1790s, Helmuth's rigidity may have helped to undermine his own system.

At least his enemies in the parishes of St. Michael's and Zion thought so. A report entered into the protocols of the vestry on August 12, 1820, after Helmuth had been unceremoniously and cruelly retired as senior pastor, reviewed the calamities. Admitting that the Francke Academy recently founded to replace Helmuth's old Latin-German academy was doing well, the elders blamed Helmuth. "If twenty or more years ago more thought had been given to the establishment of schools in which the German language was taught and spoken, there would not now be so many justifiable complaints. The blame for this neglect lies mostly with the pastors and teachers. Too much emphasis was always laid on religious instruction. It was thought sufficient to have children learn to read, write and memorize a few verses, but too little attention was paid to their understanding what they had learned and thus they soon forgot what they had never understood."[27]

Yet, in their criticism, the lay leaders conveniently forgot to mention that they had never comprehended Helmuth's plans for a total system that included the von Mosheim Society and reached down through the university to the academy and the parish schools. Not only Helmuth, but also Schmidt, Kunze, Mühlenberg as president of Franklin College, and other clerics and teachers, identified the tightfistedness and lack of vision among the Pennsylvania German laity as a primary cause of the schools' ongoing problems. Perhaps the aging Gotthilf August Francke had been right in warning Mühlenberg in 1764 against making great plans for an elaborate schooling system. Halle had built up enormous privileges and monopolies upon which to base its worldwide missionary education plans. Francke and the other Halle fathers knew, perhaps even more than their enthusiastic American sons, what it would take to run such establishments. Helmuth's vision, inspired by Halle, did not receive enough financial support in Pennsylvania, nor was the goal of perpetuating German language and culture through pietist experiential pedagogy and classical learning honored by his parishioners. Not only the farmers of the countryside, but also the artisans and humble members of St. Michael's and Zion, never comprehended how

27. Protokolle des Kirchenrats . . . (St. Michael's and Zion Congregation Vestry Minutes), Lutheran Theological Seminary Archives, Vol. II, August 12, 1820; for further details of Helmuth's difficulties, see also Carl F. Haussmann, *A History of St. Michael's and Zion Congregation* typescript, 1949, H 10 P5 M 6 L2.

such a system of learning might serve them well, both economically and socially. They were hardly alone in this, for the tendency toward practical knowledge and a narrow professionalism characterized most of American education during this period.[28]

It was Helmuth's misfortune to see his ideals of pietist-classical educational goals stigmatized as elitist Federalist politics and his reverence for the German language as un-American. Yet his project's frustration may have stemmed more from an unresolved internal tension symbolized by the choice of von Mosheim as the patron of his society. Already in the eighteenth century, von Mosheim had achieved a reputation as an orthodox but rational scholar of the early Enlightenment. By choosing von Mosheim over more deeply pietist or orthodox Lutheran divines, perhaps Helmuth meant to appeal to others sympathetic to his overall social and pedagogical goals, to whom von Mosheim, "a light even unto the British," was well known. Yet, perhaps Helmuth's rather idealistic desire to see state aid for education shorn of actual state control of educational institutions also reflected an unresolved set of tensions about how religion and national interests should be related – a tension existing not only in him, but in Prussian reformers like Wilhelm von Humboldt as well. In this, as in many other dimensions, there seemed to have been a truly transatlantic dimension to Helmuth's educational theories and goals.

Like so many of the Federalists who remained convinced of the value of a classical world rapidly vanishing, Helmuth and his view of educational objectives were repudiated at the polls in 1800. Forbidding his congregation to pray for the infidel Jefferson, Helmuth had consoled himself by publishing a lament for the departed Washington. His efforts to tie classical education and pietist Lutheran doctrine to the German language continued for another decade, in the face of growing indifference or hostility. Only in the 1820s, after Helmuth's death, did the rediscovery of orthodoxy among Lutherans on both continents lead to an appreciation of theological and pedagogical rigor.[29] And by the 1830s, the State of Pennsylvania finally responded to the constitutional mandate of 1790 to provide education for the children of the poor *gratis*. That neither Lutheran historians nor the standard writers on American education know of J. H. C. Helmuth and his

28. See, for example, Burton J. Bledstein, *The Culture of Professionalism* (New York, 1977).
29. See Clifford E. Nelson, *The Lutherans in North America* (Philadelphia, 1975), 83–101; also Walter Conser, *Church and Confessions: Conservative Theologians in Germany, England, and America, 1815–1866* (Macon, Ga., 1984). Additionally, one might point to the belated work of the Pennsylvania German Society in collecting a particularly impressive library in the nineteenth century as an indirect outcome of the purpose, if not the accomplishment, of the von Mosheim Society.

educational mission testifies to the ongoing force of a democratizing revolution in cultural standards of which he did not approve and whose triumph guaranteed his obscurity.[30]

Helmuth, like many European-trained clergy of his day, remained convinced of both the dangers of infidelity represented by the French Revolution, and the inappropriateness of the new evangelicalism and its measures that he identified with the Methodists and Baptists. Caught between the distasteful choices of allying himself and his tradition with the latter or battling the former alone, Helmuth sought for most of his life to carry out his educational and pastoral objectives solely within a pietist Lutheran context. By the time he founded the *Evangelisches Magazin* in 1811, enlisting Reformed and Moravian support for his efforts, the egalitarian rhetoric and practices in American religious and educational culture had already undercut his systematic approach to education within a confessional context. And when Philadelphia in 1818 adopted its own plans for secondary education, Helmuth's vision of state cooperation with various private religious societies was also swept away.

On the other hand, the conviction that religious education in both practical and classical learning, carried on under private auspices, might continue to benefit the republic was a notion that survived the sea change Helmuth himself barely comprehended. Despite the seeming irrelevance of German language instruction, the preference of most Americans for local control that translated practically into some version of unofficial Protestant establishment control over schools and curriculum continued for another century.

---

30. The eclipse of the classical world envisioned by many of the revolutionary generation continues to be debated among scholars; for the formulation, see Gordon S. Wood, *The Creation of the American Republic, 1776–1789* (Chapel Hill, N.C., 1969), and again in his introduction to *The Rising Glory of America, 1760–1820* (New York, 1971), 1–22; on education, 154–74.

10

The German-English Academy, the National German-American Teachers' Seminary, and the Public School System in Milwaukee, Wisconsin, 1851–1919

BETTINA GOLDBERG*

On May 21, 1901, a number of prominent Milwaukee citizens and school officials met in the hall of the Milwaukee Turner Society to celebrate the fiftieth anniversary of the German-English Academy, a German-American private associational school for boys and girls. The representative of the Milwaukee public school system, German-born Superintendent Siefert, used the occasion to pay tribute to "the many benefits" the city's public schools had received and were still receiving, "directly and indirectly," from the German-English Academy, as well as from the National German-American Teachers' Seminary, which had been affiliated with the Academy since its founding in 1878. "The German English Academy had a mission to perform," Siefert continued, "and it has performed it well." The dissemination of "rational methods of teaching," the establishment of "our magnificent Museum," and "the early introduction . . . of the Kindergarten system . . . [are] largely due to the influence of the German English Academy." Referring to the Academy's bilingual character, already emphasized in its name, and to the prominent professional positions held by many of its former students, Siefert added: "[T]hrough it [the Academy] was demonstrated the possibility of teaching in two languages simultaneously." In concluding his address, the superintendent did not forget to honor the "excellent teachers" in the Milwaukee public schools who had received their training in the seminary and who, in his words, were "exercising a salutary influence on . . . their fellow teachers . . . from other institutions."[1]

Most of the graduates from the seminary employed in the Milwaukee

*This essay is connected with my forthcoming dissertation on the assimilation process of German immigrants in Milwaukee between 1850 and 1930. Research was funded by the Studien zur Assimilation der Deutschamerikaner, 1830–1930, a research project directed by Prof. Willi Paul Adams at the Freie Universität Berlin with support from the Volkswagen Foundation.

1. Quotes taken from *Fiftieth Annual Report of the German-English Academy* (Milwaukee, 1901), 12–13; for the biography of Siefert, see John G. Gregory, *History of Milwaukee, Wisconsin* (Chicago, 1931), vol. II, 1158.

public school system were German-language teachers. German-language instruction had been introduced on an optional basis into all the city's grade schools during the late 1860s. Although there were opponents of that instruction from the beginning, enrollment figures went up, and in 1899, 73 percent of the students were taking German as an optional subject. Thus, by the turn of the century, German seemed to be a rather stable part of the curriculum, accepted not only by a majority of German-Americans but by the larger Anglo-American public as well.[2]

Less than twenty years later, in 1919, the situation had dramatically changed. In Milwaukee as well as in practically all other American cities, German-language lessons had been banned from the public grade schools. As a result, the National German-American Teachers' Seminary was forced to close because of a lack of students. Furthermore, the former German-English Academy had changed its name in 1918 to the Milwaukee University School, and at the same time had made German no more than an option in the curriculum, thus abandoning the founders' principle of strict bilingualism.[3]

In examining the relationship between the German-English Academy, the National German-American Teachers' Seminary, and the Milwaukee public schools more closely, it is not my intention to give an account of the various innovations in the American school system that – rightly or wrongly – have been attributed to the influence of German-American educational theory and practice.[4] Rather than presenting another piece of "contributionist" historiography, this essay focuses on German-language instruction, which was the main concern of the German-American educators at the time but which, in contrast to gymnastics, drawing, and other branches of learning that they advocated, failed to become part of American elementary schooling.

German-American educators and other leaders of the German-American community were preoccupied with German-language instruction for ped-

2. See Milwaukee Board of School Commissioners, *Annual Report 1876/77*, 78–9; *1898/99*, 101. See also *National German-American Teachers' Seminary* (Milwaukee, 1917), 47–55.
3. See "Gegen fremde Sprachen," *Milwaukee Herold*, August 7, 1918; Steven L. Schlossman, "Is There an American Tradition of Bilingual Education? German in the Public Elementary Schools, 1840–1919," *American Journal of Education* 91 (1983):139–86, 177–8; Frieda Meyer Voigt, *The Engelmann Heritage* (Milwaukee, 1951), 4;'*Sixty-Seventh Annual Report of the Milwaukee University School* (Milwaukee, 1918), 16, 69.
4. See, e.g., Hermann Schuricht, *Geschichte der deutschen Schulbestrebungen in Amerika* (Leipzig, 1884); Ludwig Klemm, "Das Schulwesen in den Vereinigten Staaten," in Armin Tenner, ed., *Amerika* (Berlin and New York, 1886), 33–83; Albert B. Faust, *The German Element in the United States* (New York, 1927), vol. II, 201–49; on the filiopietistic tradition in German-American historiography in general, see Kathleen Neils Conzen, "The Writing of German-American History," *The Immigration History Newsletter* 12, 2 (November 1980):1–14.

agogical reasons but, even more so, for ethnic reasons. Especially for German immigrants, who were divided along economic, political, and religious lines, ethnic identity basically had to be defined in cultural terms. The vernacular was the most prominent cultural bond, and thus its maintenance was of crucial importance for the very existence of the ethnic group.[5]

The rise and fall of German as the medium and subject of instruction in the schools will be discussed within the context of the assimilation process of Milwaukee's German-American community. Although it was during the First World War or shortly thereafter, when anti-German sentiment ran high, that instruction in the German language was given up in all public and most private grade schools, the war functioned only as a catalyst, not as a cause for abandoning German. The crisis of German-language instruction had already made itself felt around the turn of the century. It was evident in the public as well as in the private and parochial schools, although it took different forms in these systems. The crisis was not brought about by attacks from the outside, from nativist spokesmen or competing ethnic groups. It resulted, rather, from social and mental changes that had been taking place within the German-American community itself and that clearly indicate, long before World War I, and advanced stage in the assimilation process.

This essay first traces the founding and early history of the German-English Academy and similar German-American schools, and describes the efforts of their founders and supporters to reform the Milwaukee public schools, particularly to implement German-language instruction therein. Then it discusses the adoption of German as an optional branch of study in the public grade school system and its impact on German-American private schooling. Finally, this essay presents an analysis of the crisis of German-language instruction that caused its decline and facilitated its abandonment during or after the First World War.

The sources that I have evaluated include the annual reports of the German-English Academy and the National German-American Teachers' Seminary, unpublished minutes of the *Milwaukee Schulverein*, the proceedings of the Milwaukee Board of School Commissioners as well as local German-American newspapers, and pamphlets and journals published by

5. See Kathleen Neils Conzen, "The Paradox of German-American Assimilation," *Yearbook of German American Studies* 1 (1982):153–60, and "German-Americans and the Invention of Ethnicity," in Frank Trommler and Joseph McVeigh, eds., *America and the Germans. An Assessment of a Three-Hundred Year History* (Philadelphia, 1985), vol. I, 131–47; David Gerber, "Language Maintenance, Ethnic Group Formation, and Public Schools: Changing Patterns of German Concern, Buffalo, 1837–1874," *Journal of American Ethnic History* 4 (1984–5):31–61.

the National German-American Teachers' Alliance that was formed in 1870.[6]

In May 1849, Peter Engelmann, a graduate of the University of Berlin and a dismissed secondary school teacher, was forced to leave the German states to avoid persecution for his revolutionary activities. He shared this fate with quite a number of German teachers who had become heavily involved not only in the movement for educational reform but also in the general political revolution of 1848–9, particularly its radical wing. Engelmann emigrated to the United States, the favorite destination for many Forty-Eighters. After an unsuccessful attempt at "Latin farming" and a short period as a farmhand in Michigan, he found employment as a private tutor and village school teacher in Milwaukee County. Soon he was well know for his excellent teaching. Thus, when he moved to the city of Milwaukee in 1851, he was offered the position of principal of the German-English Academy that was to open in July of that year. Engelmann directed the school until he died in 1874 at the age of fifty-one. By that time, he had gained such a high reputation that the German-English Academy was far better know as "Engelmann's School."[7]

The German-English Academy was founded by a group of German professionals, artisans, and small businesspeople who, for the most part, had emigrated voluntarily and settled in Milwaukee well before 1848. Though not political refugees themselves, these immigrants came from the same classes, had comparable educational backgrounds, and held ideals similar to those of the Forty-Eighters. They shared their conviction that, in view of American nativism, political corruption, racism, slavery, and the influential position of the Protestant churches, the United States was still far from being the model of an ideal democracy, as it had been eulogized by leftist liberals of the German *Vormärz*. They also shared the strong belief in education as a decisive means of effecting ethical change and social and political reforms.

---

6. Research was done in Archives of the Milwaukee University School; Milwaukee County Historical Society; Milwaukee Public Library; Legislative Reference Library of Milwaukee; Milwaukee Area Research Center at the University of Wisconsin–Milwaukee; State Historical Society of Wisconsin and Memorial Library, Madison; and Library of the John F. Kennedy Institute for North American Studies, Freie Universität Berlin.

7. See Peter Engelmann, "Autobiography," MS, n.p., Engelmann Papers, Milwaukee County Historical Society; Albert Wallber, "Die Deutsch-Englische Akademie," in *Festschrift zur Einweihungsfeier der neuen Heimstätte deutsch-amerikanischer Erziehung in Milwaukee* (Milwaukee, 1891), 7–28, 14–15. Engelmann, the son of a Rhenish farmer, had edited a democratic newspaper and organized a democratic society in Kreuznach. For the German teachers' movement, see Thomas Nipperdey, "Volksschule und Revolution im Vormärz," in Ulrich Herrmann, ed., *Schule und Gesellschaft im 19. Jahrhundert* (Weinheim and Basel, 1977), 111–36; Wilh. Appens, *Die pädagogischen Bewegungen des Jahres 1848* (Elberfeld, 1917).

For that reason, they established musical, Turner (gymnastic), and freethinking societies, a whole network of liberal-minded associations that aimed at the enlightenment of the people. It was in this context that the German-English Academy was conceived and organized.[8]

German-American liberals, in contrast to their Catholic and Lutheran compatriots, were ardent advocates of public education. They held it to be not only the right but the duty of a republican government to provide free secular schooling for future citizens. The public schools that they encountered in the United States in the middle of the nineteenth century, however, did not meet the educational standards that they had been used to in Germany. Therefore they felt the necessity to organize their own private schools. This was true not only for the established urban centers of the East, but especially for Milwaukee.[9]

By the early 1850s, the city of Milwaukee had just been carved out of the wilderness. It already had a population of over 20,000, of whom more than a third were German immigrants, but its infrastructure was still in its infancy.[10] This was particularly noticeable in the school system, which would not keep pace with the burgeoning population: As late as 1855, less than 50 percent of the approximately 10,000 children of school age attended either a private or a public school.[11] The majority of the private schools were German Lutheran or Catholic parochial schools and thus unacceptable to Milwaukee's freethinking German immigrants. The public schools, on the other hand, did not satisfy their educational aspirations either. They did not provide any instruction in the German language; they were overcrowded and poorly equipped; and they suffered from a lack of qualified teachers and professional supervision. Learning by rote was the prevalent

8. See Rudolf A. Koss, *Milwaukee* (Milwaukee, 1871), 261ff.; Kathleen Neils Conzen, *Immigrant Milwaukee 1836–1860: Accommodation and Community in a Frontier City* (Cambridge, MA, and London, 1976), 172–84; Bettina Goldberg, "Radical German-American Freethinkers and the Socialist Labor Movement. The *Freie Gemeinde* in Milwaukee, Wisconsin," in Hartmut Keil, ed., *German Workers' Culture in the United States 1850 to 1920* (Washington, D.C., and London, 1988), 241–60; see also Eckhart G. Franz, "Das Amerikabild der deutschen Revolution von 1848/49: Zum Problem der Übertragung gewachsener Verfassungsformen," *Beihefte zum Jahrbuch für Amerikastudien* 2 (1958): 104–8, 134–8.

9. For German-American criticism of the American public school system, see, e.g., Rudolf Dulon, *Aus Amerika über Schule, deutsche Schule, amerikanische Schule und deutsch-amerikanische Schule* (Leipzig and Heidelberg, 1866), summarized in Bettina Goldberg, "The Forty-Eighters and the School System in America: The Theory and Practice of Reform," in Charlotte L. Brancaforte, ed., *The German Forty-Eighters in the United States* (New York, 1989), 203–18, 207–8; for a survey of German-American private and associational schools, see Schuricht, *Geschichte,* 56–63.

10. See Conzen, *Immigrant Milwaukee,* 10–15; Bayrd Still, *Milwaukee: The History of a City* (Madison, 1965), 111ff.

11. According to the school census of 1855, 2,013 out of 9,346 children of school age attended public schools, 1,996 private schools, and 5,337 no school at all ("Das Board der Schul-Commissäre," *Banner und Volksfreund* (Milwaukee), October 6, 1855).

method of instruction, and the subjects taught were generally limited to reading, writing, and arithmetic.[12]

To ensure their children a thorough bilingual education and, at the same time, to offer a model for the public schools, in May 1851 twenty-six German citizens, among them the editors of Milwaukee's two daily German newspapers, joined to form the *Milwaukie-Schulverein*. Less than two months later, on July 1, their associational school, the German–English Academy, opened in a rented building on the city's east side.[13] "The school aims at providing the pupils," Peter Engelmann wrote in his autobiography,

with the same sort of education which they would receive in a good German *Realschule*. The only difference is that in our school they are instructed free of all religious bias and are just as fluent in English as they are in German.[14]

In accordance with this aim, from the beginning, the school offered a broad curriculum that became even more comprehensive in later years. Elementary subjects in 1851 included not only English and German reading, writing, and grammar as well as arithmetic, but also memory exercises, object lessons, geography, history, biology, and drawing. In the upper class, penmanship, natural history, mathematics, the sciences, and technical drawing were added. Thus the school put strong emphasis on the sciences, not only for vocational reasons but also to counter the influence of religion and superstition.[15]

The German–English Academy started in 1851 with two teachers and forty children enrolled in two classes. During the course of the decade, the number of pupils increased, and in 1860 269 children received their education in the school, which employed eight teachers and consisted of six classes.[16]

The German–English Academy was the first school of this type in Milwaukee, but it did not remain the only one. Encouraged by the early development of the Academy, German-Americans living on the city's west and south sides established similar schools for their respective areas. However, the six German–English schools that opened in Milwaukee during the

12. See Koss, *Milwaukee*, 331–2; "Die deutsche Schule und Familie," *Banner und Volksfreund*, June 9, 1855; Patrick Donnelly, "The Milwaukee Public Schools," in John W. Stearns, ed., *The Columbian History of Education in Wisconsin* (Milwaukee, 1893), 436–65, 436–42.
13. See *Wisconsin Banner* (Milwaukee), April 24, May 2, 10, 14, 17, 22, 23, 26, 31; June 6, 12, 17, 28, 1851.
14. Engelmann, "Autobiography"; for a more detailed account of the purposes of the school, see *Statuten, Neben-Gesetze, Verordnungen und Regulationen des Milwaukie Schul-Vereins* (Milwaukee, 1863), 13–14.
15. See "Schul-Verein," *Wisconsin Banner*, June 17, 1851.
16. "Milwaukie Schul-Verein," *Banner und Volksfreund*, April 14, 1860.

1850s and the first half of the 1860s reached only 1,085 children even at the height of their influence in the mid-1860s. At the same time, German-American parochial schools were attended by over 3,000 children and the public schools by more than 9,000.[17] In view of these figures, even those German-American educators who advocated a comprehensive system of German-American schooling must have become convinced that this dream was rather illusory.[18] The secular German-English schools, it was evident, would never reach more than a tiny percentage of German-American children. The educator for the great majority of Milwaukee's children, including those from German immigrant families, was to become the American public school. Thus, the public schools had to be the real focus of German-American activities for educational reform.

Milwaukee's German-American liberals were involved in school politics as early as 1846, when the city was incorporated. At that time, however, German immigration had just begun, and only one out of fifteen members of Milwaukee's first public school board, appointed by the common council, bore a German name. He was Moritz Schöffler, a trained printer and the publisher of Milwaukee's first German newspaper, the *Wisconsin Banner;* later he would become one of the founding members of the Milwaukee *Schulverein*.[19] During the 1850s and 1860s, when more than a third of Milwaukee's population was German born, German-American representation on the board increased, and in 1867, for the first time, German immigrants made up 50 percent of Milwaukee's school commissioners. Like Schöffler, they came from the liberal camp, and many of them were also involved in German-American associational schools.[20]

These school officials, supported by other German-American activists, mainly from freethinker and Turner circles, strongly advocated a whole list of educational reforms. They demanded, for instance, a professional system of school supervision; the employment of qualified German-Americans as teachers and principals; the use of fewer and better textbooks; the adoption of teaching methods that do justice to children; the introduction of music,

17. Milwaukee Board of School Commissioners, *Annual Report* 1866/67: 34ff. The secular private and associational schools were the German-English Academy, the Anneke-School, the high school of the second ward, the German-English school of the fourth ward, the high school of the fifth and eighth wards, and the West Hill School. The German-American Lutheran parishes maintained seven schools, the German-American Catholics three.
18. For such concepts, see Goldberg, "The Forty-Eighters," 208–9.
19. See Jerome A. Watrous, ed., *Memoirs of Milwaukee County* (Madison, 1909), vol. I, 384; for the biography of Schöffler, see ibid., 183–4; for his membership in the Milwaukee *Schulverein,* see footnote 13.
20. See "Im Board der Schul-Commissäre," *Herold* (Milwaukee), April 27, 1867; "Milwaukee, Wis.," *Amerikanische Schulzeitung N.F.* 4, 3 (December 1873):9; *History of Milwaukee, Wisconsin* (Chicago, 1881), 269–70; for the ethnic composition of Milwaukee's population, see Still, *Milwaukee,* 574–5.

gymnastics, and drawing lessons; and last, but not least, the adequate consideration of their German vernacular in the public school curriculum.[21]

Their reform efforts not only provoked attacks from the Anglo-American nativist camp, but also met with opposition from Milwaukee's numerous German-American churches. Both Catholic and Lutheran clergy knew that the projected improvements of the already tuition-free public school system, and in particular the attempts to introduce German-language instruction, were not least intended to weaken their own parochial schools. Although the Lutherans, partly out of ethnic motives, remained comparatively moderate in their criticism, the German-American Catholic clergy launched an aggressive campaign against any innovation in the public school system, including the teaching of German, that would involve higher costs and thus result in higher general taxation.[22]

Whereas the opposition of the churches was largely to be expected, it is quite surprising that these reform efforts did not attract much attention among Milwaukee's German-American population. This was true not only for the strictly educational part of the reform program: Even the purely ethnic demand for German-language instruction was received with only slight interest. Already in 1857, Milwaukee's school board had passed a resolution providing for the hiring of German language teachers in all schools where a need for German language instruction was felt. Only the school of the sixth ward, however, whose representative on the board had brought up the issue, made an application.[23] Three years later, the editors of the German-American daily *Banner und Volksfreund* found it necessary to appeal to the German population of Milwaukee's other wards to make known to the school board their urgent need for instruction in their mother tongue. However, the local German-American press reported only on two

---

21. See the *Proceedings* and *Annual Reports* of the Milwaukee Board of School Commissioners; see also Watrous, *Memoirs*, vol. I, 390–418.
22. See the dispute between Milwaukee's German-American newspapers *Columbia* (Catholic) and *Germania* (Protestant), which lasted from November 1873 to August 1874 (esp. January 22 and 24, 1874); see also "Die Lehrerbundsbestrebungen und die kirchliche Presse," *Erziehungsblätter* N.F. 13, 9 (June 1883):9. The Catholic campaign reveals that German immigrants were far from being "unified," as Schlossman argues, "in insisting that public schools incorporate their native language into the curriculum" ("Is There an American Tradition?" 143).
23. At that time, the school board consisted of twenty-seven members, only six of them German. When the resolution was passed on June 3, 1857, nineteen school commissioners were present; not only the five German-Americans in attendance but also nine other members of the board voted in favor of the resolution. The initiator of the resolution was Ferdinand Kühn (1821–1901), one of the founders and a lifelong officer of the Milwaukee *Schulverein* (see "Collegium der Schul-Commissäre," *Banner und Volksfreund*, May 2 and June 8, 1857; *Kurzgefa te Geschichte der Deutsch-Englischen Akademie, des Nationalen Deutsch-Am. Lehrerseminars und des Turnlehrerseminars des Nordam. Turnerbundes* [Milwaukee, 1901], 23; for the biography of Kühn, see Watrous, *Memoirs*, vol. I, 134–5).

occasions about meetings or similar activities of German immigrants to lobby for the implementation of German-language teaching, and in the second case the meeting had to be canceled for lack of participation.[24]

When German was introduced as an optional subject in those schools situated in predominantly German wards during the 1860s, and when German-language instruction was eventually started citywide in 1869, this was not the consequence of political pressure from below or the result of an organized ethnic movement; rather, it was a reform from above that was achieved by collaboration between German-American and Anglo-American educators and school politicians.[25] The basis of cooperation on the Anglo-American side was less a particular esteem for the German language than the recognition that the public schools would fulfill their function as agents of Americanization only when they reached the majority of children who were to be Americanized. Offering instruction in the vernacular seemed to be a suitable means of drawing closer to this end.[26]

The system of German-language instruction implemented in Milwaukee's public schools did not follow the bilingual model used in the city's private German-English schools. Rather than becoming the medium of instruction for some of the elementary branches, German in the public schools remained restricted to one optional language lesson daily that was added to the otherwise English-only curriculum.[27] Limited as this instruction was, it served its purpose. Public school enrollment rose, especially in Milwaukee's heavily German wards. There it had been below average in the early 1860s, but it was well above average in the 1870s and the following decades.[28]

24. See "Die öffentlichen Schulen," *Banner und Volksfreund*, May 16, 1860; "In einer am 24. Mai in P. Bichler's Halle abgehaltenen Massenversammlung," ibid., June 2, 1860; "Ein Schul-Meeting," *Herold*, June 20, 1867.

25. See "In den öffentlichen Stadtschulen," *Banner und Volksfreund*, September 1, 1861, and January 5, 1862; reports on the public schools in the second, ninth, and sixth wards, *Herold*, January 17 and 25, February 2, 1867; "Verhandlungen des Schul-Rathes," ibid., October 2, 1867; "Schulraths-Verhandlungen," ibid., October 2, 1867; "Schulraths-Verhandlungen," ibid., September 3, 1869.

26. See Milwaukee Board of School Commissioners, *Annual Report* 1872/73: 113, 1876/77: 84–7; see also Schlossman, "Is There an American Tradition?", 150–8.

27. See Milwaukee Board of School Commissioners, *Annual Report* 1872/73: XXXIV, 1881/82: LXXXVI ff., 1898/99: 94, 1902/3: 145, 1912/13: 119; for the far more comprehensive German-language instruction that was offered in Cincinnati, Indianapolis, and Baltimore, see Carolyn Toth, "A History of German-English Bilingual Education: The Continuing Cincinnati Tradition," diss., Univ. of Cincinnati, 1988; Schlossman, "Is There an American Tradition?", 146–9; Heinz Kloss, "Die deutschamerikanische Schule," *Jahrbuch für Amerikastudien* 7 (1962):141–75, 146–8.

28. See the results of the school census, particularly for the predominantly German wards 2, 6, 9, and 20, published in the *Annual Reports* of Milwaukee's Board of School Commissioners. In 1877 Superintendent MacAlister declared: "We . . . have acted wisely . . . the German instruction has brought large accessions to the Public Schools from the German population" (*Annual Report* 1876/77: 84).

This increase demonstrates that German-language instruction, though not the rallying point of an ethnic movement, was nevertheless desired by many immigrant parents as part of their children's education. It also reveals, however, that it did not take a bilingual system or preferential treatment of the German language to satisfy the ethnic aspirations of these parents. As soon as they found their vernacular considered at all, they were willing to send their children to the public schools, which in contrast to private or parochial schools did not charge tuition and, for that reason alone, were attractive in any case.

German-language instruction, as well as other innovations in the public school system, caused only a relative decline of the German-American parochial schools but a significant decrease in the secular German-English schools. These schools, in contrast to the church schools, did not differ basically from the public schools. Indeed, they offered a bilingual and a more comprehensive curriculum than the public schools. Their standards, however, were much higher than the educational aspirations of the average German immigrant of the 1870s and 1880s. The majority of Germans coming to Milwaukee after the Civil War were no longer educated craftsmen and shopkeepers from the more urbanized parts of Germany, but rather peasants and day laborers with a low educational background from the agrarian northeast. These immigrants had only limited financial means, and especially during the severe economic crisis of the 1870s, they were neither willing nor able to invest in education more than was absolutely necessary. If they were religiously inclined, they might enroll their children in parochial schools, which charged a very modest fee. Otherwise, they sent them to the secular public, but not the private, schools.[29]

Milwaukee's German-English schools had suffered from a chronic lack of funds from the beginning. Since their regular income, consisting of associational membership dues and tuition fees, had never been sufficient to cover operating costs, these schools had always been dependent on additional fund-raising through charity events and bazaars, which for the most part were organized by the women's auxiliary. During the 1870s and early

---

29. See Wallber, "Deutsch-Englische Akademie," 16–17; for the parochial schools, see the statistics on private schools in the *Annual Reports* of the Milwaukee Board of School Commissioners; for the shift in skills and regional origin of German immigrants, see Klaus J. Bade, "Die deutsche überseeische Massenauswanderung im 19. und frühen 20. Jahrhundert," in Klaus J. Bade, ed., *Auswanderer -Wanderarbeiter–Gastarbeiter. Bevölkerung, Arbeitsmarkt und Wanderung in Deutschland seit der Mitte des 19. Jahrhunderts* (Ostfildern, 1984), vol. 1, 259–99, 275–83; Conzen, *Immigrant Milwaukee*, 31; Walter D. Kamphoefner, *Westfalen in der Neuen Welt* (Münster, 1982), 96–7; further evidence will be presented in my forthcoming dissertation.

1880s, because of dwindling attendance, the financial problems became insurmountable; as a result, two of the German-English schools closed and three others were transformed into public schools.[30]

Thus, by the mid-1880s, the German-English Academy was the only secular school left, and even the Academy, though a laboratory school of the National German-American Teachers' Seminary since 1878, was not in stable condition. The number of students had decreased from 450 in 1865 to only 149 in 1885, and during the same year, Isidor Keller, director of both the Academy and the Teachers' Seminary, predicted the school's demise if it did not adjust to changed conditions. Whereas the public schools, Keller argued, were rather crowded, especially in their lower grades, the Academy's elementary classes, in contrast to earlier years, showed the lowest enrollment in the lower grades. This clearly indicated, he continued, that the great majority of even the educated German immigrants was rather satisfied with public common schooling; for that reason, there was no longer a sufficient demand for the type of education that the German-English Academy offered. To have a future at all, Keller concluded, the Academy had to give up its elementary classes, end its connection with the Teachers' Seminary, and gain a profile as a top-quality secondary school.[31]

Keller's views and his efforts to transfer the Teachers' Seminary to New York City met strong opposition, and he was forced to resign.[32] But his analysis proved to be correct. Although the Academy was to maintain its lower grades as well as its connection with the Teachers' Seminary, it gradually shifted its emphasis to secondary education and developed into a college preparatory school for Milwaukee's German-American elite. This took another twenty-four years. In 1909 the German-English Academy, after consolidation with the Anglo-American Milwaukee Academy, established

30. See "Die deutsch-englischen Schulen America's," *Herold,* April 16, 1869; Wallber, "Die Deutsch-Englische Akademie," 9–10, 16–17; Augustus J. Rogers, "Private and Parochial Schools," in Howard Louis Conard, ed., *History of Milwaukee from Its First Settlement to the Year 1895* (Chicago and New York, n.d.), vol. I, 181–90, 186.

31. *Bericht des Direktors an den Verwaltungs-Rath der "Deutsch-Englischen Akademie"* (Milwaukee, 1885), 4–15; *Bericht über das Nationale Deutsch-Amerikanische Lehrerseminar und die mit demselben als Uebungsschule verbundene Deutsch-Englische Akademie* (Milwaukee, 1886), 26–7; Wallber, "Die Deutsch-Englische Akademie," 11; for the history of the National German-American Teachers' Seminary, a normal school for bilingual preschool and grade-school teachers organized by the National German-American Teachers' Alliance in 1878, see *Kurzgefa te Geschichte,* 41–62; Voigt, *The Engelmann Heritage,* 27–103.

32. See *Erziehungs-Blätter* 15, 8 (May 1885):8–10; 15, 10 (July 1885):2–5, 8–10; 15, 11 (August 1885): 6–7. I. Keller was followed by H. Dorner, a Milwaukee public school teacher (Voigt, *The Engelmann Heritage,* 30–1).

its own high school department and presented itself as a school that "offered an unbroken education *from the Kindergarten to the University.*"[33] However, the first steps in that direction had already been taken in the 1880s.

At that time, the diplomas of the German-English Academy were not recognized by Milwaukee's school board; therefore its students, unlike those from the public schools, had to pass entrance examinations for the city's high schools. In view of the growing number of parents who aimed at a higher education for their children after graduation from the Academy, Albert Wallber wrote in 1891, this situation had become more and more detrimental to the school. Thus, during the 1880s and 1890s, in order to increase the attractiveness of the Academy, its director and teachers anxiously worked to meet the demands of the public school board. By 1901 they proudly reported the accreditation of their school.[34]

The formal recognition of the diplomas, urgently needed for survival, had only been achieved, however, after a far-reaching adaptation of the Academy's course of study to that of the public schools. Since the timetable could not be overloaded, during the process of adjustment German as the medium and subject of instruction was gradually cut back. Whereas in 1863 the German-English Academy had still followed a strictly bilingual curriculum prescribing the same amount of time for instruction in either language, the course of study of 1885 already provided for preferential treatment of English. From the third grade on, instruction in English made up more than 50 percent of the weekly timetable, rising to 74 percent in the eighth grade. By that time, however, German was still the medium of instruction for a number of subjects, including arithmetic in the elementary department, natural history or science in the first seven grades, and general history, starting in the third grade. Sixteen years later, when the school became accredited, this was no longer the case. With the exception of a course in world history, German was limited to language lessons, and English had become the medium of instruction for all the other branches of the curriculum.[35]

---

33. *Fifty-eighth Annual Report of the German-English Academy* (Milwaukee, 1909), 10. Until 1920 the school only offered higher education for boys (*Seventieth Annual Report of the Milwaukee University School* [Milwaukee, 1921], 1). The list of pupils published in the *Fifty-ninth Annual Report of the German-English Academy* (Milwaukee, 1910) and *Wright's Directory of Milwaukee* (Milwaukee, 1910) made it possible to reconstruct the social composition of the student body; my findings show that almost all of the German-English Academy's 185 pupils came from upper-middle- or upper-class families.

34. See Wallber, "Die Deutsch-Englische Akademie," 21; *Einundzwanzigster Jahresbericht des Nationalen Deutsch-Amerikanischen Lehrerseminars und seiner Musterschule, der Deutsch-Englischen Akademie* (Milwaukee, 1900), 20; *Fiftieth Annual Report* (1901), 13.

35. See *Statuten* (1863), 15–23; *Bericht* (1886), 28–34; *Fiftieth Annual Report* (1901), 14–20.

Thus, by 1900, the German-English Academy had fundamentally changed its character. It still offered more comprehensive German-language instruction than the city's grade schools, but in order to satisfy the educational aspirations of its German-American clientele and to keep up with its public competitors, it had given up the strict bilingualism conceived by its founders and had made English the dominant language. In this respect, the German-English Academy was not unique. The German-American Catholic and Lutheran parochial schools had undergone a similar process for the same reasons. Milwaukee's German-American citizens, this clearly demonstrates, were well aware that a thorough knowledge of English rather than German was a necessary prerequisite for economic and social mobility in the New World. For that reason, they were ready to see the German lessons reduced; they were not willing to accept an education for their children that did not meet the standards of the public school system.[36]

After the turn of the century, German-language instruction was no longer felt to be a real need by Milwaukee's German-American population. Immigration from Germany had declined, and by 1910 the majority of German-American citizens had either been born in the United States or had already lived there for twenty years or more.[37] Many of them still subscribed to German newspapers or were members of German-speaking societies, but they did so for reasons of habit and tradition. They were no longer monolingual and therefore did not depend on their children's knowledge of German to communicate with them. On the contrary, numerous complaints of German-American educators, journalists, and clergymen suggest that English rather than German was the language spoken in most homes most of the time.[38]

This change was also noticeable in the public schools. German-American public school officials were anxious to demonstrate that German-language instruction was a generally accepted and necessary branch of the curriculum and that its results strongly justified its costs. As

---

36. For the marginalization of German in the parochial schools, see Bettina Goldberg, "The German Language in Milwaukee's Grade Schools, 1850–1920: The Case of the Catholic Schools" and " 'Our Fathers' Faith, Our Children's Language.' Cultural Change in Milwaukee's German Evangelical Lutheran Parishes of the Missouri Synod, 1850–1930," John F. Kennedy-Institut für Nordamerikastudien. Freie Universität Berlin, *Working Papers*, Nos. 17/1989, and 26/1990.

37. Computed from an ethnically mixed sample of 1,090 Milwaukee households based on the manuscript schedules of the U.S. Census on Population for 1910. Evidence will be presented in my forthcoming dissertation.

38. See, e.g., Karl Knortz, *Das Deutschthum der Vereinigten Staaten* (Hamburg, 1898), 67–8; "Die Deutschen und die deutsche Sprache," *Germania und Abendpost* (Milwaukee), June 13, 1900; Milwaukee Board of School Commissioners, *Annual Report* 1898/99:95.

early as 1902, they could not avoid mentioning, however, that for the majority of children from German-American families, what once had been
instruction in the vernacular had already turned into foreign-language instruction. They also had to admit that many of these German-American
children had little desire to learn the "difficult German language," and
that, particularly in the upper grades, they showed a tendency to drop
German lessons.[39] This indicates that despite high enrollment figures,
German-language instruction was no longer flourishing. Well before
World War I, it showed symptoms of a crisis that was brought about not
by attacks from Anglo-American nativists but by the advanced linguistic
assimilation of Milwaukee's German-American population. Thus, by 1902,
the main arguments for German in the public schools, used by German-
born Superintendent Lau in 1871 – that German-language teaching was "a
natural desire on the part of the German population" and that a knowledge
of German was "of considerable advantage in [Milwaukee's] business and
social life" – had become invalid.[40]

German-American educators, journalists, and others, who had not only
a nostalgic but a professional interest in the maintenance of the German
language, observed this process with anxiety. If German were to have a
future at all in the American public schools, they knew that it had to be
based firmly on grounds other than ethnically defined needs and claims.
The German language had to be put into an unassailable position comparable to that of Greek and Latin in neohumanist thinking. In order to ensure
such a position, advocates of German-language instruction shifted the emphasis of their argument. In contrast to Polish or Italian, they stated, the
German language was taught in the public schools not primarily for the
immigrants' sake, but for its great importance to the larger Anglo-American
public. The formal educational qualities of German, the superiority of
German culture, literature, and science, and the first-rank political and economic position of the German Empire, they declared, made a thorough
knowledge of the German language not only desirable but necessary for
every educated American citizen. And for that reason, they concluded,
German lessons would never become superfluous. The chauvinist and na-

39. See Milwaukee Board of School Commissioners, *Annual Report* 1902/3:144–5; "Korrespondenzen:
Milwaukee," *Pädagogische Monatshefte* 3 (1901/2):210–12.
40. See Milwaukee Board of School Commissioners, *Annual Report* 1870/71:40, 1871/2:58–9. The
high enrollment in German-language classes is not least due to the following rule, which largely
compensated for the fact that German was not a compulsory subject: "It will be presumed that
parents or guardians of pupils desire them to pursue the study of the German language, . . . unless
formal notice to the contrary be furnished the principal of the school in each case" (ibid., 1870/1:
90).

tionalist tendency of this argument, which clearly indicates a generational change in ethnic leadership, were to become counterproductive during World War I. When everything German was suspicious, such statements of German-American educators aided those who denounced German-language instruction as publicly financed ideological support of the war enemy.[41]

In Milwaukee, German-language teaching came under attack from the English-language *Milwaukee Journal* and some superpatriotic organizations in the spring of 1917. Although the campaign did not show the aggressiveness and violence that it had in other places, in combination with the advanced assimilation of Milwaukee's German-American citizens it proved to be very effective. The editors of Milwaukee's German newspapers appealed to their readers to demonstrate that they would not let themselves be intimidated, but except for resolutions from the Turners and from three singing societies, there was no public outcry on the part of Milwaukee's German-American community. To the contrary, educators and journalists repeatedly lashed out at "the weakness and indifference of German-American parents," who were eager to remove their children from German classes right away. Thus, attendance at German-language instruction classes went down. Whereas in June 1917 more than 30,000 students were still enrolled, in March 1918 their number had declined to less than 12,000. In view of these figures, only five months later, in August, Milwaukee's public school board, which had been reluctant at first, resolved with a majority that included its German-American members to eliminate all foreign-language teaching in the lower grades by the end of the coming school year. German remained part of the high school curriculum, but in the elementary schools it was completely discontinued in June 1919.[42]

By that time, the Teachers' Seminary had already closed and the German-English Academy, because of pressure from its high school students and a large number of parents, had changed its name to Milwaukee University School. Unlike the public schools, it had not banished German from the

41. See, e.g., "Editorielles," *Pädagogische Monatshefte* 1 (1899/1900):23–5; M. D. Learned, "Deutsch gegen Englisch oder Deutsch neben Englisch," ibid., 2 (1900/1):290–3; "Korrespondenzen: Milwaukee," *Monatshefte für deutsche Sprache und Pädagogik* 10 (1909):182–3; 11 (1910):83; Joseph Winter, "Die Zukunft der deutschen Sprache in Amerika," ibid., 13 (1912):265–9; see also Henry J. Schmidt, "The Rhetoric of Survival: The Germanist in America from 1900 to 1925," in Trommler and McVeigh, *America and the Germans*, vol. II, 204–16.

42. See "Korrespondenzen: Milwaukee," *Monatshefte für deutsche Sprache und Pädagogik* 18 (1917):268–9; 19 (1918):46, 78; "Der Kampf um den deutschen Unterricht," *Vorwärts* (Milwaukee), April 28, 1917; "Der deutsche Unterricht in der Defensive," ibid., July 14, 1917; "Michel und der deutsche Unterricht," ibid., February 9, 1918; "Beharrt auf euerer Ansicht und auf euerem Rechte," *Germania-Herold* (Milwaukee), September 12, 1917; "Gegen fremde Sprachen," *Milwaukee Herold*, August 7, 1918; Still, *Milwaukee*, 461–2.

lower grades but made it an optional subject in 1918.[43] This arrangement, however, lasted for only a transitional period.

The Milwaukee University School was well on its way to developing into an American elite school, and as can be seen from the minutes, this process had the full backing of its board of trustees, consisting of prominent second-generation German-American businessmen. They were anxious to cast off the school's German heritage, which had no meaning to its students any longer and which was felt to be harmful to the school's reputation in Anglo-American circles. In view of the desired new profile of the school, it was less and less bearable that its director had been born and educated in the German Empire. Thus, in 1925, when the contract of Max Griebsch, principal since 1903, expired, it was not renewed, and an Anglo-American educator was appointed for that position instead.[44]

During the following years the curriculum was revised, and by the late 1920s the Milwaukee University School had finally broken with its past. It had not only abolished German from the elementary department but, ironically, it had also adopted one of the major arguments of the opponents of German-language instruction to justify this change. "It is the policy of our school," the catalog for 1928 states, "to begin the work in foreign languages in the junior high, for it is believed that a mastery of English expression should precede the learning of a foreign language."[45]

43. See "German-English Academy Ledger 1913–1920," 168, 171, 194, 206, 214–15, 218, 222, 231, 247, and "Minutes of the School Association of the German-English Academy 1908–1924," 30–1, Archives of the Milwaukee University School; see also Max Griebsch, "Das Nationale Lehrerseminar zu Milwaukee," *Monatshefte für deutschen Unterricht* 22 (1930):97–103.
44. See "Board of Directors. Milwaukee University School. Minute Book 6/1920–11/1925," 230–2, and "Board of Trustees. Milwaukee University School. Minutes of Meetings. July 1925–Dec. 1931," 3, 5, Archives of the Milwaukee University School; for the biography of Max Griebsch, see Voigt, *The Engelmann Heritage*, 33; for that of his successor, Alfred Lawrence Hall-Quest, see *Who's Who in America* 15 (1928–9):943.
45. *Milwaukee University School 1928–1929* (Milwaukee, 1928), 18; for the arguments of opponents to German-language instruction in the grades, see, e.g., "Skrapnel in Talk on the Needs of the Schools," *Evening Wisconsin*, May 26, 1917.

PART FOUR

The German Influence on Higher Education

11

American Students in Germany, 1815–1914: The Structure of German and U.S. Matriculants at Göttingen University

KONRAD H. JARAUSCH

The influence of the German university on American higher education has more often been posited than proven. To sympathetic observers like Charles Franklin Thwing, it went without saying that "the German university has helped to create and to nourish the American." To skeptical contemporaries like F. H. Swift, imperial institutions rather exemplified "a baffling paradox of culture and brutality" whose effects on U.S. practice should be excised.[1] This division of opinion has proven persistent. On the one hand, ethnic apologists have tended to celebrate the impact of German learning on American development, including much rhetorical praise in their efforts to revive pride in their ancestry.[2] On the other hand, critical historians of education have resented the implication of cultural dependence and stressed native developments instead. The verdict of Laurence Veysey has become commonplace: American students "accepted the method, perhaps the vision of scholarship, but not the *Geist* of German universities."[3] The reasons for the dispute are not only different emotional attitudes toward Central Europe, but also disagreements about the nature of the evidence and the criteria of evaluation. Whereas some stress the extraordinary intellectual migration of about 10,000 students to Germany during the nineteenth century, others profess to find few continental transplants in American schol-

---

1. C. F. Thwing, *The American and the German University* (New York, 1928), 1ff; versus H. F. Swift, "The Paradox of German University and Military Ideals," *Educational Review* 49 (1915), 266–84. See K. H. Jarausch, "The Universities: An American View," in J. Dukes and J. Remak, eds., *Another Germany* (Boulder, Colo., 1988), 181–206.
2. According to W. von Schierbrand, *Germany: The Welding of a World Power* (New York, 1905), Germany was the "schoolmaster of the world." See J. Wandel, *The German Dimension of American History* (Chicago, 1979), 208ff. La Vern Rippley, *The German Americans* (Boston, 1984, repr.), 119, concentrates instead on language survival.
3. C. E. McClelland, "German Universities and American Scholars," *History of Education Quarterly* 20 (1980), 229–32. The standard work is L. Veysey, *The Emergence of the American University* (Chicago, 1969), 125–33.

arship. Proceeding at cross purposes, the debate about the German impact is likely to remain inconclusive.

During the past two decades, several scholars have grappled with the question of influence by looking at the actual experience of American students. In his pathbreaking work on *The German Historical School in American Scholarship,* Jurgen Herbst studied the transfer of culture through the ideas of five leading German-trained U.S. scholars after the Civil War. Though rich in detail and complex in argumentation, this monograph does not address the experience of ordinary Americans.[4] Based on the alumni records of American colleges before 1870, Carl Diehl subsequently assembled a prosopographical portrait of 343 students at Göttingen, Berlin, Heidelberg, Halle, and other universities. Particularly helpful for the encounter of the first two generations of American humanities students with German philological scholarship, this sample is not representative of the whole and breaks off just when student numbers exploded.[5] Since tracking all Americans in every German institution requires enormous labor, it seemed more feasible to study U.S. students in a single prominent institution in order to contrast German structures with American patterns and to draw upon the rich institutional literature. Because the university registers of Berlin remained inaccessible, Göttingen was the logical choice as the second most popular institution with American students due to its long-standing British ties.[6] Though unable to provide direct solutions to problems of cultural influence, such a social analysis can indirectly facilitate their resolution by offering firmer statistical evidence on its structural parameters.

What kind of university did American students encounter after their long voyage to the Continent? Travel descriptions abound in charming portrayals of the outward differences, such as the striking absence of a campus, which made it difficult to find German institutions.[7] Articles in educational journals or book-length analyses are full of explanations of the key features of the Central European philosophy of higher education. First, the neohumanist ideal of *Bildung,* of liberal education, permeated the spirit of the

---

4. J. Herbst, *The German Historical School in American Scholarship: A Study in the Transfer of Culture* (Ithaca, N.Y., 1965), esp. 1–22.

5. C. Diehl, *Americans and German Scholarship, 1770–1870* (New Haven, Conn., 1978), 50ff, and the statistical appendix, 155ff.

6. According to Thwing, *American and German University,* 40, about one-half of the U.S. students went to Berlin, with fewer than 1,000 in the next institution. D. B. Shumway, "The American Students of the University of Göttingen," *German-American Annals* 8 (1910), 171–254, is an excellent compilation, but it does not reveal the full story because it was published a half-decade before the First World War.

7. W. Howitt, *Student Life of Germany* (Philadelphia, 1842), and J. M. Hart, *German Universities: A Narrative of Personal Experience* (New York, 1874).

lecture halls and encouraged general cultivation of mental and aesthetic faculties. Second, the philological and scientific ethos of *Wissenschaft,* of the discovery of new knowledge rather than the transmission of tradition, animated many professors and academic youths to engage in research. Third, the more practical goal of *Ausbildung,* of training in professional skills, motivated most students to prepare for their state examinations and bureaucratic careers.[8] Memoirs of German educated academics are replete with descriptions of the sometimes paradoxical interactions between world-famous *Ordinarien* and their American pupils in seminars, laboratories, and the like.[9] Though richly evocative, this literature tends to treat the German university as a fixed entity and neglects to analyze its dramatic changes in enrollment, demographic composition, social recruitment, and career patterns. To appreciate the special problems of American visitors, it is necessary to start with a closer look at the social dynamics of their host institutions.

The university of Göttingen mirrors the national transformation of higher learning in the nineteenth century with a particular Hanoverian accent. The most innovative foundation of the eighteenth century, with renowned teachers and an excellent library, the Georgia Augusta was a midsized Hanoverian institution that attracted between 5 percent and 7 percent of all German students.[10] A systematic 10 percent sample of the matriculation register yielded a data set of 7,395 cases for statistical analysis.[11] As displayed in Table 1, Göttingen enrollment followed the national trend, starting out somewhat higher but falling behind in midcentury. Beginning with a substantial 330 inscriptions a year, matriculation boomed to 850 in 1823 and then dropped precipitously back to the initial level during the revolutionary period. Recovering in the 1850s and 1860s, enrollment rose to 710 in the 1870s, but then declined to 510 in the 1880s before joining the pre–World War I expansion to as many as 1,870 new students in 1912. It seems likely that the pronounced lag after 1866 had to do with student and faculty resentment against the forced incorporation of the Georgia Augusta into Prussia.[12] This pattern suggests a series of cyclical expansions and contrac-

8. W. Lexis, *Die deutschen Universitäten* (Berlin, 1893), 2 vols; F. Paulsen, *Die deutschen Universitäten und das Universitätsstudium* (Berlin, 1902); and A. Flexner, *Universities: American, English, German* (New York, 1930).

9. For memoir lists, see Herbst, *German Historical School,* 235ff; Diehl, *Americans and German Scholarship,* 183ff; and Jarausch, "The Universities," 201ff.

10. C. E. McClelland, *State, Society and University in Germany, 1700–1914* (Cambridge, 1980), 34ff.

11. G. von Selle, ed., *Die Matrikel der Georg-August-Universität zu Göttingen, 1737–1837* (Hildesheim, 1937), vol. 2; W. Ebel, ed., *Die Matrikel der Georg-August Universität zu Göttingen, 1837–1900* (Hildesheim, 1974), 2 vols. For the period after 1900, see the manuscript *Matrikel* in the Universitätsarchiv Göttingen. The year 1796 was used as the starting point, since it is the first year in which the father's occupation was listed.

12. G. von Selle, *Die Georg-August Universität zu Göttingen, 1737–1937* (Göttingen, 1937).

Table 1. *Demographic characteristics of Göttingen students, in percentages*

Year	Origin				Urbanization			Training		
	Han.	Prus.	Ger.	For.	Rur.	Town	City	*Gym.*	Mod.	Oth.
1796–1825	35.5	26.0	29.1	9.4	34.7	41.6	23.7	92.1		7.9
1826–55	51.7	14.8	29.2	4.3	34.2	44.9	20.9	83.5	2.8	13.8
1856–85	40.0	26.0	24.5	9.6	32.5	33.2	34.3			
1886–1911	35.8	33.7	20.6	9.6	29.2	24.2	45.6	70.1	21.6	8.4
Total no.	3,018	2,069	1,877	667	2,397	2,520	2,611	2,547	691	308

tions with an initial wave cresting the 1820s, a weaker tide in the 1860s and 1870s, and an veritable flood after 1890. Although the Göttingen student body grew only fivefold (in contrast to the tenfold German expansion), the rise in attendance from 703 (1796–1801) to 2,753 (1910–14) students nevertheless fundamentally altered its character from that of an intimate regional to a large national institution.[13]

Not surprisingly, the demographic character of the Göttingen student body changed drastically during the enrollment growth. Though growing more provincial due to Vormärz repression (over half of the students hailed from Hanover), geographic recruitment once again became more widespread around 1900. With one-third of the students coming from Prussia, one-fifth from other German states, and as many as one-tenth from outside of the Reich, Göttingen regained its national and international standing. At the same time, the proportion of students from rural backgrounds (under 2,000 inhabitants) decreased slightly from 34.7 percent to 29.2 percent. Whereas the small-town proportion (under 20,000 inhabitants) initially rose over two-fifths, the proportion of students from big cities (over 100,000 inhabitants) ultimately doubled from 23.7 percent to 45.6 percent. Hence the student body grew more metropolitan. The incomplete matriculation entries for secondary education demonstrate the establishment of the university monopoly for classical schools, raising *Gymnasium* training to over 90 percent. But after gaining access in 1900, modern schooling began to account for one-fifth of all students as well. Finally, the figures on gender indicate a complete absence of women students as regular enrollees before 1900 and their gradual arrival after 1908 (5.4 percent), gathering momen-

13. H. Titze, ed., "Datenhandbuch zur deutschen Universitätsgeschichte, 1830–1940" (MS, Göttingen, 1982), 217ff. See J. Conrad, *Das Universitätsstudium in Deutschland während der letzten 50 Jahre* (Jena, 1884), and F. Eulenburg, *Die Frequenz der deutschen Universitäten von ihrer Gründung bis zur Gegenwart* (Leipzig, 1906).

Table 2. *The social composition of the Göttingen student body, in percentages*

Years	Nob.	Elite	Economic Function				Social Class				
			Agr.	Ind.	Com.	Bur.	Ed. of.	Prof.	Bour.	O. mi.	N. mi.
1796–25	15.3	26.6	8.2	3.8	16.0	68.8	49.1	11.5	11.7	17.3	10.3
1826–55	9.8	25.2	7.8	6.3	14.8	68.6	44.3	12.9	9.2	19.9	13.7
1856–85	6.4	22.6	12.8	5.9	16.1	61.0	36.0	13.0	17.5	20.3	13.2
1886–1914	4.3	22.5	11.2	8.8	20.0	55.0	30.1	11.4	21.1	22.0	15.4
Total no.	601	1,821	753	496	1,273	4,461	2,724	873	1,199	1,485	998

tum in the last prewar years (8.0 percent). These Göttingen results reflect the urbanization, modernization, and feminization of the German student body at large.[14]

The transformation of the social composition of the student body was equally pronounced (Table 2). Although Göttingen was the most noble university in Germany, the proportion of aristocrats declined from over 16 percent to less then 4 percent between 1796 and 1914. At the same time, the proportion of sons of the elite (with power over others) shrank from merely 26.6 percent to 22.5 percent, since children of higher bureaucrats were replaced by the offspring of commercial families (with the ratio dropping from 5:1 to less than 2:1). The functional economic categories, preferred by the imperial statistical office, reveal some surprising developments: The agrarians (estate owners and peasants) increased their 8 percent share to 12 percent before tapering off. The proportion of industrialists was initially quite small (around 3 percent) before becoming somewhat more respectable (under 10 percent). Commercial families were considerably better represented (around 13 percent) but increased comparatively less (to over 20 percent). Finally, bureaucratic and professional families declined from over 70 percent to about 50 percent, thereby decreasing their dominance. Even at a socially traditional institution like Göttingen, the recruitment of the student body gradually diversified. Finally, in a status perspective, the children of educated officials decreased from well over one-half to just above one-quarter; the free professional sons held steady around 12 percent; but the propertied bourgeois sons almost doubled, from 11.7 percent to 21.1 percent. Simultaneously, the old middle class (farmers, artisans, trades-

14. K. H. Jarausch, "Frequenz und Struktur: Zur Sozialgeschichte der Studenten im Kaiserreich," in P. Baumgart, ed., *Bildungspolitik in Preussen zur Zeit des Kaiserreichs* (Stuttgart, 1980), 119–49; and "The Social Transformation of the University: The Case of Prussia, 1865–1914," *Journal of Social History* 12 (1979), 609–36.

Table 3. *Fields of study at Göttingen University*

Years	Class Standing		Faculty of Study						
	Fresh	Transf.	Pr. th.	Law	Medi.	Phil.	Na. sc.	Appl.	Came.
1796–25	58.2	32.5	17.4	47.9	17.5	4.3	5.3	3.6	4.1
1826–55	60.5	27.5	18.6	40.7	17.9	8.7	2.8	9.3	2.0
1856–85	49.4	44.1	15.4	29.4	12.1	20.6	13.0	4.5	4.9
1886–1914	32.4	53.0	9.3	28.9	16.3	18.9	19.5	5.2	1.9
Total no.	3,516	3,259	1,050	2,640	1,210	1,113	946	416	227

men) advanced from around 14 percent to 22 percent, and the new middle class (lower officials, white-collar workers) grew from 10.3 percent to 15.4 percent. But the lower class, and with it half of the population, remained virtually excluded. In accord with national trends, these figures underscore both a remarkable persistence of educational privileges and a partial opening in the nineteenth century.[15]

The pattern of university study, turning backgrounds into careers, also altered significantly during the nineteenth century (Table 3). The proportion of freshmen (first-time enrollees) increased from two-fifths at the beginning to three-fifths by midcentury before declining to less than one-third in the last prewar years. Fields of study fluctuated cyclically according to professional prospects but also exhibited some long-range trends. Protestant theology rose to over one-third during the 1810s and showed further peaks in 1828, 1859–60, and 1890, although ultimately declining to less than 7 percent. Beginning with one-half of all students, law lost its preeminence after 1826, recovered intermittently (at last to one-third around 1900), and eventually decreased to one-fifth. In contrast, medicine varied counter-cyclically between one-tenth and one-third, with troughs coming after 1826, 1871, and 1901. Under the neohumanist impulse, the philological subjects in the philosophical faculty began as marginal fields, rose to 27 percent in 1871, and dropped to 7.3 percent in 1893 (due to an oversupply of teachers), only to rebound to almost 27 percent in the last prewar years. The natural sciences also began modestly and contracted at midcentury, but expanded to 18 percent in 1881 and, after a brief pause, boomed to 24.2

---

15. For comparative figures, see F. K. Ringer, *Education and Society in Modern Europe* (Bloomington, Ind., 1979), 709ff; H. Kaelble, *Historische Mobilitätsforschung. Westeuropa und die USA im 19. und 20. Jahrhundert* (Darmstadt, 1978), 73ff; and J. E. Craig, "Higher Education and Social Mobility in Germany," in Jarausch, ed., *The Transformation of Higher Learning, 1860–1930* (Chicago, 1983), 219ff.

percent in 1911. The applied subjects such as pharmacy, dentistry, and agriculture did best in the Vormärz, with almost one-tenth, but retreated to one-twentieth thereafter. In search of an academic mission, cameralism (a bureaucratic study of legal and economic policy) was in danger of losing even its peripheral status. Despite its distinctive strength in natural sciences and cameralism, Göttingen followed the German pattern of declining theology and stagnation in law, with some rise in medical enrollment and an explosion of the philosophical faculty.[16]

The German university that American students encountered therefore changed considerably during the course of the nineteenth century. Its enrollment grew between five and ten times. The student body became more cosmopolitan, urban, modern trained, and female. At the same time, its social composition opened first to the propertied class and then to the lower middle class. Moreover, the ancient faculties of theology and law gradually lost prominence in comparison with the newer, research-driven studies of medicine and philology, as well as the natural sciences. Although following these national trends, Göttingen also continued to display some institutional peculiarities. Starting at a higher level, the Georgia Augusta grew more slowly in the third quarter of the nineteenth century; it remained more rural and Protestant than comparable institutions; it continued to attract more noble, bureaucratic, and academic students than its rivals; and finally, medicine lagged somewhat, whereas the natural sciences in particular flourished. For American students, these characteristics seem not to have proven a deterrent. On the contrary, the moderate size of the institution, its pleasant small-town setting, and its academic tone and scientific orientation proved a more congenial complement to their prior U.S. college experience than urban centers like Berlin, Leipzig, or Munich. Moreover, the increasing cosmopolitanism, reluctant acceptance of modern secondary training, decreasing bureaucratic dominance, and shift from general cultivation toward scientific research lowered access barriers for American visitors.[17]

Determining the characteristics of U.S. students in Göttingen is complicated by the incompleteness of the evidence. In 1855 the fifteen Americans in residence decided "that some historical notice of the doings of the Colony ought to be preserved for future reference." The result was a book listing all U.S. students from 1815 on and updated annually. Although providing an admirable record of Americans in Göttingen, this list also includes about

---

16. For detailed figures, see Titze, ed., "Datenhandbuch zur deutschen Universitätsgeschichte," 217ff.
17. Shumway, "American Students," 171f. It also helped that Göttingen occasionally accepted dissertations written in English.

200 auditors throughout the nineteenth century. These nonregistered Americans were either engaged in liberal education and only passing through, participating as nondegree students in instruction or involved in postdoctoral training when already possessing an advanced degree. Between 1895 and 1901, forty-five women were also allowed to attend informally before German women were admitted officially.[18] After the lost world war, the academic leadership of Göttingen hoped to alleviate the pervasive material plight by an appeal to its American alumni. Hence the university compiled several other typescript lists, based on the matriculation registers and carrying the compilations up to 1914. Unfortunately, their contents do not completely agree with the colony book, since not all Americans registered with that social group and not all of its members were matriculated.[19] The official record of students is the matriculation register, containing generally accurate information as a basis for the collection of fees and debts. A thorough search from 1814 to 1914 revealed a few additional names, including several Canadians, which the alumni compilation had missed.[20] Since little is known about the auditors, the present analysis is based on all regular students, drawn from the Colony book and the alumni list but checked against and supplemented by additional information from the matriculation register.

The pattern of American attendance at Göttingen shows a slow beginning, an explosive growth from midcentury on, and a flattening out after 1900. Although many Englishmen had studied at the Georgia Augusta since its foundation, the first recorded U.S. student was a mathematician named White in 1782–3. In 1806–7 H. Schmeichel followed from the West Indies to study law, in 1810 William B. Astor explored cameralism, and five years later F. Heyer enrolled in the theological faculty. Only after the Napoleonic wars did Edward Everett (classics), George Ticknor (Spanish literature), Joseph G. Cogswell (science), and, a little later, George Bancroft (history) arrive, beginning a regular influx of extraordinary American talent.[21] During the 1820s, as many as eighteen Americans studied in Göttingen (among them Henry Wadsworth Longfellow), but the political repression of the

18. P. G. Buchloh and W. T. Rix, eds., *American Colony of Göttingen: Historical and Other Data Collected Between the Years 1855 and 1888* (Göttingen, 1976). The Shumway transcription also reproduces entries from the second Colony book (after 1888) up to 1910 but is quite inaccurate for the last couple of years.
19. Göttingen Universitätsarchiv, drafts. For the present purpose, the most complete typescript was used for the period 1850–1914.
20. See footnote 11.
21. The traditional attention to these protean intellectuals has obscured the more practical studies of the earlier Americans. See Thwing, *American and German University*, 19ff, as well as most later authors.

Table 4. *Demographic characteristics of American students, in percentages*

Years	Enrollment	Residence					Ethnicity		Fem. sex
		NorE.	MidAt.	Sou.	MidW.	West	Ger.	Angl.	
1840s	4.1	51.1	22.2	22.2			21.7	76.1	
1850s	7.9	27.0	37.1	22.5	10.1	2.2	19.1	78.7	
1860s	9.3	29.5	41.9	10.5	14.3	1.0	28.6	68.6	
1870s	14.2	26.4	34.6	9.4	24.5	.6	31.4	63.5	
1880s	17.5	29.6	26.5	11.7	23.5	4.1	27.6	68.9	
1890s	21.9	20.7	28.0	15.0	27.2	3.3	22.4	69.5	
1900s	16.2	17.6	30.2	9.9	28.6	7.7	30.8	66.5	4.4
1910s	8.9	19.0	24.0	5.0	36.0	5.0	29.0	67.0	27.0
Total no.	1,123	280	342	139	264	39	301	772	35

1830s cut their number (such as Bismarck's friend John L. Motley) in half, a drop that continued during the revolutionary years. After 1850, U.S. attendance jumped almost ten times (facilitated by the arrival of the railroad in 1854), spurring the formalization of the American colony and surpassing an average of ten a year even during the Civil War.[22] Once peace had returned, even more American students flocked to Göttingen, pushing the average to about sixteen per year for the 1870s, reaching almost twenty in the 1880s, and peaking with twenty-five in the 1890s (the maximum was thirty-five for 1895). After the turn of the century the average declined to eighteen (with a low of nine in 1905), but it recovered to around twenty in the last prewar years. Although the establishment of graduate and professional schools in the United States obviated the need for foreign study for budding scholars, the pattern of academic migration to Germany was so well established that it is likely to have continued, albeit at a lesser level, for years to come.[23]

In line with the enrollment expansion, the demographic composition of the American colony at Göttingen changed considerably during the nineteenth century (Table 4). With religion and prior education unknown, geographic origin provides interesting clues. Although most U.S. students originally hailed from New England (as well as from the Middle Atlantic region and the South), the Northeast's share declined from over one-half to under one-fifth, and the South's proportion dropped precipitously from

22. Diehl, *Americans and German Scholarship*, 50ff.
23. Shumway, "American Students," 175, exaggerates the post-1900 drop. For the whole century he gives twelve as an annual average, including auditors. Since few Americans registered before 1850, Tables 4–6 combine these matriculations under the heading "1840s."

Table 5. *Social background of American students, in percentages*

Years	Educated official	Free profes.	Propertied	Lower middle class
1840s	23.7	15.8	50.0	10.5
1850s	25.0	16.1	51.8	7.1
1860s	28.2	16.9	46.5	8.5
1870s	20.0	20.0	44.5	15.5
1880s	26.4	23.3	39.5	10.9
1890s	18.0	16.9	47.5	17.5
1900s	19.5	18.9	40.2	21.3
1910s	22.2	25.3	32.3	20.2
Total	186	166	366	132

one-fifth to one-twentieth. The Middle Atlantic states provided the largest number of students in the 1860s but receded thereafter, whereas the Midwest's representation steadily improved to over one-third. Partly reflecting the westward population shift, this pattern also shows the continued intellectual leadership of the East, the cultural isolation of the South, and the educational distance of the Far West.[24] Equally revealing is the ethnic derivation of American students, which can be loosely surmised by categorizing family and first names. The transatlantic migration started not as filiopiety but as an academic quest, with over three-quarters of U.S. students stemming from English-speaking families. Only in the 1870s did the representation of German-American offspring increase to almost one-third, but the subsequent expansion was driven by Anglo-Americans, and around the turn of the century, the proportion of ethnic students inched upward once again.[25] Finally, female students (3.1 percent) made their presence felt only in the last seven years before the Great War. Once they were formally registered, women helped to keep U.S. enrollments from collapsing, contributing to over one-quarter of the American presence in the last half-decade.[26]

24. Shumway, "American Students," 188ff, lists New York with 219, Massachusetts with 205, and Pennsylvania with 116 as the most frequent home states, followed only distantly by Ohio with 77 and Illinois with 70. Diehl, *Americans and German Scholarship*, 61ff, calls German study a "fad" among Harvard and Yale graduates.
25. Although anglicization in the United States and Germanization of names in Central Europe make classification somewhat hazardous, the rough contours of ethnic origin nevertheless become visible when comparing students like Friedrich Heyer with individuals such as Edward Everett. Moreover, the category of "others" (French, Spanish, or names that could not be assigned) averaged only 4.5 percent.
26. The competent example of female American students facilitated the eventual admission of German

Table 6. *Fields of study of American students, in percentages*

| Years | Theo. | Law | Med. | Faculty | | | |
				Phil.	Sci.	Prac.	Cam.
1840s	13.0	17.4	8.7	58.7		3.1	
1850s	2.2	19.1	13.5	34.8	28.1	1.1	1.1
1860s	3.8	12.4	12.4	18.1	49.5	2.9	1.0
1870s	5.7	17.0	15.7	34.0	24.5	1.9	1.3
1880s	4.6	6.6	25.5	23.0	37.2	2.0	1.0
1890s	2.0	4.9	23.2	21.5	41.9	3.3	3.3
1900s	3.8	1.6	15.9	22.0	51.1	3.8	1.6
1910s	7.0		3.0	32.0	51.0	5.0	2.0
Total	49	93	193	301	436	32	19

Even if they did not all come from relatively affluent families, American students at Göttingen represented something of an elite. The vagaries associated with crossing the Atlantic in ships that only gradually were converted to steam required exceptional financial resources or intellectual commitment. The most frequent occupation of the student's father, accounting for 15.4 percent, was therefore business, whereas financiers amounted to 6.5 percent and industrialists to 3.8 percent. However, sons of clergymen came in second, with 8 percent of students, and doctors produced 6.3 percent, followed by professors (4.9 percent) and lawyers (4.0 percent). In contrast, children from more modest homes were less frequent, with farmers producing 6.7 percent and craftsmen only 1.9 percent.[27] Combined into social strata, these parental occupations reveal an interesting transformation of the American student body. Except for a recovery in the 1890s, sons from propertied families steadily lost ground, dropping from one-half to one-third. At the same time, the share of children from educated backgrounds increased from over one-third to one-half by the 1880s before levelling off at two-fifths. Although the proportion of public servants increased only until the 1860s, that of professionals rose (except for the 1890s and 1900s) to one-quarter. The marginal lower-middle-class presence decreased even further before expanding to around one-fifth of all students

women. J. Albisetti, *Schooling German Girls and Women: Secondary and Higher Education in the Nineteenth Century* (Princeton, N.J., 1988), 223ff.

27. Since classification problems bedevil social analysis, occupations were first counted individually and then combined into the categories used for the German students in order to make them comparable. See Jarausch, *Students, Society and Politics in Imperial Germany: The Rise of Academic Illiberalism* (Princeton, N.J., 1982), 114ff.

in the last three decades. Taken together, these developments suggest a gradual academization of the American presence, followed by a slight social opening when the costs of travel declined.[28]

The intellectual interests of American students in Göttingen also changed dramatically over the years. Because of the U.S. academic calender, two-thirds of students enrolled in the fall semester. Only about one in ten had studied previously at another German university, mostly in Berlin or Leipzig. Due to sectarian fragmentation in the United States, enrollments in Protestant theology courses remained slight (under one-twentieth). The historical school of jurisprudence aroused more attention, but the difference in legal systems limited inscriptions to under one-tenth, even if one adds cameralism. Since it was more transferable, the study of medicine interested one-sixth of the Americans. In contrast, the main attractions were the humanities, with over one-fourth, and the sciences, justly famous at the Georgia Augusta, with almost two-fifths; enrollment in the practical careers remained marginal.[29] The original interest in liberal education (philosophy with 58.7 percent before 1850) quickly gave way to a preoccupation with mathematics (49.5 percent in the 1860s) and legal studies (29.0 percent in the 1870s). The great expansion of enrollment was also supported by an influx into medicine (29.5 percent in 1890), as well as a renewed growth of the sciences (over one-half after 1900). The stagnation after the turn of the century resulted largely from the collapse of professional enrollments in law and medicine, whereas the humanities made somewhat of a comeback after 1910 (32.0 percent), helped by the admission of women (three-fifths of whom studied philosophy).[30] From a social perspective, children of officials were overrepresented in theology and philosophy; the offspring of professional families gravitated once again to their fathers' careers; the sons of the propertied were slightly more frequent in the humanities or law; and the progeny of the lower middle class sought to rise through the study of the sciences.

Although showing some similarities to German patterns, the profile of American students in Göttingen was distinctive. In terms of enrollment, U.S. matriculations display the same peak in the 1820s, followed by a drop and a renewed rise to the 1890s. Since it was driven by different forces, the

28. Diehl, *Americans and German Scholarship,* 64, does not analyze the father's occupation. In ethnic terms, the Anglo-American share was highest among educated officials, whereas Germans were overrepresented among professionals.
29. Shumway, "American Students," 186ff. Since science students were originally registered simply in the faculty of philosophy, it is impossible to give an exact count of scientists before the 1850s.
30. In ethnic terms, Anglo-Americans were overrepresented in theology, philology, and the sciences, whereas German-Americans preferred the professions, especially medicine.

initial influx was lower, the subsequent rise steeper (with no pause in the late 1880s), and the final stagnation flatter than German attendance at the Georgia Augusta.[31] In terms of demographic characteristics, there was a similar broadening of origins from a limited regional to a more national scope of matriculations. Both groups were likely to be similarly urbanizing, albeit on a higher level for the U.S. visitors.[32] American students were also prepared in a somewhat more modern fashion, since Latin schools were less frequent and formal matriculants had already received their BA degree. But in both countries, pioneering female enrollment was more exclusive and less professional than male attendance. In social terms, the contrasts were more startling. To begin with, there were no noblemen among American students. Moreover, the share of sons of educated officials was distinctively smaller, due to the less developed nature of the bureaucracy in the United States. In contrast, the proportion from the free professions was considerably larger, thereby compensating in terms of academic background. At the same time, the propertied strata were several times more numerous among Americans than German students at Göttingen, signifying the greater role of wealth in U.S. society. Consequently, the presence of the lower middle class was also smaller, making the visitors more exclusive than their Central European hosts and their own peers who stayed at home.[33]

The contrasting pattern of studies also reveals the different intellectual priorities of American students. Though declining even in Germany, Protestant theology attracted roughly three times more Central European students than U.S. visitors, who preferred their own seminaries (13.8 percent versus 4.4 percent). Similarly, as a conduit to a secure state office, the study of law was almost four times as popular for Germans as for U.S. citizens, who favored practical legal skills over theoretical jurisprudence (34.7 percent versus 8.3 percent). However, interest in medicine was virtually identical in both student groups, since the healing arts were becoming increasingly important in both societies (15.9 percent versus 17.2 percent). Although marginal, the political and economic knowledge of cameralism was more attractive in a bureaucratic society than in a free market economy

---

31. The U.S. share of Göttingen matriculations increased from slightly over 1 percent in the 1810s to around 2.5 percent in the 1890s. Compared to the U.S. enrollment explosion from 2,562 in 1810 to 355,000 in 1910, American attendance in Göttingen rose much more slowly. See C. Burke, "The Expansion of American Higher Education," in *Transformation of Higher Learning*, 108ff.

32. This issue could not be explored because foreigners often gave the name of the country or nearest city known to the registrar as the place of origin, thereby making the information too imprecise for analysis. Shumway, "American Students," 188.

33. Buchloh, *American Colony*, 11, exaggerates when claiming that U.S. students came "overwhelmingly from the upper classes of the East Coast." R. Angelo, "The Social Transformation of American Higher Education," in *The Transformation of Higher Learning*, 261–92.

(3.0 percent versus 1.7 percent). Similarly, the applied fields, such as pharmacy, dentistry, and forestry, also were more relevant for German than for American students, who would eventually gain some such training at home (5.5 percent versus 2.8 percent). At the core of the American interest were the humanities to which they flocked almost twice as often as their hosts (14.6 percent versus 26.8 percent). Most popular among U.S. students were the subjects with the smallest cultural or language barriers, such as mathematics and the natural sciences, where they were represented three times more frequently than the Germans (12.4 percent versus 38.8 percent). Some Americans sought to gain advanced professional skills, particularly in medicine, and others sought general neohumanist cultivation (*Bildung*). But most serious U.S. students at the Georgia Augusta were interested in the new spirit of *Wissenschaft* that was revolutionizing the conduct of scientific research.[34]

Though the precise impact of their German sojourn is difficult to determine, many of these young Americans eventually led the struggle for academic professionalization. Although they were unlikely to improve their religious faith, sense of humility, artistic taste, or personal character in Central Europe, U.S. students, according to Thwing, learned the "habit" of free inquiry, acquired the "intellectual method" of thoroughness, and imbibed the "moral conviction" of scholarship as service to mankind.[35] Though more recent authors disagree on the particulars, there is some consensus on the German roots of the principle of academic freedom, however imperfectly realized in the Empire; the transfer of the scholarly method, characterized by seminars, advanced degrees, and monographs; and the introduction of the research imperative, shifting the impetus from the transmission to the generation of knowledge.[36] In these developments, promoting the professionalization of the academic calling, the Georgia Augusta played an important role. The famous protest of the seven liberal Göttingen professors in the Hanoverian constitutional conflict helped to reinforce the principle of *Lehr- und Lernfreiheit*. The acclaimed philological seminars of the eighteenth-century Georgia Augusta helped pioneer novel methods of

---

34. See the literature listed in R. S. Turner, "Die Universitäten," in K. -E. Jeismann and P. Lundgreen, eds., *Handbuch der deutschen Bildungsgeschichte* (Munich, 1987), vol. III, 221ff, and K. H. Jarausch, "Universität und Hochschule," in vol. IV, 28ff.
35. Thwing, *American and German University*, 46ff.
36. R. Hofstadter and W. P. Metzger, *The Development of Academic Freedom in the United States* (New York, 1955), 367ff; Herbst, *German Historical School*, 99ff; and J. Ben David and A. Zloczower, "Universities and Academic Systems in Modern Societies," *Archives of European Sociology* 3 (1962), 71ff.

source research, preparing F. A. Wolf's and L. von Ranke's later break-throughs. At the same time, the moderate Enlightenment climate of Göttingen fostered a critical perspective that linked the new discoveries to social and political issues, thereby providing a broader motive for the intellectual quest.[37] Much of this innovative spirit still animated the faculty in the nineteenth century, while it was being extended into the rising sciences.

Through the mediation of the American Colony, U.S. visitors experienced a new academic lifestyle at Göttingen, blending serious scholarship with pleasant student pursuits. Even before 1855, many Americans formed a tight network, passing on information and references to facilitate their studies and remaining in contact after their return to the United States. Letters home of such luminaries as Everett or Bancroft abound with statements, stressing dedicated intellectual labor. There is no doubt that for a minority of high-minded scholars, initiation into German *Wissenschaft* in formal courses, as well as personal intercourse with famous professors, was the crucial gain.[38] But for many others, who were there for the purpose of learning German and having a good time, the free conviviality of German student life was an equal attraction. Less supervised than Anglo-American collegians but more sociable than the French individualists, Central European academic youths developed an independent subculture characterized by vigorous association. Unlike a noble *Corps* or a liberal *Burschenschaft,* the American colony functioned rather like a *Landsmannschaft,* gathering those U.S. students in need of company and mutual help. By celebrating patriotic holidays, organizing excursions into the countryside, holding drinking bouts, and so on, the "colonists" accepted German customs, such as *kneipen* and colored caps, while Americanizing their purpose. In their looser organization (being led by a "patriarch" as the oldest resident), this society contributed a tone of liberal cosmopolitanism to Göttingen student subculture.[39] The Colony functioned as an intellectual meeting ground for shared experiences and a haven for foreigners who wanted to speak their own language. Experienced Americans served as crucial mediators, guiding their compatriots' German contacts as well as in fostering Americanism among them.

37. Selle, *Universität Göttingen,* 93ff. See also G. Meinhardt, *Die Universität Göttingen. Ihre Entwicklung und Geschichte von 1734–1974* (Göttingen, 1977); and H. Bödeker, et al., eds., *Aufklärung und Geschichte. Studien zur deutschen Geschichtswissenschaft im 18. Jahrhundert* (Göttingen, 1986).

38. Quotations from Thwing, *American and German University,* 12ff; and Buchloh, *American Colony,* 115ff.

39. Buchloh, *American Colony,* 12, points to the social importance of the colony but misinterprets its organizational character. See K. H. Jarausch, *Deutsche Studenten, 1800–1970* (Frankfurt, 1984), 49ff. For occasional summaries of Colony activities by the respective patriarchs, See *American Colony,* 30ff, 70ff.

Inspired by such a positive image of academic life, the great majority of U.S. alumni of the Georgia Augusta chose a scholarly career. Fragmentary occupational information indicates that they made more outstanding contributions to the development of American higher education than to business or politics. A hand count of the subsequent occupations of the 128 entries of the Colony book to 1888 that could be found in the *Dictionary of American Biography* or in *Who's Who* confirms their heavy science and humanities orientation. Even allowing for an academic bias in these listings, all but nine individuals (three publishers and two businessmen, bankers, and politicians, respectively) were engaged in some form of scholarship. Although there were only ten theologians, twelve lawyers, and seven doctors, thirty-eight were known for their involvement in the humanities, and an astounding fifty-two conducted scientific or technical research.[40] A recombination of Shumway's listing of 181 alumni professions, based only on *Who's Who* but extending until after the turn of the century, yields a similar pattern. Only 4.4 percent became prominent as businessmen and 2.2 percent as politicians, in contrast to 12.2 percent who rose to the presidency of their college. The 7.2 percent of theologians, 6 percent of lawyers, and 5.5 percent of doctors were overshadowed by the 27.1 percent of humanities scholars and the 35.4 percent of natural scientists. The single largest group were chemists with thirty-one, followed by mathematicians with thirteen and historians and classicists with eleven. Though necessarily fragmentary, these figures do suggest that Göttingen graduates played an important role in college administration and the advancement of many disciplines, particularly the hard sciences and the traditional humanities. By reorienting their fields toward research, based on continental training and organization, German-trained scientists made an important contribution to the transformation of scholarship into an academic profession in the United States.[41]

Since structural parameters cannot capture the quality of influence, the nature of the German imprint on American education remains elusive. The contradiction between extravagant claims of "tremendous impact" and skeptical stress on native developments is likely to be irresolvable. For contemporary intellectuals, the German roots of many practices and institutions of American scholarship are somewhat of an embarrassment, since they

---

40. "Annotations" in Buchloh, *American Colony,* 115–60. This finding agrees with Diehl, *Americans and German Scholarship,* 66ff.

41. Shumway, "American Students," 175ff, 186ff. This emphasis on science also corrects Diehl's stress on philology in *Americans,* 118ff, as well as Jurgen Herbst's preoccupation with the humanities in *German Historical School,* 231ff. According to the Colony book, 174 Americans studied chemistry and 126 mathematics, in contrast to 163 who pursued philology.

represent a largely forgotten tradition. Language barriers, as well as stereotypes fostered by two world wars and the abuse of learning in the holocaust have broken the bond of older affection and obliterated the consciousness of indebtedness.[42] Conversely some conservative critics like Allan Bloom have exaggerated the impact of German philosophy into the arch-evil of the modern world by making it the principal source of "value relativism."[43] In addressing the question of influence, historians confront the perplexing task of not only measuring observable parameters but also of probing imperceptible intangibles that do not fit easily into an accepted pattern. Since it is unlikely to convince doubters with general arguments, research on the German impact needs more studies of particular institutions such as libraries and individual fields of knowledge, especially in the sciences. At the same time, future discussions require a more subtle conception of what "influence" might mean. The highly successful academic community of the United States is likely to resent even well-founded claims about the direct transposition of Germanic patterns as cultural dependence. But perhaps assertions about the indirect transmission of a sense of intellectual freedom, scholarly method, and social responsibility will be more easily accepted, since the rise of an academic profession cannot be explained on the basis of indigenous roots alone. During the second half of the nineteenth century, German models and experiences had their greatest impact not in cultural colonizing, but in stimulating an authentically American academic development.[44]

42. See the literature in K. H. Jarausch, "Huns, Krauts or Good Germans? The German Image in America, 1800–1980," in J. F. Harris, ed., *German–American Interrelations: Heritage and Challenge* (Tübingen, 1985), 145–59.

43. Allan Bloom, *The Closing of the American Mind* (New York, 1987), 141ff, attributes most current problems to German origins.

44. For a classic statement of an American professional reformer, see Flexner, *Universities: American, English, German*, 305ff. See also the brief acknowledgment in P. Starr, *The Social Transformation of American Medicine* (New York, 1982), 113f.

12

Philip Schaff: His Role in American Evangelical Education

GARY K. PRANGER

INTRODUCTION

There have been many German influences on American Christianity. Among the early settlers of America were groups such as the German and Dutch Reformed or Lutherans, Moravians, Brethren, and Roman Catholics. German "higher" criticism had significant effects on American theological studies toward the end of the century. But few people are familiar with Philip Schaff, whose life and thought spans the nineteenth century and touches both ends of the spectrum.

Philip Schaff (1819–93) is one of those marginal men whose mediating influence as a theologian touched both the evangelical and modernist camps within American Christianity. His direct and indirect influence on American evangelical education is unmistakable if one defines education, in the words of a recent historian, as "the deliberate, systematic, and sustained effort to transmit, evoke, or acquire knowledge, values, attitudes, skills, and sensibilities, as well as any learning that results from that effort, direct or indirect, intended or unintended."[1] To demonstrate Schaff's complex influence, which was conservative in nature, his background needs to be summarized before we can evaluate his role as a teacher, theologian, and church historian in its American context.

THE EMERGENCE OF PHILIP SCHAFF

Philip Schaff was born in Switzerland to a poor carpenter's family near Chur, the capital of the canton of Graubünden, on January 1, 1819. His father left the family early, and, his mother later remarried. At age sixteen he "awoke to a sense of the paramount importance of religion" and decided

---

1. Lawrence A. Cremin, *American Education: The Metropolitan Experience, 1876–1980* (New York: Harper & Row, 1988), x.

213

to become a theologian in the company of Meta Heusser, a reclusive, evangelical poetess, and the Reverend Paul Kind.[2] The former gave him the early love and Christian influence he craved while also imparting to him a love for romantic poetry. The latter counseled Schaff to attend a Christian school in Kornthal, near Stuttgart, in Germany. Here Schaff had a conversion experience that transformed his life from within, while his teachers worked on him from without. Later, at the *Gymnasium* in Stuttgart, Schaff was given a classical education in Hebrew, Greek, and Latin. With a powerful, grasping mind and a hunger for learning, he progressed rapidly.[3]

From 1837 to 1839, Schaff studied philosophy and theology at the University of Tübingen, guided by Christian Friedrich Schmid, Isaak A. Dorner, and other evangelical professors, who protected him from the extremes of Hegelianism and the biblical criticism of F. C. Baur and Heinrich Ewald. Schaff, however, did not fully reject the more radical thinkers of the time; he adopted some of their philosophical ideas while rejecting their theology. From 1839 to 1840, Schaff studied at the University of Halle under Friedrich A. G. Tholuck and Julius Müller, who gave him an appreciation for pietistic Christianity. From 1840 to 1844 he studied at the University of Berlin, where he came into intimate contact with Johann A. W. Neander, the famous church historian, who further molded his thought and directed his studies.[4]

Collectively, these professors influenced Schaff's reading and usage of George W. F. Hegel, Friedrich Schleiermacher, Friedrich Schelling, F. C. Baur, and Friedrich Strauss. From Hegel, Schaff borrowed the dialectic method. From Schleiermacher, he absorbed philosophical idealism and the view of an open theological development. Baur gave him an appreciation for critical analysis and thorough research. Neander, Schmid, Dorner, Schelling, and the writings of Johann G. Herder led Schaff to an evangelical, catholic, organic developmental theology and philosophy of history that focused on the incarnation of Christ.

In 1843 the German Reformed Seminary in Mercersburg, Pennsylvania, invited Schaff to teach Bible and church history. William Krummacher, the renowned Bible expositor, who had declined the same offer, ordained Schaff at Elberfeld as a missionary and charged him with the task of reforming and reviving German-American Christianity. Krummacher's sermon

---

2. Philip Schaff, "Autobiographical Reminiscences for my Children," 7–8, 18–23, Box: Autobiographical Miscellaneous, Philip Schaff papers, Evangelical and Reformed Historical Society, Philip Schaff Library, Lancaster Theological Seminary, Lancaster, Pa.; hereafter cited only by name, brief title, and page number.
3. Ibid., 29–30, 66, 68–73.
4. Ibid., 89–90, 94–5, 97.

upon that occasion made Schaff a modern David about to take on a new Goliath. Schaff's own sermon drew a very negative picture of the United States in general and of the state of German-American Christianity in particular. Schaff's mission became even weightier when King Frederick William IV of Prussia gave him his special backing. In traveling west, Schaff spent two months in England, which impressed him most favorably, so that he became an anglophile even after he had become content with life in the United States.[5]

On arriving in the United States in 1844, Schaff was welcomed by the Pennsylvania-German community, but German-Americans at large were outraged by the low rating he had given them in his ordination sermon. Schaff's narrow German world view quickly disappeared, however, as he observed the reality of the American situation. He found most German-Americans holding firmly to their Christian heritage. Schaff still distrusted the fanatical "red republicans" and all who proposed atheistic radical change. It appeared that just this kind of people were spreading the criticism of him in the German-American community outside of Pennsylvania.[6]

Schaff assimilated easily to American life; he ceased to distrust the new and the different and embraced an American conservatism that was itself parochial, mildly liberal on issues such as abolitionism, and always flirting with nativism or bigotry. He traded the conservative vision of German Christianity for its counterpart on the other side of the Atlantic. This made it easy for him to preach Anglo-Saxon or Anglo-Germanic togetherness.[7] Thus his conservative, middle-class outlook did not dissipate but expanded. One might say that he was as wide and free-thinking as any middle-class conservative anywhere could be. His Christianity and scholarliness made him aware of his finite, human foibles. By this consciousness, buttressed by faith and reason, he rose above his parochialisms and became transatlantic in connecting and blending cultures and trying to rise above them.

Schaff became influential in Pennsylvania-German affairs, as his intimate friendship and collaboration with the poet Henry Harbaugh evidenced. At

5. David S. Schaff, *The Life of Philip Schaff* (New York: Charles Scribner's Sons, 1897), 75–6, 82–7, 105; Philip Schaff, "Reminiscences," 103; Philip Schaff, "Ordination of Philip Schaff – Translated from Krummacher's *Palmblatter*," *Weekly Messenger* (Chambersburg, Pa., September 4, 1844): 1; Philip Schaff, "English University Life and University Reform: Oxford and Cambridge," *German Reformed Messenger* 22 (Chambersburg, Pa., April 23, 1856), 4293–4.

6. Philip Schaff, *The Principle of Protestantism*, transl. by John W. Nevin (Chambersburg, Pa.: Office of the German Reformed Church, 1845), 107–10; Philip Schaff, diary entry for December 31, 1844, Box: Philip Schaff Diaries 1844–90, Philip Schaff Manuscript Collection, The Burke Library, Union Theological Seminary, New York, New York; hereafter this archive is cited as UTS.

7. Philip Schaff, *Anglo-Germanism or the Significance of the German Nationality in the United States* (Chambersburg, Pa., 1846), 12–24.

first, he taught in German, but his students and his own rapid learning of English convinced him otherwise. Like the community around him, he cherished German culture while assimilating to American life. He married and began a family within two years of his arrival. Reformed catechisms and Grimm's fairy tales remained staples of his life.[8]

In Schaff's mind, Anglo-German unity combined ever more forcefully with Christ's Great Commission, expanded his sense of a Christian mission, and made him a forceful advocate of assimilation and adaptation of the best within German traditions to the best within American culture. The best gift Germans could give to the United States was tough-minded German evangelical scholarship in order to make American Christianity stronger, deeper, and broader in vision. Schaff accepted English as the language of the future and rejected the rigidity of those German ministers and missionaries who held on to the German language tenaciously as a sine qua non.[9]

During this "Mercersburg period" from 1844 to 1865, Philip Schaff developed his theology and began his extensive works in church history.[10] While putting future German Reformed ministers through their paces, he dreamed of developing a German-American school of theology. To court the German-American community at large, he published and edited a journal called *Der Deutsche Kirchenfreund*. In 1854 Schaff returned to Germany, acting like another de Tocqueville, to explain and defend the United States to the king and others in Prussia and throughout Europe. As an advocate of more religious freedom and transatlantic understanding, he became a missionary in reverse. Schaff then endured the rigors of the American Civil War and, as he witnessed its cruelties, became an antislavery advocate.[11]

To be closer to publishers and free to pursue wider goals, Schaff moved in 1865 to New York. For a time, he defended the traditional day of rest and worship with the New York Sabbath Committee against the encroachment of secularizing influences. He claimed that the American Sabbath "was

---

8. David S. Schaff, *The Life*, 93–5, 105, 133–4; Philip Schaff, diary entry for December 31, 1844, P.S. diaries 1844–90, UTS; Philip Schaff, "Reminiscences," inside cover; Linn Harbaugh, "the Example of a Christian Scholar" (undated and unpublished), 16–18, Box 7: Schaff Mementos and Memorials, Philip Schaff papers, Evangelical and Reformed Historical Society, Philip Schaff Library, Lancaster Theological Seminary, Lancaster, Pa.; hereafter this archive is cited as ERHS.

9. Philip Schaff, *Anglo-Germanism*, 13–15.

10. Philip Schaff, *What Is Church History? A Vindication of the Idea of Historical Development*, transl. by John W. Nevin (Philadelphia, 1846); Philip Schaff, *History of the Apostolic Church*, transl. by Edward D. Yeomans (New York, 1853; Edinburgh, 1854).

11. David Schaff, *The Life*, 163–5; Philip Schaff, ed., *Der Deutsche Kirchenfreund. Organ Für die Gemeinsamen Interessen oder Amerikanisch-Deutschen Kirchen*, vols. 1–6 (Mercersburg, Pa., 1848–53); Philip Schaff, *America: A Sketch of its Political, Social, and Religious Character*, ed. by Perry Miller (Cambridge, Mass.: Harvard University Press, [1854] 1961); Philip Schaff, "The Gettysburg Week," *Scribner's Magazine* 16 (New York: Charles Scribner's Sons, July–December 1894), 21–54.

in danger of being crucified between two thieves, Irish Whiskey and German beer." Soon, however, the Union Theological Seminary offered him a professorship, and there he spent the remainder of his life as a Presbyterian. Here he edited such colossal works as the English translation of Johann Peter Lange's *A Commentary on the Holy Scriptures* and the Anglo-American reconstruction of J. J. Herzog's *Real Encyclopedia,* which became known as the *Schaff–Herzog Encyclopedia of Religious Knowledge.*[12]

In this New York period, Schaff was free to participate in transatlantic supradenominational affairs and projects. He joined the Evangelical Alliance and became one of its leading spokesmen for Christian unity and religious freedom. In the Anglo-American effort to revise the King James version of the Bible, Schaff chaired the American contingent, which included a host of scholars from many denominations. Besides doing some translation of the New Testament, Schaff showed remarkable diplomatic powers in seeing the project through the times when it was threatened by dissension and Anglo-American rivalry. Schaff was the only scholar in this project whose native language was not English. In 1893 he participated in the Parliament of Religions in Chicago when other evangelicals felt it would mean compromising their faith. By the end of his life, Schaff had become a consummate ecumenical advocate for church unity while never abandoning orthodox reformed theology.[13]

During his American years, Schaff rose to prominence. He knew James Buchanan, Robert F. B. Morse, the inventor of the telegraph, and Cyrus McCormick, and he met on occasion such people as Abraham Lincoln, Ulysses S. Grant, and Harriet Beecher Stowe. He knew most of the important religious figures of the day, such as Henry Ward Beecher, Charles Hodge, Horace Bushnell, and Dwight L. Moody. His many trips to Europe brought him into contact with Fredrick William IV, Prince Metternich, Otto von Bismarck, and Leopold von Ranke, as well as a host of religious figures of the Orthodox, Roman Catholic, and Protestant persuasions.[14] The timid Swiss-German immigrant who had hesitated to leave Germany had become a renowned church historian, theologian, and ecumenist.

12. Philip Schaff, "The Christian Sabbath," in *Christ and Christianity* (New York: Charles Scribner's Sons, [August 11, 1863], 1885); David Schaff, *The Life,* 221–7; Philip Schaff to Norman White, June 20, 1870, Letter Box 4, ERHS; Johann Peter Lange, *A Commentary on the Holy Scriptures, Critical, Doctrinal, and Homiletic,* 12 vols. (Grand Rapids, Mich., 1960); *The New Schaff–Herzog Encyclopedia of Religious Knowledge,* ed. Samuel M. Jackson (New York: Funk & Wagnalls Co., 1908); an updated version was published by Baker Book House, Grand Rapids, Mich., 1960.
13. David Schaff, *The Life,* 253–7, 357, 483–6; Philip Schaff, diary entries for April 4 and 5, 1865, P.S. diaries 1844–90, UTS.
14. Gary K. Pranger, "Philip Schaff (1819–1893): Portrait of an Immigrant Theologian," Ph.D. dissertation (University of Illinois at Chicago, 1987), 150–92, 284–334.

Schaff's Christian life remained consistent and resilient. As an emigrant, he absorbed a moderate Anglo-Saxonism. He adapted to the United States with ease but maintained close intellectual and social ties with Germany. He formulated a developmental, organic, providential view of history and a unique mediating evangelical theology that tolerated liberal positions, yet remained orthodox and fundamentalistic. Schaff had a clear mission that expanded as his career progressed. He worked tirelessly to transplant the best of German evangelical scholarship to the United States.

THE TEACHER

Philip Schaff affected American evangelical education by introducing his students to German speculative methodology as well as German theological ideas.

From 1800 to 1865, seminaries in America provided the only graduate education then available.[15] The German Reformed Seminary at Mercersburg was the oldest of three seminaries, serving a denomination of approximately 100,000 members and, by 1860, counting 356 ministers. Although the denomination remained a small element in American Christianity, its role within the Pennsylvania German community was unquestionably important.

In general, Schaff merely followed Frederick Augustus Rauch, his predecessor at Mercersburg, who was the seminary's first president until his death in 1841. Rauch had come from Germany and established speculative methods of teaching that Schaff improved upon. It had been Rauch's ambition to develop an Anglo-German system of thought, just as Schaff hoped to create a German-American school of theology.[16] Both failed to realize these dreams, but both were ground breakers in that German thought was brought to bear on American evangelical minds. Moreover, it was not just what the students learned, but how they learned it, that became important.

Schaff made an immediate impact on the classroom by stressing a reverential attitude toward the institutionalized church and its past. Enamored of high church ecclesiasticism, Schaff, however, meant much more than the Reformed Church. Schaff inculcated in his students a tolerant respect

---

15. Mark A. Noll, "The University Arrives in America, 1870–1930: Traditionalism During the Academic Revolution," in Joel A. Carpenter and Kenneth Shipps, eds., *Making Higher Education Christian: The History and Mission of Evangelical Colleges in America* (Grand Rapids, Mich.: Christian University Press and William B. Eerdmans Publ. Co., 1987), 106.
16. *The New Schaff–Herzog Encyclopedia* (1908), vol. 9, 404.

for all Christian communions and schools of thought.[17] On the one hand, this clashed with the exclusivist minds of many immigrants and, on the other hand, challenged the fundamentalist-nativist minds in the American churches. Schaff also stressed the devotional spirit in private life as most important, far beyond the pew and mere intellectual assent. This widening of horizons that Schaff had learned so well from his mentors was his lasting legacy to his own students.

In his teaching, Schaff enjoyed ranging through all areas of theology, including much of the German theoretical work, but he insisted that practical theology take precedent over the speculative. The professor's chair should be connected with the pastor's pulpit and the seminary with the congregation. Here Schaff introduced things that were truly new for his time. He showed future pastors how to use church history properly in the creation of deeper sermons.[18] Schaff hoped that the Sunday sermon would reflect an enlarged perspective on Christianity and its living history. Much of Christian society in the United States at this time believed that Bible study by itself supplied ministers with all that they needed for effective preaching to the common layman. Church history itself served primarily to glorify a particular denomination.[19] Thus Schaff introduced ecumenical views when few espoused them.

Schaff guided students in systematic study; he tried to show them how to enjoy it for its own sake, and how to reap the rewards when it was undertaken joyfully and done faithfully with prayer and a "judicious spirit."[20] This judicious spirit helped to observe human nature and all of life with great care. There Schaff united an intellectual appreciation of many ideas with careful observation and with the usage of reformed theology.

Schaff's daily classroom habits, as reflected in his students' notebooks, revealed his meticulous preparation; his early lecture notes on church history formed the outline for the later *History of the Christian Church*. Schaff used many textbooks and had such a bibiliographic command that citations flowed easily from his mind. The usual classroom method was based on the teacher's review and the student's recitation of past lessons. Sometimes Schaff took one step back from the material, played the impartial observer, and simply martialed the facts without comment. At other times he lectured

---

17. Philip Schaff, "Lectures on Christian Dogmatics," Box: Lectures at Mercersburg 1844–66, 13 manuscripts, ERHS.
18. Ibid.
19. Henry Warner Bowden, *Church History in the Age of Science: Historiographical Patterns in the United States 1876–1918* (Chapel Hill: University of North Carolina Press, 1971), 40.
20. George H. Shriver, "Philip Schaff as a Teacher of Church History," *Journal of Presbyterian History,* 47 (March 1979), 76–84.

without notes, offering personal observations and quips that students sig-
naled with the phrase "Dr. Schaff thinks . . . " Sometimes he read from
primary sources such as the Roman Liturgy or from the writings of Thomas
a Kempis to introduce students to the rich past of the church. Schaff's own
records and his students' notes reveal thorough, up-to-date scholarship,
piety, and humor, as well as some absentmindedness.[21]

His many students over the years, from Mercersburg to New York, had
great respect for him. Schaff's influence was profound, although it is impossible to document it thoroughly beyond the notebooks of his students.
If nothing else, Schaff succeeded in deepening their faith and widening their
perspectives of the church at large, both characteristics of German evangelical and speculative thought.

THE THEOLOGIAN AND CHURCH HISTORIAN

Schaff's teachings on theology and church history went beyond the classroom when he began to publish his works. Very early he came into contact
with the American theological community at large. He drew criticism as
well as respect. For the most part, the criticism led to more, not less, interest
in German theology. In the eyes of American evangelicals, Schaff appeared
to be a novel figure just as they were beginning to study German theology
in a serious way. Schaff's theology was meant to be liberating as well as
unifying, and thus his ideas had an incalculable effect – as pollen thrown to
the wind. How these ideas settled in other minds is impossible to determine,
but we can detect the directions they gave.

Schaff's own theology was anchored in, and encompassed by, the traditional reformed theology of John Calvin. It holds that God's providence, infinity, and sovereignty are behind and decree all things,
including man's freely made decisions, and consequently all of history, to
bring about God's perfectly good will out of and despite man's evil dis-
position. Adam in the beginning, and all people thereafter, create sin, but
God allows it that he might prove his perfect love and mercy to all.
Christ, the God-man, had to come to redeem all the elect, and to plant
the seed of faith by the Holy Spirit that now draws the redeemed toward
the message of free grace. Nothing a person does can bring on salvation
and eternal life. Only God opens up the heart and gives it the ability to
accept or reject the message. Only after the secure knowledge that God
has chosen the believer and the believer's acceptance of Christ as Savior

21. Ibid.

and Lord does a life of sanctification proceed, allowing the freedom to obey or disobey God. The unredeemed are imprisoned in their own sinful natures and therefore hopelessly lost. By remaining in this world, the Christian's character is shaped by life's problems, leading to a recognition of total dependence of God. The heavenly relationship is then a reconciliation between God and his creation. The world of sin and error in this theology reveals that the place of men and women has to be with God, the Creator, not against or separated from his existence. In between God's creation and the millennial reign of Christ, the history of the world as we know it unfolds.[22]

This theology, of course, had been stressed in narrow as well as broad ways over the course of time, and Schaff's own beliefs represented a certain latitudinarian Calvinism; he rejected infant damnation and believed that Christ, out of love, had died to save all men and women. The elect were known only by God, so Christians had an obligation to love and present the gospel to all people. Pre-Christian people who had never heard the gospel could be saved by an act of Christ's mercy in heaven under circumstances only God could determine. Moreover, Schaff did not believe in a literal inspiration or dictation of the Scriptures by God to men. God used fallible minds and circumstances to present his infallible thoughts and purposes. Schaff did not believe in "the absolute inerrancy of the original autographs which nobody has ever seen or will see – for they are irretrievably lost." The Bible maintained its authority, in Schaff's view, because God's power and principles reside there. It was a living Word with the words of men. Some of these thoughts he considered unfit to be taught as doctrines, but only as speculations.[23]

Schaff's theology and what can be called his "theology of history" incorporated a modified Hegelian triad with an intensive organic development of Christianity. For Schaff, "theology" and "history" were so intertwined that they were interchangeable terms. The thesis, antithesis, and synthesis are worked out naturally by people and simultaneously by God's providence. Human development is seen as a series of tossings and turnings in reaction to the events of history, particularly the crucifixion and resur-

22. Philip Schaff, ed., *The Creeds of Christendom*, 6th ed., 3 vols., revised by David S. Schaff, vol. 3, *The Evangelical Protestant Creeds* (Grand Rapids, Mich.: Baker Book House, 1985), 7–11, 18, 307–28, 601–14, 623–4; Philip Schaff, *The Principle of Protestantism;* Schaff, *What Is Church History?*, 3–16.
23. David Schaff, *The Life*, 426–7; Philip Schaff, untitled article on infant damnation and baptism, *The Independent* (May 15, 1875), Box: Autobiographical Scrapbook, 60, UTS; Philip Schaff, *Die Sünde wider den Heiligen Geist, nebst einem historischen Anhang uber das Lebensende des Francesco Spiera* (Halle: J.F. Lippert, 1841); Philip Schaff, "Other Heresy Trials and the Briggs Case," *The Forum* 12 (January 1892): 633.

rection of Christ. No matter how chaotic or complicated things may seem, or how things may change, everything will confirm the truth of God in Jesus Christ in the end. Thus "catholic" or universal Christianity characterized Schaff's theology of history, and he used this theology to work untiringly for the unity of Christianity.[24]

Along with John Williams Nevin, a close colleague, Schaff shaped this reformed theology into the "Mercersburg theology" soon after he arrived in the United States in two works, entitled *The Principle of Protestantism* (1845) and *What Is Church History?* (1846).[25] It should be noted, however, that they never developed a complete system, as did other American theologians such as Jonathan Edwards, Charles Hodge, or W. G. T. Shedd. Nevertheless, this Mercersburg Theology emphasized an adherence to the Apostles' Creed and the Incarnation of Christ: "the Word made Flesh," Christ being fully God and fully man, who inextricably connects the spiritual and the physical. This theology held to the mystical presence of Christ in the Lord's Supper, as Calvin and many reformed fathers had maintained, and not as asserted by the Roman Catholic Church. A vigorous worship emphasized a compelling and liberating use of liturgical forms that would allow one to absorb Christ in symbol, spirit, and reality.[26]

Schaff and Nevin hoped that the Mercersburg theology would be a visible, concrete step toward bringing all believers into a unity that would still allow diversity. Thus the Mercersburg theology represented another attempt by German and English religionists to develop a mediating system that would synthesize the best of contending ecclesiastical parties and ultimately draw Roman Catholics and Protestants back together. However, Schaff believed that such a synthesis could only be accomplished "by mystical fellowship, *unio-mystica* of believers with Jesus Christ as Savior and Lord," and not by compromise, diplomacy, sacramental magic, or even logical or theological argument.[27]

Within this mediating system, Schaff argued that the Reformation developed out of medieval Catholicism. This was a bold move, as American Protestant ultraconservatives held to the Waldensian theory of church development; it claimed that the pure doctrines of the Reformation were maintained from the days of the Apostles to the age of Luther, but somehow

---

24. Philip Schaff, *What Is Church History?*; Philip Schaff, *History of the Christian Church*, 8 vols. (Grand Rapids, Mich.: William B. Eerdman's Publ. Co., 1984), vol. 1: *Apostolic Christianity*, 57–8, 72.
25. See footnotes 6 and 10.
26. George W. Richards, "The Mercersburg Theology: Its Purposes and Principles," *Church History* 20 (1951), 45–6.
27. Ibid., 46.

bypassed the Roman Catholic Church and survived underground, as revealed by the records of the French Waldensians.[28]

The Mercersburg theology made an immediate impact on the German Reformed Church when Schaff was put on trial for heresy at the instigation of a small minority. Most of the immediate church, the American evangelical community, and his mentors back in Germany were dismayed by the trial. Soon vindicated, Schaff received great publicity from the trial.[29] However, the Mercersburg theological movement failed, not because of the trial itself but because of what it represented in terms of conditions in America in general and the German Reformed Church in particular; American Christianity was diametrically opposed to ecclesiastical unification, with the exception of some sympathetic but powerless divines.

American evangelicalism had grown up in the egalitarian Jacksonian era, a time of virulent feelings against new immigration and Catholicism. The nation's identity was still felt by many to be unformed. Yet a combination of American patriotism, commonsense philosophy, and Protestant theology had forged a norm that gave the nation's demeanor and religious denominations a conservative, simplistic character. Those who held to this norm were threatened by that which was foreign. Nativism, which grew to become part of the German Reformed Church, was only the outward manifestation of this larger, more comprehensive norm that essentially gave the United States its genuine identity. Schaff's trial for heresy had spread the fear that somehow he would allow German infidelity to creep into religious education. This fear kept him from being installed as the first president of Franklin and Marshall College in 1853.[30]

Nevertheless, the Mercersburg theology affected American evangelical thinking in a number of ways. First, it forced American evangelicals to reexamine both their view of Protestant history arising from pre-Reformation times and their relationship to the Roman Catholic Church. Here Schaff was instrumental in emancipating the study of church history from its parochial confines, thus making it a much more comprehensive study with a much wider perspective. Second, it made evangelicals reconsider the nature and importance of worship. This is of long-lasting import because one can

28. George H. Shriver, ed., *American Religious Heretics* (Nashville, Tenn.: Abingdon Press, 1966), 30–2.

29. David Schaff, *The Life*, 119–20, 200; Charles Hodge, ed., review of *The Principle of Protestantism*, by Philip Schaff, in *The Princeton Review*, (October 1845), 626–36; Charles Hodge, ed., review of *History of the Apostolic Church, with a General Introduction to Church History* by Philip Schaff, in *The Princeton Review* 26 (1845), 150–92.

30. David Schaff, *The Life*, 197–8; Philip Schaff, Letter of Resignation from the Faculty of the Reformed Theological Seminary, 1865, Box 4: Autobiographical Miscellaneous, ERHS.

still hear high church evangelicals use Schaff's name in their appreciation of the deep significance he placed on liturgical worship. Third, it challenged American divines to consider whether evangelical theology was meant to be concretely fixed for all time in all of its particulars, as the Princeton school of theology of Charles Hodge claimed, or whether it was something malleable that could be enlarged and improved upon, a view adopted by Schaff's evangelical mentors back in Germany. In time, American evangelicals accepted Schaff as an authority and learned from him.[31]

After leaving the German Reformed Church behind, Schaff set an agenda of work that was meant to court the wider audience he had gained. He earnestly hoped to shape American Christianity through the volumes of his church history and his encyclopedic works in order to educate all toward a unified view of Christendom. Schaff also tried to use his theology as a mediating force that would unite conservative and liberal Protestants. This was all the more necessary in order to counter the ever-increasing effects that German higher criticism and Darwinism were having on American thought throughout the late nineteenth century.[32]

Throughout the days of debate over evolution, Schaff at first rejected and then tried to accommodate the new scientific trend. On September 18, 1876, Schaff wrote in his diary that he had heard Thomas Henry Huxley speak on the subject and curtly remarked: "But I was not convinced or even much impressed." Schaff simply treated Huxley as another biblical higher critic and refuted his irreverent agnosticism. Yet by 1893, Schaff conceded a certain validity to evolution and thought it would fit into his theory of historical development once the facts of the matter were determined.[33]

Another feature of Schaff's thought that may have confused students was his belief in liberality of study, which he held from the beginning. Schaff believed that biblical criticism kept theology from stagnation and that the Bible was not threatened by close scrutiny. Schaff's students understood his position "to be that textual research and the most destructive criticism have not disproved a single doctrine commonly held among evangelical Christians."[34]

31. Philip Schaff, "Princeton und Mercersburg," *Der Deutsche Kirchenfreund* 1 (1848), 154–7, 169–78.
32. David Schaff, *The Life*, 221; "The Professorship Offered to Philip Schaff," *The Reformed Messenger* (June 22, 1870), 43.
33. Philip Schaff, diary entry for September 18, 1876, Schaff diaries 1844–90, UTS; Philip Schaff, *The Reunion of Christendom: A Paper Prepared for the Parliament of Religions and the National Conference of the Evangelical Alliance Held in Chicago, September and October, 1893* (New York: Evangelical Alliance Office, 1893), 36–8.
34. David Schaff, *The Life*, 478–9.

In all of this, Schaff accepted freedom of religion and inquiry and rejected Christianity's intolerant past. Christian love and toleration were to be shown, not for reaching compromising positions, but for allowing scholars freely to study all things that would eventually point to the conclusions of reformed theology. This is why he participated in the Parliament of Religions and Christendom held in Chicago in 1893.

Schaff's students may have misinterpreted this mediating stance as he encouraged them to study in Germany, which exposed them to more liberal trends. Schaff, for instance, befriended Charles Augustus Briggs and promoted him to a teaching position at the Union Theological Seminary. Schaff influenced Briggs's education and encouraged him to study in Germany under Dorner. Briggs, however, was not content simply to learn German evangelicalism and began to accept much from the higher criticism regarding the authenticity, authorship, and dating of certain books of the Bible. Furthermore, it appeared that Briggs based sources of authority in religious matters on the Bible, the church, and reason, in that order. This went against the beliefs of conservative Bible scholars, who believed all authority resided in the Scriptures alone. In 1893 Briggs was put on trial for heresy in the Presbyterian Church; because the Union Theological Seminary and Schaff defended him, the Presbyterian Church severed its ties to that institution.[35]

CONCLUSION

Philip Schaff influenced American evangelical education in a variety of ways, directly through teaching and writing on reformed theology and church history, indirectly through his belief in freedom of inquiry and religion, which were implicit and explicit messages he transmitted in the classroom and in his works.[36] Though Schaff never moved from his broad Calvinistic stance, he may have pushed some students to adopt far more latitudinarian views. In the 1840s and 1850s, Schaff's students saw him as a groundbreaker and a revolutionary. By the end of his life, they saw him as an anachronism.

If Schaff unintentionally influenced students to move away from evangelicalism, he was not alone. In his time, American educators and students in general were drawn increasingly to German graduate study and to ideas

---

35. Philip Schaff, "Other Heresy Trials and the Briggs Case," 621–33.
36. Philip Schaff, "The Development of Religious Freedom," in *Christ and Christianity: Studies on Christology, Creeds and Confessions, Protestantism and Romanism, Sunday Observance, Religious Freedom, and Christian Union* (New York: Charles Scribner, 1885), 285–91.

that seemed to be liberating, such as, for example, the ethical, modernistic theology of Albrecht Ritschl and the studies of Karl G. A. Harnack in church history. Thus a whole new era in the history of education, with its changing ideas of reality, challenged the older, largely Christian-based beliefs.[37]

However, the claim that Schaff had been more liberating than his fellow conservatives is somewhat misleading. Despite his belief in freedom of thought, along with his mediating theology, all of his friends were conservative evangelicals. There is no contradiction between Schaff's meshing easily with conservative American life and at the same time directing students toward more liberating positions. For Schaff believed that religious liberty in America always moved within the boundaries of Christian civilization, which governed public morality, and that it would never transgress those bounds.[38] Schaff's conservatism would compare easily with any that comes to mind today. Even Briggs's latitudinarianism, when seen in its full light, reveals him to be what might be called a moderate evangelical and not a real liberal theologian. Moreover, when Schaff died in 1893, he viewed American progress as limitless; thus he was one more perhaps naive nineteenth-century intellectual who did not live to see the momentous problems of the twentieth century.[39]

Schaff firmly believed that Christianity helps one to transcend one's own culture and foibles in that it shapes a wide world view and brings one closer to the Savior. As modernists tied religion to the vicissitudes of culture and ultimately concluded that culture shapes religion, Schaff's belief in Christian progress was not tied to culture in the same way: In his view, God uses culture and man's foibles to accomplish his higher purposes. Thus Schaff's central beliefs transcended the spirit of the age and the unintentional effects of his ideas when his mediating theology seemed to die with him. Through his works, Schaff achieved a lasting influence on evangelical students, as his studies are still used in evangelical circles today. Though dated in some aspects, his reformed Christian theology, his views of church history, and his faith in Christ have remained timeless and have not lost their meaning.

---

37. Noll, "The University Arrives in America, 1870–1930," 100.
38. Philip Schaff, *Church and State in the United States or the American Idea of Religious Liberty and Its Practical Effects* (New York: Charles Scribner's Sons, 1888), 16, 35–6, 44–5, 53–62, 73–83.
39. Ibid., 36, 83.

13

German Influence on the Higher Education of American Women, 1865–1914*

JAMES C. ALBISETTI

At the newly opened University of Chicago in 1892–3, most of the women students were housed temporarily in the Hotel Beatrice. Shortly after the first of the year, Dean of Women Marion Talbot learned that one of the students wanted to have a party to "drink up" wine left over from the Christmas festivities at the Beatrice. Talbot, who had come to Chicago from the much more puritanical atmosphere of Wellesley, had found it difficult enough to accept that women students would drink at all; she certainly would not tolerate a party devoted primarily to the consumption of alcohol. Called to Talbot's office, the unnamed student defended her action by saying "that German professors drank at their meetings." The flustered dean replied that the issue was "American ladies, not German professors."[1]

The impact of German professors and of German higher education in general on the United States has long been a subject of scholarly investigation. In the past two decades, the history of the higher education of American women has also become a well-researched field. Yet despite the many types of evidence available, of which the incident at the Beatrice is a very minor one, the two fields have seldom intersected. In part, this neglect has resulted from the diffuse nature of the topic, which does not lend itself to as straightforward an investigation as does the transmission across the Atlantic of the kindergarten or the research seminar. The degree to which German models had a decidedly negative impact on women's education in the United States has tended to exclude this theme from the generally celebratory accounts of German influences on American culture. Most important, scholarship about German influences on American education has from the beginning simply neglected women.

A few years after the incident at the Hotel Beatrice, for example, B. A.

*I would like to acknowledge the research assistance provided by Kyle Longley and Jane Woods.

1. Marion Talbot, *More Than Lore: Reminiscences of Marion Talbot, Dean of Women, the University of Chicago, 1892–1925* (Chicago, 1936), p. 67.

Hinsdale's "Notes on the History of Foreign Influence upon Education in the United States" contained many references to Germany but none to women's education. The long chapter on educational influences in Albert Faust's *The German Element in the United States* included women only in a discussion of the kindergarten, although in a separate chapter Faust did briefly mention four German women who taught their native language at northeastern women's colleges.[2] Between the two world wars, Charles Thwing left even these women out of his discussion of immigrant professors, and his investigations of American students in Germany and of the effects of German models on American universities also gave no coverage to women. John Walz found room for women only in his examination of the kindergarten movement. In 1939, neither W. H. Cowley nor W. Carson Ryan examined the impact on women of the rise of graduate education based on German models, though Ryan mentioned in passing the exclusion of women from Johns Hopkins and Clark universities and their admission to Chicago.[3]

During the 1950s, S. Willis Rudy omitted both women's colleges and coeducation from his examination of "The 'Revolution' in American Higher Education" during the last third of the nineteenth century, and he failed to list M. Carey Thomas among the important college presidents affected by the "impact of the German university." Walter Metzger's discussions of the German influence on the development of American views of academic freedom also neglected the higher education of women, and his work leaves the impression that the only woman involved in issues of academic freedom was Mrs. Leland Stanford.[4] Even in the 1960s, Laurence Veysey omitted women entirely from his discussion of "the lure of the German university," and Jurgen Herbst explicitly restricted his research for *The German Historical School in American Scholarship* to "*men* in university departments of history, politi-

---

2. B. A. Hinsdale, "Notes on the History of Foreign Influence upon Education in the United States," in *Report of the Commissioner of Education for the Year 1897–1898*, 2 vols. (Washington, D.C., 1899), 1: 591–629; Albert B. Faust, *The German Element in the United States, with Special Reference to Its Political, Moral, Social, and Educational Influence*, 2 vols. (Boston and New York, 1909), 2: 201–49, 455–6.
3. Charles Thwing, *The American and the German University: One Hundred Years of History* (New York, 1928); John A. Walz, *German Influence in American Education and Culture* (Philadelphia, 1936), pp. 36–42; W. H. Cowley, "European Influences on American Higher Education," *Education Record* 20 (1939): 165–90; W. Carson Ryan, *Studies in Early Graduate Education: The Johns Hopkins, Clark University, the University of Chicago* (New York, 1939), p. 119.
4. S. Willis Rudy, "The 'Revolution' in American Higher Education, 1865–1900," *Harvard Educational Review* 21 (1951): 155–74; Walter P. Metzger, "The German Contribution to the American Theory of Academic Freedom," *AAUP Bulletin* 41 (1955): 214–30; Richard Hofstadter and Walter P. Metzger, *The Development of Academic Freedom in the United States* (New York and London, 1955).

cal science, economics, and sociology." Yet two years before Herbst and Veysey published their works, Thomas N. Bonner had demonstrated, in his *American Doctors and German Universities, 1870–1914,* the reality of German influence on an important segment of the higher education of American women.[5]

Historians of the education of American women have not done a significantly better job of exploring German or other foreign influences on their topic. Thomas Woody's pioneering work in the 1920s contained brief surveys of attitudes toward female education in England, France, and Germany, but he concluded the last of these three sections without stating what influence German ideas and institutions had in the United States. In his second volume, though, Woody did mention briefly how some American opponents of coeducation cited German authorities and how "many American women followed the example of American men and pursued advanced studies abroad, chiefly in Germany and France."[6] Yet works concerning American women who earned doctoral degrees written by Emilie Hutchinson and Walter Crosby Eells simply omitted these women who studied abroad, as did Mabel Newcomer's survey of the first century of higher education for American women.[7] In the last twenty years, the explosion of interest in women's history has produced many fine studies of women in higher education and the professions; but with the exception of Margaret Rossiter's examination of women scientists,[8] none of these books has addressed the question of German influence in a meaningful way. The different research agendas in American women's history account for much of this neglect, but the general provincialism of contemporary American historians and their ignorance of foreign languages also contribute to it. References in such works to women who studied abroad frequently reveal an extremely shaky knowl-

5. Laurence Veysey, *The Emergence of the American University* (Chicago, 1965), pp. 125–33, and passim; Jurgen Herbst, *The German Historical School in American Scholarship: A Study in the Transfer of Culture* (Ithaca, N.Y., 1965), p. viii (emphasis added); Thomas N. Bonner, *American Doctors and German Universities, 1871–1914* (Lincoln, Neb., 1963). Veysey discussed coeducation briefly but totally neglected the women's colleges: *Emergence,* pp. 271–2, 332–3, 374. Nothing related to German influence on the higher education of American women is included in Frank Trommler and Joseph McVeigh, eds., *America and the Germans,* 2 vols. (Philadelphia, 1983).

6. Thomas Woody, *A History of Women's Education in the United States,* 2 vols. (New York, 1929), 1: 87, and 2: 265–6, 334. In a reevaluation of Woody's work, Maxine Schwartz Seller speaks favorably of its "internationalist" outlook and does not suggest the need for revision in that area: "*A History of Women's Education in the United States:* Thomas Woody's Classic – Sixty Years Later," *History of Education Quarterly* 29 (1989): 95–107.

7. Emilie Josephine Hutchinson, *Women and the Ph.D.* (Greensboro, N.C., 1929); Walter Crosby Eells, "Earned Doctorates for Women in the Nineteenth Century," *AAUP Bulletin* 42 (1956): 644–51; Mabel Newcomer, *A Century of Higher Education for American Women* (New York, 1959).

8. Margaret Rossiter, *Women Scientists in America: Struggles and Strategies to 1940* (Baltimore, 1982).

edge of German geography and institutions, and the bibliographies and notes seldom contain works in German.[9]

How, then, should one study the German influence on the higher education of American women before 1914? This essay looks briefly at four subtopics of this general theme: the relation of the German immigrant community to female education, the impact of individual immigrants, the extent to which German institutions for female education served as models for the United States, and the effects in this country of German ideology about woman's capacities and proper place. It then examines in more detail two others subtopics: the impact on women of the adoption of the German university model in the late nineteenth century and the lure that advanced study in Germany exercised on American women.

To explore the relation of the German immigrant community to advanced schooling for women, one could look at the percentage of women students who were daughters or granddaughters of German immigrants in comparison to figures for the overall population. This would require many case studies of individual universities – a task far beyond the scope of this essay. We do know that many immigrants brought with them from Germany a strong prejudice in favor of male teachers: as Geraldine Joncich Clifford has pointed out, "Cities with greater-than-average proportions of male teachers in 1885 also were cities with sizeable German populations: Cincinnati, St. Louis, and Milwaukee."[10]

Among influential immigrants, one individual stands out above the rest: Marie Zakrzewska of the New England Hospital for Women and Children. Although she came to the United States from Berlin in 1852 with only a midwife's training and earned her medical degree in Cleveland, Zakrzewska later served as a crucial source of information and advice about universities and hospitals in German-speaking Europe for two generations of female physicians.[11] Her successful medical career did not provide a model for many other German women, however. As of 1897, for example, the Woman's Medical College of Pennsylvania had not enrolled a single German student.[12]

9. For an up-to-date bibliography, see Lynn D. Gordon, *Gender and Higher Education in the Progressive Era* (New Haven, Conn., and London, 1990); and John Mack Faragher and Florence Howe, eds., *Women and Higher Education in American History* (New York, 1988).
10. Geraldine Jonçich Clifford, "Man/Woman/Teacher: Gender, Family, and Career in American Educational History," in Donald Warren, ed., *American Teachers: Histories of a Profession at Work* (New York, 1989), p. 296. See also Woody, *History of Women's Education*, 1: 503.
11. Agnes Vietor, ed., *A Woman's Quest: The Life of Marie E. Zakrzewska, M.D.* (New York, 1924); Regina Markell Morantz-Sanchez, *Sympathy and Science: Women Physicians in American Medicine* (New York, 1985); Mary Walsh, *Doctors Wanted, No Woman Need Apply: Sexual Barriers in the Medical Profession, 1835–1975* (New Haven, Conn., and London, 1977), pp. 76–105.
12. Clara Marshall, *The Woman's Medical College of Pennsylvania: An Historical Outline* (Philadelphia, 1897), p. 73.

Medical training in the United States during the later nineteenth century would, of course, have been of little use to a German woman interested in practicing in her homeland. The same was not true in dentistry, in which American training had a much higher reputation in this period. German women had a major, and seldom acknowledged, impact on opportunities in dentistry for their American sisters. The second woman admitted to an American dental school was Henriette Hirschfeld, who entered the Pennsylvania College of Dental Surgery in 1867, one year after Lucy Hobbs Taylor had graduated in Cincinnati. Hirschfeld's successful completion of her studies in 1869 and news of her thriving practice in Berlin, which was reported in the United States by *The Woman's Journal,* served as a stimulus both to other German women and to Americans. Among the first twenty women who graduated from dental schools in the United States between 1866 and 1881, no fewer than twelve were Germans, including the first four female graduates of the Baltimore College of Dental Surgery and one of the first two at the University of Michigan. Almost all of these women dentists returned to Germany to practice, so that their impact in the United States was only as pathbreaking students.[13]

Among the immigrants who remained in this country were several important teachers of German. Faust mentioned Carla Wenckebach and Margarethe Müller at Wellesley, Ottilie Herholz at Vassar, and Marie Kapp at Smith. What he did not mention is that these "professors" were in fact graduates of German teachers' seminars, qualified at home to teach girls only up to the age of sixteen. When advanced courses for women teachers (*Oberlehrerinnenkurse*) became available in Germany, Müller and Herholz returned there – to Göttingen and Berlin, respectively – to obtain training more appropriate for a college professor.[14] German-born Klara Hechtenberg arrived at Smith in 1897 after a more thorough education, including the University of London and a first at Oxford, but after two years she left to pursue a Ph.D. at Heidelberg and never returned. In the first years of the new century, Wellesley hired Natalie Wipplinger after she obtained her doctorate from Freiburg, and Vassar added to its German department Lilian

13. Bonner, *American Doctors,* p. 10; Committee on Historical Research of the Federation of American Women Dentists, "Women in Dentistry," *The Journal of the American Dental Association* 15 (1928): 1, 735–56 (data on graduates, pp. 1, 755–6); *The Woman's Journal* 1, no. 33 (Aug. 20, 1870): 264; James Truman, "Henriette Hirschfeld, D.D.S., and the Women Dentists of 1866–73," *Dental Cosmos* 53 (1911): 1, 380–6; Franziska Tiburtius, "Dr. Henriette Tiburtius," in Deutscher Lyceum-Club, ed., *Bahnbrechende Frauen* (Berlin, 1912), pp. 187–96. Hirschfeld is the only woman mentioned in James Denton, "Some Interrelations between German and American Dentistry, 1800–1914," *The Journal of the American Dental Association* 61 (1960): 587–98.

14. Faust, *German Element.* 2: 455–6; Margarethe Müller, *Carla Wenckebach, Pioneer* (Boston, 1908); *Women's Who's Who of America, 1914–1915* (New York, 1914), pp. 383, 584, 445 (this will be cited as *WWW*). Kapp may not have even attended a seminar.

Stroebe, with a Ph.D. from Heidelberg.[15] The American women's colleges thus provided a few German women with teaching opportunities they could not find at home. These professors were certainly in a position to provide important information about opportunities for study in Germany to the young women attending these elite schools.

Evaluating the influence of German institutions for female schooling on developments in the United States requires a broadening of the definition of "higher" education. Jurgen Herbst has recently pointed out that as early as 1831 the *American Annals of Education and Instruction* printed an article about the education of women teachers in Germany, and he implies that this information contributed to the foundation later in that decade of the first normal schools for women in Massachusetts. In 1851, Henry Barnard published a not entirely accurate account of normal schools for women in Prussia, including that founded for deaconesses by Theodor Fliedner at Kaiserswerth.[16] The training of nurses at Kaiserswerth, on which Barnard also commented favorably, had some influence on the upgrading of nursing in the United States, although its greatest impact was transmitted through Fliedner's most famous student, Florence Nightingale.[17]

The deaconesses' institution at Kaiserswerth enrolled its first American woman, Julia S. Tutwiler of Alabama, in 1873. She had come to Europe as part of a "conducted party of several hundred ministers and public school teachers." Learning from a companion of Fliedner's normal school, she literally knocked on the gates and asked to be admitted. After a year with the deaconesses, Tutwiler moved to Berlin, where she appears to have taught for two years in a private girls' school, attended lectures at the Victoria Lyceum, and at least visited the commercial and technical courses for girls at the Lette Verein. These experiences, along with a later visit to the technical courses organized by Elise Lemonnier in Paris, provided Tutwiler with models for her work as the principal of the Livingston Female Academy, a normal school in her home state, and the major advocate of the foundation of the Alabama State College for Women at Montevallo, originally a commercial and vocational school.[18]

---

15. *WWW*, pp. 194, 791; Patricia Palmieri, "In Adamless Eden: A Social Portrait of the Academic Community at Wellesley College, 1875–1920," (Ed.D. diss., Harvard University, 1981), p. 308.

16. Jurgen Herbst, *And Sadly Teach: Teacher Education and Professionalization in American Culture* (Madison, Wisc., 1989), pp. 33–5; Henry Barnard, *Normal Schools and Other Institutions, Agencies, and Means Designed for the Professional Education of Teachers*, 2 vols. (Hartford, Conn., 1851), 2: 126–8, 131.

17. Barnard, *Normal Schools*, pp. 129–31; Woody, *History of Women's Education*, 2: 274.

18. Anna Gary Pannell and Dorothea E. Wyatt, *Julia Tutwiler and Social Progress in Alabama* (Alabama, 1961), pp. 26–47, 58, 98–9; Julia S. Tutwiler, "The Technical Education of Women," *Education* 3 (1882): 201–7; Milton Lee Orr, *The State-Supported Colleges for Women* (Nashville, Tenn., 1930), pp. 129–32.

More surprising than the limited impact in the United States of German institutions for women's education is the very modest influence exercised by German ideology on women's proper place and education. Henry Barnard's collection of writings by German pedagogues omitted Betty Gleim and other important advocates of women's education, but it did include a translation of Karl von Raumer's treatise on the subject, which opposed secondary, much less higher, education for girls. In the first edition of his *German Educational Reformers* of 1863 and in the revised edition fifteen years later, however, Barnard gave no coverage to women's education.[19] Even that most notorious American opponent of the higher education of women, Dr. Edward H. Clarke, did not draw on the many readily available German "authorities." Clarke's *Sex in Education; or, A Fair Chance for the Girls*, echoed in many ways the similar views published a year earlier in the equally notorious and perhaps more effective pamphlet by Dr. Theodor von Bischoff of the University of Munich; but Clarke did not cite and does not appear to have read Bischoff. Where Clarke did make use of German sources was in citing a number of correspondents who informed him that German girls had few problems with menstruation because they did not compete with boys at school, left school at age fifteen, and had complete rest during their periods. Several of the responses to Clarke also cited German correspondents on this issue, an aspect of the debate not touched upon by the many recent commentaries on Clarke and his influence.[20]

The relatively modest and very diffuse impact on the higher education of American women exercised by German immigrants, institutional models for female education, and ideological views of women's proper schooling does not hold true when one turns to the two themes that have dominated scholarship dealing with German influence on the higher education of American men: the German university as a model for new institutions in the United States and Germany as the place to go to receive advanced training. With regard to the first of these themes, one must make a distinction between the new American universities usually included in the discussions of German influence – especially Michigan, Cornell, Johns Hop-

---

19. Henry Barnard, ed., *German Pedagogy* (2d ed.; Hartford, Conn., 1876), pp. 295–367; idem, *German Educational Reformers* (Hartford, Conn., 1863); idem, ed., *Memoirs of Eminent Teachers and Educators with Contributions to the History of Education in Germany* (rev. ed., Hartford, Conn., 1878); Woody, *History of Women's Education*, 2: 265–6.

20. Edward H. Clarke, *Sex in Education; or, A Fair Chance for the Girls* (Boston, 1873), pp. 169–77; Julie Ward Howe, ed., *Sex and Education: A Reply to Dr. E. H. Clarke's "Sex in Education"* (Boston, 1874), pp. 47–8; Anna C. Brackett, ed., *The Education of American Girls, Considered in a Series of Essays* (New York, 1874), pp. 363–7. For the most recent discussion of Clarke, see Sue Zschoche, "Dr. Clarke Revisited: Science, True Womanhood, and Female College Education," *History of Education Quarterly* 29 (1989): 545–70. On Bischoff's *Das Studium und die Ausübung der Medizin durch Frauen* (Munich, 1872), see James C. Albisetti, *Schooling German Girls and Women: Secondary and Higher Education in the Nineteenth Century* (Princeton, N.J., 1988), p. 126.

kins, Clark, and Chicago – and the women's colleges universally omitted from such discussions.

Henry P. Tappan, head of the University of Michigan from 1852 to 1863, is often regarded as the first great "Germanizing" – or, perhaps more accurately, "Prussianizing" – university president. Before going to Michigan, and before ever visiting Germany, he wrote in 1851, "The Universities of Protestant Germany stand forth as model institutions." Later that year, a visit to the University of Bonn – then scarcely thirty years old – further impressed him with what Prussia had built up in such a short time. At Ann Arbor, Tappan tried to introduce as many aspects of the Prussian universities as he could, including abolition of dormitories, which he labeled "a mere remnant of the monkish Middle Ages, still retained in England, but banished from the universities of Germany."[21] When women first applied in 1858, Tappan adamantly opposed their request, considering "the admission of women as an unbearable threat to his whole concept of what a university should be." A man who in 1867 would write from self-imposed exile in Switzerland that the admission of women students at Michigan would lead to "*defeminated* women and *demasculated* men" may not have needed the model of a German university to stimulate his opposition to coeducation, but Tappan's sense of what a "true" university should be certainly contributed to what proved to be a twelve-year delay in the admission of women to the University of Michigan.[22]

Such an "elective affinity" between enthusiasm for the German research university and opposition to the higher education of women, or at least to coeducation, existed in many of the other late-nineteenth-century Germanizers, but not all. Andrew D. White was perhaps the most ambiguous case. As president of Cornell, White was one of the leaders of what Veysey has called the "utilitarian" movement in American higher education, opposed to the "pure scholarship" of the German universities. White also oversaw the admission of women to the first major eastern college or university, being moved to support coeducation in part, as he tells us in his autobiography, by the pleas of his mother.[23] Yet White was a less devoted advocate of coeducation and a more serious Germanophile than he has sometimes been portrayed. When he visited Europe in 1868 to inspect technical and agricultural schools, his itinerary included no institutions that

21. Henry P. Tappan, *University Education* (New York, 1851; reprint New York, 1969), p. 39; Charles M. Perry, *Henry Philip Tappan* (Ann Arbor, Mich., 1933), pp. 151, 232.
22. Dorothy Gies McGuigan, *A Dangerous Experiment: One Hundred Years of Women at the University of Michigan* (Ann Arbor, Mich., 1970), pp. 18, 30.
23. Veysey, *Emergence*, pp. 60, 78–82; Andrew D. White, *The Autobiography of Andrew D. White*, 2 vols. (New York, 1905), 1: 397–402.

indicated that he expected to train women students at Cornell any time soon. The limits to his enthusiasm for coeducation became especially clear in a speech on "The New Germany" that White delivered frequently after returning from his two years as U.S. minister in Berlin from 1879 to 1881. This address heaped praise on the German universities without mentioning their exclusion of women, even though, during his service in Berlin, White had helped convince the government of Saxony to allow four American women auditing courses at Leipzig to continue doing so at a time when new auditors were going to be banned. In this speech, he also suggested that the United States should imitate Germany and concentrate its resources on twenty to thirty universities that would "receive young *men* from the colleges."[24]

Johns Hopkins University, with its devotion to graduate education, its strong emphasis on the professor as researcher, and its hiring of numerous scholars with German degrees, was the American institution based most clearly on German models, despite Daniel Coit Gilman's insistence that the founders "did not undertake to establish a German university, nor an English university, but an American university." Hopkins also was, as Woody put it, "the last of the great graduate institutions of the country to admit women" – in 1907. With the father of M. Carey Thomas on its original board of trustees, Hopkins considered coeducation but rejected it, with the one trustee who had studied in Germany, Heidelberg graduate Reverdy Johnson, leading the opposition. Topping a list of books ordered by the trustees in 1874 were Matthew Arnold's *Higher Schools and Universities in Germany* and Dr. Clarke's *Sex in Education,* a striking indication of the concerns that shaped the new university.[25]

Gilman himself had studied in Berlin in the 1850s, along with Andrew D. White. While president of the newly founded and coeducational University of California in 1871, he "had forecast a university for graduate study only, 'to which young *men* will resort for the highest sort of scholastic training,' " clearly a scheme derived from his German experiences. On his trip to Europe in 1875, Gilman stopped at the universities of Zurich and

24. White, *Autobiography,* 1: 291, 338, 552–3; Glenn C. Altschuler, *Andrew D. White – Educator, Historian, Diplomat* (Ithaca, N.Y., and London, 1979), pp. 119–20; Andrew Dickson White, "The New Germany," *American Geographical Society of New York, Journal* 14 (1882): 240–2 (emphasis added). Professor Goldwyn Smith, who was from England, suggested that the admission of women would cause Cornell "to sink at once from the rank of a University to that of an Oberlin or a high school": Charlotte Williams Conable, *Women at Cornell: The Myth of Equal Education* (Ithaca, N.Y., and London, 1977), p. 77.

25. Daniel Coit Gilman, *The Launching of a University* (New York, 1906; reprint, New York, 1969), p. 49; Woody, *History of Women's Education,* 2: 337; Hugh Hawkins, *Pioneer: A History of the Johns Hopkins University, 1874–1889* (Ithaca, N.Y., 1960), pp. 259–67, 329.

Leipzig without commenting on the women students at either location. In Berlin he inspected even *Realschulen* for boys but apparently visited no institutions devoted to female education.[26] Here again, Germanophilia appears to have worked strongly against the higher education of American women.

The same was true with G. Stanley Hall at Clark University. Like White, Hall was in Germany in the late 1870s, during which time he submitted various essays to *The Nation* that were later published as *Aspects of German Culture*. Although Hall did comment on female education, his remarks centered on the ladylike deportment of the "little girls at the Victoria School in Berlin" and on how German girls avoided the "pitiable and useless half-culture in ancient languages, mathematics, sciences, etc.," in pursuit of which many American girls ruined their health – echoes of Dr. Clarke. Like White and Gilman, Hall praised the universities without mentioning the question of women students, even though he had spent a year in Leipzig before women auditors were banned and had known a woman who had studied in Germany when he taught at Antioch College in the mid-1870s. Hall claimed in his autobiography that from its opening in 1889, Clark University "always admitted women graduate students on the same basis as men"; but, in fact, the first few women were tolerated only as private students of individual professors, and none was allowed to earn a Ph.D. until 1908.[27]

The University of Chicago was the last of the major new institutions inspired to a significant degree by the ideal of the German research university to open and the only one that was coeducational from the beginning. Although one prominent citizen of Chicago asked, "How can the University be the dignified body of scholars that you intend if women are to be included?", neither the fourteen members of the original faculty with German Ph.D.s nor any other constituency offered major opposition to the introduction of coeducation, which by 1892 had over a twenty-year history at the nearby state universities of Illinois, Michigan, and Wisconsin. Women students at Chicago, in addition to whatever profits they derived from the example of German professors who drank at parties, benefited particularly from the strong influence of the German social sciences at the university, with some, such as Katharine Bement Davis, even being able to pursue part of their studies in Germany.[28]

26. Hawkins, *Pioneer*, p. 65 (emphasis added); Gilman, *Launching*, p. 13; Fabian Franklin, *The Life of Daniel Coit Gilman* (New York, 1910), pp. 204–7.
27. G. Stanley Hall, *Aspects of German Culture* (Boston, 1881), pp. 3, 305–6, 318–19; idem, *Life and Confessions of a Psychologist* (New York, 1923), pp. 202, 318; William A. Koelsch, *Clark University, 1887–1987: A Narrative History* (Worcester, Mass., 1987), pp. 72–4.
28. Talbot, *More Than Lore*, p. 64; Richard J. Storr, *Harper's University: The Beginnings* (Chicago and

If the cases of Tappan, White, Gilman, and Hall suggest that male admiration of German universities tended to work against the expansion of higher education for American women, in at least one case an American male combined lavish praise of the German university system with direct criticism of the exclusion of women. In 1871, Charles Phelps Taft, half-brother of the future president of the United States and holder of a law degree from Heidelberg, spoke to the Cincinnati Literary Club about the plans for founding a major university in that city. After recommending many elements of German higher education, Taft remarked, "Those great universities have not encouraged the aspirations of women. In this respect, at least, we may improve upon their system; for the doors of our university may be open not only to the graduates of a Yale or a Harvard, but also to those of a Vassar or a McMicken College for young women," as one segment of the University of Cincinnati was expected to be known.[29]

What influence did the German universities have on the evolution of such colleges for women? With regard to seminaries such as Mount Holyoke and Wheaton that gradually grew into colleges, it is difficult to trace any impact whatsoever. For the coordinate colleges such as the "Harvard Annex," Barnard, and Pembroke, the new women's colleges at Cambridge and Oxford served as models more than German institutions did, although in all three cases it was primarily the failure of women to gain admission to the existing male colleges that provided the most important stimulus. At Columbia, where president Frederick A. P. Barnard had proposed opening the college to women in his annual reports for 1879, 1880, and 1881, the creation of a coordinate college resulted largely from the opposition to coeducation by Germanophiles such as John W. Burgess and Nicholas Murray Butler. As late as 1892, Columbia's University Council resisted the proposed affiliation of Teachers College because it would "introduce coeducation into Columbia in a most pronounced form," something to be avoided at a time "when Columbia is becoming a university and is laying the foundations of its reputation as such."[30] Here again, German models of what constituted a true university militated against the admission of women.

Several features of the independent women's colleges created after the

London, 1966), p. 76; Ellen Fitzpatrick, *Endless Crusade: Women Social Scientists and Progressive Reform* (New York, 1990), pp. 28–9, 54–5.

29. Charles Phelps Taft, *The German University and the American College* (Cincinnati, 1871), p. 20. See also Alphonso Taft, *A Lecture on the University of Cincinnati: Its Aims, Needs, and Resources* (Cincinnati, 1872); and Reginald C. McGrane, *The University of Cincinnati: A Success Story in Urban Higher Education* (New York, 1963).

30. Annie Nathan Meyer, *Barnard Beginnings* (Boston and New York, 1935), pp. 8, 47; John Fulton, *Memoirs of Frederick A. P. Barnard* (New York and London, 1896), pp. 407–22; John W. Burgess, *Reminiscences of an American Scholar* (New York, 1934), pp. 174, 241–3; Nicholas Murray Butler, *Across the Busy Years: Recollections and Reflections*, 2 vols. (New York, 1939–40), 1: 76, 80, 183.

Civil War – the religious impulses of their founders, the cloistered housing of their students (despite the variations documented by Helen Lefkowitz Horowitz),[31] the presence of women faculty members, and the relatively young age groups served – distinguished them sharply from German universities. Yet, like White, Gilman, and Hall, the president designates of Vassar and Smith – Milo P. Jewett and L. Clark Seelye – took trips to Europe to learn about the latest developments in higher education. When Jewett traveled in 1862, he visited Queen's College and Bedford College in London but found little to inspect in Germany other than several private girls' schools. He did, however, express admiration for German pedagogy and the role of religion in the schools, and he reported to the trustees that all young women "who desire to explore the richest mines of human thought" would have to "acquire an ability to read the German." Jewett resigned before the college opened, however, and it is difficult to detect any specific German influence on Vassar's early years other than that exercised by the riding master, a former Prussian cavalry officer named Leopold von Seldeneck.[32]

By the time Clark Seelye went to Europe in 1873, many more institutions for the higher education of women were available to be seen. All that he tells us, though, is that he "visited the universities of England, Germany, Switzerland, and France, giving special attention to Girton College, which had just been opened for women near Cambridge." Seelye destroyed his papers, and nothing more is known about the effects on Smith College of what he learned on his travels. As early as 1877, however, Seelye did hire a physics professor with a German Ph.D.[33]

Neither Henry Fowle Durant, the founder of Wellesley College, nor Ada L. Howard, its first president, made any inspection trip abroad; and with its faculty composed entirely of women, Wellesley appears to have been far removed from any German model. Yet Durant's close friend and supporter, Eben Horsford, had studied in a German university, and Durant from the beginning was much more interested than Matthew Vassar or Sophia Smith in moving beyond a college to a university. Patricia Palmieri has noted Durant's openness to pedagogical innovations, "especially those which emanated from German universities. In science this meant labora-

---

31. Helen Lefkowitz Horowitz, *Alma Mater: Design and Experience in the Women's Colleges from Their Nineteenth-Century Beginnings to the 1930s* (New York, 1984).
32. Vassar Female College, *The President's Trip to Europe* (New York, 1863), pp. 12, 15, 18, 22; James Monroe Taylor, *Before Vassar Opened* (New York, 1914), pp. 135–44; Woody, *History of Women's Education*, 2: 118.
33. L. Clark Seelye, *The Early History of Smith College, 1871–1910* (Boston and New York, 1923), pp. 18, 45. His daughter repeats verbatim his own account: Harriet Seelye Rogers, *Laurenus Clark Seelye: First President of Smith College* (Boston and New York, 1929), p. 127.

tories in which students participated with a sense of independence and adventure in experiment and discovery." In 1878, Wellesley became the second college in the country to have a physics laboratory, the first being MIT. Yet some aspects of the German university were explicitly rejected at Wellesley: the English department, for example, tried to avoid "undiscriminating acceptance of the dry, detailed scholarship emanating from Germany," and many of the faculty cultivated the lifestyle of Oxford dons rather than of German professors.[34]

The last of the major independent women's colleges to open, Bryn Mawr, was also the most strongly influenced by the German university. Its founder, the Quaker physician Joseph Wright Taylor, did not have direct experience of higher education in Germany; but through years of service on the Board of Managers of Haverford College, he had come to know many men who were also trustees of Johns Hopkins, including James Carey Thomas. Taylor met Martha Carey Thomas in late 1876, when she was a senior at Cornell, and appears to have been impressed by her suggestion that women needed access to graduate education if they were to become good college teachers. Taylor's will, written soon after this encounter, pointed in two different directions, toward a women's college that might imitate either Haverford or Johns Hopkins. As the historian of the college has written, "Records have failed to reveal conclusively at just what point it was decided that Bryn Mawr, unlike any other women's college already in existence, was to have a department for graduate study."[35]

When Bryn Mawr opened in 1885, it did possess a graduate department, fellowships for graduate students, and a nine-member faculty who all had Ph.D.s, including one each from Leipzig and Munich and three from Zurich, two of whom were women, Carey Thomas and Emily L. Gregory. Thomas's own experiences during three years at Leipzig had convinced her of the importance of professors devoted to research, and she persuaded the trustees of Bryn Mawr that it was more important that faculty members have Ph.D.s than that they be Quakers. Bryn Mawr granted its first Ph.D. in 1888 to Mamie Gwinn, who had studied with Thomas in Leipzig but had not tried to obtain a degree from Zurich.[36] Thus, in many ways, the German influence on Bryn Mawr appears to have been every bit as powerful

34. Florence Converse, *The Story of Wellesley* (Boston, 1915), pp. 35–6; Palmieri, "In Adamless Eden," pp. 26, 35, 357, 334; Alice Payne Hackett, *Wellesley: Part of the American Story* (New York, 1949), p. 45.
35. Cornelia Meigs, *What Makes a College? A History of Bryn Mawr* (New York, 1956), pp. 15, 18–19, 27–9.
36. Patricia Hochschild LaBalme, ed., *A Century Recalled: Essays in Honor of Bryn Mawr College* (Bryn Mawr, Pa., 1987), p. 57; Edith Finch, *Carey Thomas of Bryn Mawr* (New York, 1947), pp. 155, 128, 212; Meigs, *What Makes a College?*, p. 52.

as on the male institutions that have been the focus of earlier studies of the impact of the German universities in the United States.

Mentioning Thomas, Gregory, and Gwinn raises the final subtopic for this investigation: the role of studying in Germany for the development of the higher education of American women. In many ways, women merely followed the patterns set by the men who flocked to the German universities, especially during the 1880s and 1890s, but several features of the women's experiences differentiate them from those of male students. An important part of the context in which serious study in Germany became possible for women was the increasing ease of travel in the late nineteenth century, which allowed for the growing practice among at least some segments of the American upper classes of sending their daughters to Europe for "finishing" at elite boarding schools, for instruction in music or art, or simply for travel.[37] This practice was widespread enough by the mid-1880s to arouse some anxieties, one response to which was the creation in 1886 of the American Home School for Girls in Berlin, which was advertised as having "the influences and care of a refined Christian home" and was managed by Mary Bannister Willard, the sister-in-law of temperance leader Frances Willard.[38]

One group of young American women who pursued higher studies in Germany, those who attended the Victoria Lyceum in Berlin, may well have been carrying out this "finishing" process at a more advanced level. This institution, which offered women a variety of lecture courses taught by university professors and other instructors, had been brought to the notice of Americans by an article in the first issue of *The Woman's Journal* in 1870.[39] The first American to study there may have been Julia Tutwiler during her two years of teaching near Berlin in 1874–6. By the late 1870s, a number of Vassar graduates, as well as several women from the University of Iowa, attended courses at the Victoria Lyceum.[40] It is likely that several other women, among them a Vassar graduate named Gertrude Mead, who, according to Carey Thomas, was studying in Berlin in 1881, also took

37. I know of no scholarly research on this theme, which would make an excellent topic for a dissertation.
38. L. H. Stone, "The Influences of Foreign Education on American Girls," *Education* 3 (1882–3): 14–23; Horace M. Kennedy, "Studying in Germany," *Popular Science Monthly* 26 (1885): 347–52; Frances E. Willard and Mary A. Livermore, eds., *A Woman of the Century: Fourteen Hundred Seventy Biographical Sketches* (Buffalo, N.Y., 1893), p. 781.
39. *The Woman's Journal* 1, no. 1 (Jan. 8, 1870), p. 3. On the Victoria Lyceum, see Albisetti, *Schooling German Girls*, pp. 117–21, 155–6, 217–18.
40. Laura Brownell Collier (Vassar), Lilian Bayard Taylor Kiliani (Vassar), and Virginia Joynes Slagle Berryhill (Iowa), in *WWW*, pp. 194, 455, 97; Ella Hamiliton Durley (Iowa) in Willard and Livermore, *Woman of the Century*, p. 265.

advantage of the opportunity to hear famous professors at the Victoria Lyceum.[41]

By 1890, however, attendance at this institution had developed into something more than advanced finishing. In that year, a woman with a graduate fellowship from an American college attended lectures in art history at the Victoria Lyceum after being denied admission to the same professor's classes at the University of Berlin. As mentioned earlier, Ottilie Herholz returned to Germany from Vassar to take the new *Oberlehrerin-nenkurse* at the Victoria Lyceum in the 1890s. At least two graduates of Smith also appear to have pursued advanced study in German literature in this fashion during the mid-1890s.[42]

Physicians contributed to a second major group of American women who sought advanced training in German-speaking Europe during the last third of the nineteenth century. Like their male colleagues, the large majority of these women already had degrees from domestic institutions before they went overseas. In contrast to their male colleagues, however, female physicians from the United States had extremely limited opportunities to study in the hospitals and universities of the Second Reich; the "German" influence on them took place primarily in Zurich and Vienna.[43]

During the 1860s, the Maternite hospital in Paris was the main destination for American female physicians seeking training abroad, and in 1866 Mary Putnam began studies in Paris that would lead to the first foreign medical degree for an American woman. By early 1868, however, Susan Dimock, a student at Zakrzewska's New England Hospital for Women and Children, had learned about the new opportunities at the University of Zurich, where after three years of study she would earn a degree in 1871. Although many other American women followed Dimock to Zurich over the next decades, as of 1897 only eight had taken degrees there.[44]

American women also began to arrive in Vienna for medical studies in the late 1860s, the first two apparently being Mary Jane Safford and Josephine Henry. By the early 1870s, Zakrzewska noted, "Not less than six of

---

41. Mary Gertrude Mead Abbey in *WWW*, p. 33; Finch, *Carey Thomas*, p. 102, which misspells the name as "Meade."
42. Helen R. Olin, *The Women of a State University: An Illustration of the Working of Coeducation in the Middle West* (New York, 1909), p. 279; Herholz, Daisy Luana Blaisdell, and Anna Sheldon Kitchel Bole in *WWW*, pp. 383, 115, 112.
43. For greater detail see Thomas N. Bonner, *To the Ends of the Earth: Women's Quest for Education in Medicine, 1845–1914* (Cambridge, Mass. 1992).
44. Mary P. Jacobi, *Life and Letters of Mary Putnam Jacobi,* ed. Ruth Putnam (New York, 1925); Vietor, *A Woman's Quest,* pp. 299–302, 347; Hanny Rohner, *Die ersten 30 Jahre des medizinischen Frauenstudiums an der Universität Zürich, 1867–1897* (Zurich, 1972). See also Thomas Neville Bonner, "Rendezvous in Zurich: Seven Who Made a Revolution in Women's Medical Education, 1864–1874," *Journal of the History of Medicine and Allied Sciences* 44 (1989): 7–27.

our pupils from Boston are at present receiving the benefits which the opportunities for medical study and research offer in Vienna." Graduates of the Women's Medical College of Pennsylvania, such as Anna Broomall, also journeyed to Vienna after earning their degrees.[45]

Mary Jane Safford left Vienna in 1871 for Breslau, where she worked with Wilhelm Waldeyer and was one of the first women ever to perform an ovariotomy. She also visited hospitals in Leipzig and Dresden.[46] The maternity hospital in Dresden, where Dr. Franz Winckel welcomed women as voluntary assistants, had been visited by Emily Blackwell as early as 1856; and in the 1870s and early 1880s, it was the only German institution easily accessible to American female physicians. When Winckel moved to Munich in the 1880s, the American physician Anna Mary Galbraith was one of his first assistants. In contrast, Waldeyer never welcomed other women students, and in 1888 he asserted – in the most influential attack on female physicians since that of Bischoff – that his one American student should remain an exception, not become the rule.[47] That he rather than Winckel represented the views of the majority of professors meant that American women, however much they shared in the general admiration for German medical training, could seldom benefit directly from it.

The third group of American women who studied in Imperial Germany were those who enrolled in the philosophical faculties of the universities – until after 1900, necessarily as auditors. How these pioneers learned of opportunities to do so is not clear, for the well-known accounts of German universities by Matthew Arnold and James Morgan Hart offered no information on this matter, nor did the later reports by Hjalmar Boyesen, Richard Ely, G. Stanley Hall, Andrew D. White, or James W. Bell.[48] The first American female auditor appears to have been Rebecca Rice, the mathe-

45. Willard and Livermore, *Woman of the Century*, p. 629; Vietor, *A Woman's Quest*, p. 359; Leroy H. Fischer, "Mary Jane Safford," and Patricia Spain Ward, "Anne Broomall," in Joe Smith, ed., *Notable American Women*, 3 vols. (Cambridge, Mass., 1971), 3: 220–2, 1: 246–7. Willard and Livermore were incorrect when they stated that Safford and Henry matriculated at Vienna.

46. Safford's own reports in *The Woman's Journal* 2, no. 31 and 42 (Aug. 5 and Oct. 21, 1871), pp. 245, 336; "Mary Jane Safford," in Egbert Cleave, ed., *Biographical Cyclopedia of Homeopathic Physicians and Surgeons* (Philadelphia, 1873), pp. 466–7.

47. Elizabeth H. Thomson, "Emily Blackwell," *Notable American Women*, 1: 166; Galbraith in *WWW*, p. 312; Wilhelm Waldeyer, "Das Studium der Medizin und die Frauen," *Tageblatt der deutscher Naturforscher und Ärzte* 61, part 2 (1888): 37.

48. Matthew Arnold, *Higher Schools and Universities in Germany* (London, 1874); James Morgan Hart, *German Universities* (New York and London, 1874); Hjalmar Boyesen, "The University of Berlin," *Scribner's Monthly* 18 (1879): 205–17; Richard T. Ely, "American Colleges and German Universities," *Harper's Magazine* 61 (1880): 253–60; Hall, *Aspects of German Culture*; White, "The New Germany"; James Washington Bell, "German Universities," *Education* 2 (1881–2): 49–64.

matics professor at Antioch mentioned in Hall's autobiography, who was taking courses at Heidelberg in 1873 at the time when the university senate voted to bar any future female auditors.[49] No American woman followed Rice's example until 1879, when Eva Channing, whose father was a friend of Zakrzewska, began taking courses at Leipzig. She published an anonymous article about her experiences in the *Atlantic Monthly,* but by the time it appeared, three other Americans had already arrived in Leipzig: Harriet Parker, a graduate of the University of Iowa; and M. Carey Thomas and her friend Mary Gwinn, who had learned of Channing's presence through Andrew D. White, then U.S. minister in Berlin.[50] Like Rice at Heidelberg, however, these four Americans at Leipzig were among the last women admitted as auditors before the Saxon government closed off access to the university.

During the 1880s, a handful of American women managed to pursue studies with professors at German universities without being officially allowed to audit courses. In late 1882, Mary Waston Whitney, professor of astronomy at Vassar, reported that "an American girl is studying under Professor Vichow [sic] at Berlin." At the same university, the botanist Simon Schwendener had two such female students in the mid-1880s: Emily L. Gregory, who interrupted her studies at Zurich to work with him, the other probably Susan Hallowell, a professor at Wellesley.[51] Late in the decade, Leipzig again began attracting a number of American women, even though auditing by women was officially banned.[52]

By the early 1890s, the Association of Collegiate Alumnae (ACA), Bryn Mawr College, and the Women's Educational Association of New England were offering graduate fellowships for women interested in studying abroad; and such organizations were able to provide up-to-date information about which universities allowed women to study. German universities drew a

49. Hall, *Life,* p. 202; Hans Krabusch, "Die Vorgeschichte des Frauenstudiums an der Universität Heidelberg," *Ruperto-Carola* 19 (1956): 139n.
50. Anonymous letter to "The Contributor's Club," *Atlantic Monthly* 44 (1879): 788–91; Harriet Parker Campbell in *WWW,* p. 157; Finch, *Carey Thomas,* pp. 88, 96. Details of Thomas's three years in Leipzig can be found in Marjorie Housepian Dobkin, ed., *The Making of a Feminist: Early Journals and Letters of M. Carey Thomas* (Kent, Ohio, 1979). I assume that Eva Channing was the daughter of William Francis Channing mentioned in *National Cyclopedia of American Biography,* Vol. 23, pp. 284–5.
51. M. W. Whitney, "Scientific Study and Work for Women," *Education* 3 (1882–3): 64; Simon Schwendener in Arthur Kirchhoff, ed., *Die akademische Frau* (Berlin, 1897), p. 282; Helen Abbott Michael, *Studies in Plant and Organic Chemistry* (Cambridge, Mass., 1907), p. 54; Hackett, *Wellesley,* p. 43.
52. Albisetti, *Schooling German Girls,* pp. 223–4, which incorrectly states that Jane Belle Sherzer was the "J. B. S." who wrote about studying in Leipzig in *The Nation* 58 (1894): 154.

significant percentage of these fellowship holders, including nine of the first thirteen ACA fellows.[53] At some universities, these women were the first, or among the first, allowed to audit courses. In the mid-1890s, American women even began earning the coveted German Ph.D., though they still could not matriculate as regular students.

Several things are worth noting about the fields studied by American women in Germany. Most remarkable was the string of fellows – at least seven between 1893 and 1900 – who pursued mathematics at Göttingen under Felix Klein and other professors, a practice originally encouraged by Friedrich Althoff from the Prussian Ministry of Education.[54] Another important cluster of American women, including Emily Greene Balch and Mary Kingsbury, gathered in the courses of the *Kathedersozialisten* Gustav Schmoller and Adolf Wagner at Berlin.[55] On the negative side, it appears that no American woman in the 1890s and no ACA fellow before 1914 pursued a Ph.D. in history from a German university.

The improving quality of and opportunities for graduate study in the United States had the same effect on American women as they did on men. Even before World War I cut off the possibility of studying in Germany, the lure of the German university for American women had begun to fade.[56] Yet in 1915, the American feminist Katherine Anthony pointed to a potential new German influence on the higher education of American women when she claimed that the opening of matriculation for women at all German universities by 1909 was "a more liberal policy than the exclusively male universities of the Eastern States of America."[57] It would take over fifty years, of course, before this "German influence," in combination with changes in American society, would help bring co-education to colleges such as Yale, Princeton, Dartmouth, Williams, and Amherst.

53. Margaret E. Maltby, *History of the Fellowships Awarded by the American Association of University Women* (Washington, D.C., 1929), pp. 13–18.
54. For Annie MacKinnon Fitch, Margaret Maltby, Mary Frances Winston, Fanny Gates, ibid.; Emilie Norton Martin, Virginia Ragsdale, and Adelaide Smith in *WWW*, pp. 543, 669, 753; on Althoff, see Albisetti, *Schooling German Girls*, p. 227.
55. Mercedes Randall, *Improper Bostonian: Emily Greene Balch* (New York, 1964), pp. 90–7.
56. Rossiter, *Women Scientists*, p. 43.
57. Katharine Anthony, *Feminism in Germany and Scandinavia* (New York, 1915), pp. 32–3.

14

Basil L. Gildersleeve:
The Formative Influence

WARD W. BRIGGS

It is generally held that Basil Lanneau Gildersleeve was the most important and influential classicist in America. What are his claims to such prominence? First, few have been formative figures in American education for longer than he, since he enjoyed a teaching career of sixty-five years. Second, was our most literary classicist at the same time that he was our most scrupulous and masterly grammarian, and he appeals to us today at least as much in the noble humanity of his style as in the humbling regality of his learning. At the time of his death, he could claim pervasive influence in his own land. His edition of Pindar's Olympian and Pythian Odes was recognized as a standard commentary on these poems of the most vexatious classical poet. His *Latin Grammar* was still in print and widely used. The journal he founded, *The American Journal of Philology,* continued to hold first rank among international classics journals and to attract the best contributors from this country and Europe. It is the more remarkable that each of these statements remains true today, some sixty-five years after his death.

To discuss Gildersleeve's formative influence on American scholarship and teaching, it is necessary to discuss the influences that formed him, sketching out a portion of his intellectual biography.

Gildersleeve was born in Charleston, South Carolina in 1831. His father, of New England stock, was a Presbyterian minister who came south after his ordination but never received a parish. Instead, he published religious newspapers first in Charleston and then in Richmond, Virginia. Gildersleeve's paternal grandfather had fought at Valley Forge in the Revolutionary War. On his mother's side, his maternal grandfather, along with the rest of his family, were Acadians who had been exiled to Charleston by the British from their native Nova Scotia in 1755. Bazile Lanneau, his mother's father, survived smallpox and malaria, was orphaned at the age of nine in a foreign land, and became a well-to-do merchant who served two terms in the South Carolina legislature. He retained a vitriolic hatred of the British for his whole life. As Gildersleeve said, writing in 1877, the year after the American Centennial celebrations:

The air is still full of centennial, of colonial memories, which are more than traditions, which are heirlooms to one whose earliest lessons were the stories of the suffering at Valley Forge, of the battle of Trenton, the attack on Fort Moultrie and the bombardment of Charleston; to one whose earliest pride it was that his father's father and mother's father on this side and that side of the Potomac alike had braved the danger and borne the hardship of that momentous time.[1]

But it was not so much the Revolution as the attempt to crush the young Union in the War of 1812 that aggravated Southern hostility to England. When Gildersleeve was born (1831), memories of that war were still alive. The British were oppressors and torturers, shacklers of a region for whom individual freedom counted above all. Although planters of the South, generally English émigrés themselves, had sent their sons to England for their advanced education prior to the Revolution, and a few even for a time after it, Gildersleeve tells us that in 1850, when he was considering his own postgraduate education,

there was no such thing as Anglomania then, except perhaps in a limited circle in which the ancestral connection with England was kept up. As against the North, we were southerners; as against England, we were national enough. . . .The war [of 1812] changed the attitude of the South toward England.[2]

Despite the new nationalism and historical hostility to Britain, the prevalent view during the years of Gildersleeve's adolescence was that American education was appallingly bad by European standards ("My American teachers did not understand their business"[3]) and English education was still held out as an ideal.

Brought up in old-fashioned ways and in an old-fashioned environment, which might almost be called "colonial," I had been taught or at all events had conceived a profound admiration of English scholarship, especially in its lighter manifestations.[4]

Before he was thirteen, Gildersleeve had copied out one of Porson's facetious contributions to the London *Morning Post,* a version in Greek

1. "An Address Delivered before the American Whig and Cliosophic Societies, of the College of New Jersey, at Princeton, June 20, 1877" (Princeton, N.J., 1878), 51.
2. "Formative Influences," *The Forum* 10 (February 1891), 609–10.
3. *American Journal of Philology* [hereafter *AJP*] 37 (1916) 495 = *Selections from the Brief Mention of Basil L. Gildersleeve,* ed. C. W. E. Miller (Baltimore, 1930), 365; hereafter cited as *SBM*.
4. Ibid.

iambics of "Three children sliding on the ice," masquerading as a recently discovered fragment of a Greek play. One of the first philological works he owned was a collection of Porson's works in four volumes, which he studied religiously. But he soon found that the most useful books were by German authors, and once this realization came, he said, "there was an end of any deference to English scholarship."[5] Already attracted to Greek, Gildersleeve seemed naturally to gravitate to German models, and the reasons are of some interest.

How did the rise of European Hellenism manifest itself in this country? Before the Civil War, the great American figures in classics were primarily Latinists: Everett, Anthon, Felton, and Woolsey;[6] for the fifty years following the war, the great figures were predominantly Hellenists: Goodwin, Seymour, Shorey, Smyth, and, of course, Gildersleeve. A number of factors have been adduced. The Greek war of independence, which occurred within a generation of our own Revolution, had a particular fascination for the English romantic poets, who taught themselves Greek in order to read Homer, Thucydides, and Sappho.[7] Another factor is the Civil War itself, which challenged men with the concepts of duty and patriotism so well expressed in Greek tragedy. But a major cause must also be the coming into prominence of the entire generation of exceptional young classical scholars, who in their turn trained the best men of the post–Civil War period at Harvard, Yale, Princeton, Johns Hopkins, and elsewhere.

Thus the tale begins with a group of highly intelligent students who sought a level of training unavailable in this country in its first half-century. Many chose Göttingen, where, Greek predominated under the leadership of K. F. Hermann, von Leutsch, and Schneidewin. The first group comprised Edward Everett, George Ticknor, Joseph Green Cogswell, and others; the last contingent before the Civil War included Gildersleeve, W. W. Goodwin, George Lane, William Dwight Whitney, and Francis James Child. The predominance of Greek can be seen in the fact that of the eleven great scholars in American classics who took the doctorate from Göttingen, seven, including Gildersleeve, Goodwin, and Herbert Weir Smyth, were Hellenists. It was a time when, as Gildersleeve said, "the pent-up streams of Greek poetry brought their crystal clearness and their refreshing coolness

5. Ibid.
6. See Meyer Reinhold, "The Silver Age of Classical Studies in America 1790–1830," in *Ancient and Modern: Essays in Honor of Gerald F. Else*, ed. John D'Arms and John W. Eadie (Ann Arbor, Mich., 1986), 1–48; reprinted in Reinhold, *Classica Americana* (Detroit, 1984), 174–203.
7. See George A. Kennedy, "Afterword," in Reinhold, *Classica Americana*, 332.

to brighten and sweeten the current of our literature. No pseudo-classicism this, but a real classicism; not a mechanical rule, but a vital principle."[8] But these were also men who had read a great deal of German literature, and in those days, to read German literature was to read Goethe. Unfortunately, we have scant documentation to show more than their admiration for Goethe, but with Gildersleeve, the situation is quite different. In his case, it was Goethe who drew him to Germany at least as much as Greek. The ideals and even the view of Greece presented by the works of Goethe (admittedly influenced by Winckelmann) meant at least as much to him as the methods of Boeckh, K. F. Hermann, Ritschl, and his other German masters.

By the time Gildersleeve was born, in the last year of Goethe's life, Goethe had been, in the words of Hugh Lloyd-Jones, "more than any other individual, . . . responsible for the immense energy devoted to Classical studies by Germany during the nineteenth century."[9] He believed that true maturity and real understanding came only with vast experience of both the intellectual and the practical kind. He so combined the scientific with the humanistic that James Russell Lowell dubbed him the "Aristotelian poet." The model of life, of course, was not the Christian ideal, but a life in accord with the pure excellence of nature, an excellence Goethe saw (following Winckelmann) as most perfectly embodied in the civilization of ancient Athens.

By setting an example of serious scholarship,[10] Goethe encouraged the improvement of the sciences of archaeology, philology, and history, but he also deeply affected the view of Greece that scholar and layperson alike would have for many years. For example, he tried his hand at epic, attempting a continuation of Homer. He read widely and deeply in Greek literature but could not keep his intended epic from coming out as a tragedy, an *Achilleid* with Achilles suffering from *Weltschmerz*. In other words, he used his knowledge of Greece to write about himself, allowing others to see in the Greeks particular analogues for their own lives and problems. This encouraged the seeking of historical parallels and the transference of experience of the kind Gildersleeve indulged in his essay "A Southerner in the Peloponnesian War."[11] Goethe's love of the Greek spirit also captivated such British scholar-authors as Matthew Arnold, Walter Pater, Hippolyte Taine, and Oscar Wilde.

8. "Address," *A Record of the Commemoration, November Fifth to Eighth, 1886, on the Two Hundred and Fiftieth Anniversary of the Founding of Harvard College* (Cambridge, Mass., 1887), 307.
9. Hugh Lloyd-Jones, *Blood for the Ghosts* (Baltimore, 1982).
10. He kept a classicist on retainer and was advised by Gottfried Hermann (Lloyd-Jones).
11. Gildersleeve, "A Southerner in the Peloponnesian War," *Atlantic Monthly* 80 (September 1897), 330–42. Reprinted in *Creed of the Old South* (Baltimore, 1915), 55–103.

The first period of American Goethe-mania flowered primarily in New England among the Unitarians and Transcendentalists, despite protests directed at Goethe's character by some puritan divines who objected to his amorality and his epicurean lifestyle. In 1840 Ralph Waldo Emerson made the astounding announcement that he had read fifty-five volumes of Goethe's writings. Many of Emerson's views on self-culture derive from Goethe, and in his *Essays on Representative Men* Emerson calls Goethe "the soul of his century." Longfellow knew German and visited Germany frequently. His *Evangeline* may owe much to *Hermann und Dorothea,* and *The Golden Legend* is certainly drawn from *Faust*. James Russell Lowell had studied German at Harvard in 1835 and visited Germany in 1852. He called Goethe "classic in the only way it is now possible to be classic."

But Goethe was also becoming known to Southern intellectuals of the 1820s and 1830s, men like Hugh Swinton Legaré, Jesse Burton Harrison, Thomas Caute Reynolds, and also Gildersleeve. The *Southern Literary Messenger* of Richmond, Virginia, printed *Hermann und Dorothea* in 1805 and published the first translation of *Iphiginie* in 1844. Indeed, the first American to write a book on Goethe was a Southerner, George Henry Calvert, who had actually met Goethe in 1825.

Gildersleeve's self-described "Teutonomaniac period" began when he transferred from Jefferson College (now Washington and Jefferson) in Pennsylvania to Princeton in the fall of 1847. At Princeton, he began to read German in earnest, and was later encouraged further by Carlyle's very popular translation of *Wilhelm Meister* (1851) and George Henry Lewes's *Life of Goethe* (1856). He says, "I doubt whether any boy of my age ever devoured so much of Goethe in so short a time. There was not much that I left unread from Goetz von Berlichingen to the Second Part of Faust. His lyrics were my delight and I learned many of his 'Sprüche' by heart . . . Goethe's aphorisms were my daily food. I committed my favorite passages to memory. I repeated them over and over to myself in my long solitary rambles, and Goethe was my mainstay at a time when my faith had suffered an eclipse."[12] In his German diaries, he even says that he would eat bread and sausage for a few days to be able to buy two plaster medals of Goethe and Schiller. Following the receipt of the doctorate in 1853, he toured Italy and wrote a German friend of his ecstasy in retracing Goethe's Italian journey. His love of Italy, which was certainly encouraged by Goethe, never left him.

References to Goethe appear in Gildersleeve's work from his early essay

---

12. *AJP* 23 (1902): 110; "Formative Influences," *Forum* 10(1891), 614.

on Lucian in 1859 to his final brief mention in 1921 and his last letters.[13] Particularly notable are his references to *Faust,* the *Zahme Xenien,* and the lyric poetry. A particular favorite among Goethian principles is the notion of the Eternal Feminine ("das Ewig-Weibliche"). In discussing the Ninth Olympian in his edition of Pindar (1885), he says, "Pindar is a manner of 'Frauenlob,' at any rate, but here 'das Ewig-Weibliche' is paramount."[14] Twelve years later, in 1897, he recalls the same view: "The Ninth Olympian is given up to the Eternal Feminine, and the lofty realm of personifications is full of goddesses."[15] A good case could and should be made for Gildersleeve's reading of Goethe influencing his criticism of Greek work, particularly Pindar, who Goethe had translated and studied,[16] and who Goethe considered the pinnacle of Greek writing.

Goethe also exercised a moral influence on Gildersleeve and his generation of young romantic intellectuals at a time when hostility to the rising waves of immigrants from Europe was leading to a decline in interest in German literature (1854–68). Goethe was a particular source of strength at the time of the death of his mother in 1859 and a half-century later when a friend died in 1908.[17] Goethe's discussion of *Kanonenfieber in Kampagne in Frankreich* clearly influenced Gildersleeve's already dutiful soul during the Civil War: "Goethe tells us that he rode into the zone of the great guns in order to find out for himself what is meant by 'cannon fever', and, mindful of his example, I have tried to analyze my own feelings under similar circumstances."[18] Once in the war, Gildersleeve found, like his other fellow scholars in arms,[19] that the true lover of literature, particularly the aficionado of classical literature, will fare better in such trials than will the common man, that study actually prepares one for such situations: "Indeed the communion with the lofty spirits of the ancient times is no bad preparation for these great emergencies that come to all, and those who confound the scholar with book-worm and pedant have a false notion of the rich life that pours itself into the veins of the true student of antiquity."[20] So Gildersleeve went to war just as other classicists like Reiske had in the Seven Years' War

13. *AJP* 42(1921): 402, where he repeats his motto, "Alles ist als wie geschenkt" ("everything is like a gift").
14. Pindar, *The Olympian and Pythian Odes* (New York, 1885), 201.
15. *AJP* 28 (1907), 64. See also ibid., 23 (1902), 111 and 37 (1916), 108.
16. For example, Gildersleeve says at *AJP* 30 (1909), 232, that *Nemean* 1 "begins with a memorable picture that always recalls to my mind Goethe's 'Sänger', 'Was hör ich draussen vor dem Thor?' " In fact, Goethe's opening may have been suggested by this famous passage.
17. *AJP* 29 (1908), 125.
18. *AJP* 17(1916), 373.
19. *AJP* 18 (1917), 392.
20. "An Address," 18.

and Paul Louis Courier had in the revolutionary wars of Italy and Germany, interrupting his study, like Lachmann, who says at the close of the preface to his *Propertius* that he must put down his pen and pick up arms for his country.[21]

So Goethe was the real impulse for Gildersleeve to join many others of his generation[22] (and his region[23]) in pursuing studies in Germany. Advanced study in the classics was merely the pretext (as was the study of law or philosophy for others) for Gildersleeve's grand tour, during which he would finish the novel that he hoped would make him famous. But upon arriving at Berlin for the winter semester of 1850–1, he found more compelling influences than Goethe in the professional scientific classical scholars who taught him, and his career plans changed virtually overnight. On the day of his matriculation he met the aged August Boeckh, whose teaching, Gildersleeve said later, "made a passionate classicist out of an amateurish student of literature."[24] "It was a great thing for an American boy to see scholars in the flesh," he later wrote,[25] and in a Lucianesque essay entitled "Professorial Types" he limned his German teachers for us as an American boy saw them, with much amusement but more admiration. Like him, they detested or disprized English scholarship (with the exception of Porson and Dobree) and many of them "did not even pretend to know English."[26] Gildersleeve promptly abandoned his novel and, for the moment, his other literary ambitions under the influence of Boeckh's dictum that "Grammar is the highest problem of science." He also studied with Johannes Franz, "the first real teacher of Greek I ever had," and with Friedrich August Maercker. With only five Americans at Berlin that semester, including the Sanskritist William Dwight Whitney, Gildersleeve felt isolated and awed by the great capital, and out of a "desire to migrate from university to university to preserve a freedom from bias," he moved to the friendlier Göttingen for the Easter term 1851. There he roomed with three old friends from Charleston and the Bostonian George Martin Lane. He took courses from Karl Friedrich Hermann, the Platonist Heinrich Ritter, and Friedrich Wilhelm Schneidewin, "one of my favorite teachers."

He moved for the spring semester of 1852 and the winter semester of

21. Ibid., 7.
22. Carl Diehl, *Americans and German Scholarship 1770–1870* (New Haven, Conn., and London 1978).
23. John T. Krumpelmann, *Southern Scholars in Goethe's Germany*, University of North Carolina Studies in the Germanic Languages and Literatures no. 51 (Chapel Hill, 1965). Between 1850 and 1860, Charleston sent more young men to Germany in pursuit of advanced degrees than the entire state of Massachusetts.
24. B. L. Gildersleeve, *Hellas and Hesperia* (New York, 1909), 42.
25. *SBM*, 141.
26. *SBM*, 366.

1852–3 to Bonn, where he studied with Friedrich Ritschl, who welcomed him into his home and became a correspondent. He also worked with Joseph von Aschbach, F. G. Welcker, Franz Ritter, and the young Jacob Bernays, who "led me into the study that resulted in my doctoral dissertation." Among his fellow students were Johannes Vahlen and the man with whom he would form a fifty-year friendship, Emil Hübner.

Gildersleeve returned to Göttingen to defend his dissertation and swear his oath on the Ides of March, 1853. After a brief European tour, he sailed for home with a paucity of prospects and a multiplicity of impressions of his German friends and teachers.

When he returned to America, no suitable employment awaited him immediately, and he wrote plaintively to his Berlin friend Emil Hübner[27] of the paucity of resources in his native land, not only of books and journals, but also of colleagues.[28] Three years later, in 1856, he was elected to the chair of Greek at the University of Virginia, founded in 1815 on the English model, which imported its first faculty largely from England, including the classicist George Long (1800–79). Long remained for only three years and returned to England to join the founding faculty of the University of London. Long left behind as his successor Gessner Harrison (1807–62), who, as his student, had been imbued with the English system that would dominate classics in the South from the period of his appointment in 1830 to his retirement in 1858.

Gildersleeve's German training at once ran him afoul of his colleague, for he believed in the new theories of Greek pronunciation and particularly the semimusical notations of Johann Hermann Heinrich Schmidt (1830–1913).[29] In addition, his perhaps exaggerated self-characterization as "a conceited youngster . . . with high honours from a German university"[30] may have some truth. His controversy with Harrison and the haughty demeanor that drew him a reprimand from the faculty for brusqueness toward a student were not soon forgotten in Charlottesville, so that when he resigned after twenty years, an editorial in a Richmond newspaper hailed his departure with the words "At last we shall have the Greek of the Greeks, not the Greek of Gildersleeve."[31]

There was simply no hope of Gildersleeve's making the most of his

---

27. (1834–1901). Epigraphist and editor of *Hermes* at the University of Berlin.

28. See *The Letters of Basil Lanneau Gildersleeve*, ed. W. W. Briggs, Jr. (Baltimore, 1987), 33–4.

29. See Schmidt's *Introduction to the Rhythmic and Metric of the Classical Languages*, trans. J. W. White (Boston, 1878).

30. "Formative Influences," 615–16.

31. Thomas W. Dickson, "Letter," *Johns Hopkins Magazine* 25, no. 5 (September 1974), 2.

German training and models. He was seriously overtaxed with tedious undergraduate work, with over twenty hours of teaching per week and no assistance. More than two decades after receiving his doctorate, he had published a Latin grammar, a series of textbooks, which he called "decided failures,"[32] his text and commentary on Persius, which he called a "vacation study,"[33] and nine articles; only one of these could conceivably be called *wissenchaftlich*.

In the 1870s, the philanthropist and railroad magnate Johns Hopkins decided to create a university in his name, as he was persuaded that America, now a full competitor on the world economic stage, could also compete in education. With an eye to the grand tradition of secondary education by Germans in Baltimore following the German model, Hopkins confected a board of trustees (largely composed of fellow Quakers) to compose a university on the German model and chose Daniel Coit Gilman for its first president. Gilman (1831–1908), after training at Berlin under Karl Ritter, the Aristotelian F. A. Trendelenberg, and the Egyptologist Karl Richard Lepsius in 1854–5, had returned to the Sheffield Scientific School at Yale as a geographer and was briefly president of the University of California (1872–5).[34] In the spring of 1875, Gilman visited Charlottesville seeking faculty for a new university. He sought those who knew the German system and had the experience, ability, and energy to establish departments with three then-unique features. The first was a *seminarium,* as opposed to the general lecture and tutorial methods of the English undergraduate college. The *seminarium* would train not just teachers, but professional researchers, who would train other researchers in their turn. It would serve as a source of *new* research that would advance the body of knowledge in the field. Thus the second feature was the expectation of faculty publication and the provision of resources for same. Each professor was expected to found a journal in his field. Gildersleeve founded the *American Journal of Philology* in 1880; Ira Remsen, the *American Chemical Journal* (1880); Herbert Baxter Adams, the *Johns Hopkins University Studies in History and Political Science* (1882); and Arthur L. Frothingham, the *American Journal of Archaeology* (1885). In addition to his support for these journals, Gilman provided the medium for their publication, as well as that of the new research his faculty

---

32. Letter to Charles Wesley Bain, 7 June 1897, *Letters,* 225.
33. Letter to Paul Hamilton Hayne, 5 June 1875, *Letters,* 50.
34. See Gilman's memoir, *The Launching of a University* (New York, 1906), and papers in *University Problems in the United States* (New York, 1898). The biography is Fabian Franklin, *The Life of Daniel Coit Gilman* (New York, 1910), and the best modern work about him is Hugh Hawkins, *Pioneer: A History of the Johns Hopkins University, 1874–1889* (Ithaca, N.Y., 1960).

would produce: the first university press in America. The third factor was that students would be required to produce theses and dissertations of publishable quality.

Gildersleeve was not Gilman's first choice for the Greek chair.[35] For most of his appointments Gilman went first to Harvard (presumably he did not want to raid his alma mater, Yale), and there he offered positions to Gildersleeve's Berlin classmates the Eliot professor of Greek, William Watson Goodwin (1831–1912), and the Latinist George Martin Lane (1823–97), who were both putting their German doctorates to use by correcting grammatical exercises. Princeton was still a sleepy rural theological school, and Yale had only the Sanskritist William Dwight Whitney (1827–94). Goodwin and Lane declined Gilman's offers, but both suggested Gildersleeve, and on a December night the two men met in Washington, D.C., to discuss the university that was to be. The result was that Gildersleeve was the first faculty appointment to the new Johns Hopkins University.

Gildersleeve was an inspired choice. Not only was he intimately familiar with the German university system, but he was eager to raise the level of his own and his country's research. In addition, he was a Southerner, and Baltimore was a city of decidedly Southern sympathies. Gildersleeve set to work at once. His first seminars produced three scientific papers on fine points of Greek grammar, and American classical philology would never be the same.

A veteran of the first great wave of Americans trained in Germany in the 1850s, Gildersleeve now set out to train a new generation in the 1870s and 1880s, the generation that would build a foundation to take scholarship into the heartland of the country and raise the level of work in all reaches. He set an imposing example: his bibliography grew to over 400 items of every conceivable kind; he directed over sixty-five dissertations; and his seminar became the model for Harvard and Yale and for the new universities of Chicago, Cincinnati, and Cornell. As the proliferation of land grant colleges in the Midwest gave rise to the need for more and more classicists, regional classical associations like the Classical Association of the Middle West and South (1905) were formed, along with new journals like *Classical Journal* (1905) and *Classical Philology* (1906), the former edited by Gildersleeve's student Gordon Jennings Laing (1869–1945), the latter by Gildersleeve's close friend Paul Shorey (1857–1934). In fact, of the seventeen members of the founding editorial boards of these great journals, eleven had been students of Gildersleeve. He edited forty volumes of the *American Journal of*

---

35. *Letters*, 52.

Philology, which brought him his greatest fame, including honorary doctorates from Harvard, Yale, Oxford, and Cambridge, as well as membership in the American Academy of Arts and Letters.

The point to be stressed throughout all of this is that German literature, particularly Goethe, was as much a formative influence in his life as German scholarship, and this level of humane science was passed on to his students and from them to their students. As Gildersleeve put it in speaking of one of his teachers, "One by one books, like men, drop into the night, and shade is lost in shadow. What is not lost, what lives forever, is the spirit of love to learning and love to the learner, which, once kindled, passes from teacher to learner, onward to the end of time."[36]

Toward the end of his career, particularly in the dark days of World War I, Gildersleeve perceived that a rapprochement between German and English types of scholarship had taken place, in direct contrast to the political hostilities between the two nations. By 1916 the English had adapted German methods of research, and the Germans had come to an understanding of how love of the classics permeated every facet of English life and proved to be a working force. The charm and humor of the English were of great value in analyzing literature once the Germans had passed on the text. As Gilbert Murray, the Regius Professor of Greek at Oxford, said in 1916, "In Germany there is more one-sided devotion and more industry, in England there is more humanity, more interest in life."[37]

Curiously, this confirmed to Gildersleeve America's true role on the world stage as the amalgam of the best qualities of both our English ancestors and our German training. As he himself put it, "America is the melting pot of the world. The English base threatens to disappear: and there are those who claim the right to a new language. I came into the world too soon to see such a glorious consummation, but I have urged with what measure of emphasis my more or less imperfect command of the language of my forefathers allows, a cosmopolitan philology, which shall aim at combining the best characteristics of all nationalities."[38]

Gildersleeve's greatest contribution, in the end, was something more important than the introduction of German methods to America, though this was as considerable and perilous a task as Aeneas's bringing the Trojan gods into Latium. Drawn to Germany by his love of the inspirational Goethe, Gildersleeve received a philological training there that essentially *made* the young *littérateur manqué* became a classicist. As a mature classicist, he

---

36. "Friedrich Ritschl," *AJP* 5 (1884), 355.
37. Quoted in *SBM,* 372.
38. Ibid., 376.

showed by his regular and voluminous writings and by the example he set for three generations of students how to combine German methods with English sensibility to create a brand new, distinctively American kind of philology. Quite simply, he gave American classicists a sense of identity.

15

A Mediator between Two Historical Worlds: Hermann Eduard von Holst and the University of Chicago

JÖRG NAGLER

I

In January 1892, the eminent historian Heinrich von Sybel, one of the main representatives of the Prussian school of political historians,[1] advised his friend and colleague Hermann Eduard von Holst to accept a position with the newly founded University of Chicago:

For a proficient man the decisive factor for the choice of his habitat must be his sphere of action. Concerning your person everything is said with that. . . . As a pioneer of German scholarship you will have an effect in a field of almost unlimited perspective in Chicago. You will not be lost for Germany, however, and you will create a yearly growing market for the best commodity of German production.[2]

Sybel's coaxing recommendation, with its terms "production" and "market" reverberating with notions of cultural imperialism, had its effect on Holst. He accepted the call from the University of Chicago, but it was not the first attempt on the part of an American university to win Holst as a history professor. Other universities had already recognized that Holst would make an invaluable contribution to the development of their still nascent history departments.[3] Since Holst was an American history specialist

1. On the Prussian school of political historians, see George G. Iggers, *The German Conception of History. The National Tradition of Historical Thought from Herder to the Present* (Middletown, Conn., 1983, rev. ed.), 90–123; on Sybel, see Hellmut Seier, *Die Staatsidee Heinrich von Sybels in den Wandlungen der Reichsgründungszeit* (Lübeck, 1961); Hans Schleier, *Sybel and Treitschke* (Berlin, 1965); Andreas Dorpalen, *Heinrich von Treitschke* (New Haven, Conn., 1957). The basic concept of that particular school of historians was the urge to discover ethical forces in history and to use these findings to become involved in political struggles of the present; see Konrad H. Jarausch, *Students, Society, and Politics in Imperial Germany* (Princeton, N.J., 1982), 200.
2. Sybel to Holst, January 4, 1892, box 12, Holst MSS, University of Chicago; quotation translated by the author. Like Sybel, prominent German-American were enthusiastic about the prospect of Holst's nomination. See Henry Villard to Holst, February 2, 1892, quoted in Alfred Vagts, *Deutschland und die Vereinigten Staaten in der Weltpolitik*, 2 vols. (New York, 1935), I:435, fn. 2.
3. These were Johns Hopkins University, Clark University, and the University of Michigan; see Eric F. Goldman, "Importing a Historian: Von Holst and American Universities," *Mississippi Valley Historical Review* 27 (1940):274.

trained at a German university, he was especially qualified for a position at an American university. A German historian with an emphasis upon German history would not have been as attractive, since German history found few American students.[4]

This essay discusses several issues that touch upon the general topic of historical scholarship in the United States and Germany, as well as the development of this discipline and its accompanying structural institutional changes in the last quarter of the nineteenth century. Holst serves as a lens through which we can focus upon common and divergent concepts of historical scholarship in both countries, as well as the impact of these concepts on the structures and institutions in higher education. An examination of Holst leads one to look specifically at the graduate school and, subsequently, at the training of professional historians in the United States. When we speak of mutual influences on higher education, Holst embodies a bilateral transfer. Not only the transatlantic transfer of ideas but also his own sociopolitical and cultural experiences in both countries shaped his mind as a historian. He thus influenced historical thinking on American history in Germany, as well as historical thinking on European and American history in the United States. In one aspect, however, the transfer was unidirectional: his ideas and ideals of higher education concerning the training of historians, derived from his German university experience. At the University of Chicago he tried to implement his notion of graduate training, which included high standards for both MA and Ph.D. exams. Beyond Chicago he endeavored to homogenize standards and foster close academic cooperation between major American universities.

How much influence do historiographical developments have on institutional changes and structures? This seems to me one of the core questions when we deal with mutual influences on higher education.

II

A brief look at Holst's biography[5] permits a better understanding of the context of his nomination as a head professor in the history department of the newly founded University of Chicago. Son of a Lutheran minister, Holst was born in 1841 in Livonia, a Baltic province of Russia. Although Russian

---

4. Richard S. Barnes, "German Influence on American Historical Studies, 1884–1914" (Ph.D. diss., Yale University, 1953), 129.
5. The most extensive Holst biography hitherto is Hans-Günter Zmarzlik, "Hermann Eduard von Holst," in Johannes Vincke, ed., *Freiburger Professoren des 19. und 20. Jahrhunderts* (Freiburg im Breisgau, 1957), 21–76.

by birth, Holst's cultural and educational environment was unequivocally German, in which he was totally absorbed. Despite the recommendation of his teachers at the University of Dorpat that he continue his historical studies under Georg Waitz in Göttingen, he characteristically chose as his mentor the political historian Ludwig Häusser at the University of Heidelberg, a leading proponent of Prussian-German nationalism.[6]

In 1866, one year after he received his doctorate, Holst found employment as a tutor in a German family in St. Petersburg. His strong belief that history and politics were one inseparable entity caused him to publish a political pamphlet condemning Russian absolutism.[7] The pamphlet prompted his exile, and subsequently he took refuge in the United States from 1867 to 1872. There, after initial hardships, he succeeded in becoming assistant editor of the *German-American Encyclopedia* project.[8] Continuing to adhere to his conviction that a historian should also be involved in current political affairs, he soon became active in party politics and in endeavors to increase the political and cultural importance of his countrymen in the United States.[9]

At first, he actively supported the Republican Party in its fight against Tammany Hall, but later he joined the oppositional Liberal Republican Movement, whose main goals were the hindering of the reelection of Republican President Ulysses S. Grant and his allegedly corrupt administration, the peaceful reintegration of the South into the Union, and the reform of the Civil Service.[10] Through his political involvement, he made the acquaintance of prominent Americans and emigrated Germans, among them Horace Greeley, Frederick Law Olmstedt, the Forty-Eighter Carl Schurz, who at that time had already advanced to the U.S. Senate, and Friedrich Kapp, also a Forty-Eighter.[11] A lifelong friendship connected him with the

6. See Eric Goldman, "Hermann Eduard von Holst: Plumed Knight of American Historiography," *Mississippi Valley Historical Review* 23 (1936–7):512. On Häusser, see Erich Marcks, "Ludwig Häusser und die politische Geschichtsschreibung in Heidelberg," in *Heidelberger Professoren aus dem 19. Jahrhundert: Festschrift der Universität zur Zentenarfeier ihrer Erneuerung durch Karl Friedrich*, 2 vols. (Heidelberg, 1903), I:285–354; Ludwig Häusser, *Denkwürdigkeiten der Badischen Revolution* (Heidelberg, 1851). Häusser was a former member of the Baden legislature.

7. The pamphlet was entitled *Das Attentat vom 4. April 1866 (16. April) in seiner Bedeutung für die kulturgeschichtliche Entwicklung Russlands. Eine kulturhistorisch-politische Studie* (Leipzig, 1867).

8. The project was directed by Alexander J. Schem, *Deutsch-Amerikanisches Konversations-Lexicon*, 11 vols. (New York, 1869–74).

9. Zmarzlik denies Holst's endeavors to coordinate German-American efforts to influence American politics; see Zmarzlik, "Holst," 36. However, Holst's letters during his first stay in the United States indicate his strong involvement in precisely these affairs.

10. For the general history of this oppositional movement and the involvement of German-Americans in it, see Jörg Nagler, "Deutschamerikaner und das Liberal Republican Movement 1872," *Amerikastudien/American Studies*, 33 (1988): 415–38; see also the letters from Holst to Schurz during this time in regard to this movement, Holst to Schurz, June 25, 1871, and August 24, 1871, Schurz MSS, Library of Congress.

11. On Kapp, see, most recently, Wolfgang Hinners, *Exil und Rückkehr: Friedrich Kapp in Amerika und*

latter two, and Kapp was to become his protegé in the United States, as well as in Germany after Kapp's remigration. Through his own historical writings and political influence, Kapp was well connected with major American and German historians as well as with politicians, among them George Bancroft and Heinrich von Sybel, and such liberals as Ludwig Bamberger and Franz von Roggenbach. Kapp used his influence to Holst's advantage, and he made Holst his successor as the correspondent of the *Kölnische Zeitung* from 1869 to 1871.[12] But much more important for his future career and for establishing his prestige as a historian was the assignment Holst received in 1869 (again through the mediation of Kapp and the endorsement of Sybel): to write a study on popular suffrage and government in America for a German audience.[13] Sybel, as the editor of the *Historische Zeitschrift,* knew Holst through an article he had published in this prestigious journal in 1867.[14] After some initial research, Holst soon realized that the scope of this enterprise was beyond the capability of one single historian. He wrote his patrons – a group of Bremen merchants – that he would prefer to write a constitutional history of the United States, which from his point of view would be manageable. He had found the subject of his *magnum opus,* which would establish his reputation as a historian in the United States as well as in Germany.[15]

Once Holst had changed the format of his assignment into a true research project, Sybel approached Holst in order to emphasize the salient political relevance this work could possess for current political developments in Germany. This notion of doing history as a comment on current politics was characteristically symptomatic of the Prussian school of political historians. As Sybel stated in a letter to Holst, one of the major purposes of this con-

Deutschland 1824–1884 (Stuttgart, 1987); see also Hans-Ulrich Wehler, *Friedrich Kapp. Vom radikalen Frühsozialisten des Vormärz zum liberalen Parteipolitiker des Bismarckreiches, Briefe 1843–1884* (Frankfurt/M, 1969); Edith Lenel, *Friedrich Kapp* (Leipzig, 1935). For Kapp's relationship with Holst, see the numerous letters from Kapp to Holst in box 12, Holst MSS. The author is preparing an annotated edition of the Kapp–Holst correspondence. Kapp's life in many ways resembled Holst's: They were both émigrés, both shared political experience in the United States and Germany, and both were writers on American history. When the Franco-Prussian War broke out, Holst became secretary of the German Patriotic Aid Society, with its seat in New York, and strove for a nationwide organization. In his function as secretary, he cooperated closely with Friedrich Kapp in Berlin. Kapp had become the organization's representative and was in charge of distributing the collected money to the German victims of the war; see Hinners, *Friedrich Kapp,* 243–9.

12. His articles for this newspaper are in box 2, Holst MSS.

13. See Kapp to Hermann Kruse, March 6, 1869, Kapp MSS, Library of Congress; see also Sybel to Kapp, June 25, 1870 (copy sent to Holst from Kapp), box 12, Holst MSS.

14. The article is "Ludwig XIV und die Hugenotten," *Historische Zeitschrift* 14 (1867): 277–316.

15. Charles R. Wilson, "Hermann Eduard von Holst," in William T. Hutchison, ed., *The Marcus W. Jernegan Essays in American Historiography* (Chicago, 1937), 63–4.

stitutional history should be to prepare a German audience intellectually for the impending and inevitable democratization of Germany. As a true adherent of a conservative liberalism, Sybel pointed out to Holst that a process of radicalization would endanger democracy and that a thorough study of the "American example" could indeed have "practical significance" for Germany.[16] Although it was not explicitly stated in this letter, Sybel, as a fervent supporter of German national unity, looked at the American example as proof of the superiority of the concept of national unity, which was finally achieved in the United States through Northern success in the American Civil War. As we will see, Holst shared this unitarian view and made it one of the central theses of his *magnum opus* on the U.S. Constitution.

Holst also endorsed Sybel's dislike for radical democracy, since he was a firm believer in the societal relevance of an educated *Bürgertum,* which, according to Holst, should play a leading role in a democratic society. Holst's political engagement, situated within the broader context of a traditional and moderate liberalism, was motivated by his genuine belief – and that of liberals in general – that *Bildung* was a panacea for political participation and emancipation. Increased education raises the moral tone of society and hence leads to an enlightened progress intertwined with freedom.[17] Without doubt, Holst's dislike of all oppressive political as well as religious systems stemmed from his own experience with Russia's stern rule over the Baltic German Lutheran population in Livonia. Consequently, in his historical writings, this attitude led Holst to concentrate on issues in which he could reflect on the negative consequences and negative moral implications of undemocratic and despotic regimes such as French absolutism, czarist Russia, the American Southern slaveholding society, and Catholicism in general.[18]

In 1872 Holst received a call to become an associate professor at the newly revived University of Strasbourg, named after the German annexation of Alsace "Kaiser-Wilhelm-University."[19] Thus Holst became the first and only incumbent of the first European associate professorship in U.S.

16. Sybel to Holst, July 4, 1869, Box 12, Holst MSS.
17. See James J. Sheehan, *German Liberalism in the Nineteenth Century* (Chicago, 1978), 14–15.
18. Zmarzlik, "Holst," 28–30.
19. On the University of Strasbourg, see John E. Craig, "A Mission for German Learning: The University of Strasbourg and Alsatian Society, 1870–1918" (Ph.D. Diss., Stanford University, 1973). Although Schurz greeted Holst to his position, he nevertheless regretted the loss of a politically active compatriot, as he indicated in a letter to Holst: "[W]e do not have exactly here an abundance of men who can analyze the events and know how to influence them." Schurz to Holst, February 1, 1872, box 12, Holst MSS. Translated by the author.

history – nine years earlier than the first American chair for American history was filled by Moses Coit Tyler.[20] Again Kapp, who had been the actual instigator for the American history professorship in Strasbourg, was the main actor behind the scenes to make this position available to Holst.[21] In several letters he recommended Holst to the liberal Franz von Roggenbach, former minister of Baden, who had been assigned by Bismarck to build up this university and to make it a model for German universities. Friedrich Althoff, later main organizer of the Prussian and German University system and promoter of *Wissenschaftspolitik*,[22] was one of the principal organizers of the University of Strasbourg, with a strong emphasis on graduate studies and *Seminare*.[23] Without doubt, Holst must have been influenced by this new direction of academic training. In 1874, one year after the first appearance in German of the first volume of the *Constitutional History*,[24] Holst became a full professor of modern history at the University of Freiburg, again through Kapp's mediation.[25]

For the next eighteen years, Freiburg became his sphere of effective influence, continually gaining him a reputation in scholarly as well political terms. For eight years he served as a member of the upper chamber of the Baden legislature, first by nomination of the Grand Duke, whose oldest son he had tutored, and later as a representative of the University of Freiburg in that body.[26] However, as an opponent of ultramontanism who supported Bismarck's anti-Catholic *Kulturkampf*,[27] his liberal vision forced him to op-

20. On Tyler, see Michael Kammen, *Selvages and Biases. The Fabric of History in American Culture*, 2nd ed. (Ithaca, NY, 1987), 222–53. The significance of Holst's work for American historians at that time is demonstrated by the fact that when Tyler prepared himself for his Cornell assignment, one of the historians he studied thoroughly was Holst; see Kammen, *Selvages and Biases*, 232.
21. See Roggenbach to Kapp, February 2, 1872 (copied letter in Kapp's letter to Holst), box 12, Holst MSS. When Bismarck insisted that George Bancroft be consulted regarding the filling of the professorship, Kapp also won approval from Bancroft; see Zmarzlik, "Holst," 38.
22. On Friedrich Althoff, see Bernhard vom Brocke, "Hochschul-und Wissenschaftspolitik in Preussen und im Deutschen Kaiserreich 1882–1907: Das 'System Althoff'," in Peter Baumgart, ed., *Bildungspolitik in Preussen zur Zeit des Kaiserreiches* (Stuttgart, 1980), 9–118.
23. See Brocke, "Das System Althoff," 49.
24. The complete German title was *Verfassung und Demokratie der Vereinigten Staaten von Amerika, 1. Teil: Staatssouveränität und Sklaverei* (Dusseldorf, 1873). The subsequent four volumes were entitled *Verfassungsgeschichte der Vereinigten Staaten seit der Administration Jacksons: Von der Administration Jacksons bis zur Annexion von Texas* (1878), *Von der Annexion Texas bis zum Kompromiss von 1850* (1881), *Vom Kompromiss von 1850 bis zur Wahl Buchanans* (1884), and *Von der Inauguration Buchanans bis zur Zerreissung der Union* (1891). The title of the American edition was *Constitutional and Political History of the United States*, 8 vols. (Chicago, 1876–92).
25. See Wehler, *Friedrich Kapp*, 151, fn. 69.
26. See Albert Bushnell Hart, "Hermann von Holst," *Political Science Quarterly* 5 (1890):678; Wilson, "Holst," 65–6; Goldman, "Plumed Knight," 514. Holst became *Hofrat* in 1879 and *Geheimrat* 1889.
27. For the *Kulturkampf* in Baden, see Josef Becker, *Liberaler Staat und Kirche in der Ära von Reichsgründung und Kulturkampf. Geschichte und Strukturen ihres Verhältnisses in Baden, 1860–1876* (Mainz, 1973).

pose the Iron Chancellor's drastic domestic measures, which for Holst violated basic civil rights. Despite this criticism of Bismarck, Holst gave national unity priority over internal improvement. This was demonstrated when he ran for a seat in the Imperial Diet (*Reichstag*) in the election of 1890 as a candidate of the increasingly conservative National Liberal Party. He was defeated when the Social Democrats supported his Center Party competitor in a runoff election.[28]

His dedicated political involvement, however, did not lessen his scholarly achievements. Holst contributed an extraordinary share to the development and rapid growth of the University of Freiburg, which at Holst's arrival had an enrollment of only 286 students. Holst dedicated his research almost exclusively to American subjects, even when he was teaching German and European history in Freiburg, attracting both German and American students.[29] For one of his American students, Albert Bushnell Hart, Holst became doctoral adviser for a thesis entitled "History of the Coercive Powers of the Government of the United States." Hart returned to the United States in 1883 and later taught history at Harvard. He became president of the American Historical Association in 1909[30] and edited the twenty-six-volume *American Nation Series,* published between 1904 and 1907, which, according to John Higham, "constituted the first great professional synthesis of American history."[31] Like other historians of his time who had studied in Germany, such as Herbert Baxter Adams,[32] John W. Burgess,[33] and Andrew D. White,[34] Hart became an adherent of the Teutonic hypothesis that traced the American democratic institutions back to their Teutonic origins. According to this conservative evolutionary theory, these institutions were

28. Hart, "Holst," 679; Zmarzlik, "Holst," 59.
29. Goldman, "Plumed Knight," 513–14.
30. Zmarzlik, "Holst," 41, fn. 54. For Hart, see Carol F. Baird, "Albert Bushnell Hart: The Rise of the Professional Historian," in Paul Buck, ed., *Social Sciences at Harvard, 1860–1920* (Cambridge, Mass., 1965), 129–74; Michael Whelan, "Albert Bushnell Hart and History Education, 1854–1907" (Ph.D. Diss., Columbia University, Teachers College, 1989).
31. John Higham, *History: Professional Scholarship in America* (Baltimore, 1983), 20.
32. Adams was a student of Johann Bluntschi at the University of Heidelberg, where he received his Ph.D. in 1876; on the influence of German historical scholarship on Adams, see Raymond J. Cunningham, "The German Historical World of Herbert Baxter Adams: 1874–1876," *Journal of American History* 68 (1981):261–75.
33. On Burgess, see Bernhard E. Brown, *American Conservatives: The Political Thought of Francis Lieber and John W. Burgess* (New York, 1951); Hans-Ulrich Wehler, "Nachwort zu 'Uncle Sam' von John W. Burgess," *Jahrbuch für Amerikastudien* 8 (1963):261–6. See also John W. Burgess, *Reminiscences of an American Scholar* (New York, 1934).
34. On White, see, most recently, Wolfgang Drechsler, *Andrew D. White in Deutschland. Der Vertreter der USA in Berlin 1879–1881 und 1897–1902* (Stuttgart, 1989); Glen C. Altschuler's study, *Andrew D. White – Educator, Historian, Diplomat* (Ithaca, N.Y., 1979) still provides more information on White's notion of German historiography.

then transplanted to England, from where they were transferred to New England with the first settlers.[35]

From 1878 to 1879, during a leave of absence in the United States, Holst did research for his work on constitutional history through a generous grant from the Prussian Academy of Sciences. During this stay, Holst was invited to lecture at several universities, including Johns Hopkins, Harvard, and Cornell. Daniel Coit Gilman, the noted president of Johns Hopkins University and admirer of German historical scholarship, tried to persuade Holst several times between 1879 and 1880 to join the history faculty. Holst would then have become a colleague of Herbert Baxter Adams and Austin Scott, at that time the only two regular faculty members of the Johns Hopkins history department. Holst was flattered by the offers, which he seriously considered, but finally decided to decline, largely because of the superior German pension benefits.[36]

What, then, did finally motivate Holst to leave his amazingly scholarly productive and politically influential position in Freiburg[37] more than ten years later? Although not explicitly evident in his letters, certain "push" and "pull" factors can be delineated. One of the push factors was that Holst's sphere of influence in Freiburg became too parochial for him. Limited resources in Freiburg concerning American history, as well as higher academic and political aspirations, caused Holst to aim at Imperial Germany's capital, Berlin. When the creation of a chair for American history in Berlin did not materialize,[38] and when Holst was defeated in the election of 1890, as we have already learned, the road to greater influence and prestige was blocked and the way to the University of Chicago was open. As a pull factor, the more than fivefold increase in income offered to him for this

---

35. On the Teutonic hypothesis, see Higham, *History,* 161; Jurgen Herbst, *The German Historical School in American Scholarship: A Study in the Transfer of Culture* (Ithaca, N.Y., 1965), 115–21; Herbert Baxter Adams, "Germanic Origins of New England Towns," *The Johns Hopkins University Studies in Historical and Political Science* (Baltimore, 1883), I:5–38.

36. At this time, Sybel asked Holst not to accept the Johns Hopkins offer: "Mr. von Sybel urged me with great energy to decline, for to gain a somewhat broader and more solid foundation for my work on the United States would not be a sufficient reason to deprive my own country of my services, where they are appreciated and bid fair to be appreciated still more in the course of time," Holst to Gilman, July 11, 1880, cited in Goldman, "Importing a Historian," 270. The correspondence between Gilman and Holst is quoted in this article. Clark University also offered Holst a position as a history professor.

37. During his tenure at the University of Freiburg, Holst produced an impressive body of scholarly works. Besides the additional four volumes of his *magnum opus* on the American Constitution, he published numerous articles in the *Historische Zeitschrift, Preussische Jahrbücher,* and two more popularly oriented books for an American audience, *John C. Calhoun* (Boston, 1882) and *John Brown* (Boston, 1889).

38. Holst's friend in Berlin, the art historian Hermann Grimm, had unsuccessfully lobbied for the creation of an American history professorship. Althoff, whom he contacted, declined for financial reasons; see Zmarzlik, "Holst," 55.

position in Chicago might have been a not insignificant factor in his decision to leave Freiburg. Another factor that might have caused Holst's move was the new mode of historiography in Germany, often defined as the Ranke renaissance.[39] Political historians such as Holst were in decline. The new generation of historians emphasized "objectivity" and abstention from overt political and moral judgment in their historical writing. Highly specialized studies replaced the more general historical works such as those written by Holst. The same trend toward specialized studies was apparent in the United States in the last decade of the nineteenth century.

III

Let us now turn to the reception of Holst's work in the United States, which reflects the permutations in historical scholarship in that country between 1876 – the year of the first appearance of the eight-volume American edition of the *Verfassungsgeschichte,* entitled *Constitutional and Political History of the United States* – and 1892, when the last translated volume of Holst's *magnum opus* appeared. Although Holst produced much more than his *magnum opus* in his long scholarly career, his *Constitutional History* had the most lasting effect on historical writing in the United States. Immediately after the appearance of the first translated volume of the *Constitutional History* in 1876, it was celebrated as the most important work on the subject, and Holst was welcomed as one of the most brilliant historians.[40] In a letter to Holst, Herbert B. Adams congratulated him for his work, which for Adams was "very generally recognized among American scholars as the most critical and, at the same time, as the most impartial and thoroughly scientific treatment to which the constitutional and political history of the United States has hitherto been subjected."[41] In the first issue of the *Political Science Quarterly,* John W. Burgess praised the *Constitutional History* as an entirely innovative work and a "new contribution to the literature of our public jurisprudence."[42] And indeed, it was one of the few general histories that covered in such a scholarly fashion the time from the writing of the

---

39. Here I disagree with Zmarzlik, who assumes that Holst was not affected by these changes; see Zmarzlik, "Holst," 43. On the Ranke renaissance, see Hans-Heinz Krill, *Die Rankerenaissance, Max Lenz und Erich Marcks* (Berlin, 1962); Elisabeth Fehrenbach, "Rankerenaissance und Imperialismus in der wihlhelminischen Zeit," in Bernd Faulenbach, ed., *Geschichtswissenschaft in Deutschland* (Munich, 1974), 54–65.
40. For the positive reviews, see Charles K. Adams, *A Manual of Historical Literature* (New York, 1889), 607; Henry Adams and Henry C. Lodge, *North American Review* 123 (1876):328–61.
41. Adams to Holst, December 6, 1878, cited in Goldman, "Plumed Knight," 519–20.
42. John W. Burgess, "Von Holst's Public Law of the United States," *Political Science Quarterly* 1 (1886): 615.

Constitution to the Civil War. Also, when compared with the historical work produced by Americans at this time, Holst's approach was far more professional than those of the mostly self-taught American historians such as Tyler, John Bach McMaster, and Edward Eggleston.[43] The books written by James Schouler and James F. Rhodes lacked Holst's more sophisticated research. In addition to these factors, the timing could not have been better: The image of German professional historical scholarship had reached its zenith, and the aura of a German historian almost guaranteed success. In fact, American historians might have been flattered by the fact that a German historian deemed it worthwhile to deal with an American subject.[44] The translators even went so far as to compare the possible interest the work might create with that of Tocqueville's *Democracy in America*.[45]

Sixteen years later, however, the appearance of Holst's last volume of the *Constitutional History* evoked more criticism than praise.[46] Ironically, it was in the same year that Holst accepted a call from the University of Chicago. What was the reason for this decline of acceptance of Holst's work and the increasing criticism by contemporary American historians? We can take Holst's case as an example of how the ideal of German historiography and its perception of how a historian should approach his subject was slowly being replaced by an increasingly German-critical community of historians in the United States, or what Jurgen Herbst once called "the rise and decline of the German historical school . . . in the United States . . . between 1876 . . . and 1914."[47] We have to be aware of the underlying forces of the general American historiographical climate that shaped this critique. The growing criticism of Holst's work also indicated a move away from the New England–dominated school of historians – who were strongly influenced by German historiography – to a more self reliant, self-conscious, genuinely American school of historiography, coinciding with a strong American nationalism that called for self-definition. Frederick Jackson Turner, interestingly enough a student of H. B. Adams, exemplified that tendency, which gave high priority to social history and thus superseded political history as the primary field of research. This new trend in American historiography also indicated the failure of the attempt by German-trained American historians, like H. B. Adams, to transplant German historical thinking to the United States. In other words, they failed to accomplish a

43. See Kammen, *Selvages and Biases,* 236.
44. Goldman, "Plumed Knight," 512.
45. *Constitutional History* I, translator's note, xiv.
46. Goldman, "Plumed Knight," 511. For a discussion of Holst's view on Jacksonian democracy, see Alfred A. Cave, *Jacksonian Democracy and the Historians* (Westport, Conn., 1964), 14–16.
47. Herbst, *The German Historical School,* viii.

synthesis between their German notion of history – basically a concept of *Ideengeschichte* – with American historical material.[48] But it was precisely through the concept of *Ideengeschichte* that Holst, who wrote history out of contemporary political interests, tried to manifest the moral dimension of history and human actions involved in the process.

Thus in the early 1890s, Holst was criticized by a growing number of American historians primarily for his philosophical notion of history as purposive and instrumental. Without doubt, this perception and preconception led him to a narrowed interpretation of American history as a fight between the forces of good and evil, with the South, as the proponent of slavery and thus evil, inevitably losing to the good cause of the Union.[49] As a firm believer in centralization and an opponent of states' rights, Holst celebrated the outcome of the Civil War as proof of the superior concept of unitarism. Since the *Constitutional History* was written under the fresh impression of the unification of the German Reich, it amplified Holst's beliefs in this direction. There are abundant references to the *Zeitgeist,* or mind and spirit, in Holst's *magnum opus,* the constructive relationship between a "national sentiment" and the identity of the individual.[50] As an exponent of a moderate liberalism, for Holst the *Rechtsstaat* – imperfect as it may be – was the cornerstone of civilization. This rather optimistic and positive notion of the state was not shared by American liberals, who assessed more realistically the potential conflict between state and individual.[51]

Interestingly enough, extrinsically the major criticism of Holst's work grew out of skepticism about German historians in general, who were identified with the interests of the autocratic German-Prussian state.[52] Holst's allegedly wrong interpretation of American institutions was viewed as a lack of experience with "free institutions" in the United States, since "these things are mysteries to German professors, because they are mysteries to German statesmen also. The German scholar simply reads in a book of things which we are always looking at and acting in."[53] In the same vein,

48. Ibid., 128.
49. Although Gilman's endeavor to recruit Holst as a history professor was approved, a response by a member of the executive committee of the board of trustees of Johns Hopkins University is revealing in regard to the assessment of Holst as a historian: "[H]is [Holst's] views on the Slavery Question . . . seemed to me to be extreme altho' natural from his point of view. He judges of what was done in forming the Constitution, and in the strife of parties since, not according to the opinions then generally entertained, or with sufficient allowance for the difficulties of the case . . . but rather as an abstract question of right considered in the light of today." Cited in Goldman, "Importing a Historian," 268.
50. Goldman, "Plumed Knight," 526.
51. See Iggers, *The German Conception of History,* 94–5; Sheehan, *German Liberalism,* 234.
52. Sheehan, *German Liberalism,* 234.
53. John Alexander Jameson, *A Treatise on Constitutional Conventions,* 4th ed. (Chicago, 1887), 658. For

Harry P. Judson, dean and later Harper's successor as president of the University of Chicago, expressed his concern on Holst's appointment – not in regard to his personal qualifications but as a potential representative of the German Reich: "Of course there was a time when German notions were a valuable leaven in America – German enthusiasm for pure knowledge and careful specialization. But I think that that day has about gone. We have learned the German lesson – quite too thoroughly. . . . I should be hopelessly out of accord with a fragment of the German empire transplanted to Chicago."[54]

This remark is revealing indeed and reflects the growing tendency to identify German scholarship with authoritarianism and antidemocratic, hierarchical structures. As Frank Trommler has recently pointed out, it reflected less the actual level of scholarship in Germany than the rising competition in this field between the two countries.[55] But it also anticipated a growing reservation and skepticism about the German (Prussian) state and everything attached to it, such as culture and education. It also should be mentioned that in the context of the 1890s, there existed a nativist and antihyphen mentality in parts of American society, caused by new waves of immigration accompanied by a growing general skepticism about imported foreign ideas and culture.[56] In fact, the attraction of studying in Germany had declined perceptibly in the 1890s, which was reflected by the decreasing number of American students then enrolled at German universities.[57] Already in 1886, H. B. Adams, the strongest advocate of German historical scholarship,[58] compared with pride the best of the American universities with German universities and stated that it was not longer the *sine qua non* for American history students to attend German universities for training in European and American history.[59] It is interesting to note that Adams also gradually changed his positive perception of the German historical profession and oriented himself with the English "democratic" historians.[60]

---

a very similar view, see also W. L. Penfield's review of volumes 4 and 5 of the *Constitutional History* in *American Law Review* 20 (1886):123–4.

54. Judson to Harper, December 25, 1891, cited in Richard Storr, *Harper's University: The Beginnings. A History of the University of Chicago* (Chicago, 1966), 159.

55. See Frank Trommler, "Years of Estrangement: German–American Cultural Relations, 1900–1917," paper given at the Third Krefeld German–American Symposium, 1990, 9–10.

56. See Alfred Vagts, *Deutschland und die Vereinigten Staaten in der Weltpolitik,* 2 vols. (New York, 1935), I:435. Vagts misinterprets Holst's call from the University of Chicago as a consciously antinativist decision.

57. See Barnes, "German Influence on American Historical Studies," 68; Higham, *History,* 19.

58. John Higham states that Adams "did more than anyone else to Germanize American historical scholarship." Higham, *History,* 11.

59. See H. B. Adams, *The Study of History in American Colleges and Universities* (Washington, D.C., 1887), 41.

60. See Herbst, *The German Historical School,* 127.

Besides the fact that in the early 1890s major American historians emerged and their publications coincided with the last volume of Holst's *Constitutional History*,[61] these intrinsic and extrinsic factors led to a critical reception of Holst's work. As Michael Kammen has pointed out, "historians have not been very successful in handling the problem posed by interpretations considered ideologically unpopular at any given moment," and he rightly quotes Holst as an example for the late nineteenth century.[62]

IV

Ten years before Holst arrived at the University of Chicago, most American colleges did not have trained history faculty, and for a long time the colleges were structured more like schools. For universities such as Chicago, this meant that in order to elevate their prestige, it was necessary to educate students for both independent research and the teaching of history.[63] Along with the general transformation of higher learning in the United States,[64] starting in the 1870s there was a notable increase in the number of history courses offered at American institutions of higher education. Whereas history was taught before that time – if at all – by classics or philosophy professors, it was now increasingly taken over by trained historians. The need for an education of professional historians, who were capable of teaching history, stimulated the growth of and necessitated the emphasis on graduate studies. American colleges had to adapt to this new trend, and reforms were aimed at incorporating graduate training that was largely molded on the features of the German university, with a major emphasis on scholarly research.[65] With the opening of Johns Hopkins University in 1876 and the emphasis on research, historical studies were professionalized in the 1880s and 1890s under the able direction of H. B. Adams. Consequently, this school awarded the first American Ph.D. in history six years later to J. Franklin Jameson, the *paterfamilias* of the historical profession in the United States.[66] But it was a mere beginning. In 1884, the year of the founding of the American Historical Association, there were only twenty regular professors of history in the nearly 400 American colleges and universities in the

61. See Goldmann, "Plumed Knight," 516.
62. Michael Kammen, *Selvages and Biases,* 89.
63. Zmarzlik, "Holst," 63.
64. See Donald W. Light, "The Development of Professional Schools in America," in Konrad Jarausch, ed., *The Transformation of Higher Learning 1860–1930* (Stuttgart, 1983), 345–65.
65. Barnes, "German Influence on American Historical Studies," 51.
66. For a conflicting view of when the first American Ph.D. in history was awarded, see Bonnie B. Collier and Christopher Collier, "Who's on First?" *Perspectives* 27 (December 1989):10–11.

United States. Others had to divide their teaching duties with other disciplines, such as political science.[67]

By the time Holst arrived at the University of Chicago, American historical studies were thus indeed on their way to becoming more professional. Increased professionalization had an effect on the expansion of history courses offered in college curricula and led to the expansion of graduate studies. In these formative years of the American historical profession, newly established monographic series such as the *Johns Hopkins University Studies in Historical and Political Science,* edited by H. B. Adams, and journals contributed to the rapid growth of the scholarly interest in history. Although the major emphasis was on American history, these efforts were still oriented to German scholarship.[68] When Holst received the call from the University of Chicago, it was this aura of German *Wissenschaft* that stimulated the interest in promoting graduate studies.

Although Holst's historical methodology was in decline, his personal reputation as a historian, scholar, and educator, especially amplified by the German scholarly aura, was beyond criticism. William Rainey Harper, first president of the University of Chicago, was indeed proud when he finally managed to recruit Holst to become "head professor" – this term was later changed to "department chair" – of the history department and, in this position, to build up the department.

As a tenured head professor – the most influential academic position – Holst supervised the department in its entirety, including coordination of the curriculum, preparation of entrance examination papers, and the hiring of new faculty members in consultation with the president. Shortly after Holst's arrival in Chicago, the history department consisted of three professors and two instructors, all five Americans. Looking at the overall number of Ph.D.s held by the university's faculty members, it is worthwhile to note that fourteen of the thirty-five held a German Ph.D. Of the thirteen head professors, five held a Ph.D., of which two were German.[69]

In his negotiations with Harper before he accepted the call from Chicago, Holst had requested full freedom for teaching and learning, *Lern-und Lehrfreiheit,* "which we Germans consider the condition *sine qua non* of a real university," as Holst expressed it in a letter to Harper. He also emphasized that he intended to build up the history department on the model of German universities. Holst opted for improvement of the education of graduate students by insisting that they be taught by historians who were

---

67. See Higham, *History,* 4. In 1880 there were eleven professors of history in the United States; see Kammen, *Selvages and Biases,* 235.
68. Barnes, "German Influence on American Historical Studies," 129.
69. Starr, *Harper's University,* 62, 76; Zmarzlik, "Holst," 59, fn. 89.

capable of independent research.[70] Harper agreed since the university was organized to emphasize graduate work and original research. In addition, one of the important functions of the university was the preparation of students for teaching positions through its graduate departments and professional schools.[71]

But still, there were conflicts between Harper and Holst about the nature of the university. Should scholarship – as Holst wanted it – become the first priority of the university, or service – as was Harper's position? After his first glance at the university's schedule of activities, Holst complained that too many lectures were offered and too much of the academic planning was tailored to the needs of students. According to Holst, quality, not quantity, should be the priority. The individual faculty members should themselves decide what they wanted to teach. According to Holst, this decision should not be subordinated to a set curriculum. The intellectual elite could only be encouraged through high-quality research and should not be influenced by "the masses who require to be guided in such matters."[72] At monthly meetings with Harper and the university senate – consisting of the thirteen head professors, a recorder, and the librarian – Holst endeavored to convince them that this was the right approach. How well he succeeded in implementing his ideas is hard to assess in retrospect, but his correspondence demonstrates how often he had to struggle and his insistence on the principles he had acquired and defended at German universities.[73] Holst's importance to the new university was shown when he delivered the keynote speech at the opening ceremony on January 2, 1893, on "The Need of Universities in the United States."[74]

In every respect, Holst was interested in transferring his ideas about the university, shaped by his German experience, to this newly developing university of the Midwest. *Akademische Freiheit* and research were the first priorities, and the second was the improvement of standards in education in order to elevate the prestige of the university. Holst repeatedly requested that, at a minimum, doctoral candidates should not be allowed to repeat their exam more than twice.[75] "The candidate for the doctor's degree in History will be expected to pass an examination upon the entire field of

---

70. Zmarzlik, "Holst," 60, 74.
71. See Thomas Wakefield Goodspeed, *A History of the University of Chicago. The First Quarter-Century* (Chicago, 1916), 374–5.
72. Holst to Judson, August 26, 1892, box 12, Holst MSS.
73. Zmarzlik, "Holst," 72–4.
74. See Charles F. Thwing, *The American and the German University. One Hundred Years of History* (New York, 1928), 92; Starr, *Harper's University,* 181. The same year, the Prussian Cultural Ministry presented itself with an exhibition on German higher education at the Chicago World's Fair; see Brocke, "Das System Althoff," 65–6.
75. Zmarzlik, "Holst," 72.

history . . . the main stress falling upon the subdivisions, ancient, medieval or modern."[76]

Beyond Chicago, Holst was engaged in the reform of the entire American university system. For example, he gave a lecture at Nebraska State University on "Nationalization of Education and the Universities,"[77] in which he emphasized close cooperation among the greater American universities, with the goal of setting standards nationwide for student registration and academic degrees. He emphasized that the universities, not the colleges and high schools, should dictate the level of education, and that education should be nationalized without being consolidated.[78] The founding in 1900 of the Association of American Universities, which was created by the presidents of Harvard, Columbia, Johns Hopkins, and the universities of California and Chicago, shows that Holst was not alone in his efforts to coordinate different universities.

Without doubt Holst was a successful teacher, as demonstrated by overcrowded classrooms and overwhelming applause after his lectures.[79] Each semester he offered a four-hour lecture and a seminar on American history subjects. In the "kollegs" he discussed subjects relating to the French Revolution and nineteenth-century history.[80] Holst did not want to train specialists in American history, but rather "to contend against this narrow and humiliating notion. . . .Still, if we want to be a real University worthy of a great nation we must train historians and not merely drill specialists for a very limited field, which itself can be properly understood only if one rises to the conception of his being but one integral part of one vast organic whole."[81]

However, when Holst spoke of the status of American history specialists in Germany, he perceived the situation differently. In an astonishingly contemporary-sounding comment, he complained that the study of American history was still not adequately accepted and acknowledged by German historians who were "stars of the first order" in a field sufficiently serious for exclusive concentration.[82]

Through his political involvement in Germany as well as in the United States, Holst embodied the German idea of "the professor as the conscience

76. Starr, *Harper's University*, 155.
77. *The Monist* 3 (1893):493–509.
78. Ibid., 506–7.
79. For Holst's successful teaching skills, see Lucie Hammond, a former student of Holst, "Hermann von Holst, the Historian," *American Monthly Review of Reviews* 29 (1904):322.
80. Zmarzlik, "Holst," 72.
81. Holst to Harper, August 3, 1890, Harper MSS, cited in Zmarzlik, "Holst," 75.
82. Holst to Gilman, April 14, 1883, cited in Goldman, "Importing a Historian," 273.

of the state" and thus active in civic affairs, an idea that "corresponded roughly to the American ideal of an aristocracy of culture. John W. Burgess, German-trained historian who inaugurated graduate work in history and political science at Columbia, hoped to produce statesmen and public officials, as well as scholars."[83] Holst lived out these principles through his active involvement in the protest against American imperialism, the Venezuela policy of President Cleveland, and the annexation of Hawaii under President McKinley in 1898,[84] the same year Harper decided to grant an honorary doctoral degree to this very president. A year later, due to his deteriorating health, Holst resigned from his professorship and returned to Germany, where he died in 1904.

Holst's position as a tenured head professor and as the founder of the history department had been a success in every respect. The University Senate Address to Holst of December 10, 1900, read in part: "You have been conspicuous for scholarship and the maintenance of scholarly ideals; in the work of laying the foundations of a new American university your preeminent conscientiousness and strenuous devotion to the highest educational aims have been appreciated and admired. . . .Your reputation . . . has been one of the foremost elements of our success. . . ."

V

In the story of the transfer of historical thinking and ideals of higher education from Germany in the last quarter of the nineteenth century, Holst is one of the rare examples in which this transfer was instigated by a German scholar and not by Americans returning from their studies in Germany. It is worth noting that this historian was not a Europeanist, but primarily a specialist in American history. To our knowledge, Holst was the only German historian who received a call from an American university in the last quarter of the nineteenth century despite widespread admiration for the German school of historians. Therefore, one wonders why more German historians were not imported. A partial explanation might be the general relationship between the ordinate and the subordinate. The gradient between German and American historiography was so intense that American historians might have been intimidated by major important representatives of the German historical profession. Wilhelm von Humboldt's discouraging comment to George Bancroft concerning the importing of German scholars

83. Higham, *History*, 11.
84. See Charles Francis Adams and Schurz to Holst, January 30, 1899, box 13, Holst MSS; see also Goldman, "Plumed Knight," 515.

– "The proposition of importing German learned men into America is not a good one. The eminent men, those of very distinguished talents, those who would be able to do good, would never be induced to quit their country"[85] – is contradicted by Holst's successful tenure at the University of Chicago. Although Holst does not belong to the top-ranking historians of the nineteenth century, his importance as a mediator between two historiographical and educational worlds is great. His effect and influence, however, might have been greater in a time before the United States entered what we would call a transitional period in which American universities liberated themselves from European, especially German, academic predominance. Holst might then have become a true pioneer of German historical scholarship, as Hermann von Sybel had predicted.

85. Cited in O. W. Long, *Literary Pioneers: Early American Explorers of European Culture* (Cambridge, Mass., 1935), 134.

16

German Influences on American Clinical Medicine, 1870–1914*

THOMAS N. BONNER

When Abraham Flexner came to Munich in 1910, he wrote his wife about the powerful impression made upon him by a lecture given by the internist Friedrich von Müller. "He delivered a wonderful lecture," Flexner wrote, "his text a patient, after examining whom, he turned to the class with a discourse on infectious diseases as such. The case was of an obscure infection: that made his theme. He swept the whole field, working it out in broad, clear strokes, illustrating, differentiating, summarizing, – and yet ever keeping both concrete, never vague, never abstract."[1]

In his resulting study of medical education in Europe, Flexner paid tribute to the clinical teaching and investigation of the German universities. The German clinician, unlike the clinical teacher in the United States, was a research scientist, a full-time university scholar, one who devoted his life to the natural history of disease. "In a soundly organized university," he told his readers, "the medical faculty is in the position of any other faculty, – that of arts, of philosophy, or of science," and "within the medical faculty there is no distinction in kind between the professors of the fundamental or theoretical branches – anatomy and pathology, for example – and the professors of the clinical or practical branches – medicine, surgery, and obstetrics." While the professor of medicine was indeed a physician, this was of secondary importance. "He is first of all a university professor; that title indicates his dominant and consuming interest." Like other scientists, the university clinician had his set of research laboratories, where fundamental problems of disease were studied by chemical and biological methods.[2]

*I am grateful to the *Journal of the History of Medicine and Allied Sciences* for permission to use portions of a forthcoming article on "Friedrich von Müller of Munich and the Growth of Clinical Science in America, 1902–1914" in this essay.

1. Abraham Flexner to wife, July 18, 1910, Flexner Papers, Library of Congress.
2. Abraham Flexner, *Medical Education in Europe* (New York: Carnegie Foundation for the Advancement of Teaching, Bulletin no. 6, 1912), 145, 161.

By contrast, clinical teaching in the United States and Canada in 1910, as reported in Flexner's celebrated study for the Carnegie Foundation, was still the province of local practitioners. The conditions that had made clinical instruction in Germany a respected profession – full-time appointments, laboratories attached to clinics, and university control of the hospitals – scarcely existed anywhere in North America, and "clinical medicine droops in consequence."[3] At school after school, Flexner castigated the weaknesses of American clinical education and contrasted them with the progress made in American basic science. "In the matter of laboratories we discovered no slight cause for satisfaction," he wrote; "within two decades the laboratory movement has gained such momentum that its future, even its immediate future, is in no doubt. . . . On the clinical side [however] the outlook is less reassuring." Even at Harvard Medical School the faculty had as yet no effective control over the affiliated Boston hospitals, and clinical teaching lagged behind instruction in scientific subjects.[4]

The system of clinical education followed by Müller and others in Germany was as yet a remote ideal in the vast majority of American medical schools. Although the spirit and methods of German science had triumphed in the laboratory branches of study, clinical teaching had remained largely true to older British and American practices. By 1900, the structure of American medical education had taken on many of the characteristics of the German system, including a new emphasis on research, an accelerating drive to bring medical education within the orbit of the university, the growing use of laboratories to teach the fundamental sciences, and an insistence on the unity of teaching and research in a first-rate medical school. But even at the Johns Hopkins University in the glory days of William Osler (1889–1905), the work of clinical medicine was largely confined to the wards and clinics of the hospital, which was in itself a revolutionary advance over the traditional didactic lecture for clinical students. It was Osler who introduced the British system of clinical clerkships in medicine at Hopkins, which ultimately became the method of teaching all American medical students. At Harvard, Yale, Michigan, Pennsylvania, and other schools, however, the clinical professor of the early twentieth century was still drawn, for the most part, from the ranks of distinguished local practitioners with a bent for teaching. None of these early clinical teachers, not

3. Abraham Flexner, *Medical Education in the United States and Canada* (New York: Carnegie Foundation for the Advancement of Teaching, Bulletin no. 4, 1910), 101.
4. Kenneth M. Ludmerer, "Reform at Harvard Medical School, 1869–1909," *Bulletin of the History of Medicine* 55 (1981): 356–7.

even Osler, contributed much to the growth of medical science, and none was trained to conduct clinical research.

For Osler, the hospital was the beginning and the end of medical instruction. Students learned progressively by treating patients; textbooks and lectures were merely supplements to their experience in dealing with disease in a live patient. They took careful histories of their patients; did physical examinations; carried out simple laboratory tests; and followed their patients' condition throughout their stay in the hospital. Every student at the Johns Hopkins Hospital, unlike those in the selective British system, was given hands-on experience in the management of patients. But clinical investigation, as in the German system, was never a significant part of the clinician's duties in any American medical school before 1900.

The future of clinical research in America was very much at issue in the medical discussions of the first years of the twentieth century. American educators were still searching for a model of clinical teaching that would combine the experimental studies of the laboratory with the hospital-based teaching of medicine. How could medicine itself become more scientific? How could the hospital become as important as the physiological laboratory for medical advance in America? How could clinical medicine avoid being cut off from its scientific roots?

A number of Americans admired the efforts of such German clinicians as Hugo von Ziemssen, Friedrich von Frerichs, and Bernard Naunyn to bring the new laboratory sciences to the bedside instead of relying on the remote departments of basic science for complicated tests and new medical knowledge. New technological innovations, such as the gastric tube and a serviceable thermometer, were pressed into the service of research at the bedside. Advances in bacteriology were also clearly important to the clinician's ability to diagnose and treat disease.[5] Von Ziemssen, who had opened Germany's first clinical institute in 1878, persuaded the authorities at Munich to build a laboratory for him in the new university hospital, with separate departments of physiology, pathology, and chemistry. Medicine, Ziemssen believed, must be turned into a natural science focused on the diagnosis and treatment of disease.[6] When Osler visited a number of the German clinics in 1884, he wrote that the wards had become "clinical

5. Russell C. Maulitz, " 'Physician versus Bacteriologist': The Ideology of Science in Clinical Medicine," in Morris J. Vogel and Charles E. Rosenberg, eds., *The Therapeutic Revolution: Essays in the Social History of American Medicine* (Philadelphia, 1979), 95–6.
6. Johanna Bleker, "Medical Students – To the Bedside or to the Laboratory? The Emergence of Laboratory-training in German Medical Education 1870–1900," in H. Beukers and J. Moll, eds., *Clinical Teaching, Past and Present* (Amsterdam: Clio Media, vol. 21, 1989), 40–1.

laboratories utilized for the scientific study and treatment of disease, and the assistants under the direction of professors carry on investigations and aid in the instruction. The advanced position of German medicine and the reputation of the schools as teaching centres are largely fruits of this system."[7]

Other observers, however, saw little of practical value for the clinician in the new studies of the laboratory. The vast majority of the thousands of American physicians who went to Vienna, Berlin, and other German centers did so in order to perfect their skills in a clinical specialty. For them, Vienna, and later Berlin, with their special short courses, many of them in English, and their abundance of clinical and experimental material, were the ideal places for advanced training. Here one could do more eye operations, deliver more babies, treat more patients, and conduct more postmortems in a week than would be possible in a year in many parts of the United States. Vienna, in the words of William Henry Welch, was the "conventional Mecca of American practitioners." Its appeal, like that of Berlin, was to those with little time who wished to learn much. Few of them paid much attention to clinical investigation or to the studies coming from the laboratories of German science. By 1910, the educational value of a short sojourn in a clinical course in Vienna or Berlin was under sharp attack. Flexner, in his report on *Medical Education in Europe* in 1912, seriously questioned the value of the short medical stay at a clinical center.[8]

Many clinicians in America and Britain feared that the German emphasis on clinical investigation would lead to the loss of traditional bedside skills of diagnosis and the management of disease. Others feared the loss of economic and professional independence as scientifically trained men began to invade departments of medicine in hospitals and medical schools. There was such a thing as clinical research anyway, and how would it benefit the physician and medical student? Was not the business of clinical teaching the preparation of future practitioners? The very concept of clinical science was, in the words of the physician-historian McGehee Harvey, "a radical one at the turn of the century."[9] In Britain, as in the United States, leading clinicians challenged the relevance of the new laboratory science to their work at the bedside. According to Christopher Lawrence, British leaders thought

7. Harvey Cushing, *The Life of Sir William Osler* (London, 1940), 225.
8. Thomas N. Bonner, *American Doctors and German Universities: A Chapter in International Intellectual Relations, 1870–1914* (Lincoln, Neb., 1963, 1987), 25–6, 69–106.
9. A. McGehee Harvey, *Science at the Bedside: Clinical Research in American Medicine, 1905–1945* (Baltimore, 1981), 19–30, 115.

that clinical medicine "needed the ineffable wisdom that came only with advanced years, a classical education and the bearing of a gentleman."[10]

Among those who forced attention to the promise of clinical investigation in the United States before World War I was the German-trained physiologist Graham Lusk, who, according to a contemporary, served as "the strongest connecting link" between the new clinical science of Germany and its development in the United States.[11] A student of Karl Voit's at Munich, Lusk preached constantly to his American colleagues the importance of scientific ideals and standards in clinical work. "The development of American medicine," he wrote in 1909, "can come only through men who have a knowledge of modern chemistry, physiology, pharmacology and pathology." But where were such men to be found among America's clinicians? "You have not a great medical clinic," he said, "because you have not properly educated men, and you have not properly educated men because you have not a great clinic." No one in the United States, he said, could be compared with Friedrich von Müller, Oskar Minkowski, Ludolf Krehl, or Rudolf Kraus as a teacher of medicine.[12]

In the same year, Samuel Meltzer, who had studied in Berlin and Königsberg before coming to America, told the new Association for the Advancement of Clinical Research that American backwardness in clinical medicine was due to the fact that teaching was still in the hands of busy consultants "who received their medical training nearly exclusively in this country." The creation of special chairs of experimental medicine in departments of medicine was not the answer, said Meltzer, for "everywhere [the] science and practice of clinical medicine [must] go hand in hand." In the United States, he told his hearers, "one observes with amazement that nearly all the factors which favored the development of a scientific spirit in Germany are absent."[13]

Between 1905 and 1907, Osler's successor at the Johns Hopkins Hospital, Lewellys Barker, greatly expanded the work of clinical laboratories in Baltimore. In contrast to Osler, Barker, who had just returned from an ex-

10. Christopher Lawrence, "Incommunicable Knowledge: Science, Technology and the Clinical Art in Britain, 1850–1914," *Journal of Contemporary History*, 20 (1985): 510.

11. Eugene F. DuBois, "Graham Lusk 1866–1932," *Ergenbnisse der Physiologie und experimentellen Pharmakologie*, 25 (1933): 10.

12. Graham Lusk, "Medical Education: A Plea for the Development of Leaders," *Journal of the American Medical Association*, 52 (1909): 1230.

13. S. J. Meltzer, "The Science of Clinical Medicine: What It Ought to Be and the Men to Uphold It," *Journal of the American Medical Association*, 53 (1909): 510–11. See also A. McGehee Harvey, "Samuel J. Meltzer: Pioneer Catalyst in the Evolution of Clinical Science in America," *Perspectives in Biology and Medicine*, 21 (1972): 431–40.

tended stay in Müller's clinic in Munich, was deeply interested in promoting research within the department of medicine. The simple microscopic, chemical, and physical tests carried out in Osler's day were now broadened to include experience in original experimental research. Under Barker's Munich-inspired direction, biological, physiological, and biochemical laboratories under independent directors were added to the general clinical laboratory.[14] "It is just as necessary for physicians and surgeons to have their own . . . laboratories," Barker said in 1908, "as it is for analine dye manufacturers to have chemical laboratories attached to their plants. . . . It will not do for the sciences of diagnosis and therapy to rely upon the laboratories of chemistry, physiology, and pathology in the medical school to solve their particular problems for them."[15]

But change was slow and uncertain. William Henry Welch told his audience at the opening of the new Jefferson Medical College Hospital in 1907 that opportunities for academic careers in clinical medicine in America still lagged far behind those in the basic sciences. The crucial lack was well-equipped laboratories in the clinics of the teaching hospitals where investigators trained in chemical, physical, and biological methods could conduct research and work closely with the attending physicians.[16] Without saying it expressly, the diplomatic Welch also decried the commercialism that characterized so much of clinical medicine in the early years of the century. Most medical schools still offered their students little more than clinical lectures, a brief exposure to their professors, and a limited amount of ward experience. Harvey cites, by way of example, the testimony of James Means, who began his medical training at Harvard in 1907: "The clinicians brushed off the preclinical scientists as mere laboratory men who knew little of medicine and the scientist looked upon the practice of medicine as largely unscientific guess work. The preclinical scientists were in the world of college teachers on the campus. They were full-time, salaried people. There were no full-time clinical teachers. . . . These men taught and attended hospital patients for love or kudos and made their livelihood in private practice."[17] As late as 1913, Abraham Flexner charged that "the clinical teacher in the German sense hardly exists as yet in America at all." Clinical professors in the United States were not respected, he said, and made little

14. Lewellys F. Barker, "The Organization of the Laboratories in the Medical Clinic of the Johns Hopkins Hospital," *Bulletin of the Johns Hopkins Hospital,* 18 (1907): 193–8.
15. Lewellys F. Barker, "Medical Laboratories: Their Relations to Medical Practise and to Medical Discovery," *Science,* 27 (1908): 607.
16. William H. Welch, "The Relation of the Hospital to Medical Education and Research," in J. McKeen Cattell, ed., *Medical Research and Education* (New York, 1913), 192–3.
17. Harvey, *Science at the Bedside,* 116.

effort to create the kind of scientific atmosphere found in German clinics. "The university spirit," he concluded, "is missing in the clinical half of the American medical school."[18]

The remarkable aspect of this early debate over the future of clinical medicine in America was the unanimity of praise for the major German clinics as the ideal model for clinical teaching. Even those who had not studied medicine in Germany, such as Flexner and Arthur Dean Bevan, chairman of the powerful American Medical Association's committee on medical education, used examples from Müller's and other clinics to buttress their case. Opponents of reform were likewise respectful of the "German system," despite concluding that it could not be transplanted intact to the United States. Friedrich von Müller, according to Lusk, was the leader in a class of medical men who had no counterparts on this side of the Atlantic.[19] Krehl, Kraus, and Minkowski, along with Müller, were called "master clinicians" by Samuel Meltzer.[20] Barker said that Müller had exerted "a profound influence upon me."[21] Like his mentor Barker, Rufus Cole traveled to Germany in 1908 before starting his career as director of the pioneering Rockefeller Institute Hospital. The historian Fielding Garrison, writing in 1913, described Müller as "perhaps the most scientific teacher of internal medicine today."[22]

What was it about German clinical teaching, and especially that of Müller, that so impressed visitors from the United States? G. Canby Robinson, who spent a year in Munich, has left us the best description of Müller's clinic and its methods. Müller, wrote Robinson in 1909, was in control of 300 beds in one of Munich's municipal hospitals. He had nine full-time assistants, all of whom lived in the hospital. They were trained as chemists, bacteriologists, or hematologists. A series of special laboratories for chemistry, physiology, microscopic pathology, and bacteriology adjoined the principal clinical laboratory and a room for animal experimentation. Müller himself did a surprising amount of teaching to both medical students and postgraduate physicians. His clinical lectures included not only the usual physical examination but also chemical and other tests performed before the class. X-ray pictures were also frequently shown. Treatment of the patient was always discussed, including the latest pharmacological remedies. Robinson valued particularly Müller's firsthand knowledge of pathology

18. Abraham Flexner, "The German Side of Medical Education," *Atlantic Monthly,* 112 (1913): 660–1.
19. Lusk, "Medical Education," 1229.
20. Meltzer, "Science of Clinical Medicine," 510.
21. Lewellys F. Barker, *Time and the Physician* (New York, 1942), 130.
22. Fielding H. Garrison, *An Introduction to the History of Medicine* (Philadelphia, 1913), 564.

and the presentation of stereopticon slides showing microscopic findings. Bacteriology, too, was brought into the clinic. "It is remarkable," wrote Robinson, "to hear a teacher of internal medicine describe in detail the Gram stain or how various culture media are prepared." Much of Müller's day was spent in the hospital clinics and laboratories, though he saw a number of patients in consultation. The important thing, in Robinson's view, was that "the main part of his life's work is focussed on teaching and on the material with which his teaching is done." This required not only an unusual knowledge of the whole field of medicine, "but the ability to see future possibilities, so that promising problems for investigation may be suggested" to students. It was evident to Robinson "that there are few medical teachers in America who even aim at an ideal such as Professor Müller represents." His clinic, concluded Robinson, "represented an outstanding example of the true university spirit which bases teaching primarily on research."[23]

Most of the men who shaped American clinical science in the years after 1910 had spent time in a German clinic. Robinson and Barker were only two of a dozen American clinical teachers who had worked with Müller in Munich. Munich was a major attraction for Americans studying abroad in the halcyon years for German medicine before World War I. In medicine alone, between 1910 and 1914, 165 individual registrations of Americans can be found in the semester lists in the *Personalverzeichnis* of the University of Munich.[24] In the summer of 1910, for example, Munich led the University of Berlin in the total number of students registered in its medical faculty.[25] In addition to Müller, the aging gynecologist Franz von Winckel, the physiologist Karl Voit, the pathologist Otto Bollinger, the psychiatrist Emil Kraepelin, and the clinician Josef Bauer attracted the attention of Americans and other foreign visitors to Munich.[26] A number of the visiting American clinicians – Robinson, Ralph Major, Nelson Janney, Walter Dearborn – completed significant research projects under Müller's direction and published them in German journals.[27] The medical clinics in Berlin, Bonn, Heidelberg, and Breslau, as well as those in Vienna, likewise attracted Americans with a serious interest in clinical investigation.

23. G. Canby Robinson, "The Modern Teacher of Internal Medicine," *Old Dominion Journal of Medicine and Surgery*, 8 (1909), 383–7.
24. *Amtliches Verzeichnis des Personals, der Lehrer, Beamten und Studierenden an der Universität zu München, 1900–1914* (Munich: Ludwig-Maximilians-Universität München, 1900–14).
25. *Münchener medizinische Wochenschrift*, 57 (1910): 1718, 2214.
26. James H. Honan, *Honan's Handbook to Medical Europe* (Philadelphia, 1912), 69; Friedrich von Müller, *Lebenserinnerungen* (Munich, 1951), 171–4.
27. For more on Müller and his American students, see Thomas N. Bonner, "Friedrich von Müller of Munich and the Growth of Clinical Science in America, 1902–1914," *Journal of the History of Medicine and Allied Sciences* 45 (1990): 556–69.

It was Abraham Flexner, a frequent visitor to German clinics, who saw the appointment of full-time clinical professors as the only way to create clinics in the United States comparable to those of Germany. But how to do that? The tradition of clinical teaching by part-time practitioners was deeply rooted in British and American experience. Medical teachers in both Britain and America gained their reputations as practitioners or consultants and had few associations with university departments or laboratory research. Neither universities nor state governments were yet ready to appropriate the huge sums of money necessary to create full-time teaching positions in clinical departments.

At the Rockefeller Institute, a beginning was made in 1910 with the opening of a small hospital committed to clinical research. All of the physicians at the hospital, led by the German-trained Rufus Cole, were expected to devote full time to the investigation of disease. Cole believed that "the physical and intellectual barrier between the laboratory and wards . . . in many hospitals had seriously delayed the advancement of medicine in this country." He worked to bring the research of the hospital into close connection with the work already being done in the laboratories of the Institute. Robinson, who was senior resident physician, found that many of his coworkers had also studied in Munich and other German clinics. Important studies were launched in lobar pneumonia, cardiology, and poliomyelitis. Within twenty years, 80 percent of the 103 hospital staff members had found positions in research and academic work in leading universities throughout the world.[28]

But the Rockefeller Institute was a very special case. How could clinical research and full-time clinical teaching be fostered in the nation's medical schools and teaching hospitals? Working closely with William Henry Welch and the Germanophile anatomist Franklin Mall, Flexner in 1911 offered Johns Hopkins University an opportunity to develop full-time appointments in clinical medicine. The clinical professor, according to the plan, would see patients in the university hospital, but the fees collected would go for departmental uses and not to the professor. The full-time plan would create in America, he believed, the new science of clinical medicine. It would make possible careers for scientifically minded clinicians who would otherwise have to enter what one reformer called the "bewitching graveyard" of medical practice.[29]

In Germany, Flexner had observed that private consulting made the smallest demand on the clinician's time, following teaching, ward work

28. G. Canby Robinson, *Adventures in Medical Education* (Cambridge, Mass., 1957), 86–100.
29. Meltzer, "Science of Clinical Medicine," 512.

with students, research, and the direction of advanced students. But in the American environment, given the long tradition of private practice and the commercial appeal of the marketplace, Flexner believed that any compromise with the greed of private practice would leave the busy practitioner still in control of educational and hospital policies. "The clinicians," he wrote of the University of Michigan, "are the problem. They are a mercenary lot. . . .The laboratory men are heroes – men of ideals who have stood up to their jobs for sheer love of science."[30] The clinical professor in Germany was primarily an academic man, one who moved freely from one university to another for *academic* gain – a more prestigious university, a larger clinic, more independence to carry on his own work – whereas the American teacher-practitioner was firmly rooted among the patients in the home soil of the city where he lived.[31] What Flexner now sought in his patient but flinty negotiations with Johns Hopkins, and later with Washington University, Yale, Vanderbilt, Rochester, Harvard, Chicago, and Columbia, was nothing less than the creation of a national system, subsidized by private philanthropy, to bring clinical teaching in the United States abreast of that in Germany.[32]

In the battle royal over the full-time plan that followed, both sides cited German examples and authorities to buttress their arguments. Lusk, who supported the idea of putting clinical professors on a strict salary basis, wrote that "objection may be raised that no man in America is fit to conduct a clinic in any way similar to Friedrich Müller's." But this, said Lusk, was an insult to the intelligence and abilities of Americans. What was needed in America was a firm plan to put clinical teaching under the control of "individuals who will be placed on a salaried basis with prohibition of private practice."[33] Meltzer likewise argued for professional support of the full-time plan at Johns Hopkins as necessary to begin creating a university atmosphere in the medical school, but he questioned whether the absolute prohibition of private practice was necessary in "all or most good medical schools."[34]

Critics of Flexner pointed out that his full-time plan was inferior to the "university plan" followed in German clinics, in which a reasonable amount of private consultation was allowed the professor of medicine. The influ-

30. Abraham Flexner to wife, December 6, 1920, Flexner Papers, Library of Congress.
31. Flexner, *Medical Education in Europe*, 146.
32. Steven C. Wheatley, *The Politics of Philanthropy: Abraham Flexner and Medical Education* (Madison, Wisc., 1988), 85.
33. Graham Lusk, "On the Proposed Reorganization of Departments of Clinical Medicine in the United States," *Science*, 41 (1915): 533.
34. S. J. Meltzer, "Headship and Organization of Clinical Departments of First-Class Medical Schools," *Science*, 40 (1914): 625.

ential surgeon Arthur Dean Bevan spoke for many when he said that "I am afraid if the Johns Hopkins plan . . . is generally adopted that it will be impossible for the medical schools to keep the best brains in medicine in the teaching profession. A much stronger plan is the well worked out German plan which I think we should adopt in this country."[35] William Osler, now the Regius Professor of Medicine at Oxford, told President Ira Remsen of Johns Hopkins University that "pure laboratory men" – undoubtedly a reference to Mall and possibly Welch – "were misleading him about the view of leading figures in the field of clinical medicine." Müller himself, said Osler, had "expressed himself strongly against the whole-time system, as directly prejudicial to the teacher and to the school."[36]

Osler was referring to the testimony Müller had given in London in 1910 before the Haldane Commission, which was charged with making recommendations on the future of university education in the city. In his remarks, Müller had stressed the importance of university-controlled teaching hospitals staffed by "fully acknowledged university professors." These professors, selected from among the best available clinical scientists, should have "a wide scientific foundation apart from practical medicine." The crucial point, he argued, was that they be good pathologists, physiologists, or chemists, who could conduct the work of the laboratories as well as that of the wards. Above all, they must consider their teaching responsibilities as their principal duty, just as did every university professor. Whatever private consulting was done by a clinical professor should be left to his own conscience, but the German academic ethos would never allow it to get out of hand. Should the clinician be barred from all private practice, as demanded by the Johns Hopkins plan? No, said Müller, that was going too far. The clinical scientist must be at the frontier of new knowledge in medicine, but he must also "be in constant touch . . . with general professional life, and the practitioners, too."[37]

A number of American clinicians who had studied in Germany were cautious in their attitude toward the Flexner plan. Although they favored the concept of full-time university professors, they feared the consequences of restricting appointments to those willing to accept no outside income. Some believed that American conditions would make it impossible to recruit able teachers and scientists in clinical medicine as full-time employees.

35. Arthur Dean Bevan to Henry Pritchett, January 1912, Flexner Papers, Library of Congress.
36. Alan M. Chesney, *The Johns Hopkins Hospital and the Johns Hopkins University School of Medicine*, 3 vols. (Baltimore, 1943–63), 3: 181.
37. Friedrich von Müller, "Medical Education and the Universities," *British Medical Journal*, 143 (1911): 1421–4.

Others were concerned about the restriction of professional income on their own future prospects. Still others believed, as did Müller and Osler, that clinical teaching itself would suffer if clinical teachers lost contact with their professional roots. Lewellys Barker, for example, said publicly in 1911 that "it does not seem to me probable that it will be desirable soon, if ever, to have all the men of the faculty composed of non-practitioners." In an oblique reference to the Flexner plan, he warned that "it would be a mistake to start with any cut and finished garment that we would ask the medical schools immediately to don." Although clinical research was important, "it was no reason for doing away with teaching and practise in the clinic."[38] Canby Robinson, in reviewing experience with the full-time plan later, contended "that no one believed any longer that clinical departments are to be manned exclusively by men who have no interest outside the medical school and who do not engage in private practice." Every member of a clinical department, he warned, "must have a fundamental interest in patients. . . . A man who lacks this interest, or who allows his desire to accomplish successful research to overshadow it belongs rather in the department of pathology or physiology."[39]

Flexner was undaunted by the argument that his plan deviated from that of the German university clinic he had praised so enthusiastically. In his report to the General Education Board in 1911, he argued that not only in America and Britain but also in Germany itself, "the next great advance in medical education" would be adoption of the strict, full-time plan. "The Germans have thus far done better than we without it," he said, "because their scientific ideals, being more potent, men have been less readily led away from science to money."[40] The following year, he questioned even more sharply the German practice of permitting private consultations in academic clinics. "It is worth asking," he wrote, "whether . . . the tendency to exploit university clinical positions may not require to be checked by concentrating the professor's activities in his clinic, exactly as the physicist's are concentrated in his laboratory."[41]

But German professors and authorities, including Müller, remained unpersuaded by Flexner's rhetoric. Such stringent prohibitions on practice or consultation for compensation, most German internists believed, interfered

38. Lewellys F. Barker, "Some Tendencies in Medical Education in the United States," in Cattell, *Medical Research and Education*, 275.
39. Harvey, *Science at the Bedside*, 147–8.
40. Chesney, *Johns Hopkins Hospital*, 3: 301.
41. Flexner, *Medical Education in Europe*, 148.

with the professor's freedom, demeaned his sense of responsibility, and denied him the advantage of firsthand contact with ordinary patients.

As Flexner continued his campaign to install full-time clinical positions in America and Britain after World War I, opposition mounted on both sides of the Atlantic. The concept of "geographic full-time," a notion similar to the German custom of allowing a limited amount of private practice within the bounds of a full-time commitment to teaching and research, was more and more advanced as an alternative to Flexner's plan. The compromise that was struck resembled the German plan outwardly but in many medical schools was actually closer to the traditional British–American practice of allowing extensive outside work.

By the end of the 1920s, the passion surrounding the debate over the strict full-time plan began to abate. Flexner's own influence declined as outside opposition grew and a new generation of foundation executives forced a change in direction at the Rockefeller philanthropies.[42] Most medical educators came to favor the appointment of career-minded clinicians with primary interests in teaching and research, but less was said about depriving them of all income from private practice.[43] The academic clinician and the practicing specialist became more and more differentiated. Clinical laboratories became a regular feature of hospital design. The stature of academic departments of medicine rose sharply. In a dozen or more universities, important clinical research was conducted. The evolving system, though characterized by great diversity, still owed much to the example of the German university clinic. By the onset of the Great Depression, the historic distance that had separated German from American clinical science had been appreciably closed.

42. Wheatley, *Politics of Philanthropy*, 140–66.
43. Kenneth M. Ludmerer, *Learning to Heal: The Development of American Medical Education* (New York, 1985), 212.

Index

For EU product safety concerns, contact us at Calle de José Abascal, 56–1°,
28003 Madrid, Spain or eugpsr@cambridge.org.

www.ingramcontent.com/pod-product-compliance
Ingram Content Group UK Ltd.
Pitfield, Milton Keynes, MK11 3LW, UK
UKHW040619240426

470322UK00010B/210